A GIRL CALLED PETER
CONNECTION - DISCONNECTION - RECONNECTION

PETER REBBECHI

CONTENTS

I am Love	1
Acknowledgments	5
Foreword	7
Introduction	9

PART I
Early Days 15

PART II
Laying On Of My Hands 17

PART III
Yappa Yappa 19

Part IV
Y2K

Life is a Journey 23

EARLY DAYS

1. A Girl Called Peter	27
2. Treesville	29
3. Heritage	32
4. Marble Bar	35
Photos 1	41
5. Dongara	42
6. Wyndham	45
7. East Rockingham	55
8. Boarding School	58

LAYING ON MY HANDS

1. Nursing School	69
2. Ward Runs	75
Photos 2	79

3. A Special Time	80
4. Midwifery School	82
5. Rottnest	87
6. Return to the Kimberley	90
7. Exmouth	96
Photos 3	101
8. Trip to London	102
9. Channel Islands	105
10. The European Experience	110

YAPPA YAPPA

11. Yirrkala	117
12. One becomes Two and Then Six	129
13. Greek Islands	148
Photos 4	161
14. Perth	162
15. Moving Forward and Changes in Nursing	171
16. Life Goes On	176
17. Wheatbelt Adventures	184
18. Norseman	207
Photos 5	215
19. Norseman contd…	216
20. New Home…New Beginnings	221
21. Roebourne and Wickham	229
22. Call outs	258
23. A New Win	276

Y2K 285

24. Y2K	287
25. Holiday Break	293
Photos 6	313
26. Holistic Nursing	314
27. Tranquillitas Healing	337
28. Rounding Up	347
29. Christmas in Europe	383
30. Life Continues	388
Photos 7	469
Photos 8	471

Epilogue	473
Appendix 1	485
Appendix 2	489
Appendix 3	493
Appendix 4	499
Appendix 5	505
Appendix 6	519
Appendix 7	527
Glossary	533
Notes	535

Copyright © 2021 PETER REBBECHI

The rights of Peter Rebbechi to be identified as the author of the work has been asserted by her in accordance with the Copyright Act of Australia, 1968.

All rights reserved.

No part of this book may be reproduced or transmitted in any form or by any means, electronic or mechanical, including photocopying, recording or by any information storage and retrieval system, without prior permission in writing from the publisher.

For any enquiries or permissions, the publisher can be contacted at petanottle47@gmail.com

First published by: IngramSpark

First Print: December 2021

ISBN (E-BOOK): 978-1-925471-49-6

ISBN (Paperback): 978-1-925471-90-8

I AM LOVE

I am Love, Love, Love, Pure Love

I am Love Love Love, Pure Love
I am Light Light Light, Pure Light
I am Energy Energy Energy, Pure Energy
I am Peace Peace Peace, Pure Peace
I am Truth Truth Truth, Pure Truth
I am Joy Joy Joy, Pure Joy .
I am one one one with ALL ALL ALL

I am one of the Earth, Sand and the Rock
A part of the Galaxies
I am one of the Sun and The Moon
I am one of the Stars and the Sky
I am one of the Rivers, Lakes and Sea

. . .

PETER REBBECHI

I am one of the fish, the dolphins, turtles sharks and whales
I am one of trees, their branches and leaves, just like the birds and the bees
I am one of the flowers, the fruit and the seed
I am one of the animals, snakes , spiders and insects too
Lions, tigers, bears, monkeys to name just a few
All interconnected, all have a purpose to be

27 May 2020, Peter

I dedicate these memoirs to my dear husband, Brian(referred to throughout in this book as Noddy), who has been by my side from the day we met, who has walked the walk with me supporting and holding me and carrying me during my life's journey through the good, the bad and the ugly times. He has never left my side. For years he has encouraged me to write a book sharing the stories and adventures I have experienced in my rich and rewarding life. I thank him from deep within my heart.

I would also like to dedicate this book to our children and grandchildren for the joy they have given us from the day they entered this world and for their love and support.

I also thank and honour my birth parents and my brother and sisters.

ACKNOWLEDGMENTS

It is here I would like to thank all who have journeyed with me throughout my life.

The people who came into my life and then left.

The many people who moved my soul to awaken me to understanding, giving me knowledge and filling me with wisdom, teaching me lessons I had to learn and leaving me at times scarred, and at times wiser.

The people who made human nature so beautiful from all races and ages - newborn to dying members of humanity.

The people who stayed in my life, have embodied their footprints in my heart and brought me to where I am today.

I cannot thank Simon Molan enough. He paid for these memoirs to be published, which led me to write them in the first place.

Fiona Jones from Author Express for her guidance.

Shoma Mittra, my editor who has undertaken the midwife's role of bringing these memoirs to birth.

And, last but not least, the second midwife, Andy Kahle, my typesetter and graphic designer who enabled the memoirs to be birthed.

In the spirit of reconciliation, I Peta Nottle acknowledge the Traditional Custodians of country throughout Australia and their connections to land, sea and community. We pay our respect to their Elders past and present and extend that respect to all Aboriginal and Torres Strait Islander peoples today.

Aboriginal and Torres Strait Islander should be aware that this book contains images and names of people who have passed away.

FOREWORD

I met Peta in 1993 after moving to the Pilbara with James. Peta hired me immediately after my interview at Roebourne hospital and asked if I had bought my uniform - if so, I could start straight away! Peta was so supportive as I adjusted from working in a big city hospital to rural nursing.

My name is Sel. Jane and I wanted to write this foreword together.

At the time, I was working between Roebourne and Wickham Hospitals. Peta relocated from Perth to be our new Director of Nursing at the time. What a breath of fresh air and energy she bought to our hospitals. Peta and Brian were so welcoming and they became a close part of our Pilbara family. We spent many a wonderful adventure exploring the magical Pilbara in the years to come.

Peta has had an incredible life and sharing her story in this book will give readers a generous insight into what a beautiful and amazing woman she is. Peta shares her passion for life and gives us inspiration to make positive changes. Both, Jane and I, are in awe of Peta - not only for her achievements, but for what she has given of herself to family, friends, patients, staff and acquaintances.

Peta is a natural and inspiring leader. She does this with her honesty and sharing of herself, by passionately doing and demonstrating. Peta has many passions. Her advocacy for mental health, social justice, indigenous belonging and care of all people from the young to the elderly no matter what their background, is empowering. Peta's overarching passion for reconnecting the mind, body and soul is key in providing positive outcomes and resolving imbalance.

The belief that we are shaped from the moment we are born and, thereafter reshaped through our life's experiences and interactions is apparent throughout the book.

Peta has shown us that pain and challenges help define who you are and what you truly believe in. Defining your passions and what you stand for become clear as we accept and move forward from any challenge. She shows us that from pain comes happiness and wholeness, which Peta has said she didn't reach until age seventy. Giving and caring, learning, being active, taking notice and connecting - these are the gifts Peta brings.

Our world is a better place with Peta in it.

Enjoy reading. We certainly have.

We are only a part of Peta's story but know so much more about her journey from this book. This is her story. A story which aims to inspire everyone to be true to themselves and rediscover their wholeness - their mind, body and spirit.

~ Sel and Jane

INTRODUCTION

Becoming the nurse-healer I was born to be.

I am sitting here on my front verandah of our little duplex and across the road is the most beautiful divine nature park surrounding Lake Gwelup in Perth, Western Australia. A little suburb, ten kilometres from the centre of one of the most remote cities in the world. I am pinching myself - is this really happening? Am I writing the preface for my memoirs, *A Girl Called Peter - Connection Disconnection Reconnection*?

I spoke with my editor, Shoma Mittra - chosen by divine intervention on the 16th July 2019. Well into the editing, Shoma had emailed me several weeks before to say it is time to write the preface. I had no idea how to write or where to start or what to say. I started to research and read many forewords and prefaces in other books. I had many discussions with my higher self, and I asked for help to just allow the words to flow. So, this is coming straight from the centre of my being. I hope you will like it and enjoy the journey of a fellow human being on this planet. It is a journey of the good, the bad and the ugly. A journey from the 'seen' world to the 'unseen' world as experienced by a registered nurse and midwife, wife, mother and grandmother.

The journey through nursing school began for me in the summer of

1965. I had just completed my Leaving Certificate at a private Catholic girls' high school where I spent five years as a boarder in Perth, Western Australia. I finished school in the November of 1964, had a very long summer vacation spending virtually every day on the beach. I had applied to go to nursing school in October of 1964. My application was successful and I was to start on the 18th of January 1965. I had dreamed of becoming a nurse, ever since I was a little girl. I wanted a 'vocation', and there was no higher vocation, as far as I was concerned than to be a Nurse. I was so naïve and innocent, having no idea about the external world around me outside of the comforts of the family home or the big brick wall surrounding the convent and boarding school I had lived in for five years.

I entered nursing school and lived in a very protective environment in the nurses' quarters. I had no idea about washing, cooking and household chores as it was all done for us. The thing that was different was that we were free. I embraced this freedom wholeheartedly. For the first time in my life, I was earning money. I was so very excited to receive my first pay check for a forty-four-hour week. A fine sum of five pounds in a little brown envelope.

I was rich.

I had no life skills, and it took many years before I developed any. I did however love the journey. I studied hard, worked hard and, at times, played hard.

I had a wonderful time, with lots of adventures and experiences along the way. With many great friends and colleagues both here in Western Australia, Sydney in NSW, remote areas in the north of Western Australia, overseas and The Northern Territory, I was a free spirit

Along this journey of life, I met another free spirit, a man with whom I have shared and been so blessed to have married. We met over forty-nine years ago. We were so blessed to have two very healthy children. Becoming a parent was for me one of the greatest lessons human life can teach you. I had to learn to cook, clean and take on responsibilities for raising happy, healthy little human beings. It was a blessing working in partnership with a totally devoted father and husband. Our lifestyle was second to none. We were both able to work. I worked in my beloved profession in a time when it was always about care and compassion. It was a time before Medicare - before health became a business model. It was a time before nurses were educated in universities; a time before the career structure was introduced into nursing in Western Australia in 1985.

The nursing journey into 'another world' began for me in this period of time until 2017, when I sustained an undiagnosed major workplace injury. Within these pages, I will describe the incident and the resultant outcomes of being a whistleblower and how this went on to affect me for many years, both personally and professionally. I found out what workplace bullying and harassment was like at a time when there was no occupational Health and Safety legislation in this state of Western Australia. Fortunately, it did not have an effect on the love and devotion of my personal family and true friends. This period of time from October of 1989 until 2017, led me on the most challenging professional journey one could ever have envisaged.

The ride led me on to so many worthwhile adventures and helped me achieve my dream of becoming a matron that I had had as a ten-year old girl. I became a Director of Nursing in 1993 for a ten-year period.

It was not long after, that I was asked to do a presentation for a workshop. My presentation was called, 'A Better Future for Our Children'. I will share this at the end of the book as it has never ever been published before. I have to say I still have this in my hand writing and have only in the last few months had it typed into the computer.

During my early years as a Director of Nursing, I had many challenges which ended in a major workplace injury because of workplace bullying and harassment, as I have mentioned above. It ended up in a severe reactive depression and breakdown after a very public attack was aired on the ABC Northwest News from Parliamentary Question time in the WA parliament in 1997.

A long recovery period commenced; but I loved my role and working with my colleagues. One morning, I received a mystical message and I made the decision not to resign despite all the politics that was going on at that time. This decision was the beginning of a second journey that I was blessed to commence. It was a true healing journey.

I started a whole pathway of Nursing Education at the beginning of 2001. For me, it was not a new pathway, it took me back to the mid 1960's when we were trained in the Holistic Model of Care. A time when we were not only in being with the patients but we were also doing and meeting their clinical needs of body, mind, emotions and spirit as a whole. I found out that the Nurses' Board in Western Australia had approved 6 Modalities of complementary therapies that Nurses were allowed to use in their daily nursing practice. Other state nurses' boards also approved these practices.

I threw myself into this educational pathway of Healing through the Power of Touch. Initially, I started with the Complementary Therapies of Therapeutic Touch and Healing Touch. I had a vision to bring Healing into the Australian Medical Model.

In 2001, I started talking very openly about the need to bring Holistic Health Care and Healing into not only The Health Industry, but other services as well. I was so honoured to be asked to write a paper by the Chief Justice of W.A. and the outcome from that paper, has gone on to form the basis of all submissions I have written ever since. I have never stopped talking about the need for holistic healing to be integrated into the Australian Medical Model, and I will continue to do so until the day I go home.

You can read this paper entitled, *A Vision Towards Developing a Holistic Approach in the Rehabilitation of Prisoners* in the appendices of the book.

Ever since the first workplace injury I had in 1989, I knew I had recovered when I started writing poetry.

Some of these poems have been included within the pages of this book. Writing became a passion for the good times and the bad.

I left my role as a DON(Director of Nursing) in 2003 and spent time out in the wilderness working in various roles in both remote areas and a regional hospital, before finally transferring to Perth to take up my last role as a Clinical Coach for Graduate nurses fresh out of University. I finally walked away in 2013 after being burnt at the stake yet again. I took nearly two years to finally follow my true passion of becoming the very best nurse/healer I could be.

In 2015, I started a little Holistic/Healing Clinic. The practice I set up was based on the ethos and principles of the first Mayo Clinic founded in the USA in 1891, by Dr William Worrall Mayo and Mother Alfred Moes, both strong willed pioneers who found common cause in serving patients. I finished the final upgrade of a Touch modality I had done first in 2000 to a Diploma.

In 2016, I was asked to write a submission to The Victorian Government Enquiry into Bullying and Harassment in the Health Industry by a well-known and recognised person in WA. The submission had to be unidentifiable. Again, I sat at the computer and started to write.

The submission was, *The Physical, Emotional, Psychological and Spiritual Effects Workplace Bullying and Harassment has on a Person*. This paper can also be found in the Appendix section of this book.

Lots of wonderful things were happening including real mystical awakenings. The writings came pouring through, I would be woken in the early hours of the morning with words coming forth - always around two o'clock in the mornings. I would have to get up, go to the computer and write. The conversations I was having with my inner voice and higher power were amazing. Little did I realise that this was the first stage of my transformational journey.

It was in the March of 2017, that I had a phone call and a meeting with a lady who asked me to see her son who had suffered from severe workplace bullying and harassment issues. I said yes, I would, if he would like to come. We journeyed together for three months. Then one day, I gave him the paper I had written for the senate enquiry on Workplace Bullying and Harassment. After reading it, he said to me "The whole world needs to read this –you have to write a book".

Six weeks later he rang me and said, "You must write the book. I have paid for it to be published".

What could I do?

A Girl Called Peter – Connection, Disconnection Reconnection was born.

Once I started writing, I realised the importance of documenting my journey. I have four beautiful grandchildren, who will one day grow into adults. I would dearly love to see the world as a much kinder and safer place for them to grow and be the very best they can be. A world that is peaceful, full of love, caring and compassion. A world were virtues and values are the gospels of the future. This is my wish not only for my grandchildren, but for all human beings.

It has been a real honour and labour of love to be able to pen the journey of seven decades on this planet.Maybe there will be another sequel to these memoirs, which will take you on another journey of the time left on my voyage of life to everlasting life.

With much love and light.

Peter/Peta

PART I
EARLY DAYS

1. A Girl Called Peter
2. Treesville
3. Heritage
4. Marble Bar
5. Dongara
6. Wyndham
7. East Rockingham
8. Boarding School

PART II
LAYING ON OF MY HANDS

1. Nursing School
2. Ward Runs
3. A Special Time
4. Midwifery School
5. Rottnest
6. Return to the Kimberley
7. Exmouth
8. Trip To London
9. Channel Islands
10. The European Experience

PART III
YAPPA YAPPA

1. Yirrkala
2. One becomes two and then six
3. Greek Islands
4. Moving forward and changes in nursing
5. Life goes on
6. Wheatbelt adventures
7. Norseman
8. Norseman continued
9. Roebourne and Wickham
10. Call Outs

PART IV
Y2K

1. A new win
2. Y2K
3. Holiday Break
4. Moving Forward and Changes in Nursing
5. Perth
6. Tranquilitas Healing

LIFE IS A JOURNEY

Life is a Journey.

Birth is a beginning
And death is a destination
And life is a journey
From childhood to maturity
And youth to age;
From innocence to awareness
And ignorance to knowing
From foolishness to discretion
And then perhaps to wisdom;
From weakness to strength
Or strength to weakness
And often back again
From health to sickness
And back, we pray, to health again
From offence to forgiveness
From loneliness to love
From joy to gratitude
From pain to compassion

LIFE IS A JOURNEY

And grief to understanding
From fear to faith;
From defeat to defeat to defeat
Until looking backwards or ahead
We see that victory lies
Not at some high place along the way,
But in having made the journey, stage by stage
A sacred pilgrimage.
Birth is a beginning
And death is a destination
A sacred pilgrimage to everlasting life
(With permission from The New Union Prayer Book. Central Conference of American Rabbi's)

EARLY DAYS

A GIRL CALLED PETER

I was born on the 2nd May 1947, the second child, and first-born daughter of John and Mary Rebbechi at the Three Springs Hospital in Western Australia. I was christened Barbara Mary Peter Rebbechi; however, I was only ever called "Peter". My parents were strict Catholics and I think they named me after St Peter.

I never asked them why I was called Peter, and not Barbara, or why my name was always spelt, 'Peter'.

Why I never asked, I do not know, but would ask now if I had the chance ever again.

I had an older brother whose name was Joseph, born on 28th November 1945 (deceased 11th June 1958). He was my soulmate and we were often mistaken for twins. I had two younger sisters, Marion born 1st January 1950 (deceased September 16th 2016), and Marie, 5th February 1955.

Early Childhood Days – Pre school

My dear brother, Joe, was eighteen months older than I and I adored him, following him everywhere. We were like a pair of Siamese twins. After Marion was born in 1950, Joe and I were at an age, where we had discovered a world outside the confines of the house. We were always outside playing, during the day.

When she was a baby, Marion was struck down with the polio virus that had broken out in Perth in the 1950's. She spent a great deal of her early childhood in hospital, and as a consequence, we never really bonded the way Joe and I did.

Marie, my other sister, was eight years younger and the age gap as children seemed rather marked. So, it was Joe and I who were best friends and played together most of the time.

My earliest memories are from 1949-50, when my parents lived in a little school house in a small community called Arrino, in the then Three Springs District. My dad was the headmaster of the Arrino school. Arrino is a small town in the Mid West region of Western Australia . The town is located between Mingenew and Three Springs on the Midlands Road

I can remember I used to play under the house which was elevated on stilts. Joe and I would spend hours beneath the house playing with unseen friends. If Joe wasn't with me, I used to be there playing on my own, alone with my 'friends' who were very real to me.

If I mentioned these 'friends' of mine in front of elders, they would admonish me. My mother recalled many years later that I would chatter away to my invisible friends; but when I was told they were not real, I would be furious and insist that they truly were real. I was forbidden from mentioning them when I was with my family.

TREESVILLE

*D*ad was transferred at the end of 1950 to another school; this time to a small timber mill town in the South of WA. Dad was the headmaster of the school in Treesville (circa 1922-1956). Treesville was located on the banks of the Harris River in the Southwest of Western Australia. Today, its remnants lie within the Lane Poole Conservation Reserve. Collie is the nearest town. The last photos of the town I saw were hanging in the Yarloop museum in 2014, which was destroyed completely by the big fire that burnt the town to cinders in 2016.

Mum had a little car, a 'Mayflower'. It was cream and we would all pile in to go swimming in the little creeks and rivers on the weekends before Marion became very ill with polio. The virus had affected her legs when she was only eleven months old so she ended up spending six months separated from the family in Princess Margaret Hospital. Family members were not allowed to stay with their sick relatives in those days.

I remember going up to Perth with my mother to see her a couple of times. During that time, we used to go by train from Harvey to Perth and then catch a tram up Hay Street to the hospital. When she finally came home, Mum looked after her and managed her rehabilitation. I remember a great celebration when she could finally walk without the splints on her little legs.

Mum and Dad, being war veterans loved to smoke cigarettes. I think they were mainly brands like Players, Craven A and Woodbine. In those days, cigarettes were pure tobacco and it seemed like 98% of the population enjoyed a smoke.

Of course, as curious kids, Joe and I were very keen to try one; but we were never allowed to touch the packet. One day, an opportunity arose for us to pinch one and take a box of matches up to the trees at the back of our house. We found a spot where we thought we could not be seen from the house, sat down and Joe lit our first cigarette and took a puff. He immediately started to cough and handed it to me. I had a puff and thought I was going to die, so I threw it to the ground and the next minute the grass started crackling.

Scared, we ran into the house as fast as our little legs could carry us. Dad came out when he saw the fire through the kitchen window. He managed to extinguish it in minutes; but the fate that awaited us after the drama was over, came in the form of the strap.

Over Dad's knee we were both put, Joe first and then me, and were given three smacks across our little bottoms with a strap. We had never had this happen to us before, so as you can imagine we were in shock. We were given stern warnings from my father never ever to play with matches, or smoke cigarettes ever again. We were both very upset at having had such a spanking. From that time on, we stayed outside whenever we could, especially if Dad was in a bad mood, which fortunately, was not very often.

I started school in Treesville. It was a two-teacher school and I had a lovely young tutor who made school fun. I was introduced to reading all about Dick and Dora. Joe and I would make up Dick and Dora games and try and teach our dogs to play these games with us. There was no such thing as homework, no television, no radio, just fun. Dad used to read lots of stories and poems to us before bed - especially

Banjo Patterson's books[1]. Our imaginations ran riot. Dad would sing songs from the war years and we loved those special times.

Mum was busy and would spend most of her time being a mum. She loved cleaning, cooking, sewing and attending to the needs of her family while also looking after the special needs of our little sister, Marion, when she returned home from Princess Margaret Hospital. Christmas was always a fun time for all. The school organising committee would have a pantomime on the last day of school. When Father Christmas came, we all sat on his knee. I happened to pull his beard down once and low and behold, I got such a shock to see, underneath the beard, was my dad.

HERITAGE

I cannot remember ever meeting my Grandfather, however, from what I have learnt through storytelling. He was born in 1870 in Daylesford in Victoria, Australia, and left school at twelve years of age. He got an apprenticeship as a farrier and became a skilled blacksmith. He left for Western Australia, and after a long voyage by ship, landed in Albany. He, and his friend, headed for 'Canning Mills', and as it was a mere five hundred miles, they set out on foot! After working there, he went to Mullewa, in the Mid-west of WA, where he was employed shoeing horses. Being a skilled blacksmith, he earned his living this way, only rarely being engaged in mining. It was here in Mullewa that he met my grandmother, Julia Maude Brady. They had six children, with my father being the youngest. Although he was a friendly and kindly man he would not step aside if he considered he was right, and he proved this several times in his life. He was a very religious man being a practising Roman Catholic. One story goes that he once got involved with a jeering itinerant group who were making crude and scurrilous remarks about the church. One of them made the mistake of coming too close to him and pouring out all his rancour, which infuriated my grandfather so much that he took to the man with much intent and spent some time in the cooler for assault. He travelled far and wide on the various jobs he had. His mode of transport was walking; but sometimes he had the luxury of a Cob and Company coach. He spent a lot of time in Marble Bar and the intense heat never worried him; in fact, he liked it.

The family were often separated because of his work, but whenever possible, my grandmother would join him. Once, when he was at the 'Joker' mine, Granny and two of her children went to be with him, travelling on a carrier wagon, with her brother, Jim. Another time, she took the children for a walk in the bush and ran into three strange men who were starving. She led them back to the wagon where her brother fed them and then advised them to go to Magnet to find work. In describing the life in those early days, she once told my dad, "They were hard days where children died like flies."

My grandfather had a good baritone voice and was a member of what is today called a 'glee' club. He was also an excellent rifle shooter and participated in competitions. He admired his mother, Margaret, for her learning and for the way she tried to promote this in the family. From his mother, he developed an interest in history and he too became a great historian.

He passed away in 1951. Even as he took his last breath, he made a joke as he spoke to Mum and Dad.

We never had a connection with any of our aunties, uncles or cousins. They were all much older than us and as we were a very itinerant family; we were never around, which, when I reflect, was one of the vital links in our upbringing that we missed. Mum, being an English war bride, had no relatives here in Australia; she had only one brother who lived in England. So, we never got to meet her side of the family as little ones. My mother told me very little of her story. She described how her father died when she was young, and she was brought up mainly by her grandmother and her favourite aunty. Her mother devoted all her time and attention to her younger brother. She went into nursing school in a Birmingham Hospital when she was seventeen years and when the war broke out she joined the Royal Air Force and once the war broke out she transferred to the Guy's Hospital in London,

One story, she shared often with me growing up, was nursing a war hero called Douglas Bader of the infamous Dam Busters[1] notoriety. It was during this time she met my father. They married after a short romance and once the war ended, she came to Australia as a war bride. She never talked about her early days in Australia. I got the impression from her, (from the rare times we talked about the past) that life was not easy for her. Mum was very English and a real lady when she came to Australia in 1945. Dad never talked about his upbringing either.

In 1998, I met an old Mercy nun, who was from the Day Dawn/Mullewa area. Over a cup of coffee, she told me she knew both my grandmother and my father when he was a teenager. She gave me a little history about how my grandmother wanted my father to enter the seminary; however, he chose to go to Claremont Teacher's Training College instead, and on completion of his Diploma of Education he took up a teaching position in Onslow in the north of Western Australia. He taught there until the Second World War broke out. He then joined the RAAF and trained as a rear tail gunner, and was deployed to England. He returned to Australia with my mother at the end of 1945, and back to his chosen profession of teaching. The old nun was the only person who has ever talked about my family background.

MARBLE BAR

In the early 1950's we were blessed. In 1953, my father was transferred once again, this time, up to the remote town of Marble Bar, in the Pilbara Region of the north of Western Australia. To get there from Perth, we had to travel with the State Shipping Line - the MV Koojarra from Fremantle to Port Hedland. There was no mining industry then apart from the gold mines at Marble Bar and Nullagine, and once we reached Port Hedland, we then had to drive out to Marble Bar which was 125.5 miles east on an old corrugated red dirt track, that was rough, dusty and very bumpy. We had two dogs, one a red setter and a black dog called, Atlas. A big red truck (an old Bedford, I think) took us out to Marble Bar. I remember my Mother and Marion, then aged three, sitting in the front seat with the driver whilst Dad, Joe and I sat on top of our suitcases in the back of the truck with the two dogs on either side by the cabin, catching the breeze and seeing what was going on.

All of a sudden, a kangaroo bounded past us, and my beautiful red setter was off the truck in a flash and disappeared into the spinifex[1] chasing this big red kangaroo.

Never to be seen again.

Dad banged on the roof of the truck; the driver stopped, but it was too late. He was gone. It was my first loss, my four-legged best friend was gone forever. I was sad for some time, missing him dearly.

The population of Marble Bar in 1954 was small, made up of Indigenous, Australian and European Cultures. A very harmonious place for a child to live and grow up in; we could run free and be safe. Life was fun and exciting for Joe and I, and full of freedom. We were inseparable and always out playing and getting into mischief. It was inevitable that we received a few whacks on our butts from the back of a hairbrush or a strap now and then. Apart from this, though my parents were very loving to us and life was wonderful. We swam in the Coongan River, with all our friends. I will never forget clambering all over the jasper rocks there.

One day, Joe and I went on an adventure on our push bikes and found ourselves at the Comet gold mine entrance. There was no security in those days. Joe dared me to get into a carriage. So, I did and it started to move. Joe shrieked as he went racing up to this man screaming with fear, "my sister is in the end cart". Fortunately, the man stopped and ran to the back cart and hauled me out. He took us home to our parents.

Not only did we get the strap, but we were grounded for a week. The worst punishment we could receive was staying indoors. We had to go to school with Dad and come home with him too.

Our toilet, known as 'the dunny' was outside and we were only allowed out when we needed to go.

I had my first religious encounter in Marble Bar. Joe and I made our First Holy Communion there in a little church on the hill.

A priest was coming to town - one only came once in a blue moon. Mum and Dad decided that as the Catholic priest was coming, Joe and I would make our First Holy Communion. We had no idea what this receiving 'communion' was about. Anyway, we got dressed in our Sunday best, and like good little kids went to church for this special occasion.

We never got sick; but we occasionally caught trachoma, still today a big problem in many outback Aboriginal communities. Trachoma is a bacterial infection of the eye that can cause blindness. I remember the few times Joe and I had this condition. My mother, a nurse, would put eye drops and ointment in our eyes and we had to stay in a darkened cupboard all day until our eyes were better.

The Health Department had a mobile dentist caravan that would come once a year to check our teeth, and I can remember every day at school at the 10.00am recess, we would line up for a can of carnation milk and an apple – all supplied by the Government.

Marble Bar is known to be the hottest place in Australia; however, as kids we never noticed the heat, nor the cold in the dry season. We never wore shoes and we used to fry eggs on the rocks. Mum would go crook if we did it too often. We had no electricity, everything was run on kerosene or methylated spirits - the fridge, the old Tilley lamps and hurricane lamps and of course, the wood fired stove. I remember the smell of the freshly baked bread my mum used to bake in a wood fired oven. She was such a great cook. Mum used to have to heat up the iron on top of the stove, when she was ironing. There was no such thing as an electric iron, no such things as fans or air-conditioning. Dad would chop the wood for the wood fired stove; and the bathroom heater had to be lit to enable us to have a warm bath. We had no washing machine, so mum used the copper and a scrubbing board in a cement trough.

We used to love the big storms, which brought the rains and sometimes the floods. The lightning strikes used to light up the night sky and with the thunder, Mum would say, "Oh! I love the thunder; it is the angels in heaven playing football." It was a magical fairy land. I have to say even today, I still love storms. The storms in those days were ex-tropical cyclones, even though we as kids had never heard of the word cyclone. They were known to us as big storms.

I have very special memories of my life in Marble Bar. In 1954, the Redex Trail[2] came through Marble Bar. My parents were on the

Committee for this major event. I remember being woken up at three am one morning; my mother getting me dressed, plaiting my hair and rushing us into the main street to welcome the Redex Drivers. I served them their sandwiches and tea. I met the infamous 'Gelignite Jack Murray and his co-driver Bill Murray and Jack Dwyer' (my younger readers might have to Google –Redex Around Australia Car Trial -1954)

We lived in a big house with glass louvers all around. It was not far to walk or ride our bikes to school. My father, being the headmaster, used to have yearly visits from an Inspector who would come from the Education Department in Perth. He would stay at the Iron Clad Hotel and would always come at least once for dinner to our house. On one occasion, he went out to the dunny (toilet), and in our dunny lived a carpet snake which dad had warned him about. Joe and I snuck outside and went behind the dunny to listen for a reaction in case the carpet snake whom we called, Sleepy decided to pay the Inspector a visit.

We would always scuttle inside (just in time before the guest emerged from the dunny) into the living room, giggling our little heads off.

I seemed to always be in trouble. One day, Dad was really cranky with me - for what, I can't remember. But it must have been bad, because I was in for a spanking. So, I shimmied up the tallest gumtree near our house, and sat up there in the fork of the tree. Dad brought out a chair and sat under the gum tree, strap in hand. I would pick a gum nut and see if I could drop it on his head. When one hit him on his crown, I knew I was in for a fate worse than death, as soon as I saw the look on his face. Wary and nervous, I clambered down.

I had a sore butt after three whacks with the strap. Then a couple of hours later, he took me down the street and bought me an ice cream.

A severe tummy ache meant that I had to be flown out from Marble Bar in a small plane to the old Port Hedland Hospital which was situated down near the wharf.

In those days, it was a square building with big wide verandas all the way around both on the inside and outside.

I was taken to theatre as soon as we arrived and then put on the operating table. I looked over at the window, a very large one and all these little Aboriginal kids were looking in. The nursing sister pulled down the blind, then a doctor held a cloth full of ether over my nose and mouth (it's funny writing about this incident, as I can still smell the ether). I drifted off and next thing I know, I woke up back in my big room, with my mum holding my hand and a kind nursing sister, telling me I was okay. They explained that my appendix was sick, so they had taken it from my tummy and I would be better in a couple of days. She showed me the little jar that had the appendix in it. It was for me to keep if I wanted. I chose not to. Post operatively, I was supposed to have stayed in bed for five days, but that wasn't me. I was up and running around the next day and after a five-day recovery period, Mum and I went back to Marble Bar.

We were so happy to be home with the whole family again. My sister Marie was born in Port Hedland Hospital in 1955. This beautiful old building was very badly damaged by a massive cyclone back in 1956 and then they built a new one opposite the yacht club in Port Hedland.

Each year, before we went south for the Christmas holidays, we would have Christmas dinner at the infamous Iron Clad Hotel[3]. As kids, we really looked forward to that meal. We used to love the Christmas pudding which was full of little treasures like half pennies, three pennies, sixpences and shillings, and if you got some coins in your Christmas pudding, you were allowed to keep the coins and spend the money on whatever you liked.

Dad had made friends with a lot of the Aboriginal kids' parents. So, often Joe and I would be asked to go hunting with them. We loved doing that. We would walk for miles, it seemed. There weren't cars back then, so we would trek through the mulga[4]. Aboriginal people, from a very young age, are kinaesthetic people. Their knowingness of being one with the universe dwells within the essence of their soul. Their senses are so sharp that they can catch a goanna with bare hands or bring down a kangaroo with a boomerang or a spear quite easily. We tried hard to replicate their agility and skill, but it was not innate to Joe or I. Mum used to look forward to cooking the produce we brought home, especially the kangaroo tails. She would always cook up a big pot of kangaroo tail stew, that the Aboriginal ladies hunted and skinned for her.

Mum, being very English was unable to do the work that the Aboriginal ladies could do. But she would reciprocate by baking cakes and bread for them. It is hard to believe, that Mum would do all her cooking on a wood stove even on days when the temperature would soar to 114 degrees Fahrenheit (45.5degrees Celsius) and sometimes the temperature would stay that high for days on end.

Our time came to an end in Marble Bar in 1955. Those two years in Marble Bar instilled in me a deep love and admiration for the lifestyle of freedom and the love of living and working with Aboriginals in their communities.

1954 - 1964

Primary School Friends and
Mr Ritchie (School Teacher)
Wyndham Primary - 1958 (above)
School Play SHGHS - 1960 (above right)
My Sisters and I - 1962 (right)

Joe, Atlas and I - 1953 (above)
Dad, Atlas and I - 1953 (right)
Sub Leaving - 1963 (below)

Mum, Joe, Atlas and I - 1953

Friends - 1962

DONGARA

From Marble Bar, my father was transferred to Dongara, in the Midwest. My memories of Dongara are mostly happy ones, apart from a very short period, when my mother was very sick, and had to have a big operation in Perth.

My father enrolled Marion and I into the Dominican Ladies College under the care of the Dominican Nuns. Joe and Marie were allowed to stay at home and Joe would go to school with Dad. A very kind lady from the Catholic community, would look after little Marie until dad could pick her up at the end of the school day. I hated being away from home and I was always getting into trouble at that school. Being locked away in a boarding school was like being in jail, and being separated from Mum, Dad, Joe and Marie was awful. Marion, however, loved it.

I would cry myself to sleep every night. One evening, I got into trouble with one of the nuns and I swore at her. I was about eight years old at the time, and this particular nun took off her black belt from which her Rosary beads hung, and used it as a strap to hit me. That night, when I knew all the Nuns were in chapel, I packed up all my belongings and stuffed them in a pillow-case. I did not tell Marion that I was going to run away. I slid down the drain-pipe from the balcony, and ran like the wind, till I arrived at my parent's house. I can still remember sitting on the front step crying, because the door was locked and I could not get anyone to open the door, despite banging on it.

Eventually, my father came out, to put out the milk bottles and got the shock of his life to find me sitting there sobbing my heart out.

Dad decided then that I never had to go back to boarding school. The nuns were very kind and said I could come back as a day pupil and I did so; but I was very happy when the time came to leave that school in 1957. It was very challenging for me, as I found school quite boring.

There were no Aboriginal kids in that school, all Westerners. I didn't make any close friends. I really didn't want to be there. There were no boys in the school to play *Cowboys and Indians* with and I couldn't wait for school to be over, so Joe and I could go out to play with our friends.

We would go down to the Irwin River to catch tadpoles, and come home when the sun went down. We would ride our bikes down to the back beach and spend hours beach combing and pretending to be castaways like Robinson Crusoe and the Swiss Family Robinson.

Two memories stand out in my childhood journey.

My parents booked me in for dance and piano lessons. In those years, I was a little podgy and hated those ballet steps, twirling around on my toes. One day, I had the dance teacher say to me I reminded her of a little baby elephant. That day, I decided I would never be able to dance and refused to go back.

When I was learning to play the piano, I always got my fingers tapped with a ruler whenever I made a mistake, which was quite often. I was at a lesson one day, and there was a knock on the window. The teacher and I turned around and standing there was Joe. He told me that old Atlas had just died. That was it for me. I took off and we ran home to see the old dog sleeping peacefully, not breathing. Dad dug a deep hole and we had a little goodbye ceremony. I cried and cried after the ceremony, and from that day on, I never returned to music lessons, much to Mum and Dad's disappointment.

We lived in this beautiful old two-story house, on the main road leading out from Dongara to Geraldton. No bypass road in those days.

It was very close to the bakery too. Mum trusted us to go and pick up the fresh bread on Sunday mornings when it was just out of the oven; but by the time we got home, there were big chunks of bread taken out of the middle. The smell was too irresistible for our rumbling tummies.

We also lived fairly close to the cemetery and as kids we would often go and play hide and seek at night. Life was fun and free. I will never forget the Sunday roast chicken. Dad had to catch the chook first, cut its head off, and then we kids would have to help mum pluck all the feathers of the chook. This was a weekly ritual. We also had a big pomegranate tree to the side of the house and I still love pomegranates. I could climb trees like a monkey and would always be the one to go right up to the top and pick the ones up there.

Now, I hug trees. I put my ear to the trunk and can hear the life force flowing through them. When I do this, the flow sounds like a heartbeat. (One of the things I love to do now, when out walking with my grandchildren is to teach them to hug trees and listen to the life force in them.)

Dad would always love acting out stories with us and would read us lots of books like *Tom Sawyer*, *Anne of Green Gables* and poetry. He was a great story-teller. He loved poetry, and instilled in us the love of literature. Some of the best gifts I have been given were books. My favourite was Enid Blyton, the author of The Famous Five books and The Secret Seven series. Joe and I would love to live out their adventures in our play.

WYNDHAM

At the end of 1957, my father was transferred to Wyndham, the most remote town in the Kimberley region of Western Australia. Once again, we travelled by ship - this time on a sister ship by the name of MV Koolama. There was such excitement when we arrived at the terminal at Fremantle Port, ready for another of life's adventures. Travelling by ship was how we got to the North in those days. It was a great holiday for Mum and Dad and an adventure for us kids. We made lots of friends and had the run of the ship, playing chasey and hide and seek.

Arriving in Derby, Dad and Mum had nun friends who worked out at the leprosarium. We caught a taxi out to the colony and met these lovely nuns who spoilt us with cordial, chocolate cakes and biscuits. We had never heard about leprosy before, let alone ever seen people afflicted by it. We went and talked to the Aboriginals living in there. This was the beginning of visits to the leprosarium, whenever we berthed in Derby. Mum and dad would visit their nun friends each time we sailed down or up the West Coast on holidays.

Excitement mounted as we sailed up the Cambridge Gulf. We knew we were nearly at our new home in Wyndham. On arrival, a taxi was waiting for us at the Wyndham meat works jetty and we were taken out to our new three-bedroom home at the Three Mile. Moving to a new town brought new adventures. It was a very exciting time, exploring the rivers, the gullies and swimming holes on our bikes. I made lots of friends both Aboriginals, Europeans and Westerners and life was fun. I was always barefoot with long plaits and I was great at running.

I was whole in body, mind and spirit.

We settled into our new home and once our personal effects were unpacked from the container, we had many hours of fun in a ready-made cubby house. The back yard had wild melons growing and they were so good to eat. Our next-door neighbours were a lovely couple, Roy and Alma Sargent, who ran the local taxi service. Beautiful people who I will never forget, especially Roy. They had two children, Vicky and Peter. They were good kids. Occasionally, Peter and I would get into some fights. We arranged a fight after school one day on the lawn at his house. All the local kids came and cheered us on. Peter and I were at it punch by punch and I can still remember the bloody nose I got from that fight. He won, of course, and my pride came off second best. I never boxed again.

The school was situated in the town of Wyndham; now known as the Port. It was a big school on stilts with three big classrooms. I was in a combined year 5-6-7 class. My father was the teacher. Each morning at assembly we would raise the Australian flag recite, "The Lord's Prayer' and sing "God Save the Queen."

The school was right next to the jail. We used to talk to the prisoners through the holes in the asbestos fence that surrounded the prison; there was no barb wire on top of the fences. We used to talk to them as most of the Aboriginal kids, were related to the prisoners, and we would often share our lunch with them. One of the teachers, Miss Glendenning, was old and taught sewing. The other teacher was a lovely young man. Reg Ritchie was his name. We got to know them quite well as they used to come to our home regularly for tea.

The meatworks was in full swing in those years, and the kids whose parents worked there lived down at a small community at the base of

The Bastion (The Bastion is now known as the "5 Rivers Look Out"). We were fortunate enough to go to the top of the lookout on a road trip in 2016 and what a view it had! I had school friends who lived at the meatworks village, but I only saw them during school hours.

We did not have a car, so once we caught the school bus home, we lived in another world. The hospital was in the town, a big rambling old building. Mum worked part time as an RN(registered nurse) in the Outpatients and Causality ward doing four hours per day, three times a week. I recall back in 1958, when the Head of Nursing for the Health Department would do her annual visit, the staffs' children would line up to greet her. She would get out of the car and walk up the path to the front steps of the hospital to a clap from all of us kids. This lady looked so elegant, dressed in her Matron's uniform. A white mid-calf dress, white veil on her head, white gloves and white shoes and stockings. The kids used to think that she was like the queen; I knew then, when I grew up, I wanted to be a nurse and a matron.

Out at the Three Mile, there were only three rows of houses with approximately ten houses in a row. On the opposite side of the road, down near where the current caravan park is situated, was a Native Welfare Hospital for Aboriginal people only. "Segregation plus." The hospital was the only building on that side and bush surrounded it. The Aboriginal people were prohibited from buying or drinking alcohol and were not allowed into the two hotels – one in town, on the corner opposite the jail and diagonally across from the court house and one out at the six-mile, opposite the race track on the other side of the road.

Sly grog[1] runs were made to where the Aborigines, known in those days as Natives, lived in humpies down in the region of the marsh on the same side as the Europeans in their little houses. Methylated spirits were very popular as an alternative to alcohol and certain cars would bring these to the Aboriginals. I can remember lots of shouting and noises travelling up from the native community to where the rows of white-only people lived. Apartheid was alive and well. That is how it was; but fortunately, it was not so in our house.

With Dad being the headmaster, we would always be the earliest to school; which was great so we could play before classes began. One day, we were told by our friends that there was a crocodile stuck in the town drain, so off we ran to see the poor old croc. We all had these long sticks and we began poking it. The poor thing could not move. Dad appeared out of nowhere with a cane in his hand. We were all duly lined up (about ten of us from memory) and we received three cuts each. That is what it was like in those days. Then we had to go back to school, stay in at recess and write a hundred lines: "I must not tease crocodiles." Needless to say, I never ever did again.

Friday nights were great. They had an outdoor cinema at the meatworks and after a full week at work, it became a ritual that on Friday nights we would go out by taxi to the meatworks to watch the movie that was showing that week. We loved going out and spending a night in the old deckchairs under the moonlight and the stars. In those days it was usually *Cowboys and Indians* movies; so, this also became one of our favourite games as kids. We all sported a Cap Gun, Cowboy suits or Indian feathered bands on our head and skirts. I loved being a squaw, with a bow and arrow and one of my favourite books was *Hiawatha*. We played out the stories many times. Mum would always pack a picnic and we would have a community tea at the outdoor cinema. The parents would sit in the deckchairs and the kids were down on the lawn at the front of the big screen.

Another memory that stood out for me was the visiting clergy. They would come to town four times a year and would always come for dinner at our house. We met the new Bishop of the North West who had just been appointed. Bishop Jobst was a very nice young German man and he would visit all the towns in the Kimberly once a year. The visiting clergy would say Mass in an upstairs bedroom in the two storey Wyndham Hotel, (owned and managed by a man called Des Gee and his wife), or at the old Court House. They had a dock in the courthouse and we used to run for our lives to be first in; because if you were first in, you would get to sit in the dock. I had no idea what Mass was and found it very boring. Mum and Dad were strict Catholics and would always say grace before meals and then pray the rosary every night. We too would have to join in, so we learnt the prayers by rote but had no idea of the meaning of the words. I was not interested in praying; I knew I had a 'special friend' who could not be seen and would always be there for me to talk to.

Wyndham was very much a live town and it had a great heart despite the tribulations of our indigenous brothers and sisters in spirit. It was the time of the Drovers[2], who would bring in their cattle by horseback to the meatworks. The meat would be packed and shipped all over the world. I can still recall the posts outside the Wyndham hotel where white men's horses were tied up out the front.

They closed the old school in town at the end of 1958 and built a brand new one out at the Three Mile. It was not far to walk from our house. Although I missed my friends from the meatworks, I had lots of Aboriginal friends and one boy from Umbulgari was my bestie. His name was Henry and he was a great fun kid.

One day, a group of us decided to become blood brothers and sisters. The Aboriginal kids knew of a native bush that had thorns on it. If you scratched it on the inside of your wrists, it would superficially scratch the skin and you would bleed. This we did and then we would rub our wrists together and become blood brothers and sisters.

I look back and smile at the carefree life I led back then.

At the end of January of 1958, my whole world was devastated. My "twin and soul mate" Joseph was sent to a boy's boarding school at St Louis in Claremont in Perth to commence his high school education. This school was run by the Jesuits Order.

I was lost at this separation and little did I know at the time that a few months later it was to become a permanent separation.

I missed Joe a lot and counted the days until he came home for the school holidays in the May of 1958.

It was a very exciting day, when the MMA plane touched down at Wyndham airport and he appeared at the door. I was as happy as the rest of the family to see him. I would not let him out of my sight that first week and we spent many happy hours playing and talking. The first week of the holidays, we were out exploring the new places I had discovered while he was away and introducing him to the new friends I had made at school.

Unbeknownst to me, I had a very selfish streak within me, and for some reason on the second Sunday he was at home, Joe was on my bike, and I wanted to go somewhere. Joe would not get off my bike, so I kicked him in his sore knee.

I must have really hurt him, leaving him on the back veranda crying while I rode off to where I was going.

I never apologised to him; something that was to come back to haunt me over the years. This event went on to have an influence on my future life. After this incident, I was never mean to anyone when someone hurt me. I became very sensitive and vulnerable.

When other children teased me, I would not retaliate; instead I would bury the hurt inside me. This had a major effect on my psyche, when a tsunami of verbal violence and subliminal bullying and harassment was aimed at me in my late thirties.

It was the 26th May, 1958, a Monday, and we had just started school again after the holidays. Joe still had a few more days before he had to go back on the MMA plane (the big bird, as we called it), to boarding school in Perth.

Every Monday morning, Gladys, an old Aboriginal lady, would come to do the washing and ironing for Mum. Dad would normally have the copper laid and lit before we went to school.

On this day, Joe said to dad, "I will fix it Dad, I will light the copper and have it ready for when Gladys arrives. We all left for school and after we had gone, Joe went out and started to light the copper fire; the grate at the back was open but he couldn't get the fire started with just matches; so he threw some kerosene on it.

Immediately, the wind brought it straight to the front and he was standing right there in front of the fire. Flames came out and his pyjamas caught fire. Mum heard him screaming and went racing out and tried to put out his burning body with her bare hands. Roy Sergeant who also heard the screams, came out of the house, jumped the fence after grabbing a blanket and threw it over Joe and rolled him onto the ground. Joe received horrific burns and my mum had severe burns on both her hands as well.

We were in school when all this happened. Dad, obviously had to leave suddenly to come home and another teacher took over supervising our class.

Joe had to be airlifted to Darwin Hospital with my mother on an MMA commercial flight. Wyndham was the last airport on what was known as the milk run[3], flying from Perth, Geraldton, Carnarvon, Onslow, Roebourne, Port Hedland Broome, Derby and Wyndham and then to Darwin. They made the two stretchers fit and flew them straight to Darwin unattended by medical or nursing staff. Poor Dad had to stay behind and break the news to us girls. It must have been a horrendous time for him and my mother.

I went on with my carefree life, having little idea of the tremendous upheaval my family had just endured. All I knew was that Joe had had an accident, Mum had her hands burnt and they would be home soon.

My poor father had to wait a few days, to get the next MMA plane, a DC3 to Darwin. Dad had to prepare us that Joe could die. I was very sad from that day on. Friends rallied to take care of us girls, so that when Dad was ready to go, he did not have to worry about us. I remember being so distressed at not being allowed to go to Darwin that I did nothing but cry and sob and kept on saying that I needed to go with him to Darwin to see Joe and say sorry to him for kicking him in his sore knee the day before his accident.

One night, during my time of grief and despair, I woke out of a deep sleep to see a beautiful man with a bright red light coming from his heart. He sat on the bed and I heard a voice say to me, "Peta, I am going to take Joe home". I sat up in the bed and the man was gone so I went and woke my father and told him what had just happened, and my father immediately said to me, that I could go with him to Darwin. To this day, I really believe it was the presence of Jesus that I saw that night all those years ago.

On arrival at the Darwin airport, we were met by total strangers - members of a Catholic family, and the parish priest, Father Frank Flynn.

They took us straight to Darwin hospital to see Joe and my mother who were in the same room. I ran straight into my mother's arms, but too scared to stay long in her arms, in case I hurt her if I accidentally touched her bandaged hands. Joe was lying in a bed covered from head to foot in bandages, and all I could see of his face were two eyes, and his lips. He could not talk, I remember telling him I loved him, and to this day I cannot remember if I said sorry to him for my meanness. I stayed with him, just looking into his eyes for some time, I had to leave then to go home with this very kind lady, leaving dad to be by their sides.

The family with whom we were staying had enrolled me into the St Mary's Catholic school, so I could go to school with their children. I was never allowed to go back to the hospital. The people we stayed with were very kind and cared for us very well. Meanwhile, Joe slipped into a coma; he was very peaceful and he passed over on the 11th day of June 1958. The saddest thing was, I was not allowed to go to his funeral as it was not a place for children in those days.

Death was not talked about. It was swept under the carpet and not spoken of in front of children. I look back and realise how all the emotions and pain must have been buried so deep at the cellular level in my parents' bodies as it has been in mine. I had no one to share my grief and pain with. I could not talk to anyone. This really affected me initially. However, I knew where my Joe was, and spent my time praying(talking) to him and for him, in my own way. I must say I have had peace around me from that time on in relation to death and dying right up to this day. I know we are all going home.

On our return to Wyndham, life changed forever; our family had been torn apart, my parents were in a state of deep grief, depression and shock. They were completely broken and until the day they died, they were never the same as they were in the early years of my life; they grieved in the only way they knew how.

In reflection, I believe a lot of that learning came from the Second World War, in which they both served, as armed forces service personnel. My father was a tail gunner in the Royal Australian Airforce, RAAF - involved in bombing raids over Germany; and my mother was a nurse in the Royal Air Force, RAF. They saw so much death and destruction, I am sure it affected them when it came to their own personal tragedy too.

Physically, things continued the same. Life went on with Dad teaching and Mum working at the hospital in the casualty section. However, once we were all at home we lived in sorrow, sadness and brokenness.

I became quite feral and defiant to orders from Mum and Dad. Dad became very much an authoritarian and consequently I received the back of the hairbrush very regularly. I spent a lot of time out of the house with both my European and Aboriginal friends. I was happy with my friends or playing on my own. I shut down emotionally and spiritually, blocking the flow of the life force, by burying my pain very deeply. Joe was never spoken of after he passed away, and I found out forty years later in 1998, from my sister Marion, that she remembered coming down on The State Ship, the MV Koolama in January of 1960 and saw Dad take a little suitcase out on the deck, go to the ship's rail, open the suitcase that had all Joseph's treasures in it, and throw his treasures one by one into the ocean followed by the suitcase. My heart broke again when I heard this story; all I have of my brother's life are three photos- two of him and one with myself.

I also remember one of the biggest treasured times I had in Wyndham as a twelve year old. I was allowed, if I had been good, to go out on the sugar tea and flour run with the Native Welfare Sister when she did her weekly runs to the twenty-mile camp on a Tuesday afternoon after school. I was never allowed to go if I had been naughty. Once we arrived at the camp, we would deliver Sunshine powdered milk, tea, sugar and flour. The Sister was a kind lady who wore a white uniform and a veil. I really liked our outings. At the camps we would sit in a circle on the ground talking and sharing tea and damper with the old Aboriginal women.

I won my first running race, a 100-yard dash on a town picnic day when the Wyndham races were held. People came from everywhere around the region. The racecourse was right opposite the Six Mile hotel, where in the winter time they would have a ten gallon tin barrel fire pit, to keep the patrons warm. I must add here that there was no such town called Kununurra then. I remember Mum having to go out with the doctor to the Kimberley Research Station (KRS) to do a clinic, once a month.

Sometimes, friends would come and take us out to the Ivanhoe Crossing over the great Ord River, which was once part of the main road to Wyndham. It was flooded after the start of the Ord Irrigation scheme in the 1960's. We had fun, swimming in the crossing's flood ways; the water was always cool, refreshing, and safe. Salt water crocodiles were never seen there in that era. The other place we used to go swimming to was "The Grotto" one of my favourite swimming holes, in the world.

One of my other beautiful memories of Mother Nature's beauty was to see all the mountains and hills surrounding Wyndham, on fire. We would sit on the front veranda and watch it, especially when the lightning strikes hit. This was being, not doing; it was being one with nature. Another beautiful memory just flashed before me. There were plains on the road between Ivanhoe Crossing and Wyndham, where you used to see Pink Brolgas[4] in full flight dancing their way across the plains as you drove past.

At the end of 1959, Dad was given notice of another transfer. This time it was to be in the South. So, we had to pack up again and say goodbye to all the beautiful people with whom we had journeyed during these two very painful years. Once again, I had to leave my school friends, both Indigenous and Westerners.

I did not want to leave.

EAST ROCKINGHAM

In 1960, Dad was transferred to the East Rockingham School as the Headmaster. I was twelve when this move happened and as a free wild spirit, I was very independent. I quickly made friends with a couple of girls the same age (who were our neighbours) and we would spend our days down on the Kwinana beach swimming and snorkelling around the old shipwreck, that was quite close to the beach.

We would ride our bikes down at 10.00am and were given very strict instructions that we had to be home by 4.00pm; or else we would not be allowed to go the next day. I soon became a suntanned blonde-headed beach girl and could have quite easily become a school dropout. I started to love listening to all the songs of the 50's and learnt the words of my favourite singers' songs. That Christmas in 1959, I received a little transistor radio as my gift.

Today, it is so hard to imagine that both Rockingham, was a very small country town and East Rockingham (now Kwinana) was a holiday village. There was no industry there then, and it was so far away from Fremantle and Perth that transport was non-existent. We had two buses a day passing our house - one in the morning and one in the late evening, to and from Fremantle. There was nothing but bush and trees around.

We lived at the end of Office Road, closest to the old Mandurah Road. It was an old school-house next door to the school. It was so different to Wyndham. We had electricity, a big rainwater tank and a huge block with lots of fruit trees. Dad still had to chop wood and light the wood stove and the water heater for hot water for our baths. Mum still boiled the kettle on the stove, baked her own bread and heated the water to do the dishes in winter. But the biggest change we had was the purchase of a television. Television came to Perth in 1959. Our first was a box TV, black and white with a dial. I remember the old days where we watched shows like Bonanza, Rawhide, The Bob Dyer Show, and I Love Lucy. I think we had just one channel - Channel Seven. The world came into our lounge room and for the first time we saw a big open picture book on a screen.

The Narrows Bridge was opened shortly before we came south in November 1959.

It was great to be in a little town and to have the milkman come and deliver fresh milk in glass bottles. The fruit and vegetable man would pull up outside the gate and we would go out with mum to buy all the lovely fresh produce. On the odd occasion we would even go into Perth on the bus. In those days, there was a big general department store called Boans, on Wellington Street, in Perth. It was built in 1895. We thought it was just the best; we used to watch the cashiers put the money in a brass container and it would be sent across the building via a wire from one counter to another counter somewhere on the second floor. We kids had never seen anything like it. It used to be where Myer's is now situated in the city. The old Boans store suffered major damage in a fire in 1979; but after being restored, it closed in 1986 when it was bought by the Myer Company Limited during the Forrest Chase development of Perth's CBD. Mum and Dad were very faithful to the three major departmental stores in Perth at that time. Boans, David Jones and Aherns.

The other thing that standouts in my memory, every time, we went to Perth was that we would always have lunch at a cafe on the corner of Murray Street. It was right next door to the Boans store exit and run by an Italian man. It was a real treat. He had a big flower stand outside his café and would sell bunches of roses, carnations and other flowers. In the winter, he would have buckets full of Boronia and Kangaroo Paws for sale. Mum would buy them fresh every time we came up to the city. That would always keep the wonderful memories of Treesville alive; beautiful smells would permeate through the mall coming from that corner on Murray Street.

Mum bought another car, an old Vanguard. It was big and magical to ride in. My father never ever learnt to drive and I do not know why to this day. One day, we went on a long drive to Mandurah for the day, and on the way we had a flat tyre. Dad disappeared into the bush and hid behind a tree, while Mum stood by the side of the car, with us three girls in the back seat. A car came by shortly and a man stopped and changed the tyre for my mother and after he left, Dad appeared from behind the tree and off we went for a picnic in Mandurah.

When one drives down the old road to Rockingham, along the Kwinana Industrial area, one could never in a million years imagine what it was like back then.

BOARDING SCHOOL

*I*n 1960, it was my turn to go to boarding school and I was sent to a Catholic private girls' school in Perth run by the Sisters of Our Lady of the Missions. There was a great big brick wall that ran right around the convent and the school. I wanted to go to the local Kwinana High School where my friends were going, not to a boarding school - but obviously, I had no say in these decisions. My mother took me to Aherns, to be fitted for my school uniforms. I had to wear a boater panama hat and a blazer, gloves and these things called stockings - and to keep them up, we had to wear a suspender belt, which had little knobs on to attach to the stockings – a time before pantyhose was invented. For our sports uniform we would wear a skirt below the knee and a top; no shorts were allowed. School shoes were the Clarks brown lace-ups, and our sand shoes were white canvas with no cushioning. My lovely long blonde plaits were cut short and blunted to my ears.

The dreaded day arrived when Mum took me to the convent. The nuns were welcoming but when the time came to say goodbye, I cried and cried. My bed was in a corridor against a wall. All the other girls had their own little cubicles. I found it was a cold and unfriendly environment for me and I became a rebel overnight, waiting and wanting to be expelled.

The nun who ran the boarding house was a rather plump older motherly woman, who tried to help me settle in over those first few weeks. I suffered severely from the culture shock. Gone was my freedom, gone was my way of life, gone were the bare feet. However, the worst thing gone was my extended Aboriginal families, my white friends from Wyndham and the new friends I had made in Kwinana. There were no Aboriginal children at this school, just girls from different socio-economic backgrounds, who did all things well, like dance and play the piano. I only knew the sound of the didgeridoo and clap sticks, and Aboriginal dances and songs from my early childhood.

I was always in trouble for talking and being the class fool. I hated school and tried to get expelled several times. I was so miserable, I decided I would run away. So, one night, I scaled the big red brick wall and found myself all alone in Mary Street. It was dark, cold and raining. I had no money and knew no-one in Perth, so I sat against the wall and cried and cried, till I rang the front gate's bell and a nun came and found me. She was very kind. She made me some hot chocolate and went to fetch the Reverend Mother. They contacted my parents and they made the decision to give me one more chance. My parents, wrote me a letter, warning me that if I didn't stay put, there would be big trouble. It was a very lonely time and I started internalising everything. On the outside I was a cheeky fun-loving young teenager, but on the inside, I felt disconnected in body, mind and soul.

School proved very different - with grades mattering more than happiness. I desperately missed the carefree life I had before I went to this school.

Sex education in those days was taboo in school and when I became a 'young lady' with significant changes in my anatomy and physiology, I was frightened at all that was happening to my body. A kindly senior boarder helped me through this, but I decided then that I hated being a girl. Mum had never prepared me for these changes.

As a border, one of my chores was to clean the large jarrah staircase and banisters that separated the senior school, (the boarding part of the school) from the junior school. I hated doing these boring jobs and would mostly spend my time sliding up and down the bannisters; until one day I was caught and given the chore of cleaning them for another whole term.

In high school, I was the joker in the class doing things that were bound to get me expelled. We had a nun who was a short round lady with black rimmed glasses. Suffice to say, she did not like me, and I did not like her. She was the French teacher.

Whenever, she would say "Je Ne Vous Par," her glasses would pop down onto her nose and I would start laughing uncontrollably as the whole class joined in.

One of my classmates told me that she did not like cats. So, one day a little kitten happened to be in the playground, and I picked it up, as it was just before our French class, smuggled it up my jumper and put it in her desk. When this nun opened the desk, the kitten squealed and jumped out. The entire class burst out laughing.

Needless to say, I failed French.

My reports were never very good, the art teacher even wrote in my art report "Art is uphill work for Peter".

To a fourteen-year-old school girl this just reinforced the message, "you are not good enough."

Most of the friends I made were the day scholars. My hero at school was a senior girl who was the captain of one of the faction teams. Her name was Sue Oswald. She was such a great sports champion and always had a kind word to say to everyone. I didn't know her well then as she was in year 12. However, I was fortunate enough to meet up with Sue at an athletics meet many years later at the State Championships where our boys were competing back in 1987. We really connected then and today Sue and her husband, Mal Gooch are two of our closest friends and I am honoured to say Sue was my eight-year-old granddaughter's first music teacher.

So, after my failed attempt to escape, I realised I had better start conforming to some of the rules if I had to stay. I started to say "Yes Sister, No Sister" and under my breath "three bags full Sister" until one day, I accidentally said ''three bags full'' out aloud. This, of course, resulted in immediate detention - which I didn't mind, except that I had to miss sports.

I played as much sport as I could, loving all the sports the school offered at that time - the swimming carnivals, netball games and athletic carnivals, but most of all, I enjoyed tennis and took it up seriously. I was taught by a lovely man called Mr Marshall, who was a great coach. Full of encouragement from him, I worked very hard and became an "okay tennis player". I think it was tennis that saved me as I used to practise hitting that poor little tennis ball against the old bumper board. I took my internal anger and frustration out on that small green ball, as it renewed my spirit.

Tennis made me take a decision about the spelling of my name. In 1963, I entered the State Championships held in Kings Park, during the January school holidays. When Mum and I arrived, we went to check the girl's draw and couldn't find my name. I was really upset. A kind official came and checked out the boys' draw and yes, I was in their draw.

I was not allowed to play, and I was so disappointed; so unbeknown to Mum and Dad, I started spelling my name Peta, even though all formal documents spelt my name as Peter. I was lucky enough to have made the Herbert Cup team in 1962 and was a member of the winning Slazenger cup team in 1963 and in 1964.

Prior to Beatty Park being opened in 1962, we used to have to go by bus to Crawley Baths for swimming lessons and swimming carnivals.The water was brown and freezing cold. It was closed after Beatty Park was opened for the 1962 Empire Games and today the bronze statue on Riverside Drive is a Perth icon. I love the flashbacks I get sometimes, when I drive past the statue.

The other thing I loved was to be part of the Choir for the Eisteddfod Competition that was held each year in Perth. We also had an Irish singing and dancing competition held on St Patrick's day. The Church had extra holidays like "Sacred Heart Day" and very special days called 'Holy days of Obligation.' On those days the boarders, after mass, and breakfast would go out to Sorrento for a day at the beach. The bitumen finished at North Beach Road and we then travelled on a sandy road till we reached the water. There was absolutely nothing out at Sorrento, except for a Dome shaped building, where we could buy ice-creams and a few snacks on the now West Coast Highway. The nuns purchased a large section of land from the Church back then, and we were told one day there would be a very big Sacred Heart School and lots of houses. Often on a Sunday, we would be taken on a boarders' outing to Kings Park to see all the wildflowers in Spring. They were beautiful and I would love those outings as it would remind me of the days when Joe and I would live in the forest amongst the kangaroo paws and boronia bushes as little kids. We were told we were not allowed to pick any flowers; I would do just the opposite and pick a kangaroo paw and some Boronia and stick it up my jumper to take back to my little cubicle.

My favourite academic subject was Speech and Drama. Our teacher was a beautiful old lady who set very high standards. I always got very good marks in the annual Speech and Drama Exams.

I went on my first retreat when I was fifteen years old, and I remember that experience helped me reconnect with a way of living internally for the five days we spent in silence and prayer. It was so nourishing for my soul. We had a retreat each year, from year 10 to year 12; however, once the retreat was over, it was back to only living in the outside world; thus closing and locking the door to my soul again

As boarders, we had only three sleep-ins a week. Four mornings a week, we were up when the bell rang and we had to go to Chapel for mass; most evenings we would have to go to the rosary in the chapel at 5pm. I was fascinated by the old nuns who would sit and pray. They all looked so peaceful. We also had prayer time every morning and night before school and bed. I had no idea what the words meant at Mass or what the Rosary really meant. Mass was in Latin and the Priest used to say Mass with his back to us. It was in my latter years at school when 'The Second Vatican Council' was held in Rome and changes were being brought in world-wide that I started getting interested in religion and a theological way of thinking. I was caught up in a dualistic mindset, closing the door to my soul and the oneness of the universe that was alive and happy and full of love, before I went to boarding school.

I have very strong memories of three major events that happened in the world in 1962 and 1963, which were life changing both globally and in our State of WA. The USA was about to send 'The Friendship 7' space craft on a mission to orbit the Earth and it would be orbiting over Perth. The Australian Government agreed to a request from NASA to leave the airports lights on at the Perth Airport to see if they were visible from space. Premier, David Brand, ordered that the street lights be left on and asked the people of Perth to respond enthusiastically. He asked us to leave our front porch lights on. When the night of the orbit came, everyone was excited. We were allowed to stay up, Perth changed overnight, and today is still renowned for the words John Glen said as he was orbiting Perth, "Just to my right I can see a big pattern of lights, apparently right on the coast. I can see the outline of a place and a very bright light just to the south of it. The lights show up very well and I thank everyone for turning them on." Perth was now an international city! We came to be known as the 'City of Lights', as this event hit the world newspapers. I can still remember the excitement of that first space journey.

The second major event that changed Perth occurred on Australia Day in 1963. At that time, many families left their front doors and windows open. On hot summer nights, families would drag their mattresses out to sleep under the stars on their back lawns. Life was free, safe and easy; there were not many air conditioners back then and we had no fans in government owned headmasters' houses we lived in. In the early hours of the morning, a man started to prowl the streets at night in the Western Suburb of Nedlands, shooting randomly. Twenty two people were targeted prior to his arrest and eight were killed.

That night Perth lost its innocence. People were scared and started locking their doors and windows at night and the practice of sleeping out on the lawn slowly died.

The third major event happened at the end of that year which was to greatly affect the world, wrapping citizens in grief. I clearly remember that Friday in November 1963, when John Frederick Kennedy was shot dead while riding in a motorcade in the USA. He was one of the world's most famous and greatest leaders in that era. Everyone loved him; including myself and I was just fifteen. I remember the school assembly where we all had to pray for JFK; tears flowed in our school for this great man.

I passed my junior certificate at fifteen and I was happy because it meant the end of formal school life. Mum and Dad would not have that; I had to get my leaving certificate. Dad insisted that I was smart and filled out my forms to do physics, chemistry and maths one and two; he wanted me to be a maths teacher.

In term 1, I failed all four subjects and didn't care. I was not interested; my brain was not wired for science or maths. I was far more a hands-on type of student and a visual learner. I loved biology, physiology, language, speech and drama, English, economics and history.

So, I said I would leave school if I had to continue doing the subjects, I had failed. This was the first time I had ever stood up to my father. I got my way and finally started passing exams, and the programming continued for another two years.

When leaving year came, it was crunch time. What would I do next? In those days, opportunities were limited. We could either choose academia or professions like nursing or teaching. There weren't many other options.

For me the decision was easy. I decided I would choose nursing as my career. When I met the Matron from the WA Health Department at the age of ten, I had already decided that nursing was going to be my chosen profession.

I was also influenced by my visits to the 6-mile township with the Native Welfare Sister and with my dear Mother, who was a Nurse, I was automatically led into nursing.

It was not easy back in 1964 as places were limited in nursing schools. The training hospitals, Fremantle, Royal Perth, Princess Margaret, The Government school of Nursing, and Sir Charles Gardiner had four entry classes a year with twenty student nurses in each class. You had to pass two aptitude tests to even get an interview to one of the training schools. The aptitude tests were done through a Government Department on St Georges Terrace. They were very thorough. On reflection, it was to identify who had the attributes for the humanities and to see if you had specific traits like empathy.

I chose to go to Fremantle Hospital. I had my two interviews with Matron Leaworthy, and was overjoyed to receive my letter of placement at the Fremantle Hospital School of Nursing commencing the 18th January 1965.

I finished my leaving certificate and passed. In those years, all the results came out in the Western Australian newspaper just after Christmas. A great night of excitement when we all gathered down at St Georges Terrace to get the first print of the West Australian and danced when we found I had matriculated.

I guess by the time I finished, I was quite a lady and having done speech and drama, I talked with a plum in my mouth.

In some subtle ways, I had changed. I had become disconnected in body, mind and soul to the way I was brought up in the first twelve years of my life. I lived in and for the outside world only.

LAYING ON MY HANDS

NURSING SCHOOL

Some of the happiest years of my life happened when I was in nursing school.

I started my nursing career on the 18th January 1965, dressed in a blue uniform, a white apron, a white cap on my head and black polished lace up shoes. We were also issued with a lovely red Fremantle Hospital Cape. We were housed in a big nurses' quarters in the grounds of the hospital.

We were taken over to the School of Nursing - old army huts in the hospital grounds on the corner of Alma Street and South Terrace. From memory, there were twenty of us, all young, all straight from school apart from a couple who were in their early 20's. Here, we met the Head Tutor of the School of Nursing, an old sister by the name of Sister Harris, a wonderful teacher with great nursing knowledge on all facets of nursing.

This is where we would spend the first two months, learning the theoretical aspects of Basic Medical conditions and basic nursing procedures in the specialties of Medical, Surgical, Gynaecological, Paediatric, Ophthalmic, Geriatric, Ear Nose and Throat Conditions and Orthopaedic.

Would you believe I have taken these headings from "FRE-

MANTLE HOSPITAL -P.B. REBBECHI -RECORD OF PRACTICAL INSTRUCTION AND EXPERIENCE". I am excited I kept it for 55 years. Never expecting to publish a book about that era of nursing.

During the third week, we went on the wards to practise what we had learnt. Oh! what a shock I had when I had to give a man a bed bath - I had never seen a naked man before and I remember being as nervous as hell. I had a senior second year student nurse guide me through the bed bath.

Great excitement came when we had finished PTS (Preliminary Training School) and were finally rostered on to the wards to work as a real nurse - in the roles of the Pan Room Nurse or the Drinks Nurse.

My first ever ward was a Female Surgical Ward, run by an older Sister whose name was Hoppy Western. She was a nice, tall, big woman who walked with a limp; hence her nickname, Hoppy. She was also a woman of few words, but she always had a smile for everyone and was kind to all the patients and nursing students. Two duties at the very beginning of becoming a nurse for the first six months, would include being the pan room nurse - we had to do a pan and bottle round every two hours, ensure the pan and bottles were sterilised in a boiling water steriliser, and ensure all the stainless steel wash bowls and tooth mugs too would be cleansed and sterilised.

In those days, it seemed like every one of the older generations had false teeth and as the pan room nurse, it was your job to clean their false teeth. I will never forget how stupid I was on my first day when as the pan room nurse, I collected all the teeth from the patients' bed side lockers (which by the way, we also had to clean), brought them into the pan room, filled up the sink and put all the teeth in together and cleaned them all. On completion of this task, I had no idea what teeth were matching and what mug they had come out of! I was trying to match them up when Sister Western came in to see the pickle I was in. She was so patient and kind with me and did not growl. She did, however, give me "the look". The Hoppy Look.

If you were rostered on as the Drinks Nurse, it was your responsibility to ensure every patient on the ward had a daily egg flip. Every day, the drinks nurse, at 10am in the morning, would go into the kitchen and make up a big silver jug with the following ingredients in it – egg, malt and full cream milk. On my first attempt, (I had never cooked or made a cup of tea before) I turned on the old vitamiser and forgot to put on the lid and whoosh it went everywhere . I then had to clean it all up.

Spending three months being the drinks and pan room nurse, was really grounding and teaching me the basics of nursing like the importance of filling in accurate fluid balance charts. If you had forgotten to calculate the fluid balance charts and had not added up the intake and output, you were called back to fill it all in.

I fell in love with nursing.

I loved the camaraderie of my nursing school mates but loved most of all, the patients we cared for. I represented Fremantle Hospital in the inter-hospital sports tournaments that were in existence in those days, playing tennis, netball (the Nurse's Quarters had their own netball and tennis courts) and I swam in the swim team. Our swimming training was in the river, in East Fremantle, in the weeks, leading up to the inter hospital swimming carnival held each year at Beatty Park pool.

I was seventeen when I received my first pay - a tidy sum of five pounds in a little brown envelope for a forty-four-hour fortnight. I had never seen so much money. Dad said to me, "You are on your own now."

It was during those years I first discovered the power of the 'Laying on of Hands,' not knowing what it was until 1999. Patients always used to say to me, 'Oh nurse your hands are so hot/warm' and that they felt so much better after I had rubbed their sore bodies. I would reply smiling, "I do have a cold heart".

Nursing is a humanitarian vocation and to this day I maintain that the human connection should override the patient being regarded as a case number and analysed by machines.

The rotations were every six weeks. There were eight rotations, Male and Female Surgical, Male and Female Medical, Male and Female Community wards, Paediatric Theatre and Casualty. The training was extensive and thorough. The senior nurses were our mentors and coaches on the wards. We had lectures on theory and assignments to do every week.

Our theoretical studies included surgical, medical, paediatrics and community health. We dealt with every condition and diagnosis except, midwifery. We would also have mentally ill patients that we had to escort to Heathcote Hospital for electric shock treatments. One heard awful stories about mental health hospitals and it was very scary to walk into Heathcote, escorting patients for shock treatment. I now shudder to think about how patients were treated back then.

Mental health was not seen as the kind of serious issue it is today. The emergence of the acuteness and seriousness of mental health issues over the last 20-30years in our society- from all cultures and all age groups in Australia, and the daily suicides that get reported, is a tragedy beyond words and until holistic health in its purest form is brought back into our society, we will only see the problem growing bigger. It is the same for all the other cohorts in our society, especially those most vulnerable, like our aged, young children and the broken members of our society.

The patients on the male surgical ward (there was only one, then) were car and accident victims, sporting injuries, hernia repairs, laminectomies, in the young and middle-aged group. In those days, the health and wellness of the ageing population was very good. Cancer was a word hardly ever heard of in those days. I really only remember two patients whose diagnosis was cancer.

I remember one day as a student nurse in 1965, I was escorting a lady with uterine cancer to the radiotherapy unit on the grounds of the now SCGH (Sir Charles Gairdner Hospital). Originally, that hospital was the Perth Chest Hospital for Tuberculosis, and other infectious diseases. It was renamed, Queen Elizabeth II (QEII) and then later to Sir Charles Gardiner Hospital.

What I also remember was nursing timber mill workers – some

who suffered with gas gangrene. It was in the days when the timber mill industry in WA was a thriving industry. If a tree fell, and landed on a tree loppers' leg, the gentleman would be very seriously injured and then transferred to either Royal Perth Hospital or Fremantle Hospital for treatment. One never hears of patients with gas gangrene today. I also nursed only two patients with tetanus during my career.

People used to stay in hospital until full recovery occurred. As a result, one got to know the patients well, and many of the male surgical patient units had a big back veranda- that was normally where the patients with the fractured femurs where nursed. In those days, traction was the treatment of choice and the average length of stay was anything from six weeks to ten weeks. Nurses and patients were informal and exchanged gentle banter. If young men were very cheeky, we would put a product called ENO and gentian violet in their urinal bottles (not much) and once they used it, it would start to fizz. There were many laughs. Ambulant patients too, if they were cheeky, would have their beds short sheeted. Jokes were a part of life and each day there was something or other happening. Laughter, they say, is the best medicine.

There were only a few allied health staff; the nurses used to be the ones who did the post op exercises and the percussions. There was a lady who would come and do basket weaving with the persons who were long stay patients once a week. The senior nurses were the speech therapists, dieticians /nutritionists and sometimes psychologists too.

There were no such thing as intensive care units. Unconscious patients would be nursed in a single room and, if intubated, would be on a ventilator called a 'birds' machine. There were only five single rooms for the very ill and all the other patients were nursed in the old Florence Nightingale wards.

The shifts were from 11.00pm to 7.30am for night shifts; day shifts went from 07.00am-3.30pm and the evening shifts from 2.30pm till 11.00 pm. Once on a roster, you would work a split shift, twice in a fortnight equating to forty-four hours per week. Interestingly enough, the sick leave taken was negligible and no-one ever had any stress leave; we had no agency nurses or casuals back then. There appeared to be no such thing as stress or anxiety. If you didn't like it, one would know nursing was not for them, and they would leave. There was no patient hoists, slide boards/slide sheets, occupational health and safety regulations and wind up beds ; only iron beds. If you had to elevate a patient, one would have to put these big wooden blocks under the bed legs and we would have to shoulder lift all the patients. To lift patients on to trolleys, we would roll them on to a canvas which was cradled in long thick wooden poles and lift patients on to a trolley.

Many a time, I would get squashed under a patient, when having to sit them up; it was not fun having an 14-18 stone man squashing you, when you were under 7 stone and 12 pounds and five foot tall. No wonder old nurses have really bad backs!

I was working on the male medical ward once and we had a very strict Charge Sister - a brilliant nurse, whose nursing knowledge was fantastic. She was a very big woman and had a booming voice; if she was cross, she could be scary at times and she could also be mean. However, she liked me, so I never got a hard time from her, like some of the others did.

It was on this ward that the first ever cardiac monitor was introduced in Fremantle hospital. It arrived in 1968; the first two beds in the ward were people who had had heart attacks and would be nursed attached to these monitors; there was no such thing as a Coronary Care unit, no specialisation units, and as a student nurse, you were trained to know the full gamut of all conditions that patients where admitted with.

It was an amazing era.

WARD RUNS

*A*fter six months, we got another cap which was plain white with a pale blue checked stripe. Fremantle Hospital in those days had male and female surgical and medical Florence Nightingale wards with verandas, plus a separate private male and female ward, a paediatric ward, two operating theatres and causality with an eight-bed observation ward and a minor theatre. We had no specialities at all. We had no intensive care units and no palliative care units. Our dying and unconscious patients would all be nursed in a private room on the ward next to the sister's office; we would ensure all had their suffering alleviated. The drug of choice back then was Mist Morphine Mixture. Nembutal was also used as a sleeping tablet but was phased out in the mid 70's.

All the IV bottles were glass. We had no plastic ones at all. We would have to count the drips into the chamber when we put up IV fluid. After calculating the rate; we had to count the number of drops per minute. There was no technology like i-vacs and machines to do that for you. I shake my head at the environmental waste that happens in the health industry today and I would consider the industry to be one of the biggest polluters of the environment. Even in theatre today, just everything is thrown away.

Workplace bullying was not a 'thing' in those days. Although that did not mean that it did not happen. During one rotation in my second year of nursing school, I was delegated to the operating theatres. There were two surgeons who had very bad reputations. You never wanted to be in the theatre they were working in. One was an orthopaedic surgeon. He would actually throw heavy metal instruments at nurses in the operating room, while operating. Fortunately for me, I was never assigned to his theatre. The other was a general surgeon. On my very first assignment, scrubbing for him, he was very rude to me. I remember shaking in my boots as I stepped back from the table, peeled off my gloves and prepared to walk out of the OR, much to the horror of those present. The surgeon could not believe it; he gave me a smile, said to me, "re-scrub". He was surprisingly nice to me on my return. The Charge Nurse spoke to me later and asked why I did it. I remember saying to her, he cannot speak to me like that. She just smiled. After that incident, he always asked me to scrub for him when I was assigned to his theatre. Duties in theatre were very different back then; we had to scrub the walls on night shift, tip the small and big trolleys upside down and scrub all the wheels after the last theatre case had finished. How did we do it! I have to say, hardly ever did patients get a hospital acquired infection. A vast contrast to 2020.

If someone died during the night shift, two nurses would place the deceased on a trolley and would have to wheel the trolley a kilometre down to the mortuary in the dark, with a torch to guide us along the path. If you accidentally left their false teeth out, you would have to go back and insert them. As an eighteen- year old that was not fun! It was quite frightening really. We had no orderlies to do this in those days - the nurses were it.

My favourite place to work became Casualty. Here is where I really learnt what it was like to be a good generalist nurse; one had to be good at everything. My passion developed for casualty work, and I spent many years of my working life in remote, rural, regional and tertiary health service units in emergency care. I have many stories to tell and maybe one day I will write a book called, "*Stories General Nurses Can Tell.*" Nowadays, it is mainly only in the smaller country health care units and remote areas, where nurses develop into generalist nurses. Regional or tertiary hospitals do not cater to this because specialisation happens very early in a nurse's career. In my opinion, this has been rather detrimental to the nursing profession and to the health care industry in general.

The great thing about training and living in Fremantle was the proximity to the beautiful west coast beaches of South Beach, Port Beach, Leighton and Cottesloe. I quickly became a beach goer every day, except when I was on day shift. Cottesloe and Leighton were our favourites. Bikinis were just coming into vogue and many a time we lost our tops catching a wave at Cottesloe beach. Leighton beach was much calmer. Through spring, summer and autumn for three years the beach was my other home. My other beach buddies and I would lie on the beach in the sun most of the day if we were on a day off, or on night shift. We would rub Johnson's baby oil all over our bodies, (we all had amazing suntans) and I had a head of sun-bleached blonde hair.

I loved my life.

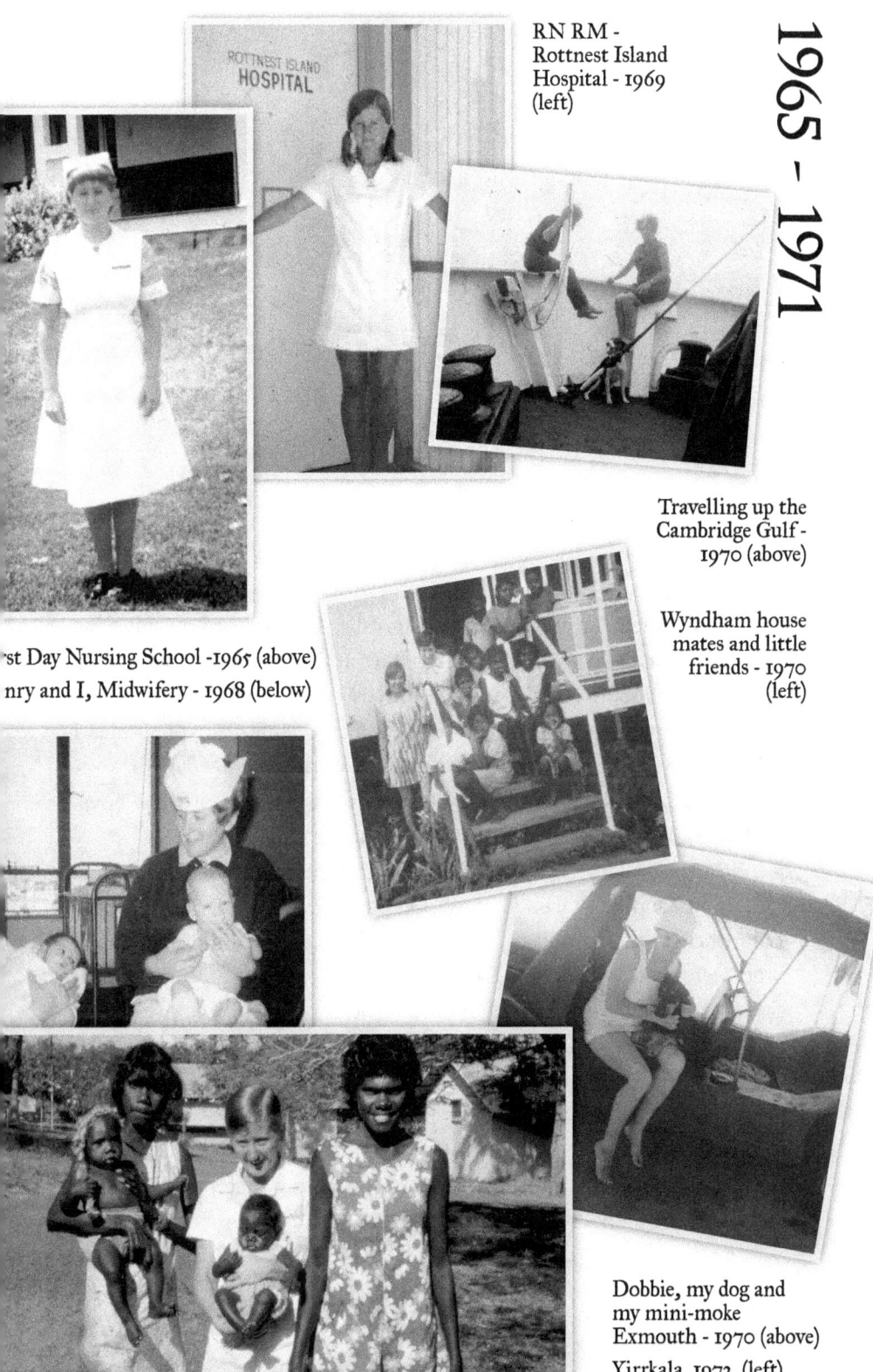

A SPECIAL TIME

Three of my friends Anne, Coralie, Barbara and myself went on a two week holiday together at the end of our first year in January of 1966. We had a week at Caves House, in Yallingup on the South Coast of WA. It was here where I met an amazing young man I fell head over heels in love with, and we journeyed together for over two and a half wonderful years. The four of us also had a week down in Albany and a week over at Rottnest Island.

Rottnest was to become a favourite stomping ground. The four of us went a couple of years in a row. On one holiday, in a cottage next to ours, there was a group of young men from the taxation department who were also holidaying. Each evening we would head to the hotel for a lemon squash and the guys would join us for a beer. We would head back to our cottages around 8:30pm, to get ready for another day of swimming, snorkelling and sun baking. One particular evening, they were giving us some cheek, so when we got home, Barbara and I snuck into their cottage (all doors were left open in those days) and smeared honey under and on the toilet seat. We heard the reaction when they arrived home an hour later. We all had a good laugh.

. . .

Throughout our training we had to live in the nurses' quarters. If you were married though, you had to leave nursing. We had to be in by 22.00 hrs if we were going out partying or nightclubbing or simply going out with our boyfriends on a date. The doors would be locked at 22.00 hrs. We had a key to get in after shift; however, if you forgot to take it on social outings, there would be trouble because the only other person who had a spare key was the house sister, a senior nurse.

In our second year, we lived in a beautiful old six-bedroom house, right next door to the new nurses' quarters where all the third year nurses and staff nurses lived. I shared a room with my friends, Coralie, Anne and Bernadette. When one was going out with their boyfriends on a date, we would leave the window open so the person who was out late could come in that way.

My boyfriend and I were very close, and at that time, I thought he was the man I was going to spend the rest of my life with. We discussed where I was going to do my midwifery. I wanted to go to the best midwifery school in Australia. My mother had lots of friends who were midwives who advised her to send me to St Margaret's in Sydney. I applied and was accepted. I very nearly changed my mind as I didn't want to leave my boyfriend at the time; however, the voice in my head kept saying St Margaret's has the best reputation for being the best hospital in Australia for training midwives. My boyfriend and I agreed that hard as it would be, we would get through this period of separation.

MIDWIFERY SCHOOL

*1*968 came around very quickly and we finally graduated that year in April. At graduation we were told, "your real learning starts now." How true were those words! I have never forgotten them. Straight after graduation, four of us from Fremantle Hospital went to Sydney Town. What a contrast to laid back Perth. The pace and rush of life and the sheer amount of people in Sydney made Perth look like a village. St Margaret's was situated at the top of King's Cross in Darlinghurst and the Nurses quarters was a ten-storey building, situated in the grounds of the hospital. We all had a room on the ninth floor with views of Sydney Harbour. I missed my boyfriend very much and we would talk on the phone in those first months apart and write letters just about every day. Then it became weekly. We had promised each other we could see and go out with others but, we would always be faithful to each other.

St Margaret's Hospital was run by 'The Brown Joseph Sisters', founded by the order Mary Mackillop. The Matron was an old nun by the name of SR Anne. She would do her ward rounds knitting and she had a little dog, which would follow her everywhere. Midwifery back then was women's business and men were not allowed into the labour ward. The women would come in, in labour and the men disappeared. We would have to give the women a dose of castor oil followed by a soap and water enema. How awful must that have been? It was here that the students became midwives, caring for women in a loving, compassionate environment, massaging them, ensuring they were relaxed with minimal intervention. The only intervention was when the student midwife observed an abnormality. She would call the Charge Sister, who would then contact the obstetrician. The Convent would be called and a group of old nuns would go to the chapel and pray. There were minimal inductions or booked caesarean sections; only emergencies as far as I can remember. I have never forgotten the feeling of conducting my first delivery under the watchful eye of a senior sister. It was a wonderful experience.

In those days, the only instrument we used was a pinard - a type of stethoscope used to listen to foetal heartbeat. There were no Doppler's, CTG machines, monitors etc. One of the things I disliked about the labour ward was that after delivery we would have to wash the linen after the patient had left the room. They had a washing machine in a big utility room. Also, in the 60's we had to boil the urine in a test tube to see if there was protein in the sample. To measure the specific gravity we would use a glass urinometer (a small hydrometer) for determining the specific gravity of urine; an important assessment tool for hydration status. Today, nurses just dip a stick into the specimen to get the same result.

I loved working with the mums. In the 1960s it was the practice that first time mums would stay in hospital for fourteen days. Women who had children were kept in for ten days post-partum. We had to bind their breasts and abdomens with binders. We would bring their babies out for breastfeeding every four hours, in a big cart with little compartments full of these adorable little bundles of love. It was the nursery student midwife's job to bathe and care for the babies twenty-four hours a day, apart from feed times. It was such a beautiful role, nurturing mothers and babies. Mums used to have leave for a night out with their husbands the night before they went home.

One of the very sad things about that era was the hidden generation of harmed mothers. The hospital had a program for unmarried mothers. The girls would be sent there by their parents because of the stigma of being an unmarried mother. They would board in the convent ground and would work in places like the kitchens, laundry etc. The student midwives were their carers in the labour ward and in the post-partum period. It was very sad at delivery time. The mothers would deliver on their sides as they did in that era, and once born, the mother of course, would hear that first cry and the baby would be rushed out of the birthing room to the nursery next door. The midwives would comfort the mother after delivery and to this day as I am writing about this, I imagine the pain, that these poor women must have suffered and a shudder goes through me. All I can say is thank God, we student midwives were there for them in their time of grief, sorrow and pain. To those women, I praise you and I am so sorry, that it was how it was forty-nine years ago.

The unmarried mums were nursed in the unmarried mother's only ward. They would be discharged on the fourth day after delivery to return to where they came from before becoming pregnant. There would have been no follow up or grief counselling then; their pain just buried and never to be spoken of again. The babies would be nursed in the adoption ward, the trainee midwives were the surrogate mothers and we cared for these babies as if they were our own. We cuddled them, nursed them, bathed them, and fed them. I still remember Henry; he was my favourite as he was with us for eight months. In fact, I still have a photo of Henry sitting on my knee. It was a happy day; when the day came for the baby to go to a home with new parents. I pray that all had a good wholesome life.

Fast forward to 2017, my husband and I watched the movie "The Lion". It really affected me at a very deep level in my heart. I cannot write a further word about this social and nursing era of Australian history, as it is too painful; knowing what happened to the Stolen Generation of Aboriginal Children. I was honoured to meet and nurse the author, Doris Pilkington Garimara, author of the "The Rabbit Proof

Fence" whilst I was working as The CNS Night Manager at PHRH in 2007.

St Margaret's had a children's hospital right next door to the Maternity Hospital. This is where we had to do our neo natal, sick and premature baby training. Night duty was a hoot as the children's hospital, where the unit was situated, was part of the Red Light District of Kings Cross. All the houses had red lights on outside their front door and in the summer, ladies would stand in the doorway in their very short miniskirts, smoking their cigarettes until a car pulled up and a gentleman got out of the car and would go inside. I had no idea what it was all about; however, I was soon educated by some of my peers. I didn't even know what a prostitute was at that time. I had never heard the word. We would sit on the window sill, to feed the babies as we watched the night life.

Life outside work and study was exciting. Sydney was just one big party town; it really was an amazing place to live. We spent many an evening at Kings Cross, dancing the night away. I was twenty-one and got introduced to spirits and loved the taste and the relaxation. I guess I was what they called a one pot screamer. We were always being very careful of who we were with. All the girls would go together to Kings Cross, and would never separate; we always looked after each other, ensuring we were all safe. I loved Go-Go dancing and even danced on tables. I just looked at a photo yesterday of the first concert I had ever attended. It was in a ballroom. Nothing like the outdoor concerts today (in fact, I have never even been to an outdoor one). The artist was none other than Tom Jones; he was one of my musical heroes back then and I still have his records in the shed.

In the summer, I would spend my days off down on the beach at Bondi, surf, sun and sand and in winter I'd go exploring. I remember my first visit to Mt Kosciusko, with my friend Coralie, at the beginning of 1969, just two years after Lake Jindabyne was flooded as part of the Hydro scheme. The Town Centre was newly opened in 1964. A Roman

Catholic Priest took us down there. He was an Oblate Priest who we had nursed back in Fremantle Hospital when he had broken his leg.

My boyfriend was on a cruise ship with his parents, that Christmas and we had two wonderful days together before he sailed out. I was still madly in love with him and counting the days down till my graduation and trip back to Perth. I went with him to my first ever International Cricket Match at the Sydney cricket ground and spent a day at the 1968/69 game between Australia and The West Indies. May of 1969 came very quickly, and I graduated with my Diploma of Midwifery.

It was now time to return home to continue with my life and be with the love of my life. I returned to Fremantle Hospital. Life was great. I moved into a flat with my friend Janet, and another girl, up on the hill opposite the war memorial in Fremantle. I reunited with the man I was madly in love with.

I started as a staff nurse in a white veil, and a very pretty pale blue uniform and after two weeks working and getting to 'know the ropes,' I was put on night shift. I loved the variety of the nursing work I was doing all over Fremantle Hospital advising student senior nurses and encouraging junior student nurses, nurturing them to be the very best they could be. I spent a lot of time working in casualty.

Socially, during my time away, things had changed. All my friends had either stayed in Perth, got engaged or married and several had gone overseas. Six weeks after returning home, my heart was broken into a thousand little pieces. The love of my life had met somebody else while I was away and he broke up with me. It was awful and again I went deep within and put on a big mask for the world to see and buried everything at a deep cellular level. I was devastated and in so much pain.

I never wanted to fall in love again.

ROTTNEST

I threw myself into my nursing career. Six weeks after the trauma of breaking up with the only man I had fallen in love with, I was asked if I would go over to relieve the nursing sister at Rottnest Island for three months. I was twenty-two years of age at the time. The resident nurse, Mrs Sullivan and her husband, were taking long service leave. The relief nurse also needed to be a midwife. As I was the only midwife with causality experience, I jumped at the opportunity. I loved Rottnest, so at the end of September in 1969, I arrived on the island. Mrs Sullivan was at the jetty to meet me. She gave me a comprehensive handover and the key to the Rottnest Island Hospital. It had a little flat on the back, facing the ocean, which was to be my home for the three months I was there. The hospital had no beds; just a little office and a treatment room. It was situated on the ocean side opposite the bakery. I can still smell the fresh bread pulled straight out of the woodfired oven that would wake me at five in the morning every day.

I was the only healthcare worker on the island. There were no other nurses or doctors; it was a single nursing post in those days and it was wonderful. No bureaucracy. I had the freedom to be the nurse I was born to be. There were no policy or procedure manuals back then, one just knew. It was here that the true meaning of why and what we were taught really came alive. "Know the normal, then you can pick up the abnormal," and I have to this day never forgotten that adage. I have applied it to my life in many ways, professionally and personally. The hospital would be open from 0900-11.00 and again from 1400-1700 hours, and I was on call twenty-four hours a day, seven days a week.

I would close the clinic at 11.00am, get changed out of my short white uniform, into my red and white bikini and then cycle down to the basin, leaving a note on the door, which read, 'Sister at Basin'. I also drew a map of exactly where I would be sun baking in-between swimming and snorkelling. However, I was never called back to the hospital. Rottnest in those days was very quiet and peaceful and the population was small. Everyone knew everyone and looked out for each other. We would have one ferry a day running from Fremantle and back. It was a blissful time.

I received a letter one day from Mum and Dad, asking me if, Marie, my little sister could come over for a week's holiday. She was fourteen years old at the time. "Of course!" I replied.

Marie came to stay for a week and we got on very well and bonded; something neither of us had ever had the opportunity to do before. I still have the slides which have been transferred on to the computer from that time with young Marie.

I only ever had one situation where I had to ring the mainland for assistance. It was to evacuate a young lady from the island. She was losing her baby at ten weeks gestation.

During this time, I started to plan for my future. I rang the Health Department of WA in Murray Street, in Perth. A department that had approximately hundred employees for the State of Western Australia and was situated right next to the fire station, just down from Royal Perth Hospital. It was small; a wonderful group of personnel who valued and respected the employees. I was offered a position in any hospital in country WA. My heart told me go home to the Kimberleys. I chose to go back to Wyndham. I would commence in January 1970.

I was very sad, when the day came for me to hand back the keys to Sister Sullivan and leave Rottnest Island and return to Fremantle hospital. I left in January, to commence the next stage of my journey through life.

RETURN TO THE KIMBERLEY

I left Fremantle on The MV Koolama and travelled up the coast, calling in at all ports along the way from Fremantle to Wyndham. I was very outgoing and made friends with everyone very quickly. I had a wonderful trip cum holiday on the way up. I met a lovely young school teacher, who was going to Wyndham to her first post from the teacher's training school. Her name was Jane and we soon became friends and hung out together during the voyage. I remember getting up at 5am for the trip up the Cambridge Gulf and I have never forgotten this magnificent sight of the sun rising over the hills. As a kid, I remembered travelling up and down that Gulf every Christmas holiday on our way to Perth.

We arrived at Wyndham port, one hot and humid rainy day at the end of January. The hospital orderly was there to meet me, and it was funny driving through the marsh, up to the main street of the town. The old two storey pub had been demolished and replaced by a modern single storey hotel. Gone were the rails to tie up the drovers' horses. All the old shops on the other side of the road were still there. I remembered Bessie Wiley's and Jimmy Le Tong's shops.

We pulled up at the back of the hospital and I was taken around to meet the matron, a lovely woman by the name of Liz; she was very tall and had an air of gentleness and kindness as she showed me around. It was kind of funny to be working in the same place my beloved mother had worked as a nursing sister ten years ago. Nothing had changed. It was even more amazing on our road trip when we were in Wyndham in 2016. We went into the museum in the old court house in the port and in the back room was a beautiful single photo of my mother and another photo of her with the cook and the Matron. Tears started to flow when I saw this beautiful smiling lady who had learnt to wear many masks, but beneath those masks lay a broken heart, buried in the pain of the loss of her only son.

I had to be escorted over to the nurses' quarters - a little house with three bedrooms; no ceiling fans, a bathroom and a little kitchen. I had a room facing the main road. It was so hot, I was advised to soak my towel in the bath full of cold water and lay that on my sheets before I went to sleep, with the window open to catch any breeze coming in off the gulf waters. I soon became accustomed to the heat and the humidity. By this time, Wyndham had been connected to the electricity grid; however, we only had electricity till 6pm. One of the duties, when you were on afternoon shift was to start the generator which enabled us to have electricity for the hospital, and the nurses' quarters for the evenings and nights. I cannot remember any blackouts. The generator was shut off at 7am. Our engineer, a Mr Dave, kept the generator in excellent condition.

Liz and Dave eventually got married and I was to meet with them several years later in Gove, in the Northern Territory.

Working in Wyndham was a great experience. There were only two nurses on duty. An enrolled nurse and a nursing sister and again I loved the generalist nature of the role. On any one day, you could be preparing for an operation with only one doctor in town. He would put the patient to sleep, the theatre sister would be called in, she would scrub for the doctor and the second nurse would bag and mask the anaesthetised patient. God really looked after us at all times as nothing ever went wrong. Next day, you could end up transferring and escorting a patient to Derby Hospital, going out to a rollover on the highway or, delivering a baby. Nurses also did everything else like physiotherapy, social work etc.

I was on night duty one night with a lovely EN(Enrolled Nurse). We had just finished our rounds and gone back to the office in the centre of the building when we heard this banging. So, we went to investigate. As soon as we got to the corner of the veranda of the women's section, the knocking stopped. All the midwifery patients were at the back of this section. Finding nothing, back to the office we would go. After about five minutes, we would hear the tapping. Again, it would stop as soon as we advanced. After about five times of this, we got wise and took off our shoes and crept silently towards the source of the noise. We eventually got to the end ward. Two post-delivery Aboriginal women from Kulumburu were there. We turned on the light, to see a head popup through the floorboards. It was one of the women's partners trying to get her out of hospital. I do not know who got the biggest fright - him or us, it was so funny. We all had a good laugh and a cuppa tea, and he put the floorboards back and promised to come back in the morning to see if he could take his wife and baby home.

Another night, the phone rang. It was the policeman from the station. They had a woman in custody in the female side of the jail who was having a miscarriage and they asked if I could come down to pick her up. I called the on-call sister in and she looked after the hospital, whilst I went down to the jail. I was shocked at what I saw inside. There were lots of Aboriginal women lying on a concrete floor with just a blanket to lie on and cover themselves. It was awful. I examined the lady and then took her back to the hospital, bathing her and putting her in a nice clean warm bed. I called the doctor in and he decided to take her to theatre in the morning. He was a very kind Christian man we called Dr Tony.

Back then this is how it was. Even though I had compassion for this woman and all the other women lying on the concrete floor, there was nothing I could do. I could see what was happening - the human misery, and the way people were treated.

The Kimberley was changing. Kununurra had become the centre that everyone was heading for. It was a new town with a brand-new hospital. Rivalry broke out between the two towns and never the twain did meet.

One of the roles of the Sister at the time was to escort (by plane) patients who were very unwell to the Regional Hospital in Derby. One day, it was my turn to do an escort. An elderly aboriginal gentleman was ill with liver disease and we had to transfer him to Derby for specialist treatment. We left around 7am and headed South West to Derby in a single engine aircraft. On arrival in Derby, we handed over the dear old man to the charge nurse at Derby Hospital and commenced the flight back to Wyndham. It was around 2pm and the pilot said to me he was concerned about the big dark clouds accumulating over our flight path, so he decided it was too dangerous to continue flying. We were just over the Gibb River station and he buzzed the homestead. The manager/owner came out in his land rover. The pilot explained our predicament. We were invited to camp at the station house for the night. After dinner, we went to bed in our respective rooms. We had to be ready for a 5 am take off the following morning. We got up at 4.30 and set off out to the strip. But oh no! We had a flat tyre and no spare; so now we were stuck. I had no toothbrush, no tooth paste, and no clean knickers – a solemn disaster indeed.

We were told we would have the tyre flown in the next morning. The tyre arrived four days later.

The delay didn't really matter to me. I became friends very quickly with an old aboriginal lady who was the cook; she took me under her wing and introduced me to her family. I felt at home again and had the best three days, cooking, dancing, and playing traditional music with the young drovers and her family. I even went on a muster with them for a day. I didn't want to go back to Wyndham. I was sad to leave the Gibb River Station; however, it was good to be able to clean my teeth and wear clean underwear once I arrived back in Wyndham.

. . .

It was also a very exciting time; the construction of the first stage of the damming of the Ord River was underway. Life was a ball, and there were parties, and more parties after hours at the construction camp. Dravo, an American construction company had been contracted to build it and as nurses we would be invited up to their Friday dinners and other social events. Many a time, we would drive up after work on a Friday afternoon, and head for home around 2am, stopping off at creeks, for swims in the dark. It was amazing to walk along the Ord River bed before the dam was built.

The Hospital was in the Port opposite the shire offices. Nothing much had changed since I was a twelve-year-old. One thing that *had* changed though, was the Native Hospital that had been out at the Three Mile had closed, and everyone was now admitted to Wyndham Hospital. They had a male side, a female side and a children's ward. The children's ward was the busiest as we would have little babies come in from nearby communities like Umbulgarri with severe malnutrition and failure to thrive. Diarrhoea was a major health issue. Sadly, we lost a few babies and little ones. Some would stay for several months until they reached their weight for age percentile. On admission they were very sad looking; however, with lots of hugs and cuddles from the nursing staff, and with proper feeds, we soon had growing, smiling and happy contented babies. We never had parents stay as lodgers at that time. We were happy to see them go home. Some of the children would never return, but some returned for regular re-admissions.

We would get frequent visitors from the head office in Perth, mainly all men and they used to have to stay in the nurses' quarters - something which I found very uncomfortable. I remember one guy, who came up, a big good-looking man; he was there for a week. He was an auditor I think, and we would often share a meal together over at the hospital. We never had television so our evenings would be taken up talking in the lounge room late into the night. On one of my days off, he asked if I would show him the swimming hole out at the Grotto. In my innocence, I said yes, I would love to. But once we were there, he tried to make an advance. I had a feeling this guy was married and so I asked him right away. Yes, he said; and then went on to say his wife was having a baby. This infuriated me and I told him we should go home immediately. He apologised profusely and was very compliant with my request. My guardian angel was with me that night - my spirit guide Joe, as I never came to any harm. I was telling my teacher friends about this experience and they offered me a spare room out in their teacher's house at the Three Mile. I agreed so that I would only have to stay in the Nurse's quarters when I was on call.

Overall, we had a great time, with lots of laughter and fun. Life was good and my savings were growing. After six months however, I started to miss the ocean, the sea breeze, the surf and cooler temperatures.

I was planning to head for England and Europe, backpacking the next April. I was getting restless and Wyndham was changing. Liz, Dave and Tony were leaving, so I decided I would move on to Exmouth to spend six months there, swimming and surfing, before leaving for England. I left Wyndham Hospital in early August 1970. I must add I also received a bonus of $1000 dollars, as I had worked there for over six months. In those days, all the Northwest hospital nurses were given a bonus for working six months when they left.

EXMOUTH

I had a two-week holiday in Perth with my family, and I purchased a little Mini Moke. With my Doberman dog, I headed up to Exmouth. I was so glad I did, the beaches were out of this world, the ocean was the most beautiful colours of blue. We could swim or surf with dolphins and turtles and go reef combing for exquisite shells. We did have to keep our eyes peeled for the deadly stone fish though, which were so camouflaged on the reef that if you were not aware of the danger, you could step on one. I only ever saw one, and it was a very ugly fish.

The hospital staff were very friendly. I met the most amazing group of nurses, who were to become my family for the next eight months. During that time, the American Naval Base was based in Exmouth and though the town was isolated, the base was alive. Most of the nurses living in the nurse's quarters had boyfriends out at the base. So, we had lots of parties and fun and camping expeditions out to Coral Bay. I soon made friends with one gorgeous girl. Her name was Rosemary Smalpage. She was a beautiful soul, tall, slim and blonde, with a very cheeky smile, and a wicked sense of humour.

The Matron at the time was a very good midwife. Her name was Lyn, and she and I were the only midwives in town.

There was one doctor in town, a man in his late fifties, who was a Polish man and had been a victim of the Second World War. The nurses didn't like working with him at all. Initially, he really liked me; however, one day, as I was walking out after duty, I found him spraying a can of Mortein on three Aboriginal patients whom he had brought back from Onslow. In those days, the Exmouth doctor used to go to do a clinic there once a week. When I saw him doing this, I said to him, what do you think you are doing? He replied, "they are Aboriginal people and they bring flies."

I was beyond furious. Grabbing the can of Mortein from his hand, I went in and told the Matron. I was visibly upset. I apologised to the patients and ensured they were safe, taking them inside and asking the staff to give them a nice warm bath and a cup of tea.

I had another 'run in' with the doctor on leaving the hospital to go home that day. Rosie was in when I went home to the nurses' quarters and I told her what had happened. Rosie hatched a plan to get back at him. She got hold of some plastic flies, and after he had gone home, we returned to his office and we stuck these plastic flies over the wall nearest to his desk.

We were both on the next morning when he arrived. We went to his office and peered through the key-hole. We watched him getting out the Mortein and spraying the plastic flies. Of course, nothing happened. So he got a fly swat and started swatting. When he realised what they were, we could almost see the steam starting to come out of his nose.

We took off and went and hid under the patients' beds. He did come looking for us, but fortunately, the patients kept mum.

We heard him yelling at the Matron, so finally we surrendered. The Health Department were informed and we got into a little trouble.

The Polish doctor went on leave, to become a doctor for a cruise company, for two months.

He was relieved by an ENT specialist. A beautiful man, very kind and compassionate. He handed all the midwifery cases over to the Matron and me.

The nurses also ran the Emergency Department. The American

Naval Base had two medical officers and they would help out in cases where extra help and support were needed.

One day, we had a lady who was in labour come in to the hospital. She had been labouring for a number of hours, and wasn't progressing. One of the doctors from the US Navy was called in to see her. We made a decision to transfer her to the regional hospital in Carnarvon, so a plane was chartered. I was on a day off so I received a phone call to escort her. The mother and I were in the seats behind the pilot. We were approximately fifteen minutes away from landing in Carnarvon when all of a sudden while I was massaging her tummy, I felt her contractions change. My heart started racing and I prayed time and again, but the baby would not wait and decided to come and meet her mum in the little aircraft.

I was all of twenty-three years of age. I have to say again, God was with me and we delivered her, with the pilot bringing the plane down to land very gently. A healthy baby and a very happy mother, midwife, and pilot. An ambulance was waiting at the tarmac. The pilot and I flew back to Exmouth the next morning, leaving our precious mother and baby in Carnarvon Hospital for a few days.

Another maternity emergency happened several weeks after our Polish doctor returned from leave. He had returned from Onslow following a clinic with several patients for admission. One of them was a rather plump Aboriginal lady who was at "forty weeks gestation". He brought her back to be induced the next day. Lyn –the Matron admitted her. I came on duty at 2.30pm and Lyn said to me, "Please go in and assess the patient for induction". This I did and to my surprise I could only feel a normal abdomen. No heart sounds at all. I went and reported to Matron Lyn.

I said she is not pregnant. Matron Lyn said, "you are right, your findings and my findings are absolutely the same." So, we had a big problem, what to do about it? Well, as it happened, we didn't have to do anything about it as divine intervention happened just in time.

An emergency case came in that evening. A man had had a very bad car accident which resulted in a major head injury. A decision was made to send him to Perth and our doctor had to go as the escort. As soon as they had left to go to the airport in the ambulance, Matron Lyn, rang the American doctors out at the Naval Base. One of them said, "look, bring her out here for an x-ray". This I did, and we had our findings confirmed that, there was no baby.

Matron Lyn arranged for the Hospital to charter a plane and send the lady back to Onslow and then tell the doctor when he returned from Perth, that the patient had absconded. All went according to plan and the lady was safely back in Onslow before he got back.

We never knew what Matron Lyn ever did in relation to bringing any action about this to the HDWA's attention. This happened in early 1971, nearly fifty years ago. It was how it was then.

In February of that year, there was a huge cyclone bearing down on Exmouth. I remember putting my little Mini Moke under the veranda at the front of the hospital. We went out when the winds were howling to see what it was like, returning back just before the eye of the storm passed.

That cyclone dumped so much rain it flooded and wiped out the power station; so we had no electricity. We had to nurse by torch light. We had no telephones and were reliant on the pedal radio. With limited communication with the outside world, it was a challenging time. It took approximately ten days to restore the power and re-establish communication with the outside world. Looking back, I would think this event would have been classified as a category 4 or 5 cyclone today

By the end of February, Rosie and I were getting ready to head off on an adventure overseas. My bank balance was very healthy, so I booked our passage on a ship, 'The Oriana', from Fremantle to Southampton in England. Rosie was being courted at that time by a beautiful man named, Del. We resigned from the Hospital on the 21st February and headed to Perth to spend a week with our respective families. Five nights before we were to leave, Rosie broke the news to me that Del had rung and asked her to marry him. So, she of course said yes and would not be coming to England with me as she was returning to Exmouth to be with Del. I was so happy for them.

Initially, I was at a loss wondering what to do. But then I made the decision to "go for it, Peter". You have been a gypsy for many years, just go.

Naturally, when I told my parents that I was still going on the adventure by myself, they tried to talk me out of it. I did have a male friend, who was also booked to come with us anyway. He was one of our friends from Exmouth, an English man who was a traveller too, so really, I was not alone. I assured my parents that I would be okay; Patrick was travelling on the same ship and that he would keep me safe. My mother took me to the overseas terminal at Fremantle Port at the beginning of March, and said goodbye to me as I walked excitedly up the gangplank on my way to the other side of the world. I can still see her standing on the wharf at the Fremantle passenger terminal, waving me goodbye.

Poor darling, Joe had left this earth and now her eldest daughter was leaving the country. (I was to experience this separation myself when my children left home). The pain she must have felt would have been deep for her; but like the amazing woman she was, she returned to her life, caring for my father and my two sisters.

First Trip Overseas 1971

The Two Irish Nurses - Island of Guernsey - 1971 (above)

Arriving at the Acropolis - 1971 (right)

Torquay England - 1971 (below)

Family of old man from Sark - 1971 (below)

Piglet post delivery 0300 Limerick Farm 1971 (above)

Stop over in Kuala Lumpur - 1971 (left)

TRIP TO LONDON

The first night on board was exciting, meeting new people, being assigned to dinner settings and enjoying the 'fruits' of what a ship had to offer in those days. I have to say it was so different to what cruise ships are like today. The journey took six weeks –travelling from Fremantle to Adelaide, Melbourne, Sydney, Auckland, Tahiti and through the Panama Canal to Curacao. From there to Lisbon and then on to Southampton. I had the best time. I made lots and lots of friends and we all had to make our own fun with the many activities they had for us on board. One of the groups we could join was a theatre group. At the end of the cruise, and prior to arriving at the destination, there would be a drama competition. I joined one of the groups and had a ball. The group were all young professionals from many different professions on their voyage of discovery and off to find their place in the world. We had a great group and we ended up becoming friends.

We actually won the drama competition with our play.

I loved our stopover in Tahiti. So primitive, isolated and unspoiled. There were only a couple of rows of houses. On the main street, just off the wharf, there were little huts with Mercedes cars parked outside. It was a French colony back then. The kids would dive into the water off the wharf to collect coins the passengers had thrown overboard. It was wonderful to walk down the main street with the smell of the French patisseries wafting through the air.

Crossing the Equator, King Neptune visited the ship[1], and I was one of the lucky ones to sit on his knee. There was great excitement on board as King Neptune spent a couple of hours mingling amongst the passengers. We travelled through the old Panama Canal and arrived at the next port of call on the itinerary.

The next port that is a memory etched in my mind was Curacao. My friends and I went to a nightclub there. It was a club where they had Le Girls and belly dancing. I had never seen such a show. I was very innocent and naïve as were most of my peers, including a lovely Catholic priest. He was travelling back to Ireland. Father Tom was with us that night, as he was in our drama group.

On leaving Curacao, we then sailed across to Portugal where the huge statue of "Jesus" with his arms spread out on top of a hill was very moving and a sight to behold.

We set sail for Southampton across the Bay of Biscay after spending a day sightseeing around Lisbon. This stretch of the journey had a reputation for being one of the roughest passages in the world. Mother Nature was very good to us; the sea was smooth all the way, just like a sea of glass. The day for disembarkation was sad. I said goodbye to my travelling companions and then headed with Patrick, off to the train station and caught an old steam train to London. Patrick and I were taken aback with the cold; it was freezing and we were not expecting it, coming from an Exmouth summer. Fortunately, the train had a warm fire in it, so it wasn't long until we thawed out.

I had made prior arrangements to stay with my mother's nephew in London, whom I had never met before; so once there, I caught a cab to my cousin's home close to the centre of London. Patrick went to stay with his friends and we arranged to meet under Big Ben the next day.

I met Patrick and we started to do the tourist bit. The streets of London in 1971, were so busy with people buzzing around; everyone seemed to be in a rush. I sensed London was not for me, a girl from the bush.

It was also a time when there was major change happening.

England was in a state of fear, as the Government made the decision to join the European Common Market. People were drawing all their money out of the bank and there were signs up everywhere reassuring people that England would flourish when they joined the European Common Market. The energy was not good and my intuition really kicked in. I needed sunshine and warmth. I discussed with my cousin that I had decided to move on after I had a good look around. His wife suggested at dinner, that I should look at going to The Channel Islands.

So, I decided to ring The Channel Island Nursing Agency. I got offered a contract straight away and I informed them of my start date.

Patrick and I had planned a road trip around the South of England. After three days of sightseeing in London I just had to leave. I was being suffocated with the size and the negative energy surrounding London at the time and the lack of sunshine in London Town. I really appreciated the care, love and advice Peter and his wife gave me. We said our goodbyes and I never heard from them again. I never contacted them again either.

CHANNEL ISLANDS

*A*fter three weeks of sightseeing, Patrick headed back to Germany where he was studying at Heidelberg University. I, with my backpack, headed over to Jersey. The agency had arranged accommodation for me at a lady's house for minimal rent. The lady turned out to be a single working mum, with a small boy. They were there at the airport to pick me up and take me to their home on top of a hill overlooking the ocean, and it felt like I was home again. She was very nice and the little boy was very cute.

Next day, I found the Channel Island Nursing agency's office, signed the contract and was given my first assignment.

The first assignment was with an old lady who lived in a Manor House in a parish town about ten miles out from the capitol parish of St Heiler. She had a farm and her son lived in a beautiful old farm house. The old lady, who liked a drop of gin –about half a bottle a night - had had a fall and had broken her arm. She also had a gorgeous little dachshund.

I was to be her nurse for one month. I had purchased a little second-hand white Mini minor and what a great little car it turned out to be. I never had a day's trouble with it. Next day, armed with a road map and directions from my landlady, I drove in my little white Mini to this lady's house. The son came out from the farmhouse to greet me when I arrived and took me over to the Manor House. It was here that my eyes opened to how the other half live.

The old lady was lovely. She made me feel very welcome, as did her little dachshund. She had a big swimming pool out in her backyard and a black Bentley in the garage. I settled into this assignment very quickly, and we connected immediately. From a work perspective, it was different to anything I had ever experienced before. I was really a carer for her there to keep her company and I embraced the role. We would go out during the mornings or laze around the house talking and sharing stories; she would have an afternoon sleep every day and my workday was then lying out in the sun in a bikini swimming and sunbathing, till she woke. And I was getting paid to do this! Life was a dream. The wages were unbelievable as the Channel Islands were a tax-free haven.

Gerald Durrell, the beloved author of many animal stories happened to be a friend of hers and one day I drove the Bentley to Gerald Durrell's house. Prior to that, I had always taken her out for lunch and coffee in my humble beautiful little old white Mini. It was a little unnerving to drive such an elegant but expensive car and I was glad to put the Bentley back in its rightful place and drive my little Mini again.

When the month was up, unbeknownst to me, she had contacted the agency and booked me for another month. I was a bit disappointed because I realised that she was becoming very dependent on me; so, when the agency rang, I informed them of her growing dependence on me and I saw no reason for me to stay. Her broken arm had mended and her independence had been fully restored. I promised to stay for another week. I was becoming very bored and although I did not want to hurt the old lady's feelings (she was lovely, and obviously very lonely) I needed something more stimulating to further my career as a nurse.

. . .

Two days later the Agency rang, and said we have another assignment for you; but it is on the Island of Guernsey. They described the assignment. An old man from the Island of Sark, had suffered a severe stroke. He was unconscious and as the family did not want him to die in the hospital on Guernsey Island, they had booked him into a five-star hotel- the biggest and the best on the Island. They wanted twenty-four hour care, around the clock. The old man was expected to pass over within ten days. They had appointed two Irish nurses who were friends and myself. I agreed to go. And a new adventure was about to begin.

The conditions were unbelievable. Each of us would have our own private room with an ensuite, our laundry and daily cleaning would be done for us, and all meals supplied. I broke the news gently to the old lady and she was very sad, that I would be leaving in four days. I assured her I would return to see her if the opportunity ever arose. We had a lovely four days together doing our daily routine and her family put on a very nice dinner for me on my second last day. The final farewell was hard and as I was leaving, she stood in her driveway, waving me goodbye. I looked back through the rear vision mirror and saw her wiping her eyes.

I thought, I want to stay forever young.

Arrangements were made by the agency for me to go over on a ferry with my car, and meet the girls over there. I said goodbye to my landlady and her little boy, and left on the Sunday morning. We arrived on Guernsey a couple of hours later. Once on terra firma, I headed off to find this hotel and I nearly passed out when I saw it. It was grandeur personified. It was certainly different from any hotel I had ever seen in Perth or Sydney and very dissimilar to the Wyndham and The Pot Shot Inn in Exmouth. This kind of opulence belonged to another world.

I registered at the front desk; my colleagues had already arrived and settled in, so I asked the man behind the large marble counter if he could ring them and let them know I had arrived.

Five minutes later, two young women appeared. They seemed friendly warm and sincere. Although they were a year or two older than I, I knew immediately that we would make a great team.

This assignment was so different. The old man's family were pleased to greet us but left soon to go back to Sark the next day. We cared for him as if he was our grandfather. We worked out the rosters ourselves, and did rotating eight-hour shifts.

Even though we worked hard, we did get out and about when we were off duty. There were no mobile telephones back then but it was lucky I had my little mini and as the Island was small, we were never far from the hotel. The main street consisted of high-end fashion and I remember buying a very beautiful pair of purple knee length suede boots there.

All the rooms were serviced daily; it became a life of luxury I had never experienced before. It was not long before we found we didn't even need to go out to party or go to a nightclub. The hotel had a nightlife all of its own. I have to say it was well frequented by three well known nurses in the hotel. We were such happy carefree spirits.

It didn't mean our jobs took a secondary role. Our patient always came first. Not one of us drank alcohol-as we were there for this old man and his family. One event that stood out for me was the weekend the Royal Air force's famous Red Arrow aerobatic flying squad came to Guernsey for a show. They stayed in the same hotel as our little nursing team. They arrived on the Friday night before the show, and as usual we went down to the nightclub for an evening of fun and dance. This evening two of us walked in all dressed up in our miniskirts and looking pretty suave.

These very handsome young men caught our eye, and we must have caught theirs too, for before long, conversation and laughter began to flow uninhibited. We had the best evening with lots of banter and laughter. They arranged to meet us after the air show on the Saturday evening and we danced the night away. The nightclub closed at 11.30pm; however, we were all, still in party mode, so we did a reconnoitre and found this massive ball room. The doors were open, and we headed for the stage where it was all set up with a piano and drums. We were up on the stage in no time and had a jam session for two hours. It was a really fun weekend, and we were sorry to see them go.

Eight weeks after receiving our tender loving care, the old man had a very graceful ending to his life. The family invited us over to their property on the island of Sark for the funeral and to attend the celebration of his life. We all went as we were a part of his final journey and we stayed three days with them.

By this time, I had made enough money, to last me for the rest of the year. I had sold my little Mini just before we went to Sark as I had planned to go to Greece from there, to stay with my surrogate parents whom I had met in Exmouth. I resigned from the agency and headed down to stay with them.

THE EUROPEAN EXPERIENCE

I travelled to Dover and caught the ferry over to Calais, then headed for Paris, and made my way from Paris, to Rome. What a culture shock it was. I was totally lost in a tsunami of people and traffic; I was certainly out of my comfort zone. It was, I have to say, an absolutely amazing experience to explore the cities of Paris and Rome. Walking and climbing the Eiffel Tower, spending time in Rome, visiting the Colosseum and the places that William Shakespeare wrote about in his plays, that I had studied in English in year 11 and 12. I still remember the feeling when I stood on many sites in this ancient Roman City from 400 B.C.

From Rome, I headed down to the bottom of Italy to Brindisi and then to Corfu, from there to Athens, where Mr and Mrs Norris picked me up. The naval base where they lived was approximately 50 kms from the Centre of Athens and I stayed with them for three months and had a wonderful time.

They loved me so much and I loved them. They were a couple in their mid-60 and they treated me like their daughter. Mrs Norris and I would spend our day doing all the things one does in the activities of daily living and would then go exploring the historical buildings. We loved the Parthenon and would spend hours up there, absorbing the energy and life of this ancient world.

Several times, when I went into the city on my own, I would be chased by guys, trying to give me a rose; I would disappear into a shop until the suitor vanished. I was really uncomfortable with this attention and Mrs Norris became my chaperone. On weekends, Mr and Mrs Norris and I would go sightseeing; they would take me everywhere, stopping at 'Tavernas' for lunch and a little ouzo and wine tasting. One very memorable tour we went on was to the venue of the first ever Olympic Games. It took me into another civilisation. The ancient Games were staged in Olympia Greece from 776 BC through 393 AD; it took 1503 years for the Olympics to return. The first modern Olympics were held in Athens, Greece in 1896. Just writing this really makes me feel so privileged to have had these experiences with these beautiful people who became role models to me; for I knew then that if I ever had children of my own, I would know how to treat them. I guess they were so much more and looking back now, I would describe them as my grandparents.

Out of the blue, I received an invitation from Father Tom, the Irish priest to spend Christmas in Limerick in Ireland. I had met him on the ship on the way over. Mr and Mrs Norris were going back to the USA in early December, so I decided with their blessing to head up to Ireland. I left, promising one day, I would come and visit them in the United States and took a train journey back to Paris.

It was a train journey like I had never experienced before. The first stop was at the border town of Belgrade. When the train eased into the station, there were a lot of uniformed men with guns ready to fire. They came on board and started taking everyone's passports. They asked for my passport I shook my head meaning, no you cannot have it. One of the soldiers raised his arm and had his gun pointing at me. All I could think of was, "remember never to hand over your passport.",

I handed over my passport, he took it and I was left on the train. It seemed like an eternity and my mind was running wild but I did not stop praying. After an hour, my passport was returned with a stamp on it. I couldn't wait to get out of Belgrade.

The rest of the journey was trouble free and I arrived back in Paris. I took a plane back to London, caught a ferry over to Dublin and my Irish journey began.

Father Tom, had sent his younger brother, a tall single good-looking Irish chap, to pick me up in Dublin. His name was William. We introduced ourselves to each other and I could sense he was a lovely young man. He was on two weeks leave from work, so we drove down to Limerick and went to his family's farm.

His parents were open, friendly and warm people and they made me feel very welcome. William and I would go exploring the countryside. He took me to see hurling matches as he played Hurley[1] and I saw lots of lovely places and scenery 'to die for'.

We would often go down to the Village Inn and have a few drinks. One night, we were at a local pub dancing and having a few drinks. I was in my purple suede boots. The pub closed at 1100 pm. He took me on a detour on our way home and stopped at a gorgeous spot. When he snuggled up to me, I got really cranky and told him to get lost as I didn't have time for this. I didn't want to get into a relationship. It had to be purely platonic or I would leave the next day. So, he backed off and we then spent several hours just talking and laughing before heading home.

We had just got back to the farm, when his father called us to the shed, where he was delivering his sow. The last little piglet was very slow coming into the world and the mother was having some difficulty. William, who remembered that I was a midwife called out to me, "Peter, can you help?"

"Sure," I replied.

I really did not have to do anything. I just rubbed the pig's bottom, in my purple suede boots and bingo out came a little piglet. We had a great Christmas day and two days later, I decided to head home; back to the sunshine and surf. So, on the 28th of December 1971, I said my goodbyes and headed back to Dublin.

From Dublin, I flew to London and took a Qantas flight back to Australia, via Kuala Lumpur. I was sitting next to a girl who lived in Kuala Lumpur and she was around my age. We talked nearly all the way there and she said, "Why don't you have a few days with me and my family?" Without thinking too much, I agreed. So, when we got to KL, I changed my flight so I could have a week with my new friend.

Her family were very poor and lived in a tin shack, among rows of tin shacks, with no electricity and no running water. They made me feel so welcome that I just became part of the family. During the day, the girl - who had lots of friends with little cars or scooters - would come and take us to explore the hidden gems of the city. We visited some beautiful temples. The family were Buddhists, gentle, humble and kind and when it was time for me to go home, I felt a pain in my heart for leaving this beautiful kind and generous family. They had changed me in some way.

YAPPA YAPPA

YIRRKALA

I arrived back home in Western Australia on the 4th of January, 1971. My mother was working in Silver Chain in Northam as a sister (today known as RNs) and she had teed me up a position at the Northam hospital as a midwife. I was to start on the 5th January.

My parents had arranged for me to live with them -something that had not happened since I was thirteen years old, apart from school holidays during my high school years. But after a few shifts, I really could not take the confines of living and working in such a structured environment anymore and be hemmed into a way of life, that now was so foreign to me.

I decided to apply for two positions, one in the Royal Australian Air Force, and one in a Remote Area, and I would take the one that came up first.

I had my interview for the Air Force, and I rang The Commonwealth Health Department in the Northern Territory. I was offered a position as a public health nurse at Yirrkala Mission in Arnhem Land. I had never heard of it and didn't even know where it was. I said yes, I would take it, and then I had to go and look up the atlas to find out where it was.

I was given a start date for the middle of January, the department would fly me to Darwin, and my start date for orientation was to be the 18th January, 1972.

I resigned from Northam Hospital, filled in all the required paperwork and was ready for another adventure.

My mother's friend had a daughter who was driving over to Adelaide to work and she was looking for a travelling companion. So, we met, and immediately connected. I agreed I would drive across the Nullarbor with her.

I knew I had to be in Darwin by the 18th Jan, so two days later we were ready to venture across this great dirt road from Perth to Adelaide.

We set off in my new friend's little blue VW. Once we left Norseman and hit the dirt corrugated road we thought, oh goodness what are we doing? But we had a wonderful journey and when we were just outside Ceduna, the VW decided it could not take it anymore. It just refused to start. We were stuck and we were on a deadline. I said a little prayer and an hour later a truck pulled up. This very kind truck driver became Sir Lancelot for us. He loaded the VW onto the back of the truck, (luckily he had a little crane on his truck) and took us right into Adelaide. He dropped the car into a mate of his to be repaired and he saw us safely settled in a hotel in the centre of Adelaide on the 16th Jan. Next morning, I got a cab to the airport and flew TAA to Darwin via Alice Springs, a flight that took about eight hours.

I was met at the Darwin airport by the Sister in charge of Rural Health in the Northern Territory of Australia. Her name was Nancy and she took me in and ensured I was settled into the accommodation that had been arranged for me in the centre of Darwin.

Darwin then was still much the same as the first visit I had in 1958. I saw the old hospital at the end of Smith Street where Joe and Mum were hospitalised at that time. On 18th Jan, I started my two-week orientation program. I loved it and knew it was made for me.

Once orientation was completed, I was flown out to Yirrkala, a two-hour flight from Darwin, via Groote Eylandt. An old Aboriginal health worker was there to meet me. She was a small woman, who had a beautiful smile. Her name was Liapenden, and again I felt a very strong connection. We set out across a dusty corrugated red dirt road and we travelled for what seemed like an hour, until all of a sudden, we arrived in paradise.

A most beautiful settlement, right on the Arafura Sea, at the top of the Gulf of Carpentaria. Green manicured grass, palm trees everywhere, with plantations of bananas, pineapples and paw paws; smiling happy children playing everywhere.

I was taken to the sisters' accommodation, a rambling big house on stilts. I had to share it with the other Sister on the community. She was quite a stern looking woman, between 30 - 40 years of age. She had worked in Africa as a missionary nurse for many years prior and as soon as I met her, I knew that I could not connect with her. Here we were from two different worlds and there was an intergenerational gap; however, there was a commitment, I am sure from both of us to work together.

Next day, I met the other team members - young pretty loving intelligent aboriginal health workers all between 18- 20 years of age and another older health worker, whose name was Luk Luk. A tall, slim lady who had a great sense of humour. I fitted right in. Liapenden showed me everything around the clinic and I felt warmth and love from this lady. She was also a traditional medicine lady who loved her work, and she made me feel right at home. The first weekend after I had started there, I was on call, and I had to open the clinic on a Saturday morning for four hours.

It was baptism by fire.

The other nurse had gone into Darwin for a few days for some rest and relaxation. I went over to the clinic and there on the concrete veranda was an old woman just lying on a blanket. She looked different, her eyes had no life, she could not speak, let alone understand me. I had only learnt a few words in dialect, by that stage. Her pulse was weak and her respiratory rate was slowing. I held her hand and sent for Liapenden. When she arrived, she said to me after examining her. "*Im finishing Yappa*" (Yappa is the Aboriginal word for sister.) I asked what she meant.

Liapenden replied, "Im had bone pointed at her last week Im finished."

My intuition said, to take her inside and make her comfortable. Liapenden got some men to help lift her and carry her inside where we made her comfortable and held her hand until she took her last breath, several hours later. I had never experienced anything like that before; it was part of life, culture and practices. That experience during my first week, had a very profound effect on me. After that day, the community just took me in as one of theirs. I was so privileged to be accepted and taught by this lovely elder health worker.

My role at the clinic involved health promotion and sickness prevention, looking after all the pregnant girls in perinatal care, labour, post-natal care and emergency care. I always had to be prepared for any emergency, from stabbings and bashings to accidents, heart attacks, severe dehydration and malnutrition or pneumonias. The full gamut of duties also included being the child health and school health nurse. A health worker and I would go up to the school Monday to Friday from 10.00am to 11.00am to run a clinic, using fresh paw paw to dress the sores. Paw paw is a wonderful healing agent, something I learnt at Yirrkala. There was no product like the tubes of paw paw one buys in a supermarket or chemists today.

March of 1972 brought a big storm.

I was on call and I got called at 11.00pm from the clinic to see a lady, who presented in labour. She was well advanced. I put her on the bed, and to my complete shock and horror, instead of a head-on view, I saw a foot-on view. So, I got one of the persons who had brought her to the clinic to go and get help from Liapenden and another Aboriginal bush midwife. I had them support the woman, while I went to radio the Aerial Medical Service in Darwin for telephone advice. The radio was so crackly, I could not hear a thing. Again, I prayed and some thirty minutes later, Liapenden and I delivered a little baby girl.

On another afternoon, I was just locking up the clinic and three young girls came racing in, "Yappa, Peter Yappa Peter come quick, come quick".

I said, "what is the matter girls?"

"Yappa, lady up the tree she is having a baby, come quick, she won't come down." Again, I went running (and praying under my breath). I arrived at the tree, and sure enough there was a lady in the tree in labour. Looking up, I realised she would only be in her second trimester, so I tried to talk her down. But she refused to come down, thinking I would send her to Darwin.

I called for the medicine man, after promising her I would not send her to Darwin. The old man arrived and I conferred with him assuring him I would not pack her off to Darwin. It was he, who managed to get her safely to the clinic. An hour later, we delivered a twenty-one week tiny baby who had passed away before birth. We had no equipment at all, so we made a little bed in a box full of cotton wool and the grandmother came and collected the little one and two days later a cultural ceremony was held. And life went on.

The third delivery was not so traumatic; someone came to the house calling at 2am for me to come to the beach as one of the ladies was having a baby. I got the delivery bundle; we jumped into the car and drove to the beach camp. The woman was in advanced labour and five minutes after we got there, the head was crowning. So here we are, under the headlights of the car, the light coming from the flames of a roaring fire, the lapping of the ocean on the beach and the swaying of the palm trees and we delivered a bonny bouncing baby. The best delivery I have ever done.

I was in the clinic one afternoon and an older Aboriginal man came limping and hopping into the clinic. He was holding some material over his right thigh and blood was gushing out. He told us that he had been out with his spear, fishing and a sting ray "got me Yappa".

I laid him on the bed, not knowing what was under the blood soaked material. Preparing myself with lots and lots of gauze square with the help of a young health worker, we took off the material and found the thigh ripped open all along from the top to nearly the knee through to the bone. We cleaned it up with Betadine and applied normal saline compresses and pressure bandages. Our patient told me his name was Wunjuk; and he was still smiling and giving me cheek. He had no pain.

After I had everything under control, I called The Aerial Medical Service in Darwin and asked for a plane to come in, as our patient needed to be evacuated to have the suturing done in theatre. The one operational plane, was not available. I was nearly in tears.

The Doctor on the other end said, "You have worked in theatre, haven't you",

I replied, "yes".

He said, "so you will have to suture it."

Prayer time again!

Once I knew that there was no help coming, I calmly got everything ready, pulled up a chair and two hours later, bingo all closed, we had done it. Wunjuk[1] was smiling even more. He was a very distinguished looking man, with a long grey white beard and he wore an Aboriginal headband. I had no idea who he was, I knew he was just a lovely man, and we became friends during the ordeal; in fact, he verbally inducted me into his family there and then after the suturing was completed. I had him come back every day for ten days so that I could monitor the wound for signs of infection. There were none.

I have been so privileged to have had these wonderful human beings in my life.

That year we also had a big visit from The Prime Minister of Australia, the Honourable William McMahon and his beautiful wife, Sonia. They had come up to officially open the Nabalco Plant. Whilst there, they also made an official visit to Yirrkala, together with an entourage of Westerners. It was terrific to be part of that piece of Australian history. Sonia McMahon also had her own toilet carted out on a truck; something we locals could not comprehend. Why would anybody bring their own toilet? I still laugh about it when I tell the story of the visit by the Prime Minister and his wife in 1972, to Yirrkala.

Life outside work was just as wonderful. I had really settled in.

I didn't know until the end of my third week there, that there was a community called Gove not far from Yirrkala. It took an hour to get there along a very dusty dirt corrugated road. One day, the senior sister said to me that I needed to take a trip to the NT Dept. of Health in Gove for a meeting. She gave me directions and off I headed in the blue government Holden panel van.

I drove on and on and eventually arrived on the outskirts of the town. To my surprise, there was a big town with a hospital, a police station, schools, a major shopping centre, a hotel, flats and houses. I found the head offices of the Health Department and right next to that was a huge big brand new community health centre. I felt like a fish out of water entering the building.

As soon as I walked in the door of the meeting room, the first person I saw was Liz –from Wyndham; she was the Matron at Gove Hospital and I was so happy to see her. Back then Yirrkala had nothing to do with the closed town of a mining company, neither our people nor the health workers had access to Gove Hospital; it was for white people only. As we were leaving the meeting, Liz invited me to come in and have a drink with her and Dave down at the Walkabout Hotel after work. I was not on call that night so I accepted the invitation.

I had a really good time and met lots of nice young nurses from the hospital, and danced the night away. It was that night I met a very handsome young man called, Noddy. He had sparkles in his eyes, was really cute and great fun, an excellent dancer and I got goose bumps all over when he asked me for a dance. I left to return back to Yirrkala around 10pm, as I was on call for the weekend. I was very happy and had been invited back to a party at the nurses' quarters the following Saturday night, when I was not on call; Of course, I accepted the invitation in the hope that this young man, whom everyone called Noddy, would be there.

I would invite all the young ones to our home on the Saturday nights I was on call and they would bring their friends so we would have a barbecue and a party. I had my first gathering this Saturday night. We had a great time swinging between Aboriginal song and dance to western song and dance. The boys would bring the meat from the day's hunting and I would make a salad and provide the salad and bread rolls. We all loved and looked forward to those Saturday nights.

One Saturday morning, I got woken at 5am with a hand on my shoulder. I rolled over and there was a young Aboriginal man shaking my shoulder and saying "Yappa Peter, wake up."

I sat up quickly and asked, "Galaru, what are you doing here?"

Galaru replied, "Yappa we go hunting; do you want to come?"

"Oh yes! I would love to but I am on call; will you bring back some meat for tonight? I asked

"Sure", he said and left.

All during the week, following my meeting with Noddy, I was excited about going to the party at one of the nurses' homes. I had been dreaming of this man all week. So when Saturday evening came, I got dressed up and I went to the party in Gove.

I was welcomed by everyone and then my eyes scanned the room and there was this handsome, cute young man I had met at the Walkabout Hotel the week before. He gave me a lovely smile and that was it, I was smitten.

We sat on the floor and talked for hours and hours. I had not felt like this before, he was so different- happy, kind, a real gentleman, who spoke so highly of his family life. He told me his Christian name, which was Brian. But his mates called him, Noddy.

When it was time for me to drive home, I invited him to come out to Yirrkala the following weekend, and said I would show him the beaches surrounding the mission. He soon became part of the community and I part of the Gove party scene.

We became a couple.

Camping would become our favourite pastime, and we were blessed with the freedom to explore the Arnhem Land Peninsular. Our favourite camp site was at Cape Arnhem, were we could fish, eat oysters straight from the rocks, swim, and spend hours walking on pure white sand. We would spend the night around a camp fire with our friends, telling stories, singing, having a few sherbets and snuggling up together in warm sleeping bags under the stars. If we were by ourselves, we would camp out at Turtle Beach, a surf beach not far from Yirrkala.

I was so happy in my role as a public health nurse and living in Yirrkala. I was playing in the Yirrkala Aboriginal girls' basketball competition once a week in Gove. I became known as the albino Aboriginal. I would be invited to join the family feast in the community regularly and my favourite feast was on the turtle nights, when turtles would be caught and wrapped in banana leaves, a hole would be dug and the turtle placed in the hole and a fire lit. It would be slowly roasted, it was an absolutely nutritious staple food, full of nutrients, and the taste was great.

If I stayed in town, overnight, we would stay at our dear friends Dave and Lyn Barclay's house. Lyn and Dave had one beautiful young baby, Andrew who was just the sweetest little fellow.

Noddy and I soon became one. He was so different from any guy I had ever met, so protective of me, so respectful of me and all women. We made a commitment to each other within a few weeks of meeting to be together forever.

It was in July of 1972, I received a phone call from the NT Health Dept, asking me to come to Darwin to help in a training program for eight Aboriginal Health Workers and supervise them twenty-four hours a day. These young girls were from Central Australia and had never been out of their communities before. We had to protect them from the outside world.,

So, I packed a bag, (even though I didn't really want to leave Noddy behind) and went off to Darwin for this assignment.

It turned out to be another adventure.

I was instructed to escort the girls out to Mandora for the weekend. In those days, Mandora was only five kilometres by sea and a hundred kilometres by road. Thirty kilometres of bitumen and seventy kilometres on this corrugated dirt road. On Friday afternoon, I was handed the keys to the troop carrier and a rifle. I had my provisions all ready for the weekend, and the girls had to organise theirs. Prior to leaving, I asked if they had enough food and drink, torches etc. No provisions or equipment were supplied by the employer and the girls said, "yes Yappa."

I was so naïve I believed them and didn't check to ensure the girls had what they needed as per the list given to all of us. I said okay, and at 2pm we left to go on our weekend in the bush away from the trappings of the city. There were eight, sixteen or seventeen year old girls, one white twenty-four year old girl and one rifle that not one of us knew how to use.

Four hours later, following a mud map, we arrived at Mandora Bay. In those years, there was no settlement there apart from a little tavern, a little jetty and the Australian Radio Relay Station.

However, it was not on our map and we didn't even know of its existence. It was just us, open sea, nature, bush, trees, and lots and lots of stars and a big full moon. We found a nice protected spot on the beach and prepared to set up camp. No tents. I had a little pillow and a sleeping bag, the girls had nothing. So, we made a camp fire, boiled the billy[2] and as I was the only one with a mug, we passed it around. The girls found enough branches for a bed each. We shared the dinner I had prepared and the bread I had brought for myself. After tea we were all so tired, we went to bed, me in my sleeping bag and the girls on the sandy beach. We slept very soundly.

We woke early with the sun and to the sounds of the waves lapping the shore. When it was time for breakfast, I said to the girls, let's eat. I got mine ready and the girls said, "Yappa, we go hunting." This they did and brought back a bucket of turtle eggs and a billy full of fresh water from a water stream about two kilometres from our camp. I tried the turtle eggs and quickly had to cough them out. The girls loved them. We had a great day, swimming, resting and hunting.

We were sitting around telling stories around our campfire when one of the girls said, "Yappa, car coming".

I could not hear a thing, but sure enough some twenty minutes later, we saw the headlights of a car, coming through the bush. They stopped about a kilometre from where we were camped. The girls were very scared. No matter how I tried to reassure them, that we were safe, they were still frightened, so after a little discussion, we decided we would go up and check out the intruders of our sacred site. So here we go, I with the rifle ready to go with eight girls behind me.

As we approached, a friendly voice called out "hello".

I said, "hello back."

They were a family of five - mum, dad and three little kids aged between five and eight who had come over from Darwin for an overnight camp. We were invited to stay for a cup of tea and biscuits. The girls were really shy, relaxed and happy and when 9pm came, we headed back to spend a restful night at our camp. Sunday morning came and went and before long, it was time to pack up and return to Darwin. That weekend has always had a special place in my memory.

I returned to Yirrkala, as soon as the second week ended and was very happy to be going home. Noddy met me at the airport and we spent a very special night together at the "Hideaway" guest house, about a kilometre from the airport. We had a very romantic dinner and with our life being united again, the two became one.

A couple of weeks after that I was asked to go over to Groote Eylandt[3] to a community called Umbakumba on the East Coast of the Island to assist in a leprosy survey for two weeks. It was a very interesting fortnight. I had seen leprosy as a child in the Derby Leprosarium, but had never nursed anyone with the disease before. I did not realise as a child the effects of what the disease had on a person or on the community. Leprosy is a bacterial infection of the skin and nerves caused by Mycobacterium Leprae, found mainly in Aboriginal and Torres Straight Island people from Northern Australia and migrants from areas where the disease is more common. I learnt so much about stoicism and resilience there.

It was also the first time and only time I actually saw violence against a nurse in the workplace by a community member. The poor nurse was suturing up a lady's head following a fight, when a man came into the clinic and did a rabbit chop to the nurse's neck so he could have another attempt to attack the victim who had been brought in for medical attention as a result of domestic violence. The police were called and the poor nurse was flown out to Canberra Hospital. It was an awful time, both for the nursing staff working on the island and the community. This happened on my second last night on Umbakumba and I was very glad to leave. I was not involved in the clinic as a nurse since I worked out of an office and in the community doing the survey. I did not witness the event; however, I was called in to help after the police left.

ONE BECOMES TWO AND THEN SIX

It was not long after my return from Umbakumba, that we discovered we were to become parents. We were so happy and overjoyed; we were having our very own love child. Our first little home was a unit in a block down near the town beach. We could just walk out the door and be on the shore of the Arufura Sea and we would spend many hours taking long walks on the beach planning for our baby and our future lives together.

The family at Yirrkala were so happy for us. Times were changing and Gove Hospital was now accepting seeing patients from Yirrkala. Our maternity patients from the Yirrkala Mission would come now into Gove hospital for delivery. More specialists were coming over from Darwin to Gove hospital. I had decided I would transfer into the midwifery unit at the Gove hospital, as the drive in and out from Yirrkala was very long.

From the very first, life was fantastic married to Noddy. Looking back, I guess we would have had our moments but I could not have asked for more. We had both been our own free spirits for so long, it took a few weeks to adjust to living full time together.

Noddy never argued or raised his voice, he would just smile and say, "yes dear," when I was growling at him for leaving his side of the room a mess or not sharing home duties. One night, I came home from work at 11pm and the dishes were still in the kitchen sink. He had been to the pub after work with his mates. I was upset to see the mess in the kitchen. I had left the kitchen very clean and tidy, before I left for work. So, I sat down and wrote out my resignation and showed it to him.

I said to him, "I will resign in the morning unless you commit to a 50/ 50 partnership with everything about the home –housework and bringing up our baby. It is your choice. I cannot be a house wife, a mother and a nurse. I want to be me, a wife, mother and continue to nurse. However, without your commitment I will not be able to do it."

Leaving it with him, I went off to bed. Next morning, he greeted me with a cup of tea in bed, and made the promise that it would always be a full 50 /50 partnership. Forty-nine years on, it is still that. In fact, at seventy nine years of age, he is still the 'Minister of Interior and Exterior affairs' whilst I pursue a dream I had twenty years ago.

We kept in contact with my family in Yirrkala. I loved life, my Noddy and our new little baby growing in us and with us, her movements, and her kicks made us ecstatic.

The political power in Australia was changing in 1972. The Liberal Government had been in power in Australia for twenty-two years. An amazing leader of the Labour party had emerged – Gough Whitlam. It was a time of much upheaval. Political campaigning was under way for change and we heard on the radio advertisement the slogan, 'It's time.' Sure enough, Gough Whitlam went on to become the Prime Minister of Australia and when the election was held that year, an enormous social revolution occurred. He declared free education from kindergarten right through to the end of university, and free health care. Previously, everyone had to pay $5.00 to see a doctor at the hospital; we never had any private doctors in Gove at that time. Self-determination for Indigenous communities came into being. A total change of society and social engineering became the norm. In 1973, we got television in Gove for the first time. The only channel we could get was the ABC and we could only have the ABC news from Queensland. Politically at that time, it was all about Joh Bjelke –Peterson and his famous saying, 'Don't you worry about that' and Flo's Pumpkin Scones. It changed our lives in many ways, bringing the news of the outside world into our lounge rooms. Around this time, I started becoming interested in politics, but had no inclination to enter the political arena.

It was also around this time I started to receive premonitions. I didn't realise what was happening to me. One night, I was standing at the sink doing the dishes and I started to get a very strange feeling inside and a voice saying something terrible had just happened; and then I started shaking. It only lasted for 30-40 seconds; however, I didn't know what, where, how or why - but I knew something had happened. I mentioned it to Noddy and went off to bed. Next morning on listening to the news, the very time that I felt that strange feeling and started shaking, a tray-back land cruiser with seven Aboriginals in the back had rolled over just outside Katherine and all were killed. The time given was when I was doing the dishes the night before. That sent goose bumps all over me and I felt a shiver run through me; so, I blocked it out. I never got any more such premonitions until many years later. Today, I really listen to my inner voice and take note of the messages I am given.

I loved working on the midwifery and surgical unit at Gove hospital and had some very interesting experiences. One that vividly comes to mind was when we had a young Aboriginal girl flown over from Elcho Island to have her baby. One night she went missing. In those days, many of our brother and sisters would regularly go missing (they would abscond). We let people and the police know out at the Yirrkala Mission. Twenty-four hours later, the young girl came back to the hospital and handed us this beautiful brand new baby. The mum was well and happy and very proud of her baby. She was healthy and stayed with us for another week waiting for a flight back to Elcho Island.

There was a bauxite ship in Port being loaded when a big fight broke out on board . The boatswain was involved and had received a major knife wound near his liver. He was in a very bad way when he was transferred to the Gove Hospital. Fortunately, our Medical Superintendent, Dr Pablo was a very good and renowned surgeon from the Philippines. He rushed him through to theatre and saved this dear man's life. He was a South African National who could only speak broken English. I was not on duty on his admission and at the time of his surgery; however, I came on at 14.30 the next day. This dear man took one look at me when I entered the ward, (as at that time I was 34 weeks pregnant) and said in very broken English, he would not let me do anything for him as I was with child. The staff had warned us that this poor man was full of fear whenever one of the nurses came to help him, as he was a black African. He thought the police would come and take him to jail like they did in South Africa and lock him up for being treated and spoken to by white people.

We got in touch with the shipping agent, who came with an interpreter from the ship and explained to him that he was safe. This was not South Africa and we would take care of him until he was well enough to fly back home. Even after this meeting he would not let me do anything for him except give him a drink of water; so when he needed assistance to sit up and get up, the second nurse and an orderly would assist him and he himself would try to do as much as he could himself. He was a true gentleman and we taught him some English words. He did try to teach us a few words in his language which we really could not grasp; but we had a lot of laughs together. After he had been with us for three weeks, he was well enough to make the journey home. So, on the Sunday prior to leaving for South Africa, Noddy and I picked him up and took him out for a few hours to show him our home and town. We had a lovely Aussie barbecue and took him back to the hospital, and said goodbye to this giant of a human being.

That weekend I started my maternity leave.

One night, when I was thirty-seven weeks pregnant, an orderly came around to our home and asked if I could do a nightshift in Midwifery, as the midwife on nights had called in sick and there was a woman in labour with no one to look after her. I said yes as I had had a very good sleep that afternoon.

Well, what a hoot that shift turned out to be. The lady was a westerner, and when I came on at 11pm, I went straight to the labour ward. When I walked in, she just looked at me and gave me a great big smile. It was her first birthing experience, so we really had a common bond and connected easily. She was in very early labour. We talked all night, in-between minor-moderate contractions, and while I was massaging her tummy during a contraction, my little bundle was saying, "please give me a massage too", I started to get Braxton Hicks contractions in unison with hers. We laughed about it.

Morning came, and sadly, I had to hand her over to the oncoming midwife. We would meet for coffee regularly over the months after that night we had spent labouring together. Unfortunately, they were only in Gove for a year, so we lost contact after they left.

Noddy, would spend hours massaging my expanding waist line over the months of my pregnancy and on April the 13th 1973, the early morning brought lashing winds and a huge deluge. A very big storm had arrived again. In those days, as I have already mentioned, there was no category for cyclones. This one would have been by today's gradings at least a Category 3.

At 5am that morning, I went into labour. Noddy was called into work as the storm was going to directly hit Gove. So, he took me over to Lyn and Dave's home where I laboured away and went for a long walk up Mount Saunders in the pouring rain and wind, to take my mind off the contractions. Liz knocked off duty early and came over to help Lyn look after me. By 6pm, I had to say to them I need to go in and have some pethidine. Liz rang to speak to the midwife on duty and said, "have the pethidine drawn up, Peta is coming in now."

Meanwhile, Noddy was still held up out at work, helping tie everything down on the Nabalco plant site. Dr. McDougal was waiting for us in the labour ward. I had my injection and went off to sleep. Dr McDougal pulled up a chair and sat by my side, holding my hand. Liz left around 7pm and I had a wonderful Irish midwife, Mrs Swan. Noddy came in with Liz at about 9.30 pm. Men were still not allowed in the labour ward in those days - but we loved breaking rules. At 21.50pm, Dr McDougal delivered a beautiful miracle in the form of one divine little baby girl into our arms. We were now a family of three. Joy filled the room and tears, laughter and love flowed.

I had to stay in hospital for a week. I had a lot of difficulty, establishing our love child on the breast; she had the tiniest little rose bud mouth, and I was rather well endowed but we just could not connect. So, she had to have top-ups. It did not help when a young midwife whom I rang for help, came in and stayed for only five minutes and gave up. As she walked out of the room she said, "You are a midwife, you know what to do."

Six weeks later, our princess was on Sunshine milk formula. In those days, it was standard practice to do episiotomies (a surgical cut made at the opening of the vagina during childbirth, to aid a difficult delivery and prevent rupture of tissues) and I had one, which caused so much trouble post- natally. The pain was excruciating and the healing process slow.

The construction workers were thrilled for us. My little angel immediately had a family of uncles. There were three main ones - there was "The Turk" from Turkey, " Mick The Backhoe"a backhoe operator from Italy, and "Harry The Horse" a mad punter from Albania, all of whom came into the hospital to meet her, and showered her with gifts. She had lots of aunties and uncles. There were a mix of Indigenous and Europeans and we felt blessed. It was a place of total non-judgemental love.

Prior to our princess being born, Nabalco – the company that

Noddy worked for- had moved us from a one bedroom unit to a little two bedroom cottage at the old contractor's village.

Soon after our daughter was born, Noddy decided that she would have to have a guard dog. An old camp dog from the construction camp, down near Wallaby beach had just had a litter of pups, all black Labradors. Noddy brought one home - a little black four legged bundle of joy. He called him Basil, after an old Turkish man with whom Noddy had worked. When our Princess was three days old, he snuck Basil, the tiny puppy, into the hospital at 10.00 pm at night. Basil was tucked up inside his shirt to meet the baby.

JA had her first swim in the ocean at one week old and never looked back. She would come to tennis with us, to all our parties and to our own dinner dates. She was the perfect baby - so engaging and happy.

Gove had a shortage of midwives and when JA was three months old, I went back to work. It turned out to be another interesting time. The Commonwealth Government workers back then in 1973 had paid maternity leave for three months, which you could draw out over six months. It was very uncommon for mothers with a young baby to work back then. My decision to go back to work caused some dissent in the community. Many did not approve.

That was until I presented a paper to the Women's Electoral Lobby on "Good mothers go to work, Good mothers stay home, Bad mothers go to work, Bad mothers stay home." It had an impact on women, who criticised working mothers. From that time onwards, I never had any further comments or judgements about my choice of being a working mother. I did night shift and I had a beautiful next-door neighbour who became JA's surrogate grandmother, whilst I slept. It worked very well. Noddy would get daddy time alone for bonding, I would get mummy time for bonding and JA would get bonding time with her carer. On the weekends, we would be together as a threesome. Life was fabulous, I just loved our little family, I loved myself and most of all I loved the fact that I could still continue in the career that I treasured. Becoming a mother made me a much better midwife.

One evening, I was on a night off, and the phone rang. It was the hospital, and the midwife who was on the afternoon shift, had called in sick. So, they had no-one to cover and she asked me if I could come in?

No worries, I said. We were going to a friend's place for a barbecue; Noddy just said he would take JA and the dog. Well, when I got home, Noddy was waiting for me to break some news, "Honey, I have lost the dog." he said. On the way home from Wallaby beach, a kangaroo had hopped across the road and disappeared into the bush. Basil saw it and jumped out of the car window and took after it, never to be seen again. Suffice it to say that I was quite cross with him.

Next morning, I went to a friend's house whose cat had just had kittens five weeks ago (I knew Noddy was not too keen on cats) and I picked out this cutest little kitten and brought him home.

Noddy returned home after work to find a little kitten lying on his pillow. What could he say? So, we welcomed this beautiful little kitten into our home. We used to read the little golden book series to JA and there was one called, *A Cat Named Charlie*, so the kitten became known as Charlie Cat.

About five days later, we heard a noise at the back door, I opened the door and standing there was one black Labrador with doleful eyes looking up at me. It was our Basil. He had found his way home. With much rejoicing, our tiny little family now became five.

When JA was fifteen months old, we were over the moon. We were blessed to find out we were to become new parents again.

We had another great pregnancy and during this time we were offered a house at Wallaby Beach. We jumped at the opportunity as houses at Wallaby Beach were as precious as gold. It was heaven living down there and we were always on the beach because our back lawn backed right on to the white glistening sand and the Arafura sea. Dad, Mum, JA, the dog and the cat. We had a daughter who thought she was a fish, a dog who thought he was a human and a cat who thought he was a dog.

One night, Charlie went for a wander and sadly got hit by a car much to our dismay. The distraught neighbour who had hit him came in to tell us about the accident. The man said he was deeply sorry. We reassured him and said that we realised it had been a genuine accident.

An hour later, after he had gone, JA and I were still in tears when we heard a knock on the front door. It was our dear neighbour and friend John, who was Katherine's husband. He had heard the story of our Charlie. He had in his hand the most gorgeous little Siamese kitten six weeks old, with the most beautiful blue eyes and handed it gently to JA. We couldn't thank John enough. A year later we were able to repay him in a way money could not.

When I was twenty-eight weeks pregnant, I went to work in theatre at the Central Sterilising Department. I worked there until I went on pregnancy leave again. We had a brilliant theatre charge sister who was a wonderful woman to work with. I really appreciated the break from the work load on the wards at that stage of my pregnancy. We had two theatre days per week and we were also on-call for emergencies. We were having a cup of tea in the tea room one afternoon when all of a sudden, the building began shaking. The fridge moved and we felt it quite distinctly. It was scary. We learnt later there had been quite a large earthquake in Indonesia. I would hate to experience being in an earthquake.

Buffaloes were everywhere around the district in those years; they were part of the Arnhem Land Region, Yirrkala Gove and Wallaby Beach. We would often be woken around 3am with Basil barking his head off. When we turned on the lights we would see a buffalo walking down the side of our house to the beach for an early morning swim. One of our favourite camping sites was out at Daliwuy Bay, which had buffaloes everywhere; but they never ever bothered us. I look back and I remember the nights we would spend out there, sitting around a camp fire burning buffalo dung, a worthy mosquito repellent. Across the river, was where all the crocodiles would sleep. We would often be able to see their red eyes watching us.

PETER REBBECHI

. . .

It was Christmas day 1994, when we awoke to the news that seventy percent of Darwin had been wiped out by tropical Cyclone Tracy. Our friends, Dave, Lyn Andrew and Danny had come over to spend Christmas with Dave, Liz, Noddy and myself. Thank God they were in Gove that day as their house was badly damaged. Public services – water, power, sewerage and communications - were all wiped out. Darwin was like a war zone and sixty-six known deaths occurred. The event was declared a national disaster. Women and children were evacuated south including Lyn and her two babies, Andrew and Danny. (Danny was the same age as our JA).

The army had been called in and Major -General Stretton was placed in charge of the rescue and recovery aftermath of the cyclone. We, in Gove, never had any rains or winds from Cyclone Tracey affect us. We still have movies of the devastation as Noddy, had gone through Darwin on a quick trip to Adelaide six months after Tracy, and managed to have a very brief stopover with Barry and Juliette in Darwin on his way South and had taken movies of what he found. Dave and Lyn still remember this momentous time in Australian history. Cyclone Tracy changed the face of disaster management in Australia, which has now become one of the biggest government services in the country.

One the 11th April 1975, after a joy filled pregnancy, I went into labour and a little bonny bouncy boy entered our world; Noddy stayed with me the whole time in the labour room. Times were changing and men were being encouraged to be with their partners throughout labour and delivery. There was a complication during delivery. They found his cord wrapped around his neck three times. But with one deft movement, the skilled obstetrician slipped the cord over his head and he announced his arrival into the world with one lusty yell. JD was born two days before JA's second birthday. So, we had decided to surprise her with a baby brother as part of her birthday present. We had a little pusher and a baby doll in the cupboard in the hospital room's wardrobe. Noddy brought her in, and what a stunning photo it would have made, when she saw and was given her baby brother as we sang Happy Birthday. Tears of absolute joy just flowed. There was no jealousy or attention seeking from JA. JD was so rich to have had his big sister, all of two, to care for him. The bonding throughout their lives has always been special. Our family was complete; we were all healthy, life was free, rich and nourishing for all of us and life continued as usual after JD was born.

I was able to feed JD. He was a pound heavier than JA and I had an abundance of milk so I kept a stash in the freezer for emergencies. One day, the phone rang. It was our dear friend, Katherine.

"Peter," she said, "can you help me?"

John and Katherine's mother cat had just had another litter of six Siamese kittens; she was sick and had no milk to feed these two week old kittens. "Have you any spare breast milk in the freezer"?

"Sure", I said and took over a basketful of containers of breast milk. The kittens all thrived and mother cat recovered.

So many beautiful stories to be shared - it was a different time, a different era, and I am so proud to say we lived through these times.

I took a year off - six months maternity leave and six months leave without pay. I loved being a stay-at-home mum. We would spend most of our days on the beach, with other mothers and little ones who lived in our community of twenty-six houses which was about twelve kilometres from Gove and two kilometres to the Nabalco Plant. We often went camping at Turtle Beach, one of the few surf beaches in the area. It was one of our treasured spots. Or, we would go to Daliwuy Bay about every third weekend. JA was growing and maturing very quickly and became Little Miss Independent. Our home was a magnet for the little ones in the street, so we always had a house full of love and laughter. JD was up and walking at eight months, he was such a determined little fellow and showed, even at that age, a competitive streak. "What the big kids do, so can I," was his motto.

December of 1975 was Gove's turn to have a cyclone, eleven months after Cyclone Tracy. Noddy and JA had gone down to Adelaide and

Perth to see our families and were on their way home via Darwin. JD and I didn't go. We stayed home in Wallaby Beach. It was very rough weather and all the men had to be called back to work at Nabalco for tie downs. Eight of the women had little ones in tow, with babies being breast fed; so we all congregated to care for each other at Katherine and John's home - with a flagon of sherry, I might add.

I already had a roast dinner cooked and a table set for dinner for when Noddy and JA came home. John had gone out to the airport to collect them at around 4pm, only to find out the plane, had been turned back to Darwin as the airstrip was under water. He reported the winds were so strong that it was hard keeping the land rover on the road. John was called in to work as soon as he got back. By five pm, we lost all power. By seven, we had all the little ones bunked down together. By this time, the ladies were hungry. Katherine did not have enough food to feed us all, so I volunteered to crawl over to our house -two doors down- to rescue the roast from the oven. The winds were roaring at about 150 kms per hour. I got the food out of the oven and crouching as low as I could, I scurried back to Katherine's with our dinner.

There were eight mums and nine little ones. We had a fun night sharing women's issues, story-telling and supporting each other. The cyclone also coincided with a high tide, so we were evacuated into Gove House at about 2am that morning.

It was a great relief to arrive back home later that day and find that there was no damage done. However, Noddy and JA were stuck in Darwin for another two days as our airport was still under water. It was a happy day when they arrived home on the third day after the storm.

Politically, Australia was in disarray in 1975– there was scandal after scandal, war had virtually broken out in Canberra after it was revealed that Australia was running out of money. Overseas borrowings had hit record highs; National debt was out of control, towards the end of that year (Oct 16th-1975). The Senate resolved not to pass supply until the Government agreed to call a general election. This meant the government would soon run out of money to pay public servants, provide pensions, pay its contractors and provide services.

This culminated in Gough Whitlam and his Government being dismissed by the Governor General of Australia on the 11th November 1975, and replaced by Malcom Fraser as caretaker Prime Minister. I was in the kitchen in our home and listening to the news on the radio; it was 2pm in the afternoon and I can still hear Gough Whitlam's speech on the steps of Parliament, "Well, may we say God Save the Queen, because nothing will save the Governor General"

The whole nation was in absolute shock and turmoil. Everybody throughout Australia was stunned, even the MP's on both sides of the house. This resulted in the proclamation of dissolving parliament for a double dissolution election. Malcom Fraser went on to win government and became Australia's 22nd Prime Minister.

Just before I returned to work, we had another major cat disaster. Top cat, the Siamese would go for a walk in the evenings to say hello to all her pussycat friends. We went off to bed, and as always left the backdoor open for her. We heard a knock on the front door around 6am. It was our neighbour, five doors down, with this poor little cat in his arms. She had been very badly injured. Kevin explained, that he was on his way to work. He got into his car, turned on the engine and heard a thud. He immediately got out, looked under the bonnet of the car and found that the fan blade had sliced through her forehead, down her face and cut her jaw in two on the right side of her face. We took her from him, and thanked him for his care.

There was no vet in Gove, so Noddy rang his long term mate, Terry Simpson, who managed TAA (Trans Australian Airlines) and asked him if he had a plane going to Darwin. Terry said, "no, however, we have one ready to take off at 8am for Cairns". Noddy, then told Terry what had happened and we needed urgent veterinary assistance. Terry said, "leave it with me." Ten minutes later he rang back and said he had spoken to the pilot and that yes, he would take the cat with him in the cockpit to Cairns and asked us to organise for a vet in Cairns to meet him at the airport and he would hand her over to the vet. Our next door neighbour was a cat lover; she had heard the goings on and came in to see if she could help. She went straight home and brought back a cage for her transfer. Noddy rushed Toppy out to the airport and handed her over to the pilot. I knew one of my nursing colleagues was from Cairns. I rang her and asked if she knew a vet in Cairns. It turned out that her friend was married to one. Joan contacted her friend and he said, he would be at the airport when the TAA flight arrived and he would look after her. I could relax then and assured the kids that it wouldn't be long when Toppy would be home.

At 7pm, the vet rang from Cairns and told us he had wired the right side of Toppy's jaw and sutured her pretty little face. However, he would have to keep her in Cairns for six weeks to take out the wires before he flew her home. Six days later, we had a call from the vet asking if he and his family could keep her as she was fretting so much in the animal hospital that he and his family had taken her home to their house. Everyone there fell in love with her. She was happy surrounded by the kids. Of course we said no; she is part of our family. The vet was just so nice. We would ring every second day and speak with him and Toppy over the phone. The day we got the call that she was coming home we were all so very happy. We went to the airport to pick her up and there was much joy as the Captain carried her across the tarmac. That cat never left our side from that day on until she went home for good in 1991. She was sixteen years old then. The cost was $150 in 1976.

I went back to work, when JD, was a year old. I chose to work in Causality as that was one of my favourite specialities. In Casualty, one never knew what was going to happen from one minute to the next. We always had to be prepared for whatever the patients were presenting with. We had a very cohesive and excellent nursing team and great doctors. Noddy and I used to work opposite shifts so the children were never too long away from our care.

By this time Yirrkala and Gove Hospital were becoming far more integrated. Specialists would come up to do clinics instead of patients having to go to Darwin to see the Specialists. I worked mainly evenings and on my own. I knew ninety-nine percent of all the Aboriginals who came in from Yirrkala and they would be so happy to see me, and I them. I could nurse the way I loved to nurse. Often they would arrive, and knowing that they would love a hot shower(Aboriginal housing or camps had no hot water for shower in those days), I kept a stack of towels and small cakes of soap under the desk and would offer them a hot shower, make them a cuppa tea and then sort out their complaint. One night, a stranger brought an old man who had a minor presentation. I asked him if he would like a hot shower and he said "yes please, Yappa." So, I took him to the shower, made him a cuppa tea and I offered the white lady, a cuppa too, but she declined.

Once I had addressed his presenting complaint, he left very happy. When I arrived at work the next day, I was called into the Administration office as an official complaint had been received from head office in Canberra. The woman who had brought the Aboriginal man in the evening before was the complainant. A visiting sociologist from Canberra said I was a racist nurse, going on to explain how I had told this Aboriginal man to have a shower, and that I would not do the same to a white man. The Matron and the administrator were very understanding and supported me; I was told not to worry about it, that the administrator would deal with Canberra and I never heard another word about it. I was able to continue with my nursing practice as I had always done. Nursing was all about caring for the whole person, body mind and spirit and being one with the patient.

On another instance, it was a Sunday afternoon when we got a radio call to say we had a major emergency coming in from Yirrkala. A little five year old who had been stung by a deadly box jellyfish, had arrested and they were ten minutes away. Immediately, we had a team ready for her arrival. It was a Sunday afternoon. She was rushed straight into resus and we were desperately trying to save this little one's life.

I was co-ordinating the team, and the front bell rang so I had to run down the long corridor just in case it was another emergency situation and there was a man asking for my attention. I asked this guy, if I could help him.

He said to me, "I have just scratched my big toe. I need a band aid." I looked at his toe and could see just the tiniest mark.

I gave him 'the look' and advised him to go to the supermarket to buy a packet of Band Aid, then go home, wash his toe and put on the Band Aid. He got the look and the tone of voice and hightailed out the door.

I raced straight back to resus. After trying for forty minutes, the medical officer called it a day; we all agreed and the little soul/spirit went home. It is always very sad and an emotional time when we lose someone in resus. However, in those days, most staff were enlightened and awakened health professionals that really cared about their patients and each other and ensured all involved were looked after.

We were family. We met for a cup of coffee, talked it through, we knew we had done the best we could, and it was meant to be. We had not failed this little girl or her family.

At that very same time that the man (whom I been a bit stern with earlier) was leaving the grounds of the hospital, Noddy was coming in to do a car swap and put the keys in my bag. This guy said to him, "I wouldn't go in there mate, there is a real bitch on".

He replied "Thanks mate," and smiling he came and went without me even knowing he had been. Noddy told me the story after I got home and we had a good laugh about it.

Life was fulfilling with lots of beach and camping adventures. The kids loved camping. One weekend, we went out to this remote river that an old water authority guy told us about. It was about 100 kms from Gove and the track was overgrown, making the journey slow; the worst part was traversing over narrow little crossings. There were about six car loads of families and we found our way during the day, without trouble. At about 5pm, JD started to have a cough; at first it was just an annoying irritation, but by 9pm the cough had developed into a full-blown croup attack. There was no way we could get out of the camp to get medical attention. So, I boiled the billy, put a tablespoon of Vicks vaporising cream in the billy can, got some eucalyptus leaves, brought them to the boil and laid him over my lap, with a towel saturated with this medicine over his head for a few hours. I slept with him on my chest this time and just prayed and prayed.

Sure enough, when the sun came up at five, JA and the other kids were up. JD's cough had disappeared and he too was up and about running around with all the other kids. We decided about nine o'clock to head home, as we did not want to be stuck out in the bush just in case the cough returned. We arrived home safely about five hours later and JD was fine. Four days later, it returned with full vengeance and he was in an oxygen tent in Gove Hospital. I too was in the tent nursing him. It was a scary experience for a little boy and his mum. He was fine after three days and back home four days later.

We were fortunate as we were allowed to go anywhere along the east Arnhem coast and we had some amazing camp outs with Roy Marika. We visited some pristine isolated beaches during our years in Gove.

I arrived for duty one morning and had to race straight down to resus. One of our beautiful young doctors had been out early with his friend to take photos of a buffalo in the bush over the road from where they lived. They were about to sail off on their next voyage (they were on their round-the-world sailing trip) and wanted a good close up photo of a buffalo. They had been with us during the monsoon season, and as the dry season was just commencing, the winds had changed. They only had one week to go before leaving town. In his enthusiasm, Alistair had got close to a mother and her calf and said to the mother buffalo, "chase me now." She obeyed, put her head down and came charging straight for him, gorging and fracturing his femur in three places and also fracturing his pelvis. He was in a very bad way. RFDS flew him straight to Darwin, after we had stabilised him. From Darwin he was transferred down to Melbourne and after many months finally recovered and eventually joined his friends some eighteen months later. We missed him very much, as did the community.

Causality Nursing was such a great speciality to work in as you really got to see conditions and learn something new every day. I was also very fortunate to see conditions I have never seen in the Southern States when rostered on to work with leading Cardiologists, Physicians, Paediatricians, Gynaecologists' and Obstetricians who would come to Gove monthly or from Adelaide every second month. We did have one of the best and most gifted surgeons I have ever met - Dr Alan Bromwich[1] (1924 -2015). He was friends with everyone and we were privileged to have many a dinner with him on his monthly visit to Gove.

He arrived in the Old Darwin Hospital situated at Myilly Precinct, overlooking Darwin Harbour in 1958 as the Chief Surgeon – it was the year, my darling brother had died. With only seven doctors in the Hospital, a general surgeon had to be versatile, carrying out procedures that today would be performed by specialists - orthopaedic surgeons, gynaecologists, ENT surgeons etc. He could remove an appendix in seven minutes and perform almost every type of surgery. I was relieving in theatre once, while Mr Bromwich was over, and a young girl came in with a ruptured uterus at forty-one weeks gestation; he saved both the mother and the baby. He alleviated many people's suffering with his skills. He had also led the surgical response to Cyclone Tracy. Alan came over a month after Cyclone Tracy and came down to have dinner with us; his stories were amazing. Such a giving and humble man and he was very much loved by all.

I saw children with Huntington's Chorea and Rheumatic Fever. It was in the early days too of petrol sniffing out in communities, and we saw the conditions developing in young children's brains. It was more of a major problem in the inland communities rather than in communities living by the ocean. Drugs may have been around; however, we never had any one come to casualty or admitted with drug related psychosis.

Alcohol, however, was a problem and there were times when we would be called down to the Walkabout hotel to pick up a patient who was very inebriated, and had fallen off a bar stool or who had got into a fight. We had patients with malaria and other tropical diseases too. We also would have our share of industrial accidents out at the plant, and of course there were some major car accident cases. One of our dear friends and neighbour was killed in one. He was one of Noddy's besties, and I was glad I wasn't on duty the day David Tate, only ever known as "Buffalo," was brought in.

GREEK ISLANDS

It was two months before JA's fourth birthday and JD's second. I suggested to Noddy that we go to Bali for a week's holiday. Bali was in its tourism infancy then and it was very cheap to fly from Darwin.

Noddy said, "No way, I am not taking the little ones there, they might get sick".

I tried all the tricks in the book, to get him to change his mind, but he would not. He had never been overseas before and was more cautious than I was. Well, one night, I came home from an evening shift and he was watching a British TV series, "Who Pays the Ferryman." It was set in Ageas Nicholas at the bottom of Crete. He was telling me about the story and said it is so pretty, a great place to make a TV series.

I went off to bed plotting.

Okay, if he will not go to Bali, I will take him to Greece to Ageas Nicholas for a holiday! This was Saturday night, so on Monday morning I went to the local travel agent Carol, who happened to be a friend of mine and we prepared an itinerary and planned to have JA's fourth and JD's second birthdays in Greece.

My friend told me, if we left before their birthdays; there would be no cost for the children's airline tickets. Children up to the age of four, in that era, travelled free. So, I booked and payed a deposit.

I took the itinerary home and said to Noddy, "Honey, would you mind booking your holidays for this time?" showing him what I had done that morning.

He just looked at it and said, "You win."

It would be the first time ever for him to leave Australian shores.

Once it was known around the town that we were heading to the Greek Islands, our local Greek friends suggested that we should spend Easter on their Island of Kalymnos. In fact, one of the guys gave us a letter of introduction to his uncle who managed a hotel on the island called the Knossos Palace, and promised that we would get a very special rate.

Noddy and I, both had our holidays approved, and within weeks, were off on an adventure. Dad, Mum and two kids. JD was still in nappies at night. We flew from Darwin to Athens via Kuala Lumpur where we had a short stop over. It was a time of civil unrest in Malaysia and there were armed force personnel with these machine guns everywhere. We had never seen anything like it. The kids' eyes were as wide as saucers; if the men came near them, the little ones would give them a big smile. The soldiers would stop and pat them on their heads. We had a refuel stop at Bahrain but we were not allowed off the plane. We arrived in Athens exhausted. The kids were as bright as buttons as they had slept most of the way from Darwin. The air hostesses were brilliant. The meals were served on china plates and silver cutlery. They took the kids up to the flight deck where they met the captain of the Qantas plane and the flight crew. The pilot would walk down the plane, talking to the passengers, in those days.

On our arrival, in Athens, we were surprised at the number of uniformed soldiers on guard at the airport. The kids would go up to them to say hello, and they would put down their guns and rub their hair. JA had streaks of blonde hair and JD was all blonde. In Greece, they had a myth that said if you rub the head of a blonde child you will have good fortune for the rest of your life. So, you can imagine how many pats on the heads the kids received.

We spent four wonderful days exploring Athens walking with the kids in their strollers. We went to the Parthenon and loved it.

From Athens we flew down to Heraklion. It was in Heraklion that I had to purchase ferry tickets to take us from Ageus Nickolas to Rhodes. The children travelled free and the tickets were very cheap. Then we were taken to a new Hotel complex in Knossos that the travel agent had booked for us. You can imagine our shock and horror when we found out that the hotel had not been opened yet. However, they were very accommodating and found us a little unit to stay in the complex.

We explored this ancient community, which had its origins in the 9th century AD. After four days, we travelled down to our destination, Ageus Nickolas, by bus. What a bus ride down winding old roads, through valleys that were deep and beautiful. On arrival, our heart was stolen by the magic of the 'golden jewel', this tiny little fishing village. It reminded me of Rottnest Island. We stayed at a hotel right on the waterfront within walking distance to the ferry terminal. The staff of the hotel were fantastic and told us about all the interesting places to visit.

Our next island we visited was Rhodes. What a beautiful island Rhodes was to explore! It was full of ancient ruins and remnants of occupations of crusaders back in ancient times. In 1977 it was quiet and laid back with every one going about their business in slow motion. It was not the bustling tourist mecca it is today.

From there, we headed over to the island of Kos. I loved this ancient town, standing under the tree of Hippocrates. (Hippocrates was to become one of my hero's in 2016, and I share his humour theories with people and reflexologists today.) We spent three glorious days on Kos. The kids really enjoyed themselves as little ones do when they are free spirits. They got lots of attention from the locals.

Kalymnos was our next island on our journey. It was here we celebrated JA's and JD's 2nd and 4th birthdays. We were staying at a brand new hotel, right in the middle of the town square, opposite the island's harbour. The Aegean Sea was the clearest blue; it was easy to be mesmerised just staring at the water.

Many of the construction workers and contract workers in Gove were from Kalymnos. They asked us to let their families know they were doing fine. We were even invited to a traditional Greek wedding.

After ten days, we headed back to Athens and then caught a train up to Thessalonika. The scenery from the train was breathtaking, over lots of old railroad bridges that had stood the test of time. Thessalonica was relatively new, built in 1917 after a fire had destroyed most of the old town centre. Our holiday was drawing to a close and sad as we were to leave the beautiful Greek islands; however, we were also starting to long for home.

Once home, we settled back into the routine of daily life again. At the Fisher family, Betty was a stay at home Mum; their boys were all at school, so Betty and Jeff were very happy to become surrogate parents while we were working. Like Kath and Alan, they were the best and our children were very happy being part of an extended family.

Betty was a very good tennis player and we had many a fierce competition on the tennis court. One Sunday, we were at home and the phone rang. Noddy was the President of the Gove tennis club and the man on the other end of the phone was the President of the Mt Isa tennis club. He asked Noddy, if the Gove tennis club would be happy to be involved in an exhibition match that Ken Rosewall and Tony Roach were doing as part of their exhibition tour in Northern Australia.

Noddy said, "I am sure that would be fantastic for Gove to be involved on the circuit". He called an urgent committee meeting that night and everyone voted for our tennis club to be included in their tour; he rang the man back and said yes.

What excitement in the town! 'Nabalco' sponsored the event and the whole community became involved in the planning and preparation. The cost to procure their services was $1000 each. Fundraising was organised and Nabalco provided all the scaffolding to erect seating for the exhibition. The tickets were sold for $10 dollars a head to enable the payment for the players.

The plan was that they were going to play a singles match,

followed by a mixed-doubles. Betty and I were given the honour of being chosen to play with these great Australian champion tennis players - as Betty was the Gove's tennis club's runner up and I the champion woman player that year. We were so excited and could not wait for that evening in June to arrive. The committee had taken out insurance which included an adverse weather event.

Gove never had rain in June; but the morning Noddy picked them up from the airport, it started to rain. Everyone's heart was in their mouths, praying for the rain to stop and clear. It rained all day and into the evening. Undeterred, the community filled the seats surrounding the court. Betty and I were all ready to play, as were Tony and Ken. There had been a break in the weather so Ken and Tony started to play their singles match; the men had to sweep the court prior to the game starting as the court was very wet with puddles everywhere. Ten minutes later, the heavens opened again and the match had to be suspended. It started to pour down really hard and then the event had to be cancelled. However, as true champions they spent two hours in the undercover area sharing with the community their tennis life journeys. They were great story tellers and everyone thoroughly enjoyed the evening with our visitors.

After every one left, a few of us went to the Walkabout hotel, enjoying a few ales and wines with our honoured visitors. On the way to the Walkabout, Noddy and another committee member checked the town's water gage and it measured two millimetres short of what we could have claimed back from the insurance company. Noddy and his mate were tempted to add some extra fluid, but as good upstanding citizens and too honest, they decided against it.

Although we didn't get to watch their singles match and neither did Betty and I get to partner them in a mixed-doubles, we did have a great night.

As Noddy had arranged to take Ken and Tony out to Yirrkala Mission on their way to the airport the next day, they came out to spend some time in with us on Wallaby Beach in the morning. I have a lovely photo of Noddy, JD and Ken standing outside our humble little home with a book Ken Roswall had written back then, signed and presented to one small bright-eyed boy.

In the September of 1977, I was asked if I would do a six-week holiday relief for the Aerial Medical Service (the equivalent of the RFDS) in the Northern Territory. I readily accepted the offer, even though I wasn't a fan of flying, I thought it would be a great experience and I did settle very quickly into the role.

It worked in well with family life too. A story that really stands out in my mind from those six weeks, was that one day we received a call to go down the Gulf of Carpentaria to a community called 'Roper Bar'. There was no air-med plane available, so a four-seater single engine plane flew us down. That section of the gulf had experienced some quite heavy September rains and as we approached Roper Bar, I happened to spot people running up the beach with buckets and pouring, what looked like sand, from the buckets onto the runway.

I said to the pilot, "what are the people doing"?

He said, "Filling up the pot holes so we can land".

I muttered a quick prayer under my breath.

Sure enough though, they fixed the strip; we picked up our patient and flew back to Gove, delivering him safely to the hospital. The six weeks went very quickly, and I was privileged to do clinics out in Elcho Island, Millingimbi and other remote communities.

Whilst I was relieving in that role, two new positions were created in Community Health - one was the Director of Community Nursing position and a Director of Medicine, as the administration of the East Arnhem Health Service was transferred to Gove at that time. The appointees where –Dr Max, a delightful man and a nursing Director, SR Ellen Kettle.

As soon as I was introduced to her, there was an immediate connection. We soon became friends and Ellen would spend many a night sharing a barbecue with us out at Wallaby Beach, sitting around a fire with the lawns stretching straight down on to the Arafura Sea telling us many stories of her life here in Australia and Papua New Guinea. We listened, and learnt so much from this amazing woman.

A community nurse position came up towards the end of the year, and Ellen offered me the position as the school health nurse in Gove. Another heart decision and I immediately said yes. I knew I would learn so much from this great mentor and teacher. Ellen Kettle was the nurse and midwife who pioneered mobile health care in towns and isolated communities in the Northern Territory in the 1960's. She had a very long and distinguished career, culminating in an MBE.

I said goodbye to the acute care setting and became a Monday-Friday 0800 -16.20 hour worker. There were three nurses and one doctor employed at the Community Health Centre. My role encompassed a variety of work. We would have a psychologist come out from Darwin for two days once a month; while in between times I was his go-to liaison on the ground in Gove.

I grew and learnt so much from this role. It was my first experience dealing with people with whom I had never associated before, listening and counselling and supporting parents with extremely high needs children who had severe behavioural issues. Introducing programs like Parent Effectiveness Training taught me to be a better parent too. I was also the East Arnhem Gove Health Department's and Nabalco's audiology nurse. I had to go to Darwin for a two week intensive training program in audiology. Nabalco had a very early OSH program, so I was contracted to them one day a week to check their employees hearing and I also had to do all the audiology testing on the children both in the primary and high school. I would also help out the child health nurse when she was busy or off sick. I found, I loved this role and developed a new skill set in my nursing career.

One of the best things about living at Wallaby Beach was the access to the prawn boats that would tie up at the Mission wharf on a Friday afternoon. These boats were on their way back from fishing in the Gulf of Carpenteria. They would always come in around 5pm, after the banks in town had closed. So those of us in the know would be down at the wharf, and would buy a ten-kilo box of king prawns and morten bay bugs for $5.00 a box; the kids loved them. We would get a supply once a fortnight and I am filled with gratitude to have been blessed to live, work and play in this place and era.

It was in Gove I first heard and nursed patients with Ciguatera fish poisoning; a food borne illness caused by eating reef fish, whose flesh is contaminated with certain toxins. The toxins are made by a small organism called *Gambierdiscus toxicus* that grows on and around coral reefs in tropical and subtropical waters. These are eaten by herbivorous fish, which in turn are eaten by carnivorous fish The fish most often implicated are barracuda, grouper, moray eel, amberjack, sea bass and sturgeon. Some patients would be so ill, they would have to be evacuated to Darwin Hospital. Two of our special doctors were given some fish –a grouper from a grateful patient and became so ill they too were transferred to Darwin. I never saw an Aboriginal patient with Ciguatera poisoning. The community became very aware of the dangers of eating the these fish species after our doctors recovered.

On the social front, life was full; our home was a hive of activity. The kids loved swimming and spent all their time on the beach, swimming in the sea in the dry season or in a 25 metre pool at the end of our street in the wet. We would have all the tennis club social events at our house, and just loved our life. There was a beautiful swimming and divine camping area situated about ten kms from Gove. To get there one had to travel out on a very rough track on a four wheel drive. It was very popular with snorkelers, catching painted crays.

It was here, that one of the saddest events happened during our time living in Gove. A young couple on their honeymoon were doing a camping holiday around Australia, scuba diving and snorkelling. They had come in the dry season and were able to traverse the country via a very rough road from Katherine through to Gove, a distance of 710 kilometres. Only in the dry season was it possible to cross the Goyder River as there were no bridges.

They were talking to some locals on arrivals who were also scuba divers. They took the opportunity, to take the honeymooners out to Rainbow Cliffs to do some snorkelling. One Sunday afternoon, unbeknownst to the people, who would frequent this piece of paradise, there was a big crocodile who happened to be lying in wait. All of a sudden, there was movement in the water and the newly wedded husband was taken by that crocodile, while his wife and the other lady were sitting on the beach. They saw the whole horrific event happen. It was a very sad time for the young wife and the families of the newlyweds and the kind couple who took them to Rainbow Cliff. It was also a sad time for us as we would never be able to go out any more to this beautiful bay. In the years that have passed since this tragedy, I clearly remember the day I was walking back to the health centre from the school, the police brought the dead croc in on a giant trailer into town for the whole community to see. They had caught and shot the crocodile. I think this was in 1978 or 1979.

We then had a crocodile move into the waters off Wallaby Beach that would be seen swimming regularly up and down our little piece of paradise. One morning, one of the neighbours had croc pads up his lawn. The creature had been stalking their Rhodesian Ridgeback dog. The owner used to let the dog out every morning at the same time. We would always be very careful wading from then on in the Arafura Sea in the dry season. We would never swim in the wet season because of the box jellyfish.

Both JA and JD were really into books. JD's favourite was "Peter Pan." He really believed in Peter Pan, and JA in Wendy. One night, I made them a promise that when JD was four and JA six, Daddy and I would take them to Disney Land to meet Peter Pan, Wendy and Captain Hook. In July 1979, we were true to our promises and off we went to Disney Land.

Arrangements were made, and an itinerary put together for a trip to meet Peter Pan and Wendy. We also took the opportunity to go and visit all our friends and family living around America. So, at the beginning of August 1979, we flew from Gove to Cairns to Sydney and then across to the America's, arriving in San Francisco and then we took an internal flight down to Los Angles. I had friends, Dave and Ruth Sudakow from Exmouth, living in LA and they very kindly made us welcome in their home, picking us up at the airport and sharing their experiences and their city with us. The second day we were there, we arrived at the gates of Disney Land. The little kids were so excited; but so were the big kids, I would have to admit. The first characters we ran into were Mickey and Mini Mouse, and Goofy the dog; the little ones' eyes were as big as saucers and I was so happy that we could introduce them to all these wonderful characters and shows. We have never forgotten seeing the looks on their faces, when we finally arrived at the Never Never Land and Peter Pan and Wendy were flying through the window. It was worth more than winning the lottery. We spent two days exploring the *Happiest Place on Earth* - this was Disney Lands slogan back then.

Ruth and Dave took us out to Knotsberry farm and on day outings to the famous, beaches around Los Angles . It was here we saw the first Golden arches of a MacDonald's stores. MacDonalds had not taken hold in Australia at that time.

From there, we headed over to the Beautiful Bountiful Ballwin County red neck county to spend a week with Mr and Mrs Norris, my surrogate parents /grandparents from Exmouth and Greece. It was so lovely to meet and stay with then again, this time with my own little family. We had three glorious days resting and having a few local tours, as we were a little tired and so were the kids. It was nice just to be present with them. Mrs Norris gave a beautiful wooden doll house furniture set to JA to take home, and to this day our little granddaughter has had many happy hours playing with this set. It was sad to say goodbye, as we knew we would never see them again; however they are always in our hearts, in our story telling and they would be so happy to know that they have been included in these memoirs.

From Tampa we flew up to New York; it was a good time to be leaving the area, as a massive hurricane was moving across the Gulf of Mexico and expected to cross near Tampa five days after we left.

Del met us at the airport in New York, and thank God he did, for it was something from another world. Thousands and thousands of people, aeroplanes, cars, sky scrapers - we had never seen anything like it. One can imagine what it would be like, coming from one of the most remote and isolated towns in Australia, in 1979 where the population was around 3000 people where life was so laid back and free, to the big sprawling metropolis of New York City, with millions of people racing around. The noise, the traffic and the bright lights were all just too much for us.

Del and Rosie lived upstate New York in Schenectady, near Albany the capitol of New York State. Del had arranged for us all to stay at some friends of his in the Bronx area. We met them and they were very lovely people. As we were all very tired, Del suggested, we should go straight up to Schenectady. We were happy with this decision as New York was too much for us to absorb.

Noddy and Del had never met, but within an hour of meeting, it seemed like they had been best friends all their lives and they talked for the three hour drive whilst the kids and I slept all the way to Del's. Rosie and her two beautiful children Michael and Justine were waiting on the front lawn when we arrived. It was so exciting to see them that all tiredness left us and we talked and talked for hours. The kids immediately connected and for ten days we had the best holiday experience. We loved them; it was like we had never been separated. Rosie and Del had both taken holidays and we went on adventure after adventure daily.

A memorable one was a night in The Honey Moon Hotel at Niagara Falls. All the beds were vibrating ones and it was rather an interesting night's sleep with JA, JD, Noddy and I all in the one room with two double beds. Every time someone would turn over, the bed would gently vibrate for a few minutes, but we all managed to have good night's sleep.

From there, we went up to Whiteface Mountain and to Santa's North Pole workshop. To see the faces of four little people, their smiles and excitement is something that money cannot buy.

We finally arrived back at Schenectady, dreading the next few days when we would have to say goodbye to our extended family, Rosie offered to get me a job as a RN at the hospital she was working at; however, having already been spoilt by the nursing conditions we had in Australia, to go down to one week leave a year just did not fit our lifestyle. So, we decided not to stay on in the US. Del, Rosie and the kids took us down to JFK airport in New York where we said our goodbyes and headed down to South Bend.

Noddy's sister and her family lived in South Bend. We met Pauline's family for the first time and the children met their first cousins who were all grown up and had finished school. Pauline had an indoor heated pool, so that is where many happy hours were spent. We did a week's touring around South Bend, and we even visited the famous Notre Dame University, the icon of South Bend.

We spent several days visiting Lake Michigan and there was great excitement when we toured the Henry Ford museum. JD was in seventh heaven as was Noddy and Alex, Pauline's husband. Following the visit to South Bend, we headed home to Gove, arriving back safely after five wonderful weeks in the USA.

Noddy was coming up to his 40th birthday.

Times were starting to become tough for anyone over forty to get a job in Australia at that time. Perth, was where we had decided to raise our little family, so we decided to transfer to Perth in the New Year so that Noddy could get work. It also meant that the children could be educated in Perth. The city had opportunities that were far more abundant than in a remote community setting or Darwin in that era and we wouldn't have to send them away to boarding school. The children would be surrounded by extended family, grandparents, aunties and cousins - an opportunity I never experienced.

Over the years, Noddy had fallen in love with Perth when we visited my parents. He loved the drive from Scarborough right up the coast. After much deliberation we decided to leave Gove on the 1st January 1980. This gave us three months to get used to the idea, pack up everything, sell the cars and put in our resignation.

Time flew and we had rounds and rounds of farewells to attend.

Our friends, John and Katherine Flynn had already left Gove and Jackie and Alan Miners, Muriel and JA's best friend, Suzanna were all leaving around at the same time. Working for the Commonwealth Government, I was able to transfer straight down to the Hollywood Repatriation Hospital in Nedlands, WA. I took three months leave and on the 1st January, 1980 we left this 'heaven on earth' to bring the children up in a city, so they would never have to suffer those cultural shocks that I had experienced in my earlier life.

RETURNING FROM OVERSEAS

Noddy and I - Party time .1972

Traversing the Nullabour - Jan 1972 (above)
Out camping Arnhem Land - 1975 (right)
Kids on the Greek Island of Kos (below)

Evening at Gove Tennis Club - 1978 (left)

Nursing Yirrkala with Mother's and babies - 1972 (above)

Yirrkala Basket Ball Team - 1972 (left)

PERTH

My dear Mum had rented a house for us just around the corner from where they lived. As grandparents to the little ones, they were great. The kids enjoyed going to Granny's where they were spoilt endlessly. I am sure that time was a healing process for Mum and Dad. Mum would always talk about how JD was the mirror image of Joe. Mum had also booked them into a little Catholic school, which had opened recently. JA was in grade two and JD in a Government Preschool/ Kindergarten that he didn't like at all. It was not far from where we were staying, so he would just get up and walk to Granny's home. It took a while for him to settle into the city life.

As he got older, he would often have a tummy ache first thing in the morning and not want to go to school. I was soft and would let him stay home if I was on a day off. As soon as it was 9am, he would feel better and say, "Can we go to the beach mummy, or can we go to the zoo?" So off we would go for a few hours. I have to admit this continued for several years.

It didn't take long for Noddy to get a job. JA settled into school quickly and made friends very easily because of her beautiful happy disposition. She turned out to be the best swimmer in lower primary. We signed her up in a little swim squad at 'Pitcher Whitford's' and she was so happy there, training with a lovely group of talented swimmers. We got involved on the committee too. JD was not so keen on swimming, although he joined in. We enrolled him in gymnastics, which he excelled in.

We built a new house and moved in. City living was certainly not like remote living, the neighbours kept to themselves, as there were high asbestos fences surrounding their homes. In Gove, we had no fences and as neighbours, we were always there for each other.

The women never needed to see counsellors; in fact, in that era there were no counsellors in Gove nor for that matter many professional counsellors at all in Australia. Everything would be discussed and shared whilst hanging out the clothes with your neighbour, or with a friend (or friends) over a cuppa. America was just seeing a growth in this professional group. Today, counselling and therapy in Australia is a very big health speciality.

It was time for me to return to work in the April of 1980. Mum and Dad jumped at the opportunity to look after the children for us, taking them and picking them up from school. JA and JD were very happy to be with Granny and Grandfather, as they called my Dad.

I had transferred to The Hollywood Repatriation Hospital in the Outpatient clinic. The sister in charge had been there for forty years. To a newcomer, she was not very friendly, as I was never sitting in the office. I was always outside in the waiting area talking with the old diggers. The specialists were all very kind; one in particular I admired, was a plastic surgeon. He was kind and gentle and had much respect for the old diggers. He would record a lot of their history, and I was allowed to stay in and listen to the stories. A great privilege and learning experience; but I would then be late in finishing the files and getting ready for the next day. Apart from being with the diggers, the work was very boring; however, I knew it would be only a matter of time, before the new Wanneroo Hospital would open and I would apply to become a midwife there.

Midwifery, I knew, was calling me back in 1980.

Mum had a contact, who would keep her informed when the positions at the new hospital would be advertised. So, as soon as they appeared in the West Australian, I applied and was selected for an interview and was lucky to be appointed as one of the founding midwives.

On the 8th August 1980, Wanneroo Hospital was opened. It was a state-of-the-art secondary hospital. Mind you, no monitors, no intensive care, coronary care, dialysis or mental health units. The hospital had a four cubicle emergency department and a minor operating theatre, an X-ray department and a Pathology unit on the ground floor. The first floor housed a maternity suite, which had two labour wards that led around to two operating theatres. The next floor was a thirty-bed surgical unit and the third floor housed a medical ward with four paediatric beds. It was situated in lush surrounds where kangaroos and emus would lie leisurely on the lawns and gardens surrounding the hospital. The only other building was the shire council offices situated over the road from the hospital. The closest community was Edgewater- then nothing but bushland- and the main road in, was off Marmion Avenue. We would turn down Ocean Reef Road until we got to Edgewater drive and there were no traffic lights. Heathridge was just developing, as was Beldon where we built our first house. There was no other development. We would be driving to work and have to wait for the emus to cross the road and we would also have to be on the lookout for kangaroos. I think, it would be very hard for anyone to imagine this today.

Ms Taylor was the first matron and John, the first administrator, and they were both very experienced and respected professionals. We had an Assistant Director of Nursing and four charge sisters, the midwives and general nursing staff. There would have been around forty of us all up.

The Emergency Department was staffed by a RN and GPs who had admitting rights. They would be called in if the nurse needed a medical officer's help. There were eight GP's contracted to supply the medical needs of emergency care. The staff were from different walks of life and all very skilled and heart centred professional nurses. I made some lifelong friends there.

Midwifery had ten beds and the surgical unit thirty beds on the second floor. The medical unit was on the third floor. It had twenty six beds and four paediatric beds. Initially, the maternity unit, was very slow to take off, and a decision was made to close it and move the unit up to share with the surgical ward.

I was honoured to deliver the first set of twins at Wanneroo Hospital in 1981.

Although it took some time for midwifery to start, once it did, it became a very busy bustling maternity ward and had an excellent reputation. We shared the second floor for approximately fifteen months and then relocated back to the original maternity floor. With the rapid expansion of suburbia in the Northern District, Wanneroo Hospital became a really important part of the HDWA (Health Department of Western Australia) infrastructure. All the specialists started coming out and the visiting specialist surgeons with admitting rights also increased.

Coming to work in a new state and a new hospital as a nurse, from an independent practitioner in a remote community was not easy. In actual fact, it was quite hard and the hierarchical system under which we worked took me awhile to get accustomed to. Also, missing were Aboriginal people because at that time there certainly was not the multicultural mix that our society is made up of today. It was here again that I experienced another cultural shock. I had to have a doctor's order, just to give out a Panadol. It took me a few months to adjust to the system. I missed Gove so much. My husband was very supportive during this period and kept reminding me, we were in Perth for a purpose and as soon as the children were ready to leave the nest, we could return to the North. Wanneroo hospital had not been opened very long when an opportunity arose for me to be able to return back to my role of a generalist nurse and I began relieving in all areas of that hospital. I loved this role and got to know many great people. I got on with almost everyone, with the exception of a couple of specialists who thought nurses were their handmaidens. We had no Residents or Registrars' working there in the first couple of years that Wanneroo was functioning.

The family were doing well. Noddy loved his job. JA was settled and very happy loving her new school and the swimming club she was in. JD had started school in 1981and was into football and athletics.

I heard in 1981, that there was going to be a new service starting in Perth. It was to be a new home-based one for the Care of the Dying, to be run by the Silver Chain Nursing Service –the first in Australia. I immediately thought this is what I would like to do. The Institute of Technology, was offering a post graduate certificated course in Palliative Care, so I put myself in the best possible position to be successful in joining this new service, specifically for the dying members of our society.

I studied and obtained a post graduate certificate in Palliative Care. My lecturer was a wonderful woman by the name of Joy Brand. She was a great teacher and a mentor. She introduced me to a lady author, who became a mentor through her writings. She was Elizabeth Kubler Ross, and although I never did meet her, I learnt many valuable things from her writings. I started to read and finished every book she had written and did really well in this course. Joy was instrumental in ensuring I would become one of Silver Chain's first Palliative Nurses after they ran a brief trial. I was so glad I was led to this amazing work.

In May of 1982, I commenced working in the first Palliative Care service in Australia, with the Silver Chain Home Based Service. I chose to work permanent night shift -seven nights a fortnight. It turned out to be good for family life.

The Palliative Care Support movement was growing very strongly in those years and the Perth Community worked very hard to fund and build the first purpose- built free standing Hospice in Australia on Crown land which opened in 1987. It was a glorious peaceful place for those who would be admitted and those who worked there. One could feel the peace when you drove into the visitors' carpark. As you walked in through the front door, peace permeated through you. It was an indescribable feeling. Sadly though, it was closed in the health care reforms in the early 2000's. I was lucky enough to visit there in 2004.

. . .

This was also time of great Spiritual growth for me. During this period, I was continuing my work as well as personal development. I journeyed with amazing persons to their Passover. I witnessed souls radiantly leaving their bodies as they took their last breath. One night, I witnessed a soul leaving a body and move through the walls in her bedroom. It happened in the presence of a family member - the dying woman's husband also saw what I saw. This blew the two of us away and really changed my belief in life-after-death on a much deeper level.

I commenced meditating with the Raj Yoga group in Perth and even wrote some meditations myself, which sadly I never kept. One very old lady, aged eighty-three, lit a fire in me and I will never forget her. She was a beautiful Buddhist lady, who lived on her own in a little cottage in the Western Suburbs of Perth. I used to visit her every night at around 11pm to administer her morphine. She would always be waiting for me on the back veranda of her home, with a small bottle of wine and two wine glasses. Once she had a glass of wine and I a wee sip, I would give her the morphine and tuck her in for the night.

Up until her last year, she would travel to Kathmandu every year for a retreat. We would have very deep philosophical discussions - such was the connectedness between us. On my last visit, (I knew it would be the last time I would see her as I was going on days off), I asked her to ask her family to play 'Chariots of Fire' when she was leaving her home. I received a beautiful letter from her family and in the letter, they told me they had played the melody I suggested when she left the house. From this totally enlightened wholesome woman I learnt so much and I loved her. It was indeed an honour to have shared the final journey with her, as it was with all the patients and their families I journeyed with, in those early years of Palliative Care in Perth.

Palliative Care was very well funded. Back then, nobody died alone; we would have a nurse 'special', who would be with the patient in the last days of his/her life. Nurses working in Palliative Care were and still are very special heart centred people.

Another person that I have never forgotten was a man who lived in the Homes West flats near Hay Street, down on Robert's Road. The poor old man had no family and no person to look after him, only the palliative care nurses. He had asbestosis, but would enjoy a tipple of alcohol now and then. During my five am visits, we would have a cup of tea together and talk. I would clean his little bedsitter for him and take his clothes home to wash. I said my goodbyes to him too, after four weeks of visiting him every morning during my working week, because I knew he would not be there after I returned from nights off.

It was also a good time for nursing. Palliative Care had not become a business in the medical speciality it is today; nurses were the lead carers. It was all about caring for the person and their loved ones in their journey to transition. It did not matter whether people were with us for a few short days, weeks or months. There were only two hospitals that had specific hospice beds and one of those was Bethesda with six beds. Often our patients had respite there. The other one was Hollywood Repatriation Hospital where Dr Rosalie worked. She was instrumental in ensuring our returned service men received a dignified passing. Later on, Palliative Care became a medical speciality and again this change had an effect on service provision but fortunately, I had left by then.

Sometimes, we had to do things for the families of the deceased and one of the hardest was the night; a nurse and I had to wash and then dress an Italian man in a full suit after Passover while he lay in the centre of a water bed. I will say no more, and leave it to your imagination, the difficulties of doing this in an appropriate manner.

I had another remarkable spiritual visit from Jesus. In those years, I was still a practising Catholic and would go to mass every Sunday. The Church had not yet been built so we would have mass in a classroom in the school which our children attended. I took Communion one Sunday and on returning back to my seat, I closed my eyes and I saw a big white robed man with this great big red heart sending out light. I was transfixed for approximately four minutes. He didn't say a word, just sending light pulsating through me. I didn't want to let go of that moment. I was brought back to the outside world when the kids asked for money for the second collection.

. . .

1983 came around very quickly and it turned out, we had a major decision to make regarding JD. He did not like school and would regularly take sick days. JA loved school and never had a day sick. JD found school boring and one day a teacher who taught JA in year 3, said to me, "JD is so different to JA. He is a cocky little boy."

Well, I really reacted and I was angry with her.

I said, "Of course they are, they are two different people. Do not ever compare my children again, and change your words from 'cocky' to 'a boy with high self-esteem.'

As soon as I got home, I rang another school and asked if they had a vacancy left for year four. I was asked to come in for an interview with Noddy and JD. I certainly did not want my children to be compared to each other.

My sister, Marion who was three years younger than I, was compared to me all the time when she was younger and when she went to boarding school at Sacred Heart, Highgate from year 8 to 10, and I knew it was a horrible time for her. Having missed so much school in her primary years because of polio, she found academia and sport rather difficult. She suffered from low self-esteem all her life and this affected her as she matured. I was not going to have that in my family. Fortunately, when Noddy arrived home from work, he agreed with me. We had a family meeting and the four of us discussed it. Initially, JD said he didn't want to go; but Noddy convinced him, that this was a very good school for children who loved sport.

JD was offered a place and he commenced school there in 1984. He never missed a day's school from that time on, and was never compared to JA again.

Politically, in Western Australia, things were changing again. Labour won office for the first time since 1974 and Brian Bourke became the Premier in WA. Bob Hawke was Prime Minister of Australia. WA was the state of excitement. Alan Bond had entered the Holy Grail of

Yachting and challenged to win the America's Cup. Perth was awash with money and new suburb after new suburb was being developed. The Northern Suburbs exploded with huge population growth. Freeways were being built and infrastructure projects like schools, sports clubs and gyms multiplied.

Great excitement mounted in August /September 1983 when Australia II won the right to compete for the America's Cup against the Americans. The finals were to be held in the USA. When the finals commenced everyone in Perth was fixated on their television sets. Even patients in the last nights of their lives would wait for me to come in to ask me how Australia 11 was doing. You can imagine what that last race in New Port, USA, did for all of WA. People were up all night. I was working and whilst driving listened to every single minute of the race, and arrived home just fifteen minutes before Australia 11 crossed the finish line.

Bob Hawke proclaimed the day a National holiday unofficially. Alan Bond and his syndicate and the America's cup crew, captained by John Bertram became national heroes. Fremantle then became the focus for the transformation to allow Perth to be the Centre of the world's fraternity of Yachting. Perth and Fremantle changed for ever, life was unbelievable, and the capital was in the fast lane.

MOVING FORWARD AND CHANGES IN NURSING

Towards the end of 1985, I was beginning to feel somewhat burnt out working in the service, as I was nursing men and women dying of cancer with children the same ages as our children. I decided it was time to have a break from Palliative Care. So, after several weeks considering my next career move, I decided the best thing to do was to go back to midwifery.

I wanted to return to Wanneroo Hospital and spoke to a new DON (Director of Nursing). Her name was Irene Herry.

Irene said to me, "If I didn't have a position for you, I would create one anyway." So I resigned from Silver Chain Palliative Care, which was one of the greatest honours of my nursing career and returned to work in midwifery in 1985.

I really loved being able to help with birthing. It is wondrous to watch the miracle of life unfold every single time. It was not long before I was relieving throughout the hospital in the units of Midwifery, Theatre, Emergency, Surgical, Medical and Paediatrics.

Nursing was changing, very quickly. The Australian Nursing Federation and the Nurses' Boards around Australia were urging Nursing to become recognised as a Profession. As a nurse, I for one had always been treated as a professional. I really did not understand the need for this change at this time. Nurses were now being trained at the Institute of Technology, now Curtin University. It was the only place one could do the Nursing Degree course. The degree was now mainly science based with only minimum practicum periods.

Our DON supported changes and asked me to go to study one semester a unit, called the Nursing Process and come back to Wanneroo hospital to implement education on documentation of what nurses did in their daily work. I had a lecturer who was a visiting Professor Nurse Practitioner from the USA. Being a nurse practitioner was being like a remote area nurse, as far as I could see. This is what I was over at Rottnest in 1969, and out at Yirrkala in 1972. We would only call the doctor if there was an emergency situation in those years. Until I did this unit, (the nursing process), I wondered what all this documentation was about. However, I saw great benefit in using it in practice, especially as the Australian Health Care System was becoming so much like the USA's in litigation indoctrination. We, as nurses, had to start documenting what we did, and develop written plans of care. The HDWA (Health Dept of Western Australia) was introducing a whole new set of paper work for nurses to enable this implementation. Things had to be done differently.

We would have hours upon hours of staff development for these changes to be introduced. Three new manuals were introduced over a period of several years that gave newly graduated nurses from the Tertiary institutions guidance to follow in their nursing practice.

The first one was Standards of Nursing Practise in 1983; then Standards for Nursing divisions and Nursing Quality Assurance 1985 to cater for the change from hospital-based nursing to a tertiary based training model.

Implementing a program such as this and all the changes to the HDWA forms was rather a difficult one, as change of practice in what we as nurses had always done was hard.

To make it easier for nurses, I commenced writing standardised nursing care plans, for procedures patients were having done, or for medical conditions like pneumonia. Each document ensured individualising the patients' extra needs as required. I had to keep reminding staff what we are now doing. It was all about writing all that we do in our daily work practice. With support from senior staff we finally got there. Even the Accident and Emergency forms were changed and the SOAP (Subjective Objective Assessment Plan) and DAPE (Data Assessment Plan Implementation) models of documentation became second nature to all. I have to say I embraced it and loved doing it; but some of the older nurses found it more difficult. It did take more time, than our previous report writing model.

It was a time too for changes in conditions for nurses, in those years between 1985-1987. For the first time since the abolition of the 44 hr week in 1967, the hours of work changed. It became law that nurses had to have a nine-hour break. So, instead of working from 14.30 to 2300 (If you were in labour ward you may not finish till 1am, and have to be back on duty at 0700.) It changed to a 1pm -9:30pm shift and night staff did a 10 hour shift, 9pm -07.30am The career structure was being introduced and the Charge Sister's role was being abolished. The ANF and the HDWA were developing a four-stream pathway for nurses; management, clinical, education and research. One didn't *have* to go into a clinical stream; one could go into management, education or research without any or with minimal clinical experience, once they had completed their degree. University qualifications became the holy grail of nursing and the wise older nurses who had walked the walk and could talk the talk, were being left behind.

A lot of nurses were set on management which made communications with clinical staff difficult. It was hard for them too as they had not had clinical experience, so talking the talk was difficult for the younger ones. They introduced a different hierarchical structure from The Director of Nursing down to Clinical Nurse Specialists, Nursing Manager and Educator. In Wanneroo, the model changed to a Clinical Nurse Specialist (CNS) for maternity, a CNS for ED theatre, the surgical unit and infection control, and a CNS for medical and paediatrics. This was followed by five clinical nurses per unit who were to become the new charge sisters on the wards. As senior nurses, we had to apply for the Level 2 positions and then registered nurses with a grading of 1-8 and then the enrolled nurses. It certainly was a time that saw many good nurses leave and many other senior nurses not go up to become clinical nurses. Job description forms became part of the recruitment process and when one was applying for a position one had to go through an intensive selection criteria process, which was very different to the previous models of employment. Human resource management was coming into all industries, and changing workplaces forever.

My life was very busy with supporting my children and husband. My family was my first priority and my work came a close second. I never had time to be involved with the ANF, nor the forums for managing this change process and neither did my colleagues. Everything just happened around us, and we wore the consequences of these changes for the rest of our nursing career.

Nurses were also fighting for a pay rise in 1987 as they had not had one for years. The WA ANF held a big campaign to win the nurses a pay rise. At that time, WA was lagging behind Victoria. There were nurses calling for strike action; this had never been heard of in all the years I had been working as a nurse. The nurses at Wanneroo Hospital would not support the call for a nurses' strike. The ANF called a big union meeting six weeks before the 1987 WA Government election. A few of us from our hospital went to this meeting. I had never been to a union meeting before and was mortified to hear chants for nurses to go on strike.

A very big Scottish man had a very loud voice and was really stirring and leading the members in, calling and voting for strike action. Where I mustered up enough courage to actually stand up at that meeting, take the microphone and have a say, I do not know. I remember going all red and I was shaking like a leaf as I had never spoken like this in a public place before. I appealed to the Nurses not to go on strike that there had to be another way.

I said, "We have the greatest tool in our hands. There is a State Election in six weeks and we as nurses can campaign against sitting labour members in the State of WA. The whole community supported the Nurses campaign for nurses to be given a pay rise. By going on strike, we will lose credibility with the population of WA. I believe the best way is to begin a campaign for the upcoming State election". I sat down.

But the call for a strike continued, led by our Scottish member of the ANF. Two weeks later we were contacted by the ANF to campaign against the sitting labour seats. Within a week, we were successful in getting a well-deserved pay rise.

LIFE GOES ON

It was life in the fast lane in those years, for Noddy and I, with lots happening on the home front. JA was growing up fast, swimming was her life. She trained twice a day from Monday-Friday and Sat mornings. She participated in the Sorrento Surf Club on Sunday mornings in the summer and in winter it was Netball on Saturday's. She was a beautiful young rose, blossoming into a teenager; we never had a day's worry about her. She had lovely friends, loved school and commenced at Sacred Heart College, Sorrento in 1986. It was funny to see her dressed in the same school uniform, that I was dressed in, from 1960 to 1964.

She settled in there very quickly and soon had a group of new friends. JD, too, was doing very well at his school both in sport and academia.

With both competing at state level, Noddy would run one way and I the other. Looking back, I just do not know how we did it.

We learnt a big lesson in 1987, when "The recession we had to have" was just about to arrive. Noddy had just opened a small business, in partnership with a friend. Our home was used as a guarantee for the business. The recession hit and the business was not making any money. I could see that we were struggling and debts were growing. As a couple we decided to sell our home to pay off the loan, as Noddy refused to go bankrupt. Through sheer hard work, grit and determination, he kept the business turning over and we managed through the Grace of God and family love. However, there was no money for holidays, and other material trappings. We would have the odd family get away for a week to Kalbarri or, a few days up at Port Dennison. The kids never complained and as a foursome we remained tight, with JA and JD helping Dad out whenever they could.

In late 1988, the Clinical Nurse Specialist for theatre, emergency, the surgical unit and infection control, had an accident and had to go off on sick leave, never to come back, unfortunately. Irene, the DON asked if I would step into her role. I said yes, as I had very sound knowledge of all those specialities and I knew all the staff very well. I settled into the role very easily and became more involved in quality assurance, something that was new in hospitals in Western Australia.

This year brought another cycle of strict monetary policy. Bourke had left politics in a very dramatic fashion; the state was broke yet again. Businesses were going bankrupt left, right and centre. Suicide rates increased and it really impacted the health and wellbeing of many people.

Premier Dowding was now the State's Premier and changes in health funding started happening. This was to have a major impact. Health was to become a commodity business, not a service provider model and run on similar lines like the giants in the mining industry. I remember the Medical Superintendent and the DON calling in all the CNS's for a one to one chat on budget restraints for our departments.

They said to me, "Peter we have to move from a Rolls Royce Health Service down to a Holden Health Service." I also went with other nursing staff to meetings with the hospital administrator who educated us on this new way of 'doing business'.

I was not happy about medicine and nursing being run as a business when we were dealing with human beings. To me, it was all about being a service delivery model. Health, Education, and the Police were all essential services, and as such, I was adamant that they were sacrosanct; but obviously no one listened.

I loved my role as a Clinical Nurse Specialist, especially when I worked in the emergency department; all the units were very well managed by the Senior Clinical Nurses. The staff was first class and apart from the extra paper work, nurses now had to do, they just got on with providing a Rolls Royce service to the community.

I had many amazing experiences in ED, which have held me in good stead for my career in the future. ED now had 1st and 2nd year residents working too. They would come from SCGH(Sir Charles Gairdner Hospital), many with no ED experience at all. Here again, nurses stepped up to assist them in their work. All the residents, apart from one, were grateful for any assistance and advice we offered. We did not have Registrars or Emergency Specialists, back then. Any category 1 or 2 patients would be transferred immediately by ambulance to SCGH.

Two cases really stood out for me during that time, that I remember like it happened yesterday. One night a man presented complaining of a droopy eye. Fortunately, there was a switched-on resident on duty, who had worked in neurology. I asked him to see this patient as a matter of urgency. All his vitals were okay, however intuitively, I knew something was wrong. The doctor listened to me and examined him. and he asked me to arrange a priority transfer to SCGH.

He said, "I think he is having a mid-brain stem bleed." He was transferred and when we rang the next day, he indeed had had a mid-brain stem bleed.

Several months later, I was at reception when a lady walked in with her husband and asked to see a doctor. It was around 9.15pm, and her presenting complaint was a droopy lip. She told me she and her husband were out for dinner and she was wearing a new Estée Lauder perfume. She told me she thought she may have had a reaction to this new perfume. As soon as I saw her, I took her straight through to our emergency room and asked this rather pompous young resident to see her immediately. Although her vitals were stable, my intuition told me, she was also having a mid-brain stem bleed.

When I expressed my concern to this first-year medical resident, he laughed at me. By this time, it was time for me to go home and although I really wanted to stay to ensure he saw the lady as a matter of urgency, I couldn't. I was on the next morning and the night sister assured me, (after I explained to her my assessment), that she would ensure she would care for this lady. I left to go home. We were a great team and had faith in each other's assessments. When I came on the next morning at 0700, the night sister told me, that the resident decided to admit her overnight and send her home the next morning. At 0500 am they called a major emergency and transferred her straight through to SCGH as she had lost her swallow reflex. They had rushed her straight for a CT and reported that she had had a mid-brain stem bleed. I was naturally very upset for her but when I got an opportunity to speak to the resident, he brushed it all aside. I asked him to please listen to the nurses and then ended up speaking to one of our visiting physicians about her and the attitude of the young man. It was reassuring to know this well respected and knowledgeable physician said, "Peter, whenever you get these intuitive messages, just ring me straight away and I will always come in."

The other case was on a weekend. There was a big motorcycle race on at Barbagallo's racetrack. Riders from all over Australia came. One of the riders came off his bike at approximately over 200kms per hour causing major trauma to his body. When he arrived at Wanneroo ED, he was in a very bad way.

We knew he was on his way, so everything was ready, the orthopaedic surgeon had been called in, another general surgeon was there with an anaesthetist, two very experienced ED nurses were also on and theatre nurses who had just finished a case, were there to assist as well. This man's injuries were horrendous, his femur broken through the skin and his pelvis broken in eight places. We started blood transfusions. I saw the look on this man's face drifting in and out of consciousness. I was happy that all was under control for managing his physical injuries so I went up to the top of his bed and pulled up a chair, held his hand and kept talking to him whilst stroking his forehead and reassuring him, he would be okay. Once stabilised, we transferred him to SCGH.

Several months later, hospital management received a letter from this man, thanking Wanneroo Hospital for their care and with a special thank you to the nurse who held my hand, stroked my forehead and for her reassurance. She kept me going, he said.

Things seem to have changed today. Nurses are taught to only look at the presenting complaint. The mind, body, spirit connection does not seem to matter at all for the profession. Perhaps, it is not their fault. It is the result of nursing education and nursing bureaucrats that follow the system that wants to make health big business. It is educating the nurses in "doing" only and not in "being" in synch with the patients not ensuring and embodying the true holistic model of care which includes the connection of body, emotion, mind and spirit.

I was funded and sent to Fremantle Hospital to do an intensive two-week Infection Control Course. A specialist Professor of Medicine from Germany had been flown in to run the course. What a course it turned out to be. Infection Control was something that we as hospital trained nurses were innate at practising; now it was being married up with the science of infection control. It was fantastic and my knowledge on this subject enabled me to read into scientific evidence and related it to hospital infections and interventions.

In June of that year, the Hospital Executive and the Medical Advisory Committee gave permission to a visiting specialist to do a trial procedure on an age old women's problem. It was not long after he started the trial, that I had a very strong intuitive message this was not going to turn out well. I was seeing things in readmissions and pathology reports that rang alarm bells for me. I flagged my concerns both verbally and in writing with the Surgeon, the Director of Nursing and the Medical Superintendent. But as it was a trial, it had to continue for six months. I was told there was not enough evidence.

After the trial period ended, a special meeting was called and clinical privileges of the surgeon running the actual trial were withdrawn.

Little did I know that this was a direct result of my report writing. I did not know a special meeting was held the night before with the gentleman concerned and that he had had his clinical privileges for the trial withdrawn.

I was going to scrub for this doctor the morning after the meeting and whilst I was preparing the theatre trolley, he came into the setup room in the theatre. He appeared to be brimming with hostility with the words that he expressed and the look on his face as he entered the room was one of disdain. He did not care about the other nurses' present. I asked him to leave the sterile area and I would be out shortly. A senior nurse took over from me and I went to speak to him. He was waiting in the theatre tea room.

After he finished his diatribe, I went straight down to the Director of Nursing's office and my voice was numb with shock. My emotional and mental body became very unbalanced. I shaking all over. Never before had I had such an attack on my work practices and my inner being in my twenty one years of nursing. Despite management's words of caring, he was never held accountable for his actions.

One day, he spoke to me and informed me that I was ignorant, stupid and had no concept of what he was doing. I thought to myself, I know what you are doing. I have observed the procedure you are trialing and I have realised that you were harming vulnerable women. I was informed during this conversation that the trial had been done on animals at the University of WA and they had been successful. I felt absolutely nauseated and sick; and as a woman, violated.

I was angry inside my being and was tempted to raise my voice; however, I never said anything to him. I turned my back on him and walked away. A couple of days later, I received a letter from him, telling me I had to change the infection control criteria. I took no notice of his letter.

I coped with it just as I had always done since I was a young girl. I took it all internally and buried it at a deep cellular level. I pulled on a mask and went about my work as usual, pretending that nothing had ever happened. At that time, there was no awareness of psychological workplace injury and there was no counselling. You just needed to go on.

This experience really changed my life. Intuitively, I could foresee what was happening during the six months of the trial that was to result in a disaster; so, I kept documenting in my diary the conversations I had with him. From that time on, I became a fierce patient advocate.

Like everything, I kept a stiff upper lip, but dark forces gathered and the incivility (smart bullying) escalated, both vertically and horizontally by a very small cohort of staff members. I did not know at the time that what I was experiencing, was workplace bullying. A senior clinician began to escalate this insidious workplace incivility by putting this in writing.

In ED, there was a machine that was meant to be used only for a patient coming in with an acute asthma attack. It was not to leave the department as we had a very high presentation of asthmatic patients. One afternoon, this clinician called for the machine to come to the surgical unit for a pre-operative patient who was fit and well. I asked if the patient could come down to ED, and I would do the test there, as this was the normal practice. The practitioner became very angry at me and accused me of being obstructive and subsequently wrote a very mean complaint to management. Our old DON had retired a few months earlier and the DON who replaced her was new school; she had no idea of the history of what had previously transpired. She listened to the dark forces and made my tenure at the hospital very uncomfortable.

I never challenged them for their behaviour or attitudes. I guess that was my big weakness, although I knew it was all caused by what had happened in the past. I kept it all bottled up inside and I wore a thick mask, happy on the outside but holding the buried stress inside me. There was absolutely no support from senior nursing management. As a nurse you did not complain or tell anyone you were not coping because of workplace issues because if you did, it was seen as a sign of weakness, that you could not fulfil your role as a CNS, and I really loved this role.

. . .

By this time, JA and JD were growing up and I had to start undoing the apron strings. Swimming and sport were still a very big part of their lives. JA was seventeen and began taking driving lessons to help run JD to wherever he needed to go. She hoped to get into primary teaching the following year.

JD started to become very interested in a sport which really was just kicking off in Perth at the time. He found himself doing very well and together with his training program was super fit. Noddy was keeping his head above water in the little business he was running and I was wondering where to from here?

WHEATBELT ADVENTURES

We had two years left in the city before returning to the North, and I knew I couldn't do the degree program because I had enrolled twice but found it so irrelevant to nursing practice from when I began nursing in 1965, that it forced me to quit. The only way for me to get a country DON position, was to go and get all the hands-on experience I could. JA had finished her TEE and JD going into year eleven in 1991; so after a family meeting we decided it would be a good time for me to go and obtain the experience I needed for my future.

I approached the Health Department's Emergency Nursing Service. The manager was a lovely woman; we immediately connected and I was offered a position as a relieving Director of Nursing (DON) as required, and a Registered Nurses' role which was to commence in January 1991. The plan was for me to spend time initially in both the Wheatbelt and in the North, for short periods of 4-6 weeks. She offered me a remote area stint and I accepted. I knew I would love it. I eventually resigned from Wanneroo in early December 1990, giving me a couple of weeks to adjust to leaving a role I loved and get ready for the next chapter in the journey of life.

JA had just finished her exams, and together with her five best friends from school, set off for Leavers' Week.

They had a wonderful time and came home much rested, independent and happy. JD was really into training for his chosen sports and had a busy training schedule, all in-between helping Dad. Honestly, these two young people were absolutely the most beautiful youngsters one could ever meet and as parents we were so proud of them. They supported us throughout our challenging times, never complaining or asking for anything.

Mum and Dad were beginning to age quite markedly. Mum's back was making life difficult for her even though she never complained. Dad had just finished his Bachelor's Degree in Ancient Roman History. After retirement, he could go to university for free. But when the Howard government brought back having to pay for tertiary education, he continued his love for learning through reading.

My sister, Marie had married a lovely man and was very settled into her career as a teacher. Marion was caring and raising her beautiful family.

On the 7th Jan, I started my first A/Director of nursing role at Corrigin Hospital. Corrigin is a small wheat belt town 225 kilometres from Perth. This was great as I could come home for weekends. I would leave there at 4.30pm on a Friday afternoon and be home by 7:30pm. Then leave Perth early Monday morning to be at work by 7am.

The Hospital was small but well equipped and very well managed. The staff were very friendly and welcoming. It took me a very short time to settle into the role and the community. It was so lovely to be in a place full of positive people. From the gardener, the cook and the cleaners, through to the nurses and the one doctor in the town. Country people are so warm honest and open. The hospital had six funded aged care beds and six acute beds.

I loved to talk to the older persons in the nursing home section, and we only had one in-patient for most of my stay with a very quiet emergency department. The weeks went by too quickly, and before I knew where I was, it was time to say goodbye to this beautiful little workplace.

Kate, the manager from the Health Department Emergency Nursing Service, had called me a week before this assignment had finished and, asked me if I would take a ten-week assignment in Fitzroy Crossing as an RN? I discussed it with the family and they gave me their blessings to go forth. I was very happy as I was going back to the Kimberley and to an Aboriginal township. The wet season was in full swing and already the monsoons were bringing big rains and floods to the region. After a lovely farewell from the staff at Corrigin,(who asked me to come back anytime) I headed home, for my last weekend with the family. I have to say after I spent just three weeks in my new role, I loved it.

I boarded a TAA plane from Perth on the Tuesday and arrived in Derby a few hours later; from there another flight on a small aircraft took me out to Fitzroy Crossing. Oh! my goodness. I had forgotten how green the Kimberley was in the wet season. Rivers and creeks overflowing and water everywhere.

When we arrived, the strip was covered in water, but not enough to prevent us from making a safe landing.

As soon as I had disembarked, the humidity nearly knocked me for a six. I was met by an orderly who was very nice and welcoming and took me to the Hospital. Behind the hospital were some little houses /units for nurses and a big old building which was the nurses' quarters. This was used for relief staff. It was a fairly big rambling old building and we were surrounded by a barbed wire fence. The quarters had an above ground swimming pool, where I spent quite a bit of time when I was off duty, during my stay at Fitzroy Crossing.

Sue, the DON was a lovely lady, who welcomed me with open arms. The hospital provided all the meals so I did not have to cook and I was given permission to use the hospital car after hours if I needed to go anywhere. I was on shift work which I enjoyed.

The work itself was amazing. There was a little ED-cum-treatment room, a passage way and a female ward on one end with a male ward on the other. There was a children's ward right opposite the nurses' station, and a Community Health Centre attached to the Hospital.

Times had changed since I had left the North in 1980. There were hardly any admissions of malnourished, dehydrated little ones since my time in Gove and in Wyndham in 1969/70 -1972/1980. I was also happy to see that the infant mortality and morbidity had fallen so much. The Community Health Nurses were doing a wonderful job with ensuring babies and children were kept out of Hospital. The kids were very happy in the community and were thriving. All the pregnant women and girls would be sent to Derby for delivery as there were only two midwives in town - one of whom would do permanent nights.

I was asked to do the antenatal classes for the Aboriginal women and young girls; this was wonderful because I was able to teach them as I was intuitively led to do. The girls as young as fifteen would come once a week at 2pm and it was so different to doing ante natal classes for Western Women. I had to use my imagination and come up with a simple program that was meaningful for them. I made up some lovely little dream time meditations for them "for when baby coming".

I loved the variety of work and the interactions of the staff and the families, who would bring in bush tucker for their family members in hospital and many a day, they would share some goanna or kangaroo meat with the staff.

There were two great resident doctors working up there, both young and committed. One of them, I knew from Wanneroo hospital. I was fortunate enough to be asked by Donna to come and do a clinic out at a community approximately 100 kms from Fitzroy Crossing. I jumped at the opportunity and had a great day out with both Donna and the Community Nurse, both of whom were well respected by the community members. We spent a lovely hour having a picnic lunch sitting on the banks of a river under the trees, watching the black cockatoos with bright red tails - just being one with nature the community and us. The river was up very high as the monsoons had brought so much rain this year and the fish were plentiful. It was so good to be out in the bush and meeting these beautiful down to earth people, from a different culture.

I would ring home every day. Life was good and the kids were doing well. Noddy was well and keeping things ticking over on the home front. I met the two nuns from the Order of The Brown Joseph's who had been up in Fitzroy for years and I would spend a lot of my free time with them, when I was not on call. There were only two nursing staff on duty at any one time, one RN and one EN.

The ambulance service was run through the hospital - the orderly, the driver, and the nurse on call would be called to do the emergency call-outs. There was no theatre at Fitzroy, so any person requiring surgery would have to be transferred to the regional hospital in Derby.

One night, I got called to transfer a patient who needed to go to Derby. Poor darling had had a miscarriage. She had an IV line in and needed to go to Derby for a surgical procedure. We set off around 9pm, to do a half way. What is a half way you may ask? Well it is where an ambulance is dispatched from Derby Hospital and one from Fitzroy Crossing Hospital, and we would meet under a big Boab tree half way between Fitzroy and Derby. A handover would be done there, then the Derby ambulance would return with the patient to Derby and the Fitzroy ambulance return to Fitzroy Crossing. It was a distance of approximately eighty-seven kilometres that we would have to travel to reach The Boab Tree. We were there first on this night and had about a ten-minute wait until our colleagues from Derby arrived. This whole process took twenty minutes, and we turned around to travel back to Fitzroy, when all of a sudden the driver slowed right down.

I was dozing, and woke with a start, "What's the problem?"

"Nothing," said the driver. "Take a look up there." And right in the middle of the road was a calf having a feed from her mother. We waited and watched smiling. This took longer than the handover. Eventually, they moved over and when the road was clear, off we went back to our destination. 'Only in the Kimberley.'

I was on day shift and working in ED. The ward nurse had gone to lunch, so I had gone to make sure all her patients were well and enjoying their meal. As I left the men's ward, I looked down the passage to see a young couple nursing a little baby. So, I went down and asked if they needed some help.

"Im cold sick, sister," the man said, unfolding the blanket and as soon as I saw the baby, I knew how sick the baby was. He was in severe respiratory distress with bronchiolitis. I rang the doctor and asked him to come over straight away. He was there within minutes. The baby was about four months old, and small, so I was able to act as the first responder commencing oxygen therapy straight away. We had no technology up there like pulse oximeters or cardiac monitors like the emergency room at Wanneroo Hospital. One just had to use one's clinical skills.

With a little Aboriginal baby, it is really hard to see if they are cyanosed by their skin colour; however, a quick way to check is by looking at the colour of the inside of their mouth and gums. This little one had slight cyanosis. An intravenous line and antibiotics were started immediately. The doctor decided that this baby had to go straight to Derby. Dr Donna called RFDS to come on a priority basis. Unfortunately, the rain had been relentless for six days and our strip was under water so a plane could not land. The road to Derby was also impassable, so we were asked to transfer the baby down to Cadjebut mine, some 71kms south of Fitzroy Crossing as Cadjebut mine had an all-weather air strip. The RFDS would meet us there.

We left in a big Ford Ambulance after ensuring we had all the resuscitation equipment with us, as there was a chance the baby might need intubation. Mum sat in the front of the ambulance, with the driver, whilst Donna and I were busy with the little one in the back. We also had with us a thirty-seven-week pregnant mother who was going to Derby for delivery. As it had been raining for a few days, all the creeks were up. All of a sudden in the middle of a huge expanse of water, the ambulance just stopped. Water was flowing through the cabin of the ambulance; Keith just could not get the engine to turn over. Water started lapping up near the rear tailgate.

We were well and truly stuck.

Luckily, we had an escort in front of us. The driver had got through just five minutes before the ambulance and the vehicle he was driving was a four-wheel drive Toyota Landcruiser. He had picked up a guy a couple of kilometres up the road. Keith, our driver, was able to radio him, informing him of our situation. He turned and passed us stopping on a non-flooded stretch of road about 150 metres away. The guys from the Toyota came wading towards us; the stranger carried the pregnant lady; Mick, the escort driver carried the mother with the baby. Keith had the IVAc with the drip and Donna and I were left to carry the remaining equipment and close the back of the ambulance with water swirling rapidly around us. We were both small and had to wade through the rising swell carefully, carrying the equipment above our heads. This included the resus box which was quite heavy.

The water was flowing very fast by then. It was a sight to behold. The Flying Doctor would have nothing on our party. Once the stranger had the pregnant lady back safely on the wet road, he came back to give me a hand. We all got into the back of the Toyota and headed back to Fitzroy Crossing, leaving the ambulance to drown. Kimberley Health were going to be minus one ambulance now.

The baby's condition was stabilised, but if the baby took a turn for the worse, we would have had to send the baby out by helicopter. The baby stayed with us overnight. Thankfully, neither the baby nor the adults were any the worse for the adventure. It was certainly very different from doing a transfer down the freeway from Wanneroo Hospital to Princess Margaret Hospital.

We arrived back at the Hospital at 5pm. I didn't sleep very well even though I was exhausted as I kept thinking of our failed evacuation and the drowned ambulance. The little baby, was still seriously ill. I was assigned to special the baby when I arrived on duty at 7am; fortunately, we managed to get them out on a little charter flight at 3:30pm that afternoon.

After work, I went down to spend time with the nuns, and we went down to the Bridge. It was nearly under water, with the Fitzroy River raging, almost to the edge of the bridge. The Fitzroy Lodge was flood bound, and the bridge closed. However, as the Lodge was not on the banks of the river and set back on pylons, it was on a higher position. I was informed that this flood was as big as the 1986 one. The roads were cut two kilometres from the town. It was hard to believe we were on the road the day before at this exact time. They say that the Fitzroy River in flood is something to be seen and when in flood is the largest and widest river in the Southern Hemisphere. The amount of water flooding the river could fill the Sydney harbour in half a day and supply Perth with enough water for one year and six months.

Several days later the Fitzroy River reached its peak and the water almost flowed over the Bridge. Oh my God, it was a flood to be seen; even the pub on the banks of the Fitzroy River was flooded and under water. A lot of community members were hoping the pub would be washed away and many cans of beer and bottles of spirits would be floating away down the river. To see this part of the river washing away the alcohol was a sight to behold. To see the Fitzroy River in flood would have to be a once in a life time experience and I witnessed this amazing force of Mother Nature.

I hope they never dam the river. The Fitzroy River arises from the Durack Range in the East Kimberley and flows for five hundred and twenty-five kilometres south west through the King Leopold and the Geike Gorge. It then turns northwest through rugged country and plains emptying in the Indian Ocean at King sound.

Returning home around 6pm, I slept soundly and awoke for another early shift the following morning. After work, which was very quiet, one of the other nurses and I headed down to the convent with the nuns. We went for a drive down to the bridge again. It had peaked at 10pm the evening before. Now it had just started to go down and the water was flowing very fast. Whilst there on the bridge, I witnessed the most amazing sight of what seemed like thousands of white cockatoos perched on the tree tops of the big gum trees in a small section of the river where the water flow was not quite so fierce. The water seemed spread out for miles and miles, it really was incredible .

The police did a great job - above and beyond their normal call of duty - keeping every one safe. They were out on the raging waters in a boat rescuing two Aboriginal boys stuck up in a tree on the Derby side of the road at one stage during the flood. The roads north and south were impassable. We were now totally isolated and the only way out would have been by air. Looking skywards one got the feeling we were in for a lot more rain. The aboriginal kids were all swimming outside their front doors because the streets had turned into little rivers.

I was on night shift one night, and received a call from a man who was quite distressed. He was on his way in with a lady in labour who was approximately thirty-four weeks gestation. He had just crossed one of the little tributary rivers, and as he got to the other side down went the vehicle. It was bogged. The lady was on the back of a Toyota tray back ute.

He was calling me to ask whether we could send an ambulance. I was rather nervous at the thought after what had happened the previous week. I rang the DON and she suggested I ring the police, which I did. I also collected the emergency delivery pack and some baby blankets. The on call nurse came in and I handed over to her. I would have sent her; however, she was not a midwife, so I had to go. The police were very good; they escorted us to this little river. Low and behold by the time we had got there, the delivery was all over. I checked out Mum and the baby, ensuring the baby was well rugged up. I transferred them to the ambulance and took them back to Fitzroy. I put this little premature baby in an incubator. This time after we called RFDS, they were able to land. However, instead of flying, the mother and baby to Derby and then on to Perth, they had contacted Darwin Hospital. They had an incubator available, so they came straight out and collected the baby and mother and left for Darwin. Both Mother and baby did very well. We were informed through our daily conversations with Darwin hospital's neonatal unit.

Sue would often go with her husband to their favourite water hole for a swim and a glass of wine after work as the water hole was fairly close to town. If I was off duty, they would take me with them. I enjoyed Sue's company. She was a very gentle woman who had a huge challenge as the Health Department was changing and restructuring. Derby was becoming the regional health centre for the whole of the North West. Decentralisation of everything from Perth to the Regions was the new Government Policy. I able to support her as we had undergone so many changes at Metropolitan hospitals that I had witnessed in the previous two years.

School holidays were fast approaching, as was the end of my tenure at Fitzroy Crossing Hospital. The staff had a small farewell dinner at The Fitzroy River Lodge for me. Sue and her husband were having a little break in Broome and as I was flying home on the Sunday morning, they invited me to come down to Broome with them and spend the night at The Cable Beach Resort. I was on my last night shift, the Friday night before. Arrangements were made to pick me up at 8am. At six in the morning, the police brought in a poor woman who had been beaten up and had a very large laceration from the right side of her forehead across to the left. She was very strong and had no pain. There had been no loss of consciousness. After I had cleaned her wound and her face, my heart broke as I looked into her eyes. They were bloodshot and very sad. I thought here, I am going back to a loving home, to a lovely husband who does not have a violent streak in him and whom I have never ever seen lose his temper, and here this poor lady had to go back into the community in which she was not safe. 'It was how it was'.

Anyway, after suturing her wound, which took a long time, I could at least give her compassion, love and care for the time I spent tending to her physical needs. On completion of the suturing, I made her a cup of tea and toast. The police were very kind and took her home. I was very sad to leave, but I knew I had to return to be with my family until my next assignment. I really loved the work and admired the people who lived up there, so much.

Sue was right on time to pick me up, and we set off for the 397km drive to Broome. The Kimberley in the wet is so beautiful, the landscape completely different to any other time because of the rains. The Willare Bridge goes over the Fitzroy River and it was amazing to witness the raging flood waters as one passed over this magnificent river. We arrived safely at Cable Beach and stayed in a lovely villa. I had just finished five night shifts in a row, so took the opportunity to put my head down for some much needed sleep. On awakening, we went out for a stroll through the town and had a lovely meal before heading home to bed for a good night's sleep before an early rise to catch the plane home on Sunday morning. I was very appreciative of the care and kindness Sue had shown to me during this period. I was feeling good about myself and recovering from what had been a very painful period of my work life through the late 80's.

* * *

Noddy, JA and JD were there to meet me at Perth Airport and I just fell into their arms. It was fantastic to be home again and they were all very happy to have mum back. Noddy had a surprise waiting for me. He had booked us - just him and I - into the Capricorn resort up in Sun City, Yanchep for two nights. JA and JD were as excited about this as we were, because this would be the first time we had ever left them on their own. They were growing up. JA had her licence and had given up swimming training and was enjoying being an 18 year old. JD was in year 11 and only interested in his sporting dreams. We could trust them without any doubt and we left for a romantic getaway. It was wonderful to be able to spend that time together. I just so loved my husband and his total support of me all our married life. He was happy because he could see I was becoming my own self again, and by allowing me the freedom to go on a healing journey of self-care and self- love, it was the best gift I could have had.The two days went very quickly and before we knew it, we were back to the reality of life.

* * *

Towards the end of the first week of being back, Kate rang and asked if I would do a DON's relief down in Southern Cross, a community 369 kms from Perth, for four weeks. I said yes, I would go, as I could drive home every weekend.

So come that Sunday afternoon, I packed up the car and headed down to Southern Cross. I received the handover from the DON, and she left for a four-week holiday. The hospital was small with ten beds - four acute and six aged care beds- and a small A&E (Accident and Emergency) department. The community was small; made up of farming and mining families. The mine Koolyanobbing was a BHP one where they mined iron ore. The nearest regional hospital was Kalgoorlie and the big CY O'Connor water pipeline ran straight past the hospital, where I would go for a run after work every evening. The doctor was a very nice man; he was a family GP who practised a Holistic model of medicine and homeopathy. I got on very well with him and we shared many deep philosophical discussions. The nursing staff were made up of a small mix of RN, EN's and nursing assistants.

I was on duty not long after I arrived, and much to my surprise was handed the DD keys by the nursing assistant. I asked her why she had them, and was told we all carry them, myself the EN's and RN's. I immediately put an end to that as it was totally against the law as written in the Nurses' Act. What I experienced there, was like another time zone. The hospital appeared to me to be run on a very laissez-faire type of nursing management. There were no policies and no procedure manuals for staff to refer to. It was like stepping into the 1970's model.

As a relieving DON, it was not my role to change anything; however, it was my role to ensure that all nursing standards were in accordance with the standards implemented through the 1985-1987 period and nurses practised in accordance with the Nursing Act. There was no nursing Staff Development programmes, so I set a goal of educating nurses on documentation and care planning during my month long stay. I had a visit from the Regional Director of Community Nursing, a lady by the name of Margaret who came from the regional office in Kalgoorlie and spent the day with me. We connected straight away and she gave me permission to try and implement some changes.

The documentation and staff development project went down very well, augmented by the fact, that I had been summoned to The Supreme Court in Western Australia for a trial of grievous bodily harm. The incident which caused this, happened at Wanneroo Hospital in June of 1990. I was working an evening shift on a Sunday night and was bandaging a gentleman's leg. I heard the front doors to Emergency open and these two male voices panicking, "Sister, Sister help." I dropped the bandage and went to see what the urgency was. Two men were dragging this lady in and were only just holding her up. As soon as I appeared, they literally threw her at me, and scurried out the door. She was as white as a sheet. I noted a blood stain at the fourth intercostal rib cage closest to the sternum and realised that she had been stabbed. I yelled for help and asked the ward clerk to send for the anaesthetist, who had just finished in theatre. I sent another nurse off to collect two units of O-positive blood from the blood bank and rushed her straight into resus. The ward clerk called for the ambulance for a code 000, as we prepared to get her ready for immediate transfer through to SCGH. The clockwork with all the practitioners involved was amazing. We had her already for transfer in twenty minutes with blood transfusions running and our patient intubated. One of doctor's escorted her down and they did not even stop in the emergency department at SCGH. They rushed her straight into theatre and opened her chest wall up as she was bleeding very heavily. I cannot remember how much blood was in her chest cavity, but they saved her life. Fortunately, a couple of ward staff members were sent down to take over from the ED team to enable them to attend to the non-urgent presentations. I was just about to go home; it was 10pm and after an incident like that, we had a lot of tidying up to do to ensure Resus was ready for the next emergency. The ambulance crew had notified the police and they presented to ED just as I picked up my bag to go home. As I was the one that had had the first contact with the patient and I had seen the two men who brought her in, I had to stay back and give a statement there and then to the police. This I did; and thank God I did as I was summoned to the high court twelve months later. My documentation had been so accurate that the Judge thanked me for my quick action and said, "If I had not done what I had done, we would be attending a murder trial."

Sharing that story on my return to Southern Cross, with the staff, made my job so much easier. It turned out her brother had stabbed her when they had had an argument about a car. I felt very sorry for the family, both the victim and the perpetrator.

There was a lovely ninety-year old Italian lady who was a permanent resident in the aged care section; she quickly won my heart. She reminded me of my grandmother and I would spend a lot of time laughing and joking with her. She had come out from Italy as a young bride and had come straight to Southern Cross. She was full of stories and I loved listening to them. She had a beautiful attentive family, who when I left gave me a book on, *The History of The Yilgarn* as a gift when my assignment finished. It was a great read.

Again, I was sad to leave. Home for a week's rest and then my next assignment was to Wongan Hills for a three week period, as a relieving DON. This was good as it was only 189 kilometres from Perth. Wongan Hills is in the wheat belt, and had a small well-equipped hospital. It was not a busy hospital at all, and I had minimal work to do, so I was rather glad to complete that assignment. The family hardly knew I had gone away.

We had a little holiday up in Kalbarri following that assignment - just the four of us for a week, which was great.

* * *

My next assignment was back to the North to the Jigalong Community. It was a two-nurse remote area nursing post for an eight week assignment. Jigalong is situated 1070 kms away from Perth and 110 kilometres from the BHP town of Newman. The population at that time, was approximately 300 people. Jigalong was established in 1907, for the construction of the Rabbit proof fence[1]. In the 1930's, it was used as a camel breeding site. In 1947, the land was granted to a Christian Church organization and they set it up as an Aboriginal Mission. The land was returned to the Commonwealth Government in 1969 and was granted to the Martu people in 1974 when self-determination for Aboriginal Communities was enacted by the then Federal Labour Government. Jigalong was the home of Molly Craig. The young Aboriginal girl whose 1,600 km trek from the Moore River Native Settlement back to Jigalong was immortalised in the book, *Follow the Rabbit- Proof Fence* by Molly's daughter, whom I had the honour of meeting in Port Hedland Regional Hospital in 2007

I packed my bags, and was soon on my way to the most amazing place out on the edge of the Western Desert with the most resilient people one could wish to commune with. Noddy, I would have to admit, was a little worried about me going up there, because of the negative stories being published in the press about Newman and Jigalong at the time. I assured him I would be fine and I would ring him every night if possible. I boarded the plane excited about this new adventure and returning to the Pilbara after thirty-six years. We arrived in Newman three hours later. It was the dry season and the weather was glorious. I was rugged up to 'the nines', when I had left Perth, as it was the middle of winter. I was even silly enough to have a pair of stockings on. A beautiful aboriginal lady, a health worker, met me at the airport in a Toyota troop carrier, and we had to pick up some supplies from the Newman Hospital before heading out onto the Northwest Highway. We called into the shopping centre for a cup of tea and had a bite to eat, and then set off. We had just turned on to the Jigalong road when the health worker - I sadly cannot remember her name - all of a sudden pulled up and got out to examine something.

When she climbed back in, I asked, "what is the matter?"

"We have a flat tyre," she replied.

"Oh, what do we do now?" I asked.

"Change it." she said.

I hopped out of the car and realised I was quite useless. I had never changed a tyre in my life. I had to change from my good clothes, take off my stockings behind a tree and come out dressed in shorts and tee shirt to try and help change this flat tyre.

By the time I got back to the car, my new friend was smiling she said, "We wait, there is no spare."

So, we sat on the side of the road and waited and waited until all of a sudden she said, "There is a car coming".

I couldn't hear it, nor see it. Sure enough, thirty minutes later, around the bend, came a troop carrier. The occupants pulled up; it was full of Aboriginal men from Jigalong, on their way into Newman. I was introduced to them, as Peter the new sister. I shook everyone's hand. Twenty minutes later, we were on the road again. I felt safe and knew I was going to really enjoy this assignment no matter what was thrown at me.

It was a long dusty drive out and we finally came to a huge creek crossing on the outskirts of the community with a fair amount of water in it. We had no problem crossing it, but it was quite dark by the time we arrived.

I was met by the charge sister who made me feel very welcome and she took me to my flat, a modern little unit, which was well appointed. The Charge Sister was a grey headed older lady who must have been in her mid-sixties; she had worked out there for several years and loved the community. We were just about to sit down to a meal she had prepared for us, when there was a knock on the back door. I answered it. Standing there was this Aboriginal man saying he had a headache and needed to see the Sister. She went with him over to the clinic. She was back very quickly. Apparently, the man had entered the clinic after her and as she went to shut the door, he put his hand up above her head and indicated he wanted her in a sexual manner. But the sister was too quick for him; pointing to her hair, she said, "here see this colour hair, no white woman does it when they have this colour hair." She returned very calmly and laughed it off. The incident did not deter me or frighten me in any way. I thought the old sister was very clever about how she managed the situation. I dread to think what could have happened, if this had been a young nurse out doing her first assignment in remote area nursing.

The clinic was a fairly busy one, which was good; there was always something to do. Whilst Sister did the Child Health, I did the School Health program. Thursday afternoon was the time for going out bush with a group of elders to collect firewood. A tremendous experience for me; the old ladies were all very agile and would walk kilometres bare feet and share their knowledge of the bush with me. It reminded me of the time when I was a little girl.

We ran a sick clinic in the mornings for the first three hours. We would have a visit from the Newman Doctor once a fortnight for the day, once again like, the doctors in Fitzroy Crossing, Dr Dorothy was full of kindness and compassion. I was very moved by witnessing this doctor and an Aboriginal Medicine man discussing an old man's condition at the end of his life. There was some talk of moving him to the sterile confines of a white man's hospital, a bed, clean white sheets and strangers. All he wanted was to die in his humpy in his community with his dogs; he didn't want to go to Newman. So, the Medicine Man and this beautiful young female doctor Dorothy agreed he could stay in Jigalong if I would look after him where he wanted to die. He was very near transition and knowing how it was so important to die in country for this old man, I said I would look after him. I ensured he got fluids or a mouth clean every two hours and would come and bathe him every day. He lasted forty-eight hours and slipped away peacefully, surrounded by his dogs. It was amazing the dogs never moved or growled at me during the times - day or night- when I went to his camp to take care of him. It was indeed an honour to be there for this human being.

I have many stories to tell about my stay there. I loved never knowing what I would be called to do. Late one afternoon, it was almost night fall when one lady presented to the health centre with a severe asthma attack. I administered initial treatment and kept her in the clinic. I realised she was in trouble so I rang RFDS; but there was no plane available. I was instructed to commence a Ventolin infusion and administer some Adrenaline and transfer her by road to Newman ASAP. Sister came over to help me and prepared all the emergency equipment for the 110km trip. I had an aboriginal health worker come with me. So we set off at 7.30pm that night. The three of us in the front seat and we headed for Newman. It was dark, the creek was up and it was raining, so we had to drive slow and careful. We arrived safely two and a half hours later. Our patient had improved slightly. I can assure you the power of prayer works. We arrived back at Jigalong at 1am exhausted, but satisfied.

. . .

A GIRL CALLED PETER

One day, a dear old man turned up at the clinic, in terrible pain due to a badly infected tooth. We were able to get him an appointment with the dentist in Newman that afternoon for a tooth extraction. After we left the dental surgery, we went into town for a cup of tea before heading back. It is funny, the looks one gets when they see a white lady nurturing an old Aboriginal man. I ordered some sandwiches to eat on the road home so that the old man could eat later. We pulled up half way home and hopped out. We sat on the ground with the tyre as a back rest eating our sandwiches and having a drink of cool water. Since he had no money, I had purchased enough for the two of us. We talked for quite some time; he told me of his growing up at Jigalong and that he was an artist. On our return, he was very grateful and three days later as a thank you, he brought me a heavy wooden shield, he had carved for me as a thank you gift. Today, whenever I dust this shield, I remember this very humble man. My little grandson, Max, will be the beneficiary of this shield as he loves this story and the heavy shield.

Jigalong was a dry community, meaning no alcohol was allowed to be brought in, which was great. I saw only three cases of domestic violence in the community - two presented physically to the clinic and one that I was called to in the community one night.

I saw a community that could well have been in one of the poorest and worst camps in a third world country. One night, at around midnight, I was called up to a camp at the top of the village to see an old lady who was screaming in pain due to what appeared to be a knee injury. She told me someone had hit her with a piece of wood across the knee. The poor old lady could not move. Her camp was a tiny tin shelter that I had to crawl into to be able to examine her knee by torch light. I left the headlights of the car on, to enable me to see better. I cannot describe her little shelter, but what I will write is, no human being in Australia in 1991 should ever be living like this poor old lady was - on the ground with nothing but a blanket and her two dogs. On examination, I could see her knee had a serious injury. I woke a couple of her neighbours and they transferred her into the Troopy for me and we brought her back to the clinic. I rang RFDS to get some strong pain relief for her and arranged for her transfer to Port Hedland Regional

Hospital. (For any pain relief stronger than Panadene, nurses are not allowed to instigate without a phone order from a medical officer).

Another time, I was called out late one night to a young man, who had self-harmed by cutting himself many times across his thigh. This poor young man had a long history of mental illness. Again, the housing situation was indescribable, it was so bad.

In 1991 with the millions of dollars that has been poured into Indigenous health over the years, I had to ask myself why weren't we not progressing and helping people make a better life for themselves and their families? The pain was incredible to see, but I had no power to do anything. I could only nurse them with care and love the person who was suffering.

I witnessed men having a 'secret men's business' meeting, all sitting in the red dirt just outside the perimeter of the town. I had to give the Elder running the meeting, a message for the men regarding a health issue. I had to wait for a signal from the Elder to move forward, to give the message to the Elder, and leave as soon as I had handed it over. Respect is what you have to show when dealing with any person / persons and with people with such a rich culture, we must respect their tradition. The respect is then reciprocated. This is something I had learned when I was a junior nurse in Yirrkala.

During this assignment, we had five WA Government Senators come to the community. They were all brought in on a charted plane. We had to pick them up from the little airstrip in the troop carrier. They looked so out of place; especially one politician who came out of the plane wearing a long dress, with a flowing long top covering it, and high heel shoes. The men were in suits and ties.

We had had quite a lot of rain during the night, so in the morning there were puddles of mud everywhere. It was quite a sight seeing them all trying to navigate around the mud and puddles. We took them around the community, pointing out the problems which affected the health and wellbeing of the residents including the homes and little shelters, and the broken sewerage systems and appalling conditions people had to live in. The charge nurse and I shared some of our experiences with them. They all listened intently and we were glad when they flew off, as I am sure, they felt very uncomfortable. What the outcome of their visit was, we would never know. What the cost of this visit was back then, I would not know either; but it gave me no solace to know nothing would come out of the visit. I had experienced similar events in the 1970's. This was still so evident to us when we were in Halls Creek and Fitzroy Crossing in 2016.

I had an old man come to the clinic one day; he held out his rather large hand and said, "Sister, you take out my stitches." I could hardly see them. I asked him what he had done and how long the sutures had been there. He told me he had been out bush for several weeks and had cut himself so he sutured it up himself with a needle and cotton he kept in his glove box, just in case he had an accident. Bless him. He had done a good job of suturing it, and there were no signs of infection; the wound was beautifully healed. It must have taken me near on an hour to remove these sutures they were so embedded. The Indigenous people are tough and I admire them so much.

My time at Jigalong was a very enriching and healing time for me. I am so grateful to all the wonderful people who made this assignment so memorable. When it was time for me to pack up and say goodbye, I knew I would miss the sister in charge and the two health workers and a community that had no material wealth but were rich in a way that the Western world would find too hard to comprehend.

Back on the plane and back to the fast pace of city life; I was changing and getting back to a zest for life and starting to look forward to the day, when Noddy and I could pack up our lives in Perth (once the children were ready to stand on their own two feet) and go back to the North. JD had only sixteen months left until he finished school and JA had a year off before she headed for university to study for her teaching degree, something she had always wanted to do. Everyone was happy to see me home, husband, kids, cats and dog.

* * *

. . .

My next assignment was a month down at Pinjarra Hospital in theatre, where my old friend Kate, from Wanneroo Hospital, was the DON. It was great as I could go home even during the week if I finished at 3.30pm and not come on till 1pm the next day. I clocked up a few miles running backwards and forwards. After work, if I didn't go home, I would go down and spend some meditative time sitting on the banks of the Murray River. It was so peaceful and I was communing with the oneness of nature for the first time since my palliative care days. I even wrote a number of poems whilst sitting by the river.

My first one:
The Light
As I sit here, Lord Jesus to rest
I ask you to enter and be my guest
Surrounded by water, trees and wild flowers
Your gentle voice is all I can hear
Calming me, reassuring me, that you are near
Peter dear the negatives are there no more
Gone forever the doubt, the loneliness and fear
In their place Light has entered
Bringing peace of mind, of heart and song
Nurture it, cherish it and never fear for always by your side I am near
PB Rebbechi 3rd October 1991

I was healing and growing spiritually, becoming fully immersed in the tree of life –the virtues again.

I wrote Tranquillity three weeks later.

Around the bend, in the river she flows
Gently gently like a sheet of glass she glows
When one looks in a reflection of the universe beholds
A picture of tranquillity, of freedom and of song.
Gently gently she pushes on, then out of nowhere
A formation of rocks stops her flow
Her movements change to a cascading mound
As over the rocks her, waters pound 'swirling in here, swirling in there
Until down around the river's bend, her foam starts to clear
And with no more rocks submerged
Back the tranquil waters emerge.
As the sun goes down and I am sitting here, surrounded by trees with flowering gum
I take a breath and thank my friend, my God for bringing me here to this little corner of his/her universe.
PB Rebbechi, 25th October 1991

The theatre unit at Pinjarra was a great place to work, although I did get a few flashbacks about the doctor who had bullied me at a previous hospital; however, I was able to quickly get rid of them by burying the thoughts deep within me. Here all the surgeons and anaesthetists were very respectful. I had one great experience with an obstetrician who did a near bloodless caesarean section. I was so amazed at his skill that as soon as I went home, I sat and wrote a poem about it, I took it to work when he had his next list; he was thrilled with what I had composed.

The Expectant Mother.
The Expectant Mother arrived to enable the doctor to put in the line
The pain to be controlled was his purpose to behold
With gentle skill and good technique her bottom half he put to sleep

Excitement mounted in the room as the Surgeon did appear
Are we ready he did ask, to undergo this delicate task?
With the absence of any pain the Surgeon cut the skin to gain entry into the womb beyond
With skill and grace and swiftly too
His hand ,with minutes a little baby's bottom found
The scene to follow a miracle behold
As a little baby girl he did hold
My breath I had to hold My tears I could not hid
The tears of joy and happiness
A newborn baby girl or boy doth bring
The miracle of life that only our God could create
Peter Rebbechi -9th October 1991

I used to call and see my parents on my way home. They had moved to Armadale to be close to my sister Marion, as their health was deteriorating, especially mum's pain which was due to her nurse's back, and her osteoporosis. The poor darling was becoming debilitated and they would so look forward to my visits. They moved from the beachside suburb of Hillarys where they had lots of friends, to Armadale, a suburb at the time, well known for antisocial behaviour and break-ins. My sister, Marie and her husband had moved up to a five acre property in Gidgeganup.

My parents became prisoners in their own home and were burgled a number of times. Mum couldn't drive anymore, and their social network just dried up, I am sure loneliness caused them a lot of pain and grief too.

NORSEMAN

After Pinjarra, I had a posting down to Norseman, the gateway to the Nullarbor as the DON (Director of Nursing) for six weeks. It was too far to come home during this time as it would have been a 1400 km round trip for a weekend, so we decided we would have lots of phone calls; at least two a day for the time I was away.

I fell in love with Norseman. It had all the charm of yesteryear. I had the nurse's quarters to myself most of the time and a nurse from Esperance, would come for a couple of days per week and stay there. She was lovely and great company. The weather was very cold and the old rooms in the quarters were so big, there was no way you could warm them, the hospital too was quite rambly, but it had a character all of its own. I felt at home as soon as I walked in.

The Norseman journey was a very special one and I guess after having lived in the city for eleven years without having time to be in communion with the natural world, I had somehow lost touch. For the first time in many years, I actually had time to slow down to stop and realise the beauty of Mother Earth.

. . .

One Sunday, on the 8th of September 1991 (it was my day off), I went with a very nice family and another gentleman , who also worked at the hospital on a picnic out to Cave Hill Nature Reserve. A lovely senior nurse was relieving me this day with another nurse who was on call. We travelled up the highway, about 60 kilometres from Norseman, until we came to the turn off at Higgensville and headed off road at the Higgensfield Pump Station, then down a very narrow dirt road. The road was excellent as it had just been graded. I was delighted to spot an Emu. I wondered at Nature's magic – The emus blended in so well with the surrounding environment that it was hard to spot them at a glance.

We travelled about another 40 kilometres and came across an outcrop of rocks. It was an amazing site in the middle of the vast track of dense bush land. The rocks were massive, so we stopped here awhile and went exploring. Beautiful little lizards could be seen darting all over. We had to be observant though because they too blended with nature and the landscape. I find it incredible the way Mother nature looks after each and every creature. There were several little rock pools with tadpoles swimming around; and there were also lovely specimens of little wildflowers and trees. We did not realise how high up we were until we got to the top, and surveyed the surrounding bush land. After stretching our legs, we headed to our destination, Cave Hill Nature Reserve.

This section of the road wasn't so good as there were deep ruts. There were corrugations in the road, where some travellers had got into trouble recently. We took it very sedately and meandered our way through the bush land. It was beautiful and serene to be amongst the trees. All of a sudden we came to a big notice board that said we had arrived at the Nature Reserve. As we headed in, out of nowhere, there appeared in front of us this mammoth (and I mean really mammoth) expanse of rock with a big cave on the top which was really spectacular.

We stopped for lunch, joined by what seemed like millions of bush flies. Yuck yuck yuck. But we were hungry and enjoyed our barbecue lunch, shooing the flies away with , 'The great Aussie Salute.[1]'As soon as lunch had finished and we had cleaned up, the flies were gone.

We then clambered over the rocks, exploring the caves on the way up to the top. The weather was ideal for this sojourn. When we arrived at the peak, it was a majestic sight. The wind was blowing and there were rock pools everywhere and all you could see for miles and miles were trees, and beyond the trees, the hills in the distance. I could have stayed up there in the heavens for days wishing Noddy was here to enjoy the panorama and kaleidoscope of colour. I did not know places like this existed in the Goldfields.

Australia is such a beautiful country. I did not want to leave but it was getting dark and we headed back to Norseman arriving around 6:30pm, exhausted but refreshed from a wonderful day out with these lovely travellers.

I realised how grateful I was to go back to working as a country nurse. I couldn't imagine going back to city nursing -in fact I hated the thought. But my family came first and I had to do what was best for them, and if it meant going back to the city, that is what I would have to do, after my year finished. Noddy rang to say that he was happy I had such a great day out and he and the children were so looking forward to me coming home on the 19th September.

I loved to go up after work for a walk up to Jimberlana Hill, and what a beautiful big hill with an equally magnificent site from the top that would take your breath away. It was worth the puffing and panting to get to the top. Sitting up on the highest point reflecting, praying and thanking God for all the beautiful feelings I had was just so peaceful. No one but me and my God and my thoughts and the splendour of Mother Nature.

. . .

I was invited to go with an ambulance driver on the weekend to do an ambulance swap out to Cocklebiddy on the Nullarbor. I had planned to go and visit a friend in Esperance on the weekend; but changed my mind, and decided to go on this trip to Cocklebiddy. I preferred to go to Esperance for a holiday with my husband at a time when the opportunity arrived.

Saturday, the 14th, came very quickly and we left at 06.30am to traverse the Nullabour to Cocklebiddy. We had arranged to call in to Balladonia Station to visit the old homestead and view the art gallery there, on our way. As we headed out to Balladonia it was an overcast morning with a very strong head wind blowing. We got about thirty kilometres out of town and I witnessed a beautiful site. A big emu with his six little chicks, all in single file, walking down the side of the road. It was so heart-warming to witness nature at its very best, blending in with the environment, watched over by the big tall green trees along the edge of the road. What a pretty drive. We turned into the Balladonia station, which was another amazing place. We were treated very warmly by an elderly couple who were caretaking for the weekend. An old lady who had lived there all her life had passed away at the age of ninety-seven, three years earlier. Her family now ran the station.

What was so amazing about this place was the Gallery of Paintings depicting what life was like at the turn of the century. It blew me away; every painting told a story. I would have loved to have known her - she was so creative and her love for animals was evident in her paintings. I heard she was painting up until she passed away. We were also shown through this lovely old station house and we were invited to have morning tea, which we did and headed off shortly after for the next leg of the journey which was 246.3 kilometres away. I also purchased a little book called, 'Verses from the Nullabour' prior to our leaving the homestead.

A couple of hours later we arrived at Cocklebiddy, had lunch and swapped over the ambulances. I have to say the stretch of road between

Balladonia and Cocklebiddy was very different from the stretch from Norseman to Balladonia. There was no green expanse of trees, just plains of very dry looking land. Outside the ambulance, the wind was bitterly cold. Out of nowhere, words entered my head. I picked up a piece of paper and started to write a poem.

I called it *"The Long Grey Road"*

The Long Grey Road

All we want to do is cross the road,
to get from one side to the other
Hoping Hoping Hoping we come,
will we make it?
Yes, let's go.
Suddenly a bump, where did it come from, where did it go?
My friend is now gone laying dead
A resting place by The Long Grey Road
He is now a target for the Eagles and the Crows
When will I go?

They come soaring, flying low
They come for a purpose.
Slowly Slowly they glide to a halt
Standing tall, Majestic
The winds blowing through the feathers on their strong brown legs
Steadily they walk towards their target watching and listening
They settle pecking and pulling until suddenly they stop
A noise, danger and with a single movement
They soar higher and higher to a safer haven

Down they glide again and land safely
Away from the sound of danger
Away from The Long Grey Road
Watching, waiting for the sound to disappear
Then they return, to pick and pull until
they have had their fill

While the mind was focused and I had pen and paper in hand, a second one came to my mind .

I called this, 'I wonder'

I wonder

> I am amazed
> I am frightened
> The Earth is dead
> The trees once green are dead
> Grey, they now stand
> Not a leaf on them
> Just grey dead branches
> Hanging lifeless listless
> Now the trees don't talk
> The birds nowhere to lay their nests
> Is it just by the road they are dying where travellers pass
> spewing the air with toxic fumes choking life
> or is it just old old old age?
> I wonder

. . .

I put the pen and paper away, still wondering where these words came from. I could not come to terms with the enormous amount of dead kangaroos I saw on the side of the road with the eagles and crows having a good feed. Mother Nature.

We finally returned to St John's ambulance depot and thanked my friend for the wonderful journey.

RETURNING TO WA

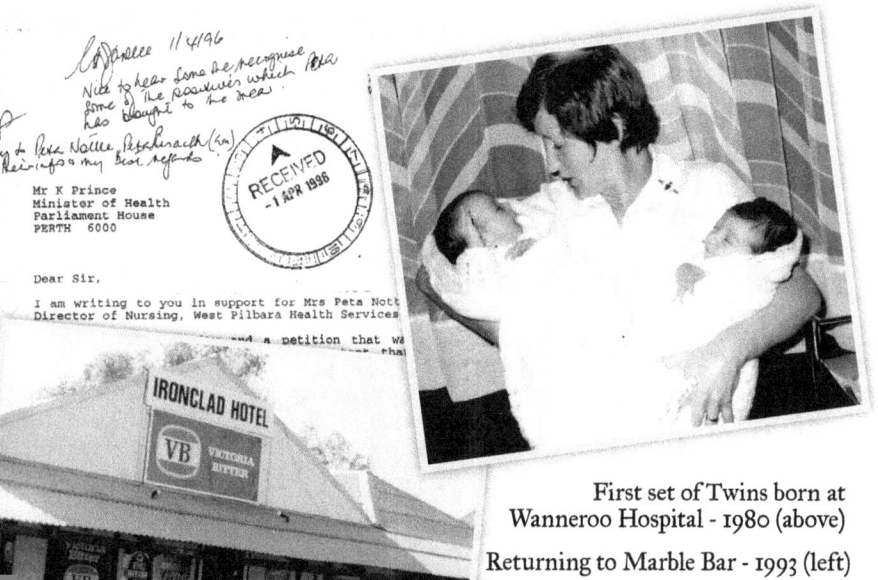

First set of Twins born at Wanneroo Hospital - 1980 (above)

Returning to Marble Bar - 1993 (left)

Fitzroy River Flooded - 1991 (below)

Camping at Cape Leveque - 1996 (above)

Enjoying a drink from The Melbourne Cup won by Rogan Josh (below)

Flooded De Grey River - 2000 (top)
Comforting Lady De Grey River Station - 2000 (above)

NORSEMAN CONTD...

I joined the local tennis club and fitted into the community very quickly. The people were all very friendly. The Hospital's regional centre was Kalgoorlie. The staff were very good, and the DON's management skills excellent. So, it was easy to step in as her relief. The doctor was nice too; an overseas doctor who would leave you to run the hospital and only come in if needed, which was not very often.

I had to call him one Saturday afternoon to assist in the management and treatment of a very dear old couple who were participating in the Australian Rolls Royce Owners' Association on a round Australia trip –crossing the Nullarbor. One of the owners, whose wife was driving at the time had a nasty roll over. Norseman had paid St John's ambulance officers and they went to the scene which was just the other side of Caiguna Road House, and brought them back to Norseman Hospital. They were such nice old people. They were old farmers and thankfully their injuries were not life threatening. The poor old darlings were in shock and badly bruised, but with the gentle loving care they received from the team, they were up and off again within ten days. Their poor car wasn't though.

One of the rally members came to see them, and during a conversation I said I have never been for a ride in a Roll's Royce, so this kind gentleman said, I will pick you up and take you for a ride after work. I have to say, what a great treat that was.

Another evening, at around 8pm when the emergency bell rang and a man was standing there carrying his kelpie. There was no vet in town and this poor man was very upset. His kelpie had tried to jump a barb wire fence, chasing something and his left hind leg had been caught. He sustained a very deep laceration right down through muscle and ligaments, so I invited them in and lay the Kelpie on the stretcher, gave him some Panadol and cleaned up the wound. I used some local anaesthetic on the wound site and packed it with saline. The owner rang an Esperance vet and they left to have the dog treated by the vet.

Esperance was 203 kms away. The things one has to do.

I received a big thank you from the man several days later. Small random acts of kindness is what makes nursing out in small country towns and remote communities so worthwhile. It really defines the meaning of the word Nurse, 'to care with compassion'. By caring for the man's dog, I had cared also for him.

The time at Norseman went very quickly. I loved the people I was working with, the staff were caring human beings and the hospital was very well managed. The permanent DON was very respected and by the way the hospital was run, her leadership skills were very evident. I wanted to stay and it would have been be a place I would be happy to work in as a RN.

***

Once the assignment was over, I returned to Perth for a couple of weeks' rest. The Health Department was winding down the Emergency Nursing Service and phasing it out. So, I was offered a position down in the South West at Manjimup hospital as a Clinical Nurse/Midwife.

Manjimup is situated 290 kms from Perth. It was approximately a four hour drive, which meant I could be a drive in drive out, wife, mum and nurse very easily, and also be home for my days off.

The DON was a very nice lady, very well educated in nursing circles and a good administrator. Sadly, she was subjected to some major workplace issues, which greatly impacted on the morale and management of the staff. It was at the time of the two infamous doctors, from Manjimup who ended up in jail for defrauding Medicare funding from the Commonwealth Government in 1991. The tension between the Board and the Hospital administration was palpable; I knew immediately I could not stay there too long as I did not want to become embroiled in any of the politics. I did have some interesting times though, especially with one of the above infamous MDs.

I was working in ED, and a man presented for an outpatient procedure to be done in ED by the doctor. On examining the man, I asked what he was having done.

He said, "I am having the lump removed from my neck."

Visually, one could not see anything on the front or sides of his neck, so when I went searching for this lump and I found a lump the size of an orange behind his neck. I thought, this needs to be done in an operating theatre, not in an emergency department. I spoke to the DON who came up and had a look. She agreed with me; so when the Doctor arrived, he was asked to speak with us, prior to him speaking to his patient, and I informed him that I had not set up for the procedure purposely, as in my opinion it needed to be done in an OR, under a general anaesthetic.

He told me no it was to be done here in the emergency department. But I stood by my assessment and refused to assist him. As fate would have it, the Chairperson of the MAC came in and the doctor spoke with him. The chairperson then came and examined the patient, and said yes he agreed, that it needed to be done in the operating room. Fortunately, for this man, the theatre was functional that day and he was added to the list. The cyst was successfully removed; however, it had been a difficult excision, as I was informed later.

Another time, the doctor had a patient come in and he saw him in the consulting room. After he left, I went in to prepare the room for the next consultation, to find empty syringes, needles and rubbish lying on the desk, with a sharps container there for the sharps. I was very stubborn in terms of infection control, and rang him up in his surgery, and very politely asked him to come back and leave the desk as he had found it, with the needles to be placed in the sharps container. He did come back and did as I requested, coming in through the back door so I would not see him. After my experience in the late 80s, I was no longer prepared to tolerate any hand maiden roles that nurses once did for some members of the esteemed profession who expected nurses to be their door mats.

I was a nurse who had found her voice.

Life was good. I would go for drives after work and find lovely little places to stop and meditate and commune with nature, something I was becoming very accustomed to. I could feel myself starting to become strong again and the self-healing was happening.

There was a lovely nurse staying in the Nurses quarters from England. She was younger than me and we got on very well. We would spend hours talking in the evening, if we were both on our 'offs' together. The staff were in general, nice. However, some were more friendly than others. One could feel the fractions and brokenness in the nursing division.

Some of the staff who had been there for many years were quite aggressive to the junior nurses and to anyone from 'the outside' with new practice ideas in the 1990's. Culture has such an impact on efficiency and effectiveness of an organisation. I was so glad to know I was only there for a short contract. I attended several staff meetings and would come away quite distressed over the way people who would complain and speak about other staff behind their backs and not be accountable for resolving issues. Tension and bitterness were embedded. As soon as I could, I started to look to return to work in a metropolitan hospital.

The patients were lovely at Manjimup and it was a pleasure to nurse them. One lady, I remember, was an old woman at the end of her life; her family lived in Melbourne so she was on her own. The ward was very quiet; at the most 3 -4 patients all self-caring, except for this old darling. It was a privilege to journey with her to be able to care for her with love and compassion and to ensure a graceful ending. I would liaise with her family every day and was able to bring them comfort even though they were so far away. Midwifery was very quiet. Mothers chose to either deliver in Bridgetown or go to Bunbury for their deliveries; I think I had only one delivery in the whole time I was there.

NEW HOME...NEW BEGINNINGS

Noddy was looking to buy a new home for us and one day he found a little golden gem in a suburb I had never heard of, the suburb was the smallest in Perth, it was called Gwelup. Ten kilometres out of the city close to the beaches and the freeway, it was a really fabulous location. There were only two houses on the street and a small shopping centre, all around was ex market garden land. It was a small three bedroom- one bathroom duplex. The cost was $79,000. We bought it and I cannot express how wonderful it was, to be under a roof of our own again. We were home. JA was starting University to study teaching and JD was in year 12 and as for my dear husband he was ever so happy.

Mum was doing okay with Dad looking after her well. They were very unhappy out at Armadale, and I am sure that they were in a very advanced stage of depression. They were prisoners trapped in a home and suburb they did not want to be in and they could not do anything about it. We felt very sorry for them but no matter what I said or did, it made little difference. It certainly made me determined I was not going to age like them. My sister Marion lived in Armadale and committed to be their carer during their ageing process. She really looked after them well.

I was ready to return to nursing in Perth. I applied to go back to Wanneroo Hospital. Wanneroo, at this stage, was transferred to a private government contractor and was now known as the Joondalup Hospital. There were massive expansions planned to grow the hospital. Much to my disappointment, one of the staff members (who I would describe as one of the a dark force back in 1990, when I left), was now in a Senior management position and advised me that there were no positions available for me to even apply for and if there was, I would not have my application accepted. I had moved on, so I was not distressed by this turn of events. I eventually managed to find a Level 2 Clinical Nurse position at SCGH in Nedlands, after having failed to be considered for two registered nurse positions at Fremantle and Royal Perth Hospitals, in their emergency departments. The feedback I received was that I was too experienced to work there.

Things were really changing in nursing, junior nurses who had university degrees were being given the positions over hospital trained nurses, who could walk the walk and talk the talk. For the first time, I witnessed and realised the saying that was so common in nursing - nurses eat their young. I was now beginning to realise that they were also eating their older, more experienced nurses. (I was 43 years old).

My role at SCGH was on a short stay ward with lots of junior and graduate nurses; I enjoyed it very much, being a mentor and coach to the young nurses, especially the graduates on their first rotations. In those days, they had a new performance appraisal system and nurses had to do an evaluation on you which was a practice of anecdotal notes on what one did well or not so well. I was so blessed and received many beautiful anecdotal notes from nurses, who appreciated the nurturing and comfort I could share with them.

I even ran some meditation sessions for the staff which was very well received in Staff Development time. One of the things I really noticed, that was so evident, were the number of nurses, who would walk around with clip boards under their arms. Doing what, I do not know. They would not stop to see if there was anything they could do to help take the pressure off the nurses who were working so hard on the floor to ensure patients were looked after well. It was a very different environment for me to work in. The clinical nurses all had a patient load, as well as all the supervisory /mentorship and management of a busy ward. There were four of us. I was happy as I was busy all the time.

I had in the back of my mind the need for me to work in ED as Noddy and I were planning to leave to return to the North in 1993. After completing three months working on the ward, I transferred to work in ED. It was hard to say goodbye to all the beautiful nurses on the ward. I had to do a two week full orientation program, working through triage, with emergency on one side and resus on the other and through the 'walking in consulting rooms.' Today the emergency is very different to what it was back in 1991.

The orientation was very thorough. I was told as I was very junior in the department I would have to be fully supervised for the first three months, especially when my experience was all written up in my CV and I had been interviewed regarding my experiences by the CNSs of the department; however, I accepted this as a newbie. I didn't want to rock the boat or appear a know-it-all. I said nothing about my previous ED experience and decided actions would speak louder than words.

I had been working there for two months when I experienced a culture shock. Everyone who turned up in ED had to be seen by a doctor, no matter what they presented with. No nurse was allowed to initiate treatment. The nurse was to merely carry out the doctor's orders.

I was working in triage one evening shift. The volume of patients in the Emergency Department was high with some patients waiting for up to five hours to be seen. Some had come in with very minor presentations but they still had to been seen by a doctor regardless of their presentation. A young man had presented at around 2100 hrs. He was complaining of a sore elbow. His history was that he had banged his elbow on a bench, and he experienced pain. He was not prepared to wait, so I assessed his elbow and forearm and there was full movement and no swelling and it was not tender to touch. I suggested to him, that I would give him two Panadol, put his elbow in a sling and that he should see his GP if it was still giving him discomfort in the morning. I wrote all this is up in his ED notes. Two days later, I was summonsed up to the level 4 Nurse Managers' office and had to account for my actions; the manager was very rude and I was given a stern reprimand. This is how it was; nurses get disempowered so quickly, as I was to find out through this journey. I never ever found out, how it escalated to that level without this being discussed with myself first. That is how things work in some workplaces.

I had however, settled in very quickly and really enjoyed the work; I always found everything really easy. In the tertiary system, like remote and country hospitals, one really had a mixture of everything. We were getting the whole gamut of the human experience - physical, mental, emotional and spiritual emergencies. It was a workplace where everyone who worked in emergency, wanted to be there, the nurses and doctors were great. There were a few junior nurses who had just graduated or were doing the 12 month intensive care course and some doctors were on their first or second rotations as residents.

At that time, Emergency Medicine was just beginning to become a speciality in its own right. I joined the Emergency Nursing Association, a professional body, and had a great learning experience. I found out on my journey that when you work in a speciality area, if there is a speciality association, it is really important to be a member of that nursing association, the knowledge, one obtains is invaluable to professional growth and development. The nurses on the floor were fantastic, experienced and very good at what they did. There were also some lovely level 2 clinical nurses who were committed to a safe and happy workplace.

Once, one of these lovely nurses asked me to swap a shift with her. I agreed readily; however, when I came on the next day I was spoken to by one of the clinical nurse specialists, who told me in no uncertain terms that I could not swap with the clinical nurse, as I was too junior in the department. (I had been working there for 3 months at this stage). The clinical nurse was very upset about this and spoke to the CNS, but to no avail. People wonder why good nurses leave. I really loved the night shifts that came around every month, so I ended up going on permanent night shift. I enjoyed the work even more, as the atmosphere was so much more relaxed. There were 5 nurses on and 2-3 doctors, and I would have to say it was a great team environment and a good place to work.

It was so good to be home. Noddy was still working hard, and glad to have me permanently home; we had grown even closer than we had ever been. The drive-in drive-out wife and mother came home healed from her experiences at Wanneroo hospital; she was happy and very proud of her family unit. JA was a mature sensible young lady who loved life and always had such a happy positive disposition; so much like her father. Her best friends were still all the girls from high school, all out doing and preparing themselves for their future. She loved University, and I was so glad she was studying what she was born to do-teach. Noddy had got her a job at the Wembley Golf Club on weekends and she loved it, she would work there until she finished University always getting plenty of extra shifts.

JD loved his chosen sports careers as well; school work really was on the back burner, he did not really know what he wanted to do at all. All I wanted was for him to be happy. He was such a good young man I knew he would always be his own person, full of faith in himself and integrity. He was passing all his exams well despite the lack of study. He loved nothing better than being home with mum dad and his sister. One Saturday, he borrowed the car for the afternoon to go to an athletics training session at the university athletic track. He had just finished training, and he was leaving the training venue when a car came speeding around the corner and ran into him. The guy got out of his car and threatened him, that if he did not say it was his fault, he would find out where he lived and would come round and fix up his family. One distressed son came home. Noddy took him straight down to the police station to report the incident. We never heard another word, as he was only 17; we had to pay a $700 excess. We still didn't have any spare cash for this excess, but we scrambled together what we could and had the car fixed, much to his relief.

On the Monday, following the event, he went to school and told a mate about it. By lunch time a kid came up to him in the playground and said to him JD if you sell this for me, you will have the money to pay your mum and dad for the damage to the car. My dear son looked at him and said, "if I ever took this money home, my mother would take me straight down to the local police station mate, so get lost." When he told me about the events of the day, I quizzed him to who the young man was. He would not tell me, this was what was happening in some schools in Perth in 1992.

In the October of his TEE year, JD decided he would like to have a gap year and go off to the East coast for a year as he wasn't ready to go to University, so we gave him our blessing. He decided to go on the 8th of December, giving me a few months to prepare myself for the final cutting of the apron strings. I have to say it got harder and harder the nearer the date came. Meanwhile, we continued with our busy lives and life was good. I kept up my prayer and meditation program and although I didn't go to church too often, I found I was having spiritual awakenings, and getting far more out of doing things my way, than I did out of going to Church.

Summer came and I would spend a lot of time down at Trigg beach in nature, with JA's dog, Silly a cross between a cocker spaniel and a beagle. I was happy

The TEE came and went and the day was fast approaching when JD would be leaving home. I took a few days off to prepare and recover from the separation. We put him on the plane to Adelaide, Noddy JA and I and oh the pain of watching him walk over that tarmac was just too much for me to bear. JA took it very badly too, Noddy, was stoic, although he had a tear in his eye and I knew he was hurting as much as I was. But he was there for JA and I. We waited till the plane was out of sight and went home. We were all very quiet, and hardly spoke all evening. Our family life had changed; my heart was broken and I thought the pain would never go. Slowly it did, after a week of emotional pain, I knew this was part of life; it was my job as a mother to get the children to the edge of the nest and then let them fly.

I am glad I experienced this pain of separation and it has helped me help others in a similar situation. Love does continue to grow regardless of the degree of separation. Many letters were exchanged over those twelve months and parcels of his favourite treats sent. He travelled through South Australia, NSW and finally Brisbane. He was very happy, which made me happy. A Mother's love for her children cannot be described; it is so powerful. A mother will move mountains for her children, as I am sure dads would too. Noddy's love for JA and JD was also deep; however, he showed it in a very different way. He adored them both, and would always be there for them through thick and thin.

JA, Noddy and I were working hard. Life, financially was improving, there were no more school fees, and JA finished her first year at University and had a three month break from study. We had lots of quality time on the beach together and life was good. The New Year came and we were planning that as soon as JA turned 20 we would head back to the North - although where to, we did not know. I would be on the search for a Director of Nursing Position and if it felt right I would go for it. The economy was just starting to pick up and Noddy made the decision he would walk away from the little business he was in. JA would have her best friends Mary and Peta come to live with her in our house, rent free and we would pick up all the bills for the electricity water etc.

Two Director of Nursing positions were advertised in the West Australian, one up in North Queensland in an Aboriginal community and one in Roebourne and Wickham in the North of Western Australia, in the Pilbara. I applied for both and got shortlisted for both. Everyone told me, 'do not go to Roebourne, it is a really bad town', I said 'no I will go', as that was the one my heart was telling me to take, if I got offered it.

Roebourne, at the time, was a very broken town and there were lots and lots of problems. The Royal Commission for Aboriginal Deaths in Custody had not long before been completed and it was in Roebourne where the catalyst for the Royal Commission started. A young Aboriginal boy died in custody in Roebourne and riots broke out and relationships between indigenous and western agencies in the town broke down; so no matter what people said to me I was determined to go if I was offered the position.

I applied and had an excellent interview with both organizations and I was offered both jobs. Decision making time, it was really pretty easy - the Roebourne /Wickham position was the best, it met all our needs. Roebourne was a town mainly made up of indigenous people. Wickham was about 18kms away from Roebourne - a closed mining town operated by Robe River Iron Ore. Karratha was 50 kilometres from Wickham and there were approximately twelve schools in the Shire of Roebourne and it would mean that if JA wanted to come up to teach when she finished her degree, the opportunity for her to get a position would be high, and she could come and live with us. Having Mum and Dad there to support her on her first role would be invaluable for her. The job opportunities for Noddy too were high. The decision was made; I accepted the position and the whole family were very happy.

I put in my resignation the next day I was at work and when I informed my colleagues and friends they knew it was what I had been working towards since Wanneroo hospital days and they too were happy for us. It is what I had dreamed of, since I was a ten year old girl - being a country Matron. Of course there were the usual knockers of us going to Roebourne, but we took no notice. The ED staff organised a beautiful night out in Northbridge for me and presented me with a lovely book of poetry, which was fast to become my favourite. They all knew how I loved poetry.

ROEBOURNE AND WICKHAM

The next few weeks were caught up saying goodbye to all our friends and colleagues, packing up all we needed to start our new adventure on life's amazing journey. We started to organise our personal effects ready for transfer. The conditions of the role were very good; we had a three bedroom air-conditioned house which was fully furnished and I also had a government car provided as part of the package, which enabled us to leave our home furnished and ready for the girls to move in. We left for Wickham and Roebourne the day after JA's 20th birthday. The family was excited, JA had her freedom, JD his independence, enjoying his adventures on the East Coast and we were going back to our beloved North. We planned to be in Wickham a few days before my start date to enable us a good rest prior to starting my new career move.

We left Perth on the 14th of April with our car packed to the roof which also included, Silly, JA's dog. We had lunch in Geraldton and headed for Monkey Mia. It was a very hot day and we would have got around 250 kms up the road from Geraldton when all this smoke just started to pour out of the engine. What a disaster that turned out to be. We had to get towed to the nearest roadhouse and then an RAC truck had to come and pick us up and takes us out to the nearest mechanic which was in Denham - at some cost I might add. The bad news really hit us the next day, after the mechanic found the problem; we had cracked the head of the motor. It would cost around $600 to repair and it could take a couple of days as he had to get a new head in from Perth. We booked into a very nice cabin in the Denham caravan park, close to the beach and local community. Luckily, the new head arrived on the early morning truck the next day. The mechanic worked on it immediately, and had us back on the road.

We drove and drove until we finally arrived at a little roadhouse north of Carnarvon called Minalya, late that evening. We were exhausted when we arrived at Minalya and decided we would have to sleep in the car as there was no accommodation available and the heat had knocked us around, we were certainly not used to it and had forgotten how hot it was in summer above the 26th parallel. We tossed and turned, but were refreshed enough by 0500 to head for the next stop, Wickham, a distance of almost 600kms. We arrived at 3pm totally wrecked. The heat was extreme and the travelling conditions in that heat had been intensely uncomfortable.

How happy we were when we finally arrived at Wickham Hospital! I went in to pick up the keys to the house which was in Poinciana Road No 13. The acting senior nurse met us there and took us inside this well laid out little home. One problem – there was no air-conditioning. It was broken and as it was a Sunday afternoon there was no one available to come in and look at it. With deep sighs, we thanked her and said, "please do not worry we will be okay, and I will see you in the morning."

We were so tired that we could have slept anywhere even in a furnace; we were lucky and grateful, to have a comfortable bed and the ceiling fans to keep us a little cooler. After she left, we hurriedly unpacked the essentials from the car, had a bite to eat, and headed for a cold shower and bed.We slept like the proverbial and woke very refreshed the next morning.

I arrived at Wickham hospital ready for work at 8am and was met by the acting senior nurse who proceeded to hand over to me reluctantly. She went on to tell me she had applied for the DON's position and that she had expected to get it. She explained how she had been there since the Hospital had opened in the early 70's. I was also informed there was another applicant, a twenty six year old nurse who had her degree in nursing management. I was introduced to the staff on duty, all of whom appeared very friendly and welcoming and commenced my orientation and then went over to Roebourne Hospital. When we arrived there I was shocked as the hospital front doors were locked. Apparently, it was their policy and I was told that Roebourne was unsafe by the acting senior nurse.

Once we were let in, I was introduced to all the staff, who were also very friendly and welcoming . I spoke to them about the front door being locked. They were quite reluctant to speak in front of a second person. I thought I would be very diplomatic and address the issue as soon as I could, once I was alone with the staff since the energy between the two places was so different.

The Roebourne Hospital 'energy' was great and I immediately knew I would rather have my main office there. I was informed that the staff at Wickham would not work in Roebourne. Wickham was for the European population. It was a closed town solely for the mining community. The hospital had ten beds and the very occasional admission; in fact, on many days, there were nil admissions. It had an out patients Department, a resus room, a labour ward and a theatre that had been closed for some years, and there was also a resident general practitioner who had his consulting rooms within the hospital. All the theatre equipment was still there in the hospital. I must add that the distance between these two towns' was 12.9 kilometres.

Roebourne had ten beds and unlike Wickham had no resident Medical Officer in the hospital. The medical service was run through Port Hedland Regional Hospital Emergency Dept. A doctor would come down on a Monday morning and return to Port Hedland Thursday lunch time. On the three days that Roebourne had no doctor, the nurses would liaise through Port Hedland's Hospital Emergency Dept. doctors, for cases they needed medical advice about. The Wickham Doctor, at the time would not come to Roebourne and neither would any of the doctors from Karratha. There was an Aboriginal medical service in the town that at times had a doctor and at times did not have one. There were also Community Health Centres in both towns. The bed average in Roebourne was 4-5 self-caring patients. It too had an Outpatient Dept, separated by a sitting room and a corridor, with a gorgeous little indoor garden, from the main part of the hospital and the emergency room for resuscitations. Each hospital had a 2x2x2 nurse roster and complemented by cleaning and kitchen staff, with two orderlies. They came under the auspices of this very beautiful and efficient administrative assistant Vicki; she was a great person to work with and made me very welcome.

Down the road, 33 kms from Roebourne and 43 kms from Wickham, was a 42 bed Hospital at Karratha called Nickol Bay Hospital, again with a very low bed average. For white people only, so the Aboriginals used to say, 'nay the twain shall meet'. It just reminded me of the Gove days in 1972; the duplication of services was just so evident. Any patient who presented that required more than primary care was transferred out to Port Hedland or transferred to Perth. The hand over took two days, and then I was on my own.The senior nurse who was acting in the DON's role, did not want to have anything to do with senior management again.

The Pilbara Health Region was divided into the East Pilbara(The Port Hedland region and encompassed Port Hedland Hospital and Community Health and the Health centres, Newman, Marble Bar, Nulligine and Jigalong were by this time under the management of an Aboriginal Medical Service) and the West Pilbara –The Roebourne Shire, which also encompassed the towns of Tom Price and Parabadoo. There was a Regional Director in charge of the whole Pilbara and a District Manager for both the regions. Each region had its own Human Resource and Finance managers There was also a regional staff development office for all the hospitals. Community Health was a separate entity and all hospitals had a Director of Nursing, with the Director of Nursing of the Regional Hospital being the advisory DON for the other DONs to liaise with if there was a problem. There was a senior medical officer in Port Hedland Regional Hospital to deal with any medical administrative issues. Also the HDWA had a Chief Nursing Officer, a truly wonderful woman, who became a support person for me over a five year period.

From the Wednesday I took over. I began being on-call 24 hrs a day, 7 days a week; this was part of the DON's role. No country DON was paid to be on-call; however, it was part of our job description. We would have the hours back at time and a half, and double time for weekends, if we were called in. There was no funding to have a have an on call roster to enable the DON to have an evening, night, or weekend off. Whilst on call, she had a big heavy box mobile phone.

A week into my role, I had a visit from the District Health Manager, a man around forty years of age who had been in the role for some time. He dropped in on his way back from Port Hedland and invited me into the district executive meeting at Nickol Bay Hospital to be held on Friday, to meet all the other senior staff. That week, I finally had the opportunity to meet the GP in Wickham, a tall slender man in his early sixties who appeared very friendly. It took me a few days to meet all the staff and arrange to have staff meetings in both hospitals for the following week. From what I was hearing and seeing , there was a real disparity between the two hospitals; one was very quiet and the other had a much higher level of activity.

I connected very quickly with a senior clinical nurse who was the staff development nurse at both Wickham and Roebourne. Her name was Seleana Powell. She was young, intelligent and a very experienced clinical nurse especially in mental health, as that was her speciality. She was a very warm and friendly woman who made me feel very welcome. She recognised the need for changes in nursing practises; she too had only been there for a few months prior to my arrival and really had her finger on the pulse. Seleana saw things with new eyes, and there were also some younger nurses who were not long out of university and found working in the environment challenging at times because the hospitals were not up to date with the nursing practise from the 1970's Model of Care. The three senior nurses had been there for years and years and were set in their ways. I knew immediately I had to take a 'slowly slowly' approach if I was to make a difference and to try and involve them in any change processes. It was very early days.

The other problem was that the nurse who did not get the DON's position was very popular with the old staff, so I knew that I had to overcome some hurdles there as well. I realised very early that I would always be compared to her and the old DON, who was a real party woman. Here was I, a nurse from the city, forty four years old, a total stranger, a non-drinker and a non-smoker. I also had a philosophy that as a Director of Nursing one could not to become personal friends with any of the staff members to ensure that there would never be an opportunity to be accused of favouritism, - in case, you had to address an issue with a staff member, one could do so without damaging relationships. I guess, this to me was a lesson, I had learnt along the way from all my mentors in senior management - treat all equally and with dignity and respect, no favouritism, as this leads to nepotism, one of the major issues in workplaces today.

I also remembered reading a book when our children were very little, called, "*Happy Children*" by Steve Biddulp. In that book, there was a paragraph that has always stayed with me, that there were three ways of raising children.

1 An Authoritarian Approach
2. A Freedom with Order Approach
3. A Lassez-faire Approach.

I loved, "The Freedom with Order" model and as a senior nurse, ensured that this was my management style. As nurses we had to be accountable for what we did, and had in place legislative frameworks within which we practised. This was how I, as a Director of Nursing chose my management style, which was very different to my predecessor's.

Meanwhile, Noddy was doing a great job setting up our home and unpacking all our personal effects that had arrived from Perth and exploring the local surrounds. We had met our next door neighbours, a delightful Yugoslavian family, Dragon and Milena Bulatovic and their two beautiful children Tomo and Tanya, aged 5 and 3, such gorgeous little kids. Noddy had been in to Karratha and described a metropolis to me; he had also discovered Port Samson was 10 kms away, and he would take Silly (our dog) down every morning for a swim. The weather was still very warm, around 40 degrees every day, we had to have the air-conditioning cranked up. He took a good break before he started to look for work as he needed a rest after working the business, doing long hours for 5 years. JA was settled at home with the girls and all enjoying their new found living conditions and freedom. JD was happy and had moved up to Brisbane and was starting to be involved in his favourite sport there. It was hard to believe he had been gone for 5 months, only 7 to go until he returned home

I went into Karratha for the first time on the Friday, and found Nickol Bay Hospital(NBH). I was shown around by the district health manager. He introduced me to everyone we met along the way. NBH was very well appointed and laid out; it had two theatres and two well-equipped labour wards. The Outpatients Emergency Dept. was very modern; it was great to see they had the resus room as part of the ED not like Roebourne and Wickham where they were some distance apart. Roebourne for example had two big doorways and a big vacant passage way, to navigate, and Wickham's Resus Room was at one end of the hospital. Nickol Bay Hospital was like a private hospital, and there seemed to be a lot of staff. I eventually got to meet the rest of the management team, including the DON of Nickol Bay Hospital. He had been there for six years and was very well established. He was very popular and well respected by all the staff. He too put patients first and was very clinically orientated which I respected. It was how DONs were back then.

Once the meeting started, the district manager informed us that we were 2 million dollars in the red and that there was no further money coming until the end of the financial year. All spending had to be stopped and no overtime to be worked at all. This was a side as a senior nurse, I had never been involved in before, so I had to get up to speed very quickly. Luckily, I was pretty good with figures and had a fair understanding of what the economic situation was like within health. Wanneroo Hospital had incurred this in 1987 right through until I left in 1990. The language, however, was the same, Cut Cut Cut. Where to cut, was the question I was asking in my heart and mind. I would not compromise on patient or staff care and neither would the DON at NBH. At RDH and WDH we only worked a 2x2x2 roster so there were no margins there, the Directors of Nursing did all the on call and overtime. I decided I would need to go back and call staff meetings to learn their thoughts and review rostering practises. It was rather a hard time, as the Management side, both in the District and the Region seemed to be growing all the time, with cars and all the other perks. Nurses could see this, and it did not help the situation, in regards to hospital nurses taking any notice of budget issues. They also saw their community health counterparts spending big and with no apparent outcomes and they were always going on study days and professional development sessions. Hospital nurses were not afforded the same equality. I was glad to leave and go back to Roebourne and Wickham once the meeting closed, to ponder and plan as to how we could address the directive.

The first week finished at 16.30 hours on a Friday afternoon and at last I had two days off. That evening, Noddy and I went down to Point Samson for a fish and chip dinner and home to bed for an early night. I was quite exhausted but very happy to be there, although I could foresee many challenges ahead. I was off Saturday and looking forward to a relaxing weekend, helping Noddy finishing off the unpacking and reviewing our garden, deciding what to do to make the house into a home for the next few years. We went to the beach the next day, for a nice long walk and swim.

Not long after we had got home the phone rang, a nurse from Roebourne was on the phone and was very upset. A woman had knocked at the front door of the hospital and when she opened it, there was a very distressed naked Aboriginal woman who stated, 'she was being chased by a man with an axe'. I advised her to keep the woman safe, make sure all doors to the hospital were locked, and ring and ask the police to check out this perpetrator. I said I would be over in 15 minutes, and we would work out a plan for this poor lady's safety. On arrival at the hospital, I met the lady, and was relieved to see that she was warm and safe. I found out from this lovely nurse, Pat, that there were no safe house or women's refuge in Roebourne, but there was one in Karratha. I rang the refuge in Karratha and fortunately they had a spare bed, so I asked Pat to take her in as she was very experienced in dealing with victims of domestic violence in a former life. She was very kind and the woman trusted her. I stayed to cover the hospital needs with the second nurse, and I learnt a lot from listening to the nurse during this time Pat was away. I was beginning to see the issues that were so out in the open in Roebourne.

On Pat's return, I spoke with her and said that I would arrange a meeting with her in the next week or two, to see what support we could give women in this situation. The rest of the weekend was very restful, and I was able to curl up with a good book and be spoilt by my dear husband.

Monday morning arrived, and I went to work at seven am to meet all the night staff and for the hand over. As per usual there were no inpatients and no outpatient presentations overnight at Wickham Hospital. I did not know what the nursing staff did in their ten hours for which they were being well paid. I decided I would spend the first couple of hours at Wickham doing all I needed to do at that Hospital and get to know all the staff. I had already set a plan to empty out the theatre and send all the extremely good and expensive instrumentation and equipment like the Boyles' Apparatus (anaesthetic machine) and the theatre table up to Port Hedland. The Wickham GP got to hear about my plan of emptying the theatre and asked me to put it on hold as there was a new surgeon coming to Port Hedland, and that he was considering opening the theatre, and he would do the anaesthetics. I agreed to wait and several weeks later, he invited the surgeon down. The old staff were very supportive of this move to reopen the operating theatre.

They asked me to come to a meeting one Saturday morning which I did. The two men were very friendly and I think that they thought I would agree to their wishes. After presenting me with their plan, I firmly said I will not be doing this, due to the fact that Nickol Bay Hospital had two very well-equipped theatres, and trained theatre staff that were on call 24 hours per day, seven days a week, and 52 weeks a year. Wickham's theatre had been closed for 4 years and we did not have the skill set or the staff to open up the theatre, and we did not have the budget to run the theatre. I said if the surgeon wanted to operate he would need to speak to the powers to be, and do so in Nickol Bay Hospital. Immediately the tone of their voices changed and they both became quite aggressive in trying to convince me to reopen Wickham Hospital's operating theatre. I took very accurate notes of this meeting, much to their disapproval. After ten minutes of passive aggression from these two males, I closed the meeting and excused myself from their company. Copies of these minutes were sent to the regional director, the senior medical officer and the district health manger. I have to say I was not very popular with the GP after that, and the few staff who wanted the theatre to reopen.

Within those first few weeks, I could see what was happening with rostering. It seemed that permanent staff were requesting and having days off together, and casual staff would be brought into cover. This was creating a huge cost to the staff budget. I sat down at staff meetings and explained rostering systems and I tried to do this with a one-on-one meeting with the senior staff member whose responsibilities included rostering, but she would not listen to my logic. She really believed that staff had the right to have days off with their friends and it was okay to fill their place with casual staff. I had to in the end, to show her the job description of all the nursing positions of the staff and her specific JDF and point out the responsibilities for human and material resource management. She still argued with me and continued to roster as she had always done, which resulted in the end, in me taking over the rostering myself and introducing a self-rostering model, after seeing how well this model worked in SCGH. It was fair and equitable and again, I made several nursing staff very unhappy. They were mostly the old timers.

The next big challenge arrived when a package appeared on my desk from the regional director. A community member had written a letter of complaint to the Parliamentary Ombudsman of Western Australia regarding the way she was treated by three members of the nursing staff at Wickham Hospital. The incident happened well before I had started and oh boy what a challenge, that turned out to be. Reading the documentation forwarded to me and being directed to address all the issues raised, I had to do it very thoroughly and realised it was not going to be an easy task. The staff members involved were staff that had been there a very long time. I had never had to do anything like this before. I prayed for the wisdom and courage to do the right thing. Before I spoke to the staff I reviewed all the medical records and there was absolutely no supporting nursing documentation of what had been done for this patient, just very brief sentences, like 'slept well' or 'good evening, no complaints', no care plan, no admission forms and nothing that told me what had occurred. After reading the very detailed complaint written by the patient, I met with her, and then I met individually with all the staff involved.

This turned out very badly and it was very difficult to manage. The staff took it very personally and involved the nursing union. I also sought help from the ANF. It was very hard, however all the details or interviews and conversations were carefully and accurately documented. I had to put the staff members on a three month performance management plan. This made me even more unpopular. Prior to any documents being forwarded to those concerned, I had them all checked out with the regional director and the human resource manager at the head office. I know I was fair. It was a tough time for all concerned and I was very pleased once I had completed the investigation and forwarded all the correspondence to the regional director to forward on to the Ombudsman. I know the nurses never forgave me for following this through.

Apart from these challenges, life was good; the staff at Roebourne were fabulous, keen, compassionate and managed everything that presented. I had one challenge, which had not been addressed before my arrival. The challenge was not with the staff, but with a poor old Aboriginal man who had been very badly damaged mentally through alcohol, and was a permanent patient who had caused great concern and stress to the nursing staff for several years. One night, one of the nurses was up in the outpatients department reviewing a patient, the second nurse was on the floor on her own, this old man was wandering in and out of the children's ward and when the nurse redirected him back to his room, he put his arm around her neck. She managed to loosen his arm and ran for help to the other nurse. I made a commitment to them that I would have this man transferred to a psychogeriatric centre in Perth for assessment and management.

These events were not uncommon; nobody listened to the nurses despite the nurses having to work every single day and night with this poor patient; and all the powers that be did nothing about the safety issues of the patient, the other patients or the staff working there. This would never be tolerated in any other workplace. I tried the district management and the regional management for help in having this old man transferred to a more appropriate setting. No help was forth coming, no-one wanted to know about the problem. I was told you just have to keep him in Roebourne – 'you just have to keep him there'. A 2x2x2 roster cannot cater for the high needs of a patient with the ongoing medical diagnoses this poor gentleman had. I started to canvas help from wherever I could, the nursing home in Port Hedland, the senior medical officer at Port Hedland and the answer was always no. He had to stay in Roebourne. I rang geriatrician after geriatrician in Perth until one day, a week after the event, I spoke to one who actually listened to me and said you cannot keep this patient up there, he needs care in a special unit. He accepted him into a Psychogeriatric unit at RPH and we sent him to Perth.

As a result of the above incident, we emptied and moved the storeroom which was a big room and we made a treatment assessment room right opposite the resus room. This made the place so much safer and easier for the staff. I moved my office to a spare office between the outpatients and ward to give the nurses a little tea room and quiet place for their breaks. Anything to make life easier for them.

Professional development was compulsory for senior management at that time. An Occupational Health and Safety act had been passed in the West Australian Legislative assembly and as part of our role we were responsible for ensuring all acts were adhered to. The HDWA was moving to a totally decentralised system throughout Western Australia - resource management, financial management and human resource management.

As an outcome, management training had to be increased to deal with the changes which were coming into effect in the new financial year. The other area of training the DONs had to be involved with was disaster management and be a representative on the local emergency management committee.

I really enjoyed the disaster management training which was held over five days. Representatives came to teach from Mt Macedon in Victoria. It was interesting to learn how far the events of Cyclone Tracy created a whole new industry in Australia, a necessary one. Over a year long period there where many trips away to Port Hedland for all the training for the implementation of the coming changes and we had several week long training sessions up in Cable Beach in Broome. The HDWA had brought out experts from the National Health Service (NHS) from the UK to train us in the new model of health care. The Funder Owner Purchaser Provider Model. Broome was the most central location for both the Pilbara and the Kimberley Health Services that was being based in Derby.

I managed to be able to save some money for Roebourne and Wickham Hospitals by introducing the new rostering programme. I was asked to transfer the money to assist the community health budget, which had really blown out. I said no, as I desperately saw the need to re-invest the money into the staff development programs for the nurses at RDH and WDH. A number of nurses at Wickham, recognised the need to upgrade their Professional practices, especially in terms of their documentation and adherence to current standards of practice and became involved in the change process by taking responsibility as per their JDF's. This I have to say made my job a lot easier and I was grateful for their support. Seleana was a great support and met the educational needs to assist the staff in growing to become the nurses they were born to be and who I would be happy to have them look after my family or myself if ever the need arose. The staff at Roebourne were very supportive of the new way of doing things. There was no problem with keeping the front door open except at night. Patients were very well looked after and faith was being restored in the hospital by the community.

I had done a lot of networking with the Aboriginal Medical Service and saw them as being very proactive in preventative health. We even managed by working together to get funding for a "Safe House in Roebourne". I met the senior community nurse, who could not understand why I was not working for Community Health, for as she said to me on our first meeting . To be a community nurse you have to be "the cream of nursing". This of course did not resonate with me at all, so we agreed to disagree on this statement.

She asked me to come up with a suggestion for some non-recurrent funding for child health in the community. I suggested it would be ideal if we could set up a dreaming/meditation programme to deal with the stress levels of some of the children who had to return to their home environments after school, which were at times, not conducive to ensuring children were cared for and nourished physically emotionally mentally and spiritually. Especially after witnessing the 'John Pat era' where the children were exposed to things no children should ever be exposed to. This went over like a lead balloon and I never heard another mention of the subject. I think it died a very sudden death, too hard, or to out of the box was the question I would often ask myself?

One of the things I started to discuss with Seleana and Pat after my first weekend experience on call over the following weeks was having a portfolio's for nursing staff, as a way forward for them to be empowered and become the 'go to person' for a specific speciality like Domestic Violence , Asthma Management etc. Over the months, these roles were developed and embraced by the staff. I was really enjoying the role of being able to develop what was to become a great team, thanks to a great effort by forward thinking nurses.

At the request from a family who's loved one wanted to be able to pass on at home, we managed to fulfil that need. The staff were wonderful and we met their needs through a joint effort of all nursing staff, hospital, community health and management. It was the first hospice type nursing in Roebourne Shire. The family were so grateful.

During this period of getting to know the people of Roebourne I met some amazing old Aboriginal elders. One of my favourites was an old man called Yilbie Warrie, a senior Yindjibarndi law man. He was a leader and such a divine old man, for whom I had so much respect. He was short in statue but he was a giant of heart and spirit; he was also very gentle and articulate. I was honoured to be present at meetings in Roebourne's old stone Hospital on many occasions that Yilbie was present, (as I had turned this into a community service meeting house, where all community leaders would come together). It was at one of these community meetings that the birth of the Roebourne Safe House was born with the Aboriginal medical service and women Elders bringing the safe house to life by obtaining funding for the building and staffing of the centre. His death brought great sadness to the Pilbara and the Roebourne Community and I was able to be present at his memorial and funeral.

Noddy and I took the opportunity to go back to Marble Bar to celebrate the Centenary Celebrations. During the drive in from the turn off from the Northwest Coastal Highway, I was taken straight back to January 1954 and experienced many flash backs and a butterflies in my abdomen. I have often wondered if this was something that the meaning of 'roots' meant. I was six years old when we arrived in this corner of the universe to live. Marble Bar's main street was still the same and the Iron Clad Hotel was still there, just the same as I remembered it, back in 1954. The little Church on the hill was in good condition, I remembered the old clinic and we were simply overwhelmed by the very historical old stone buildings that were in the town. I took Noddy down to the Coogan River and we walked over the jasper rocks, which were stunningly beautiful. Marble Bar was packed and a big party was in full swing. The Iron Clad hotel and the Caravan Park had been booked out well in advance, so we camped in the overflow campsite on the school oval. I was so happy to take my darling husband to a town that was for me was a very happy place to live and grow during this period of my childhood. We brought a book written for the centenary called, "Back to the Bar". My dad, John Rebbechi and my uncle Richard Rebbechi were recorded therein.

I was fortunate to witness the first showing of a powerful two-part film, "The Exile in the Kingdom". It would be that movie that had the most profound effect on me for the rest of my life. It was co-written by Roger Solomon, a Pilbara Aboriginal Man from Roebourne. He was a distinguished leader, lawman and Indigenous Heritage Officer, and contributed enormously to the protection of cultural heritage in the Pilbara. The nurses and I were deeply honoured to have nursed him and ensured a graceful ending to this wonderful human being's life during his last days at Roebourne Hospital. His passing had a huge impact on the community of Roebourne and the Pilbara and we all went to his funeral. It was this film that prompted me to take a huge stand for Roebourne Hospital when the Government was considering closing it and keeping Wickham as the District Hospital. The Government/HDWA was at that time rationalising Health Services throughout the State.

In fact, I wrote the following letter:

Dear Sir,

Following our discussions regarding the restructuring of the Health sites of Roebourne and Wickham, I would like to express my grave concerns regarding the possibility of making Wickham Hospital the Acute Care facility for in patients and the 24 hour emergency Care Centre and not the reverse.

My concerns include:
Social Justice Issues

1. *The people of Roebourne as history has shown have been dispossessed since the first settlers arrived here in 1861.This was recently well demonstrated in the documentary 'Exile and the Kingdom',and I see by taking the 24 hour health service cover away from this community is again dispossessing them of an essential service.*
2. *The Roebourne Community in terms of health issues is a far sicker community with many complex, chronic disease issues, than the Wickham community. Within the Roebourne community, the effects of alcohol, are continually being manifested, as they have been for years as in European communities, in a variety of ways. Examples include heart disease, respiratory disease, diabetes, kidney disease and domestic violence, from the very young to the very old to name just a few. In Roebourne, nothing is unseen, it is all out in the open, nothing is hidden behind doors, as in a white western society/culture*
3. *The Roebourne Community is far less affluent than the Wickham community and this, in itself has major ramifications.eg-transport. It further adds to the Western Population perception of the Roebourne community as a 'welfare community', whereas in actual fact it is not. People, both Aboriginal and Europeans, are very proud to be "Roebourne People "and the community, although not affluent in monetary terms is affluent in many other ways.*
4. *The community in Roebourne are not as educated as the people in the Wickham's western community and as a result are unable to be as assertive as far as their health needs are concerned. The people of Wickham have choices, as to where they go for their health care, and I know a number who choose to go to Karratha to have their health needs*

met. The Roebourne community appears to not have that choice.

5. *The statistics show that over the years, the acute emergencies that arise occur mainly in Roebourne. The amount of open domestic violence and non-compliance in health matters, occurring in the community requiring nursing and medical intervention, is far greater in Roebourne than at Wickham. Roebourne would only need to have a death, in an emergency situation with no 24 hour emergency care available on site to create a situation where once again a great injustice to this community could occur.*
6. *The trust and respect that has developed over 125 years for European nursing and medical staff, will be severely compromised within the community, and at a time of reconciliation, as called upon by the Prime Minister of Australia, Paul Keating, I urge us to be leaders in this field. I am putting a lot of physical and mental energy into building bridges with other service units and they are coming together to work on improving outcomes and support for both peoples and organisations to all we serve. We know that by not having the only 24 hours service available within the community of Roebourne that these bridges will again be broken and may never be rebuilt.*
7. *I believe, and it must be acknowledged that accessibility to Roebourne hospital from the great Northern Highway and the surrounding stations is an important issue; especially in terms of emergency care and in the event of a disaster - for example a roll over on the highway. It should also be acknowledged of the Roebourne Hospital's, close proximity to the Roebourne airport, for RFDS evacuations*
8. *Thousands and thousands of dollars, have been spent on upgrading the Roebourne District Hospital and I believe this would be a total waste of taxpayers' money if this option is taken*
9. *I acknowledge that decisions have to be made however, as*

community leaders; we need to be advocates for people who are not as fortunate as we are.

I appreciate the opportunity in expressing my concerns and firmly believe if we are unable to keep Roebourne Hospital as the acute care and emergency centre that we need to consider the other alternative and not close one site but keep them both open 24 hours per day. This I know is not economically feasible.

Yours faithfully
Peter Rebbechi
Director of Nursing Services
Roebourne /Wickham Health Sites

Unbeknown to me, it was fairly common knowledge amongst the communities that proposed changes were on the cards, and had been talked about for some time. (Oh my goodness, what the next few years brought was unimaginable.) I had a visit from a senior member sent from the regional office, a few weeks after I wrote this letter, and was told I was not to be involved in community affairs or social justice issues.' I took no notice. How could I not, the problems in Roebourne and the health of the population were all a direct result of social issues and ultimately social justices issues. Over the next year or too, there were meetings in both communities, neither wanting their "hospital closed ".Rumours innuendo's and lies " were spread about me being the instigator of the closure of Roebourne or Wickham Hospital by a very small cohort of practitioners and life became very very difficult for me creating often very stressful situations. Of course layers and layers of another mask went on and I buried it all down at cellular level again; however what I did do was record everything in diaries to help cope with the toxicity of humanity that was being vented towards me by the very small minority of professionals in the health care units.

A few senior members of the Health Dept of WA came up from

Perth for some big angry and ugly community meetings during the next 12 months, it all died down at the end of the year; the HDWA had to change tact and spend a lot of money doing a needs analysis and develop a health care plan for the Shire of Roebourne. I have to say it took 12 years for anything to happen (Wickham Hospital closed its' doors as an acute hospital in 2005/2006) and Roebourne remained as the acute care facility.

One of the things I loved about Roebourne was the old stone buildings and the history; I could foresee we could develop the old stone hospital in the future into a wonderful medical museum, something I did discuss with one of the Health Minister at the time of his yearly visit to The West Pilbara.

Times changed a lot in terms of medical management. The HDWA had to employ a full time doctor for Roebourne as a visiting medical officer. When a practitioner rang to find out about the position and he introduced himself to me. I was very happy as he very nice on the phone. However, once I informed the staff, that this man was going to be given a private contract (with all the sweeteners like peppercorn rent and incentives like a free nurse), a couple of nurses who had worked with him in the past and had very negative experiences came to see me individually. These nurses told me about a number of incidents that had occurred. Alarm bells rang in my mind and I had to refer my concerns and seek advice from The senior nursing officer of the HDWA. Meetings were held with senior officials of the Health Service and the senior medical practitioner, from the Regional Hospital and the nursing staff who knew the practitioner, to ensure the safety of the nursing staff with written assurances. I wanted to ensure that if there were workplace bullying and harassments occurring, that the nursing staff would have recourse to address the situation if they arose in the future.

The Government just had to have a doctor in Roebourne and as he was the only applicant, he was employed .The Practitioner rang me before he accepted and as I had to go to Perth on business, we arranged to meet for lunch. When we met, he was absolutely charming. I did not see the character of the person who so upset nurses in the past; so I accepted his presence with no judgements and would wait to see what would unfold.

Dear Seleana had the opportunity of furthering her career as a forensic nurse in the Roebourne Prison. Although I did not want her to leave our service, I was very happy for her, and there was also one big advantage, we could then mix socially and this then led to a very life-long deep friendship with Sel and Charlie, who I would have to describe as the most loving fun filled, generous, honest people whom we have ever known. We love them very deeply; Sel was a person who saw goodness in all. I have never heard her say a bad word or tell shady jokes. She was perfect as you could get as a person and friend, she was a real lady.

Charlie was an entrepreneur in his own right, who would do deals on a handshake and would help out any human being or animal. Charlie, well Charlie was the world's greatest story teller, a man who had a very colourful vocabulary and told jokes that were very bold. He used to say to me Peter close your ears when he told one that was shady and not fit for my ears and when he swore, would turn to me straight away and apologise. He had the biggest heart of any man I had ever met beside my dearly beloved Noddy.

Roebourne hospital was very fortunate we had another nurse join our beautiful staff at Roebourne, a young woman by the name of Jane Best. She had had a previous role as a staff development nurse at the Hollywood Hospital and stepped up to fill Sel's shoes when she left. The nurse who worked in the outpatients for years and years, who was so loved by the indigenous community, moved on to the ward, rather than work under the new medical model and another nurse started to work there. She was a university graduate, a lovely woman, who was very caring and compassionate.

The doctor once appointed expressed his dislike for university trained nurses and within weeks I would have the nurse who was assigned to his practice, presenting to my office in tears, and a medical officer complaining that university nurses were hopeless. Keeping the peace was difficult. Also, all of a sudden the bed numbers shot up from 4-5 admissions to having no empty beds. The activity had increased by over 75 % and he started to admit patients to Wickham Hospital with very minor problems. Questions were being asked, as to why our bed numbers were up by 75% to near 100% occupancy, in both hospitals. People would be admitted at 1600 hrs and discharged at 0800 next day, with absolutely no treatment given. The medical practice model would be to do two rounds a day and ensure he got paid for the two rounds per day. Of course, I had to question this as I had never seen this practise before, so I handed it all over to the senior health manager, as I saw it as a medical issue, not a nursing one. This made me very unpopular and this practitioner then started a very covert campaign to cause as much trouble for me, as he could. He was beginning to make things very uncomfortable for the nursing staff, playing one hospital off against the other, and teaming up with another medical practitioner in Wickham who didn't like me anyway, especially after I refused to open the operating theatre.

The Health Department by this time was introducing a new model of service delivery known as the Funder Owner Purchaser Provider Model. They were having a District DON for Roebourne Wickham Karratha and the five Community Health Centres. Dark clouds developed through this change process and the knives really sharpened and everywhere I turned there was someone waiting to stab me in the back. The community nurses were neither having nor being accountable to a hospital based director of nursing and fought tooth and nail to over throw the District DON model for the Pilbara. I was told outright that I would not be accepted by them and that I knew absolutely nothing about community nursing and if I did apply and get the role, life would be made very difficult .

I kept smiling all the way through this insidious campaign, of course hurting inside, I loved my diary and wrote up the day's happenings every night trying to get them out of my system. My experience in the past taught me the importance of documenting the day's activities. I also sought help and assistance from senior management both at local and state for help, dealing with all the negativity generated; again nothing was done. Fortunately, the senior nursing officer at the HDWA would be my support person on the phone verbally. There was the acting DON up in Port Hedland; he was brilliant and supported me to the hilt. One of the staff from Wickham even called a meeting of the nursing staff in at Nickol Bay Hospital to warn the staff about me, the DON of that hospital was very professional through all this and advised the staff in there to not get involved in the internal nursing politics that were being played out in Wickham and Roebourne Hospital. Even the doctors spoke at the Nickol Bay Hospital Medical Advisory Board, that I would be a very bad choice for the DDON position. The toxicity was so bad that one of the perpetrators and one of the orderlies took their concerns to a council meeting one night. (I still have the minutes in my paper work.) All this of course, happened behind my back; however I was informed of some of the skullduggery by a senior health official. I kept my head high as I believed I had never done anything wrong by anybody, I ran a very professional organisation and patients care and safety came first and I supported the staff even the ones ,who I knew were my adversaries and remained fair and equitable in all matters relating to issues that did arise

I did have a very good team of professional nurses, however in these situations it made it very hard for them to remain absolutely free from the negativity that permeated through the organisation. The group that were responsible consisted of a gang of six personnel.

One morning, I was called over to Roebourne at 9am; they had had a sudden and unexpected death in the resus room. When I arrived the staff were very distraught. I listened to the course of events, and debriefed them over a cup of tea and asked them to write up their documentation as a matter of urgency. What I had been told disturbed me very much, I rang the police as I knew it would be a coroner's case and the chief nursing officer for second opinion and was advised on two courses of action I could take: contact the Medical Board or, go and see the senior medical officer in Port Hedland. I chose the second option.

Once statements to the police were made, the staff felt so relieved, and we did the necessary processes to prepare the body for the coroner, the staff were then ready to move on with their day. My heart bled for them; however, they knew I was there for them. I could not go up and see the doctor at that stage, as I needed to come to terms with what to do, before I could speak to him as I knew the reaction he would have against the nurses involved and I just could not face it, until I had discussed the situation with the Senior Medical Officer in Port Hedland. I spoke to the District Manager and informed him of the situation and said I would go to Port Hedland the next morning.

The job was getting harder and I was between a rock and a hard place, however I was strong and knew that my inner strength and fortitude would suffice, whatever was being thrown at me. Little did I know that the officials of the HDWA would not stand by their words of support made both in writing and verbally to the nurses prior to this practitioner starting.

I met with a senior medical officer and shared with him the documentation, regarding the events of the day before and asked him to come down to speak with the nurses who experienced and witnessed the medical management of this case, and to please do a review. He absolutely refused to do this and I went away feeling a real failure, for not having my request even listened to.

By the time I got back to Roebourne, the Medical Practitioner concerned was waiting for me and went on the attack about the incompetence of the nursing staff involved in the emergency the day before. I asked him to meet first with myself and then the nursing staff. He was really angry at my defence of the nurses, who over the months had become very competent in emergency care through the staff development programmes that were being run. Their documentation was very objective and on reading the notes one could see that they had done all they could for this patient. He left my office refusing to talk any further and refused to speak with the nurses.

Several weeks, later the police asked him for a statement in relation to the case and he came down and told me that the police would want to speak to the nurses involved, I told him that the police already had their statements and that the statements were done on the morning of the man's death. I had become accustomed to his negative reactions whenever he came to me with complaints about the nursing staff. This became a daily occurrence. In hindsight, I made the wrong decision in not sending it all off to the Medical Board; however, I did believe in the HDWA promises and commitments to support the nursing division. Both nurses resigned not long after and were sadly missed by all.

Personally, the attacks on my character deepened, a Senior Official, rang me one afternoon and asked me if I was okay. I asked why, he informed me that he had just got off the phone from the said practitioner and that he was 'very concerned about my mental health'. He reported I was not communicating with him and that I had not spoken to him for weeks, this was a total lie. I told the manager that really this man had to be stopped, and that he could not go on treating some members of the nursing staff nor myself like this, would he please come out and address the issues.

He came and met him behind closed doors, and I was not privy to any discussions following the meeting, no correspondence, no minutes nothing, it was all too hard. The biggest issue for me was that several days after this meeting; my daily work diary had disappeared from my desk. I was very upset about this invasion and reported it straight away to the police and a senior official of the new West Pilbara Health Service. It really was the last straw for me as I was becoming more and more introverted and developing a negative thinking pattern in whom could I trust. I felt very alone no-one to share it with professionally, only my beloved husband. However, little did anyone know I had written a concise and factual daily diary for a number of years, at home this was a nightly ritual and gave me solace over those years. I was told not to worry about the diary, it would turn up. Turn up it did. A senior official, rang me several months later and told me that he had been informed by a Nickol Bay staff member that it had been circulated at a private nurses party, a lot of nurses from the district were in attendance. He was even given evidence of a photostat of the front page. He requested that it be handed over as I really needed it returned. From that day forth I never heard of it again - another buried trauma.

Even though work was so hard, my home life was just so very comforting and our little home was a deep refuge, Noddy had been by my side from the first day. He ensured I received so much love and happiness and always had a meal cooked and ready when I got home around 5.30 -6 pm, ensuring I had no housework and no cooking to do. I would start the day, swimming every morning for an hour, getting up at 5am; my meditation would be in the pool swimming up and down the community pool at the end of the street, for an hour. We had become very friendly with our beautiful next-door neighbours and were very happy to be Tomo and Tanya's surrogate grandparents. We spent a lot of time with Sel and Charlie as after she went to the prison to work, our friendship developed into a very special one. I was invited by one of the nurses to join the Wickham theatre group. This I did and had a great time, participating in a play, out at the Old Bond Store at Cossack. Cossack is an old historic ghost town located on Butchers Inlet at the mouth of the Harding River. The town was founded 1866 and was the birthplace of the Western Australian Pearling Industry, until a cyclone in 1881damaged the town and every pearling vessel either was badly damaged or destroyed, and in 1886, the pearling industry moved to Broome, after a parliamentary select committee back then, recommended the closure of several pearling banks in the area due to depletion.

We were so lucky to be able to spend most weekends in Cossack over a three month period, when our dear friends Seleana and Charlie lived there, as a relief caretakers at that time.

Wickham high school had arranged for an exchange Japanese teacher to come to do a semester to teach Japanese to the students. One of the nurses was one of the organisers for this project, a problem occurred just prior to his arrival. They had no-one in the whole community who would billet him, despite weeks of trying to organise a billet. In desperation she asked Noddy and I if we would help out. Of course we said yes and this again gave us a deep cultural experience. His name was Sak who prior to his retirement was a highly skilled executive for a huge Japanese company and wanted new experiences during retirement, so he would travel to different countries teaching Japanese to English speaking kids. He was lovely and it was an honour for us to share his experience and stories, we learnt a lot from this very humble man.

We invited two old friends for tea occasionally, an unlikely couple, one was a famous Australian Artist whose landscape paintings sold for thousands of dollars and even hung in parliament house. His name was Gordon Binstead-(See National Library Archives in Canberra)we got to meet him one day in the supermarket in Wickham, by smiling at him whilst out shopping , we stopped and had a chat with him the connection made then,went on to develop into friendship. His best mate was an old Aboriginal elder who used to be a dog catcher back in the 1940's in the Pilbara'.The stories that these 2 old men could tell were beyond belief, they were fantastic, even acting out the stories. His name was Gordon Lockyer.[1] We just loved their company, watching with bright eyes, and listening to the pair of them outdoing each other in the story telling of their experiences out in the bush. We were again so enriched by sharing time with these humble men who loved coming together at our home, for a meal. Both Noddy and I were present for Gordon Lockyer's memorial and funeral service.

JA was doing very well and came up to see us at semester breaks for a few weeks, as she was very keen to come to Karratha once she finished university at the end of the year. JD arrived home and they both came up for a couple of weeks over the Christmas holidays. We were so looking forward to having a wonderful Christmas day. It was our first Christmas as a family for two years, I should have left town for Christmas, for on Christmas morning the phone rings about 10.00, a staff member who was rostered on Christmas day had called in sick for the afternoon shift, and there was absolutely no-one to cover her shift. She had been very well on Christmas Eve and was very well when on duty on Boxing Day. I said I would be in at 15.30; we had a lovely Christmas lunch booked down at the Port Samson Hotel restaurant; however, I was sad I had to go to work. I went to work, it was very quiet and as I never got paid for any overtime, callouts or extra shifts and I would never be able to get the time back, it put a question mark in my mind was this a genuine sick day? My perception was that it was not. It was so lovely to have them home when I came home at 9:40pm and we had a few more days together celebrating being a family again. The weather was very humid and hot that year and JA decided to take Silly, her dog home with her. The kids left in time to spend New Year Eve in Perth. JD was commencing University in March and JA was going into her third year. The girls who had lived with her whilst JD was away, had moved back to their respective homes so it was good for Silly to go home to Perth for security for the kids , and then we would not have to leave the air-conditioning on 24 hours a day for the dog. Noddy was working for a bus company; however, he was offered a job as a crane driver out on the Burrup Peninsular with a construction company building big new gas storage tanks at the beginning of 1994. He was happy, as he loved construction. It was not long and he had won the respect of all he came in contact with. He would be up at 4am every morning and drive 120 kilometres to work and arrive home at 1800 hrs, Monday through to Saturday lunch time.

I was not getting my hours back so I negotiated with the District Manager for approval for funding for an on –call system to enable me to have some 'Peter time' on weekends. I would be on-call every second week, and staff who lived in the district would cover the other weekend, it was a much needed change as the hours worked being called back was incredible. Fly outs, emergencies, staff calling in sick, no agency to ring for a replacement and if a casual staff member was not available and no-one able to do a double shift, it was the DON who covered, often working a night shift. This is what happens in all 2x2x2 hospitals in WA as I have documented before, since time immemorial.

Noddy and I would spend many happy hours when I was off, exploring the hinterland around the district. We started to do a lot of camping again and just enjoying being out at Millstream and exploring water holes around Karratha with friends. We would spend many a happy evenings with Sel Charlie and their dear friends Jane and James Best. Jane had resigned from Roebourne mid 1994, as she received a health department scholarship to do her midwifery through Curtain University. As she was independent now of Roebourne, we were able to develop a wonderful friendship which today is so valued.

The six of us would spend many happy hours out bush. Charlie became the caretaker of Cossack for some months, whilst the permanent caretaker was away and many happy hours would be spent playing cards upstairs on the veranda of the Art Gallery overlooking the little harbour there, watching the moon gleaning over the waters when the tide was right. I was the non-drinker, so you can imagine who won the most games; I would go home with nice little loot. On the odd occasion I was able to enjoy a drop of wine and a two dog lemonade or two. Personally I did not like alcohol but sometimes one or two drinks on the Saturday night, when I was not on call, helped me through some very difficult weeks, Sel and Charlie, Jane and James totally understood, what I was going through, like Noddy they were rocks, who gave nothing but unconditional love and they were so non-judgemental. I loved them dearly. Not that I discussed with them, the politics or how I was hurting inside, they just knew.

CALL OUTS

I have so many memorable call outs to share. Sel was on night duty in Wickham one night when a tiny little Aboriginal baby about three months old had been admitted during the evening with severe bronchiolitis and placed in a humidified crib. Sel rang me just after she had taken over in charge of the night shift. She said she was really worried about the baby. She explained that she had not worked in paediatrics for many years and would I come to the hospital and help her? I went over immediately to support her. She called the doctor in and arrangements were made for RFDS to come down and transfer the infant to Port Hedland Regional Hospital (PHRH) and within two hours we had the baby safely in the hands of a paediatrician who came down on the RFDS plane to pick her up. When I rang the next morning to see how the baby was, we were told well done, this baby is still very unstable and being 'specialled'. The mother came back to see us a couple of weeks later to thank us.

Another night, the phone rang at 10.00pm. It was the night nurse from Roebourne seeking my help. They had a patient who was suffering very badly from alcohol withdrawal; IV sedation was doing nothing He had already been given the maximum amount he could have. Would I come over and assess the situation as the doctor requested I be called. I had no idea who the medicine man was or if Roebourne even had one.

On arrival at the hospital, I saw the issues immediately and spoke with his next of kin, asking if there was a medicine man in Roebourne? The woman said, yes. After discussion with the team it was agreed that as there was no other solution and it might be worth trying with the medicine man. I had had no idea who the medicine man was or if Roebourne even had one. However, the Aboriginal lady said she knew him and where he lived. So, here we were in Roebourne, close to midnight driving around to find him. Finally, we were directed to a house in the village. The lady went and asked him in language to come and see her husband. I waited in the car whilst they talked. He said yes, but he wanted to bring his wives with him. The lady came back to the car and asked him if his wives could come. I nodded, yes.

I rang the hospital and asked them to have a couple of mattresses ready for the old ladies. He was a very old man; I estimate around eighty. We arrived back at the hospital, and he went with the staff and the doctor and started to work. It was so good to see. The old medicine man did have some difficulty settling this patient although it took a number of hours and it took two days for the patient to finally recover. It is such an awful experience to witness a patient coming out of the delirium tremors.

Another new experience occurred when I was sitting at my desk in Roebourne and there was a knock on the door. A man entered and introduced himself as Dave. Dave had just started a local funeral service through the Aboriginal Church in Roebourne. The cost of funerals prior to the church commencing the service, was astronomical for the people of Roebourne. He told me he was making a coffin, the first he had ever made, and the man who passed, was in our mortuary. He asked if I would take him to the man and so he could measure the deceased man to ensure the coffin was big enough. I obliged, and escorted him to the mortuary. We did what we had to do and the coffin had to have another one foot added. As I have said before, you never know what you as a country DON will be called to do.

. . .

The time came when the District Director of Nursing Position was advertised. I applied for it and had to write a presentation on the Role of The District Director of Nursing in The Funder Owner Purchaser Provider Model of health service delivery. I had never had to prepare a presentation of a position before. The panel consisted of the West Pilbara General Manager, the Director of Nursing from Royal Perth Hospital, who was a woman I had met before and admired very much. It was this beautiful woman, who set up the School of Nursing at Notre Dame University in Fremantle. The other panel member was a Director of Nursing from Community Health for the HDWA. I was slightly nervous on the day of the interview however, once the interview commenced, I was very comfortable presenting the prepared paper.

It was a great relief to have it all over. I was hoping I would get the role as a lot of the changes and progress to a progressive health service was already happening at Roebourne and Wickham. I had a vision for the Shire of Roebourne which was endorsed, and I received the phone call several weeks later to offer me the District DON's position. I was very happy and would look forward to the challenges ahead, although I knew that things may not be easy, as there was still an element within the establishment, who were obstructive and were not happy with the appointment. A Nurse Manager was appointed to Roebourne and Wickham as well as a Nurse Manager at Nickol Bay hospital and a Community Health's Advanced Nurse Practitioner. It was their role to manage the day to day running of the nursing services in their units and be answerable to the DDON, who was the executive director for the whole health nursing service in the Roebourne shire. The three managers and the DDON made up the nursing executive.

Steve, a well-educated nurse, who was an absolute gem of a person and committed to quality patient care and standards of care, was appointed to the Nurse Manager's position in Roebourne and Wickham hospitals. Steve had a honeymoon period; however, it only lasted about three months when the dark forces started to circle. The forces were from the same quarters that had captured my soul and had played havoc with my mind for so long. My role as their manager was to keep Steve and the staff safe from the lies and innuendos that these forces spread. They had the capacity to assassinate your character.

I had the Executive of The Health Service endorse the Code of Conduct and Ethics as set down by the HDWA. Whilst this, in some ways helped resolve some of the behaviours of certain members of staff, it did not curtail the stem of lies and innuendoes directed at Steve or myself. The Doctors did not come under the jurisdictions of the Health Services; they were not accountable to anybody except themselves. Steve was a professional young man but it was not long before he was victimised and harassed by the gang of five. I was very sad when Steve, at the beginning of 1996, could not take the culture any longer and ended up resigning. The lack of support from senior officials and the HDWA hierarchy about their behaviour only added to the feeling of isolation and harassment for Steve.

He was good nurse and manager; I was distressed at not being able to stop the avalanche of character assassination. Eventually, the HDWA Senior Nurse and a Senior Doctor were brought up, to try and assist in resolving the issues. After that visit, things went quiet for a few weeks and then out of the blue, another volcano erupted which started the assassination of myself all over again.

I had a very experienced nurse with extensive management experience at SCGH, join the staff, after Steve left. Kathleen was a mature aged woman who was an ex Nurse Manager from SCGH. She had stepped up to act in the position for a few months, until another permanent Nurse Manager could be appointed. Fortunately, we were able to recruit another very experienced and highly skilled nurse manager Toni, a most beautiful soul. She was a strong assertive and a beautiful young woman married with three children. She had very good clinical and midwifery skills. She had worked as a remote area nurse for many years.

Noddy and I were loving living in Karratha; we had a very large group of friends and were always busy socially. JA had obtained an appointment at St Paul's Primary School as a school teacher for the beginning of 1996 and we were very happy that she would be living with us at home. JD had settled at university doing physical education and training his heart out doing very well in his chosen sport. He would be up twice a year and we were still a very close family unit. JA had planned a two year contract in Karratha, and then she intended going to join her group of friends from high school in London for a year. Noddy was working on construction long hours, but was happy. He looked ten years younger. We started to have and plan holidays again. Life was good and we felt so blessed.

Meanwhile, back in Perth, my mum was having severe back pain. She had been diagnosed with extensive osteoporosis and her spine had collapsed. Her doctor referred her to an orthopaedic surgeon. At that time she was 76, and her health was failing. He told her about a back operation he was doing at St John of God's Hospital in Perth. My poor mum was in so much pain, she believed every word he said and he convinced her to have the operation. I did try to talk her out of it. But she would not listen. Sadly, the operation failed to alleviate any of her pain and no healing took place. She was never the same after that and became an invalid. She accepted what happened to her and took on a brave persona, but it was painful to watch the deterioration of a once proud wife, mother, grandmother, and nurse, who had done her best in life renegaded to a life of pain and suffering; just existing, not living - taking both strong opioids and other medications. She was well cared for by my sister and my dad.

I have to tell the story of what happened to JA in her final practicum. The poor kid rang me very distressed one night. She was in her second week of a full semester of teaching at a little school in Perth. Previously, she had great practicums and did very well; however, this night she was breaking her heart over the phone. Apparently, the teacher had taken a total dislike to her and told her she would never pass and how she had been allowed to get so far was beyond her comprehension. This teacher said to her, that she had no chance of graduating and was a hopeless teacher. I was furious and ready to get on a plane and go to address the teacher. But I just assured JA she would be okay.

Next morning, I went to work, and the first phone call was to the Dean of the University Education Program. I told him what had been said to JA the day before and I shared with him, that there were two student nurses at Wickham and Roebourne Hospitals and if any of our staff had treated these students the way my daughter described how she was being bullied, then there would be ramifications for those involved. He was lovely and thanked me so much for bringing it to his attention. He assured me he would follow it through. Sure enough, he rang me back in the afternoon to say he had sent out an investigator and she witnessed the abuse of this teacher towards JA. She immediately made arrangements for her to be transferred to another classroom and she, this time had a great mentor coach and passed her practicum with flying colours. When JA rang that night, she was very happy and told me what had happened. I never ever told her about what I had done that morning until many years later.

The staff at Nickol Bay were professional nurses. Their nurse manager was also very skilled in nursing management and her clinical skills were of a very high standard. She was such a support person for Steve and Kathleen in their times of need as well, for which I was very grateful. Unbeknown to me during this time, the dark forces were working very hard gaining support to destroy me yet again. I only found this out when the senior health official, handed me a letter that had been sent to the then Health Minister of WA

It read:
Dear Sir
Minister of Health
Parliament House
Perth 6000
Dear Sir,
I am writing to you in support for Ms Peter Rebbechi-Director of Nursing West Pilbara Health Service.

Due to recent publicity and a PETITION that was circulated around the community, I feel it is important that support of achievements is recognised.

I have lived in the Pilbara for 3 years now. My first 12 months I was employed at Wickham and Roebourne Hospitals; the last eight months I was there as a Staff Development Nurse. I am currently a nurse for another Government agency and as I have my own community to attend to, it is important to me that I have the support of the medical services in the area.

The resignation of the former Director of Nursing and the appointment of Peter Rebbechi brought about many professional changes to Wickham and Roebourne Hospital. Peter Rebbechi is a great advocate for the nursing profession. Her management skills include her ability to listen to staff, to keep staff well informed of change and restructuring. She allows others to have input and upgrade professionalism. Peter's support for staff development is overwhelming and she recognises the special needs for country nursing. Working in country areas, nurses are expected to be able to deal with all aspects of medicine. I wish to list some of the changes Peter has been responsible for.

1. Emergency care: - Peter gives special emphasis on emergency care, she allocated clinical nurses to set up and re-arrange treatment rooms to become well organised and workable emergency care rooms. This also included the introduction of disaster kits. Peter's guidance in this area is highly commended.

2. Special hospice care for patients and their relatives.

3. Care and respect for the community. Peter was able to re-establish the communities' trust and confidence not only in her but with the total health care service.

4. Professional nursing assessments for Clinical Registered Nurses, Registered nurses and State Enrolled Nurses.

5 Support for professional and self-development.

6. Introduction of key nursing staff to take on specialised areas of responsibility such as asthma management, paediatrics, diabetes, etc The nurse responsible for individual areas then became an important contact for other nurses, doctors, patients and community.

7. Hours and hours of support when patients were very ill and required RFDS transfer.

8. Hours of her own time devoted to encouraging groups such as the local Lions Club to assist in buying new equipment for the emergency rooms.

The list is endless. Peter was able to bring the West Pilbara Health Care Units into the nineties; I am proud of her achievements and hope this letter will give you insight. Thank you for your time in reading this letter and I urge you to continue your support for Peter Rebbechi, in her very difficult role.

Yours sincerely

_-----------------.

There were copies of this letter sent to the Commissioner of Health, The HDWA Senior Nursing Officer and the General Manager of the West Pilbara Health Service

The Minister of Health wrote a note on the top of the letter,

"Nice to hear someone recognises some of the positives which Peter has brought to the area." Copy to Peter and The General Manager for their information and my best regards.

This letter floored me to the core of my heart. At the time, it was very hard going and for the communities and the wonderful nurses I had worked with. I realised it was worth every single step along the way. I was taken aback, but I let it go. However, I thought about the poor Matron out at a hospital in the wheat belt town around the Great Southern Region, who had gone through a similar journey in the early 1980's. I think too, I also buried the betrayal of the perpetrators at a deep cellular level, yet again. I also did not understand how the Minister of Health, and the Heads of the HDWA did not comprehend the enormity of the problem or if they did, why was it that it is always the nurses who were hung out to dry through insidious workplace violence, when the rare practitioners –in this case five- purposely went out of their way to make some nurses lives unbearable? No one listens to the nurses who are victims of the horizontal and vertical violence. This again re-enforces nurses are neither valued nor respected. They become the dispensable ones when there is conflict between nursing and medical practitioners, in my experience. Although I have been damaged by three medical practitioners during my working life of fifty-four years, I have a great deal of respect and admiration and love for the majority of doctors and specialists I have had the honour to work with.

Next day, I received another letter which read,

Dear Peter,

I have enjoyed working within the framework of the West Pilbara Health Service model. Working in the position as an Acting Nurse Manager, I found it invaluable to be part of the management team to have the support necessary to manage the various dynamics, problems, challenges and personalities of Roebourne and Wickham Hospitals

I believe if Wickham and Roebourne were separate units it would be very a difficult task for an individual to manage these two areas without support. Because of the various dynamics I have observed and experienced it would be a very difficult to maintain high nursing standards and maintaining, high nursing standards, is the bottom line.

I believe that if Roebourne and Wickham hospitals where separate units they would become a law unto themselves. I believe certain individuals have genuine concern for the patient but their thinking is not relevant for today's expectations from society and indeed the nursing Profession.

I have heard such comments from a medical practitioner that he would like to see the hospitals fully occupied with sixteen or more patients regardless of how many nurses are on duty and the funded bed numbers. During the period I was Acting Nurse Manager this medical officer endeavoured to admit more than the funded bed numbers. Many times I explained why he could not do this and he acknowledged and understood the reasoning. However, he still attempted to do this which caused much stress to the nurses on duty. There is also a core of nursing staff who would like to see the hospital services return to the "Good old days" who felt it was a lot busier then, but we coped .

My job was made a lot easier and more enjoyable having the *support of the Nursing Management team. Roebourne and Wickham need to be part of a health unit and nursing management needs to be part of the health services nursing management team to ensure nursing services are kept abreast of current trends and moves into the 21st century with the knowledge they are up there with the best of them.*

On receiving this letter, I was re-affirmed in my belief of the model we were working under, and having walked the walk before the persons who came after me as unit managers, I was able to support them in a very deep holistic way. It did give me some insight then, as to the petition circulation. What became clear was, they wanted to go back to the past and have their own DON and autonomy to do what they liked

I was offered a role with the HDWA being a team leader for a three month project benchmarking hospitals in Western Australia. I decided to accept this role, for it would be a good learning experience on benchmarking and also it would enable me to see how the hospitals in the Roebourne Shire were performing, and benchmark our health service. So, with Noddy's blessing I became a member of the project team. The Government would fly me home on weekends during this three months' project. I have to say I really enjoyed it, travelling around different regions talking with many nurses and other hospital staff. The West Pilbara Health Service (WPHS) was up there with the best of them; it was interesting too, to realise we were not the only ones not being supported by the higher echelons of the HDWA and government. Nurses it seemed to me were there as a necessity and a very expensive commodity.

(This was also evident, when sitting at the negotiating table during Enterprise Bargaining Agreements and I was present at several of these discussions. To be honest, they were not pleasant. The negotiators for the HDWA appeared to me to be very anti the nursing profession. The WPHS senior official during one of the EBA negotiation periods brought all the Directors of Nursing together and requested that we all move over to the public service union. He said, "The trouble with you nurses is that you are too 'nursey'." We all stood united and would not budge from our stance).

The benchmarking project also gave me a chance to have a break from the front line of attack for which I was truly grateful. I certainly needed time out, and the senior community nurse relieved me during this period. The nursing executive was a very strong force and put out fires that kept on being lit by the negative forces. These did not involve me at all, thank God; it was all internal politics over at the Roebourne and Wickham hospitals.

Once the project was over, I came home much to Noddy's delight. I returned to my gazetted position, which the senior community nurse was happy to hand back to me. I think the magnitude of the problems experienced by the nursing executive in supporting the nurse manager out at Roebourne and Wickham were overwhelming for them.

***

On the family front, we did lots of camping which included the best week ever up at a remote area called Cape Leveque in the Kimberely, a great getaway that was so nourishing for Body Mind Emotions and Spirit. We would walk for miles and miles along white sandy beaches and towering red cliffs and we met amazing people from all over the world including world famous artists who would spend months camping up there to capture the beauty of this amazing landscape on canvas. Our campsite was right on the beachfront and close to an amenities block. We took a magnificent flight over The Horizontal falls in the Dampier Archipelago; we flew out over Kulin Island, which brought back happy childhood memories of coming in to shelter in the bays around Kulin Island to get away from cyclones in the late 1950's - coming to and from Wyndham to Fremantle and Fremantle to Wyndham on the State Ships.

One afternoon, we were sitting at our campsite reading, when a rather distinguished middle aged lady happened to walk past our camp. She did not look well and was a bit messy. We asked her if she was okay, she stopped and told us, that she had been sick all over her clothes on a flight from Broome over the Horizontal Falls, because she had celebrated far too hard in Broome the night before. She was up having a break for a week from Sydney. I gave her a clean pair of knickers, a clean crop top and shirt and shorts. My clothes looked a bit big on her as I was quite a chubby pear shaped woman while she was much slimmer than I. I gave her a towel, a cake of soap and a tube of toothpaste and took her up to the shower. On her way back from the shower, she felt so much better, took our address, gave the toiletries and towel back and left. About two months went by and I had forgotten all about the incident. I received a parcel in the mail, the clothes had come back and enclosed was a lovely gift and a little letter, where she expressed that she was ever so touched by what we did. It was nothing to us but a small gesture to someone in need; but to her it meant so much.

I felt relaxed and rested on return from the Cape.

Noddy had finished in construction and was offered a permanent position subcontracting as a permanent courier to Woodside, a role that he loved. I was swimming daily and enjoyed a great social life. Christmas came. At the end of the year we had a lovely Christmas holiday, exploring the East Coast of Australia in a hired car, catching up with family and friends from Brisbane to Melbourne through to Adelaide.

Cyclone season was very active every year while we were in the Pilbara and we had a number of cyclones bear down on us, bringing lots of wild weather and rain. As the Health representative both on the Local Emergency Management team and the District Emergency Management team, I was very busy when the cyclones were passing the West Pilbara coast. One of the roles of the DON was to remain on duty in the Hospital until the red alert was called off. Fortunately, Noddy was able to stay with me in the hospital during all the cyclones. The worst one during my time was Cyclone Bobby which was the Cat 5 cyclone that had crossed the coast near Onslow where seven fishermen sadly drowned. There was severe damage to the mining community out at Pannawonica. Then again in 1998/99, Cyclone Vance crossed the coast at Exmouth and created havoc on the town; but fortunately, there were no deaths with that Cat 5 storm. I was involved in the recovery phase following Vance.

Nickol Bay Hospital was becoming quite busy with specialists services increasing rapidly. Midwifery was always busy and the Emergency Dept. was well used. As the DDON, I did not have to do any on call. However, I would be on the theatre call out roster a couple of times a week and would be available any time for emergencies. It had always been my belief that you have to be prepared to be there for the staff when the need arose.

I received a phone call one night around 4am. There was a man threatening the two nurses in ED with a knife. He wanted drugs. We had a duress alarm system and the staff pressed it and then waited for the police to arrive. I went straight in; the staff had given him what he was after, and he was trying to put the tourniquet on to shoot up. The staff were amazingly calm and in control. I kept talking to the man about this and that, trying to get him into conversation and distracting him until the police arrived. It was a relief when they walked in the door and took him away with the evidence. This was the first time and last time I have ever experienced an event like that.

One night, we were invited along with Sel, Charlie, Jane and James to a fancy dress Christmas party put on by the Woodside company in Karratha. I was on call that night. I went dressed as a nun and Noddy as a monk. My phone rang around 10.30pm and I was called in for an emergency caesarean section. I had no time to go home to get changed and as I ran past some persons waiting in the ED waiting room, their eyes nearly popped out of their heads seeing a nun running towards the theatre. The nurse followed me to the theatre and we had a good laugh when she saw me getting changed into my theatre attire. I left far more sedately though, post safe delivery of a new born baby. Whoopie Goldberg could not have done what I did.

. . .

The year got off to a good start for me; things had settled somewhat at Roebourne and Wickham due to a certain member of the staff resigning, and leaving town. However, dark forces started to raise their heads early in March of that year. I was asked to intervene in some major clinical issues which had occurred over in Roebourne and Wickham district hospitals.

I did what I had always done and accepted responsibility for addressing poor performances by certain staff members. The Nurse manager was having great difficulty dealing with them, especially in relation to midwifery. The dark forces started attacking again, letters were written to the General Manager - they were always signed by the same person. Meetings were held to try to resolve the worsening situations, even the local politician had been coerced into supporting the dark forces. He had been in the district for many years and the difficult practitioners knew him very well. They kept feeding him misinformation and lies about midwifery service plans for Roebourne and Wickham, convincing him by repeatedly stating that midwifery services were being closed, when in actual fact they were being strengthened to a primary care model. This was a direct response to The Royal Commission that was held into the problems and deaths in King Edward Memorial in the early to mid 90's.

It was my responsibility as the DON to implement the recommendations in accordance with the new policies from the HDWA. This then was the cause of the continued bullying behaviour which had been happening for years and I started to slowly become separated in wholeness and was enveloped in darkness. I recognised I needed help as I was starting to have nightmares about the main perpetrator confronting me in the middle of the night. I went and saw a caring and compassionate GP in Karratha. She wanted me to take some time off. However, I did not listen to this advice because I thought it meant showing weakness. I wasn't physically ill, after all. Instead I agreed to go on some anti-depressants. I was adding further layers on my mask making it thicker and thicker. I started to really bury everything even deeper inside even though on the outside I tried to be myself. A few astute nurses could see I was struggling and began protecting me.

The human resource manager at the time also picked up the toxicity that was being directed at me. This resulted in a note from here which read, "Dear Peter, although I have not known you for very long, you have been very helpful and a friendly warm person to me. I thank you for that and I am very proud of all your efforts and the genuine concern you have for your fellow human beings. God bless you Peta, you deserve only the best in life."

This good lady did not stay very long and neither did another lovely human resource manager.

Things did not improve and just a couple of weeks after my fiftieth birthday in 1997, I was home one day as I had been called out for an emergency overnight and had taken the day off. I was listening to the ABC radio; it was 12.30 and the regional news was on. A politician had brought up the whole issue of midwifery services in Wickham and Roebourne and was very derogatory about the District Director of Nursing in Parliamentary Question time. This really tipped me over the edge. It was the proverbial straw that broke the camel's back.

A couple of days later, I got hold of the tape from the ABC and took it to the General Manager, who told me, "Do not worry about it, do not react." I will send it to the HDWA and get our public relations office to handle this."

I made an appointment to see the politician and asked what grounds he had to be making these false claims and accusations. He told me he had every right that concerned staff members (the five practitioners) who delivered maternity and obstetric services at RDH and WDH had had a meeting with him and he was following it through at question time in Parliament. I contacted the ANF for help. I was gutted and a week later, I went and saw my GP who immediately, put me off work. I was diagnosed with severe reactive depression. I just felt I could not face the world anymore and I went to bed and curled up in a foetal position. I cried inside and out. Noddy, who had never seen me in this state before, could all but nurse and nurture me over the months that followed.

The reality was, I had a severe breakdown and just closed down completely. I could not talk to anyone in the health department at local or state level; they all knew about the issues that had been happening since 1993 and still nothing was done to address it. I could only talk to Noddy and would see our closest friends. My doctor had the visiting psychiatrist come and see me at home, as I would not go outside the front door of our home. The psychiatrist was a kind man, and together with my doctor, came up with a management plan. They decided to send me to a private hospital in Perth under the care of an old French female psychiatrist.

My light had just about been extinguished and if I did not have my family, I may not have been here to tell the story. When the psychiatrist first saw me in Perth, and asked me to tell my story, I started to tell her what had been happening to me since I became a DON. I told her my story and about the attempts that had been made to have me run out of town and remove me from my role by five health professionals. I gave her the name of the main perpetrator. She said these words to me, "It is not you-I know this person."

I felt a little flicker in my heart and knew that I was finally listened to. Three weeks later, I was discharged from hospital. My emotional mental and spiritual health had improved and the world was not such a dark and scary place anymore. I was on medication which was titrated accordingly as I improved. JD would come every night while I was hospitalised and sit with me until I fell asleep; his vigils were very healing for me. Noddy would ring three times a day and was so happy to hear me laugh again. My friends too were also calling every other day.

Not once did I receive a call from either the Management of the Hospital, the Health Department, nor the Nursing Executive. I had been off and it was thought I was extinguished.

As JA was in London, we decided to keep all of this from her, not wanting to cause her any worry or distress. After six weeks in Perth, I was ready to come home under the care of my darling husband, GP and the visiting psychiatrist. During the recovery stage, I had contact with the ANF, so before I went home, they referred me through to a Barrister on St Georges Terrace to handle the Workers Compensation Case that had been lodged.

Once I returned home, I was stronger in myself, although I still could not bear to go out publicly.

Sel would come and massage my back at least once a week. Melena and Dragon would come each week and bring the young ones, it was so lovely to see them. I started to get back in to prayer and meditation again slowly in my own way, in my own home.

I had walked away from the church prior to moving to Karratha as the nursing perpetrators were all Catholic women who regularly attended church. I would offer my hand in peace to them as Catholics do in mass and they would turn away. I returned to attending church regularly, and became friends with a beautiful family from East Timor. We spent many happy times with them during the journey. Part of my healing journey started when I began reading autobiographies and one autobiography had a huge impact on me. It was Mary Mackillop's story. I realised even she had been so badly bullied, victimised and even excommunicated from the Catholic Church. She too suffered physically, emotionally and mentally from senior clergy, for what she was doing; that she would spend weeks in bed suffering and withdrawing from society and her life's work, recovering each time to keep on doing the wonderful work she was doing.

I was really considering resigning at one stage, and applying for the advertised position of Director of Nursing in Nimbin in NSW, but one morning I got up, looked in the mirror and I heard a voice say, "Peter, if you run from this you will be running for the rest of your life. You are a strong woman and you will recover from this."

I thought back to the late eighties and I decided there and then I would not resign and that it did not matter how long the recovery took, I would recover. So, I set myself a small goal - one day at a time. By this time, I had been off work for six months. There was not one word from anybody from the Health Service, not even a letter or a phone call. In conjunction with my GP and Dr Guy, I started cutting down on the large doses of anti-depressants and I introduced a gentle exercise program. I was still not interested in food at all and my weight had dropped to 50kgs. Noddy, and our dear friends, would take me out bush for a Sunday barbeque by one of our favourite water holes and I started to see the world with a much better and clearer perspective. My GP continued to fill in the workers compensation claim, as all medical staff were in no doubt that this was a direct result of a workplace injury, not physical, but a severe mental injury, caused by what had been happening over the 4 year period. This caused further stress for me, as I then had to go through all the workers compensation process, which included seeing an insurance psychiatrist.

Whilst I was in Perth seeing this insurance doctor, I had an appointment with the Barrister whom the ANF had sent me to. Unfortunately, he was not the right man for me, as he told me he knew one of the main perpetrators. This was obviously very stressful for me. By this time I had set myself a return-to-work date for the beginning of March 1998.

A NEW WIN

*I*t was just before Christmas and I was reading the Saturday, West Australian newspaper. I came to the positions vacant for the Health Department and low and behold there was my position advertised, "District Director of Nursing, Roebourne Shire" in black and white. I was shocked and actually speechless; I could not believe what I had read. At first I cried at the cruelness and the lack of care and compassion that was endemic throughout the Health System. Then I experienced an emotion I had not had in years.

A fire and anger burned within me. So, I decided on Monday morning, I would ring the Administrator and ask what was going on. Monday morning came, and I rang the senior official and asked how, what, why and where this advertisement had come from. This gentleman I spoke to however, was unknown to me.

It seemed the official that had journeyed with me over the worst times had resigned and a new senior official, had been appointed in the meantime. He told me there had been a mistake, I informed him that I was recovering and that I had planned a return to work in March. I reiterated that I had not resigned and that I had no intention of resigning. That phone call gave me strength and then I worked very hard to hasten the reconnection my Body Mind and Spirit over the next three months. Spending time in nature, exercising-swimming up to two kilometres every day, praying and meditating, reading lots and lots of healing books, listening to healing tapes and enjoying being reunited with my own inner self once again helped me heal.

The love between Noddy and myself was growing deeper and deeper; he was my rock, my confidant and my carer, he and I were one. Our time spent with Melena and Dragon Tomo and Tanya were treasured; having the innocence of children in your life surrounding you with their positive energy is healing. Babies and children are our little healers. Sel, Charlie, Jane and James who had journeyed through the very dark clouds that totally enveloped us in the last few years, were instruments too of faith hope and charity. I ended up with my confidence restored and was able to integrate back into a great community life again and much of it was because of the support of dear friends and family.

Prior to returning to work, I had to have psychiatrist clearances both from Worksafe and from my own psychiatrist. I have never forgotten the words my private psychiatrist said to me when he gave me my final clearance for going back to work. "Peter, I know you are a strong woman and thank you for your self-healing, you have had more than your share of human toxicity and I wish you all the best and I will always be here for you".

He was truly one of the most compassionate specialists, I have ever met. By this time, I was on a very mild dose of an antidepressant and felt like I was back to being my normal bright caring self. I was on an inner journey as well, spending a lot of my time in prayer and meditation reading and growing within. I had a far deeper appreciation of what people suffering from depression were going through. I made a commitment to myself to ensure mental health became a focus of the health service and wellness amongst staff, a priority; I also committed to myself, that I would really put myself first, something I had never done since I was a small child. My father would say that, 'to put one's self first was a sin, to love yourself was a sin of pride and if I did any of these I was selfish.' I realised at this time that this is not how it was meant to be. I had always believed deep down that, "How can you love others when you do not love yourself, how do you care for others unless you care for yourself, and how do you respect others unless you respected yourself?" In fact, I did a presentation on this very subject after the first experience I had from workplace bullying and harassment. I blocked it out pre breakdown over a four year period but now it was time to start again living my true belief.

I returned to work at the end of March in 1998, the worker's compensation case had been accepted and having lived on Noddy's wage and my sick leave and holiday leave entitlements for so long, it was good news to hear. I had all my entitlements, holidays, sick leave, and northwest leave re-instated. I was so glad I had such a bank of leave owing. After having gone through the experience with the insurance company, I knew what the stress and anxiety of 'workers compensation' could do to a person without savings, without financial back up and not having a spouse with an income. The system is really heavily swayed on the side of the employers, it is not there to support the injured personnel. Is it any wonder then that good people resign, and walk away or even in some instances commit suicide during the long process?

I have to say it took me a few months to really get my confidence back in the workplace, as I had to get used to a full new team of colleagues at the executive level. The clinical, the administrative and cleaning staff were very compassionate and welcomed me back with no judgement and much love and care. I think one of the things that really helped me get my confidence back was the day I returned to work and received the hand over from the person who was assigned to relieve me. I had a new tool on my desk- yes, a computer. Can you believe everything I had done before 1997 was done by hand and given to the executive secretary to type? We had two of the most amazing women I had ever worked with, who would do all my typing of letters, memos etc. for me, and their command of ensuring the editing was done and the typing perfect, was fantastic.

I was scrolling through a list of emails and all of a sudden, I stopped when I found an email which offered up to $80-000 non-recurrent funding for Hospice /Palliative Care for rural and remote communities. One of my visions prior to the breakdown was having a palliative care room specifically designed and set up for dying members of our communities in Nickol Bay Hospital.

I knew I had to act quickly, as the submissions had to be in by 5pm that day. I started to work on submitting for a slice of the cake offered by the government, worked very hard all afternoon and would you believe it, I had it sent off by 5pm. Several weeks later, I received notification back that the money had been granted to The West Pilbara Health Service for a stand-alone Palliative Care Unit at Nickol Bay Hospital. Although this had gone out to all Health Service DONs and Health Service Managers four weeks prior, only two DONs responded. There was a small problem however, the submission had to be re submitted to meet the ever increasing requirements of the standards of writing submissions. I went in to the General Manager and he, I think, really got a shock when I took the confirmation letter to him. We agreed to give re-writing of the submission to a gifted Occupational Therapist, who had a lot of experience in submission writing at this time.

The money arrived and with some top up funding from the HDWA to build our new palliative care unit, upgrade the Northwest Mental Health Unit and new offices for the West Pilbara Executive. After eighteen months, we were ready for the move back to the new offices where the Health Service Executives were to be housed, with the exception of the Director of Nursing's office. The Director of Nursing's office was in the front foyer of the hospital and had glass all the way around, so I was totally accessible to the public. The palliative care room was superb, the community of Karratha were absolutely fantastic and donated a full sized television, a lovely leather lounge and two recliner rockers, a fully furnished kitchen plus other items for music, paintings for the walls and soft lighting to make the room ambience very peaceful. A construction company also at a later date constructed a serenity garden. The doors were designed wide enough to be able to move a bed in and out for anyone who chose to sleep under the stars outside. When the day came, and the Minister of Health arrived to open the Mental Health and the Palliative Care Units, it was a very joy filled day for me.

***

Things out at Roebourne and Wickham hospitals had not changed; nurses were not staying and our Nurse Manager was at her wits end - she too was receiving the brunt of the culture. By this time, I was prepared to stand up yet again to have the behaviour, that would be so damaging to Nurses, stopped once and for all. I rang the union and asked to be referred to another lawyer. They referred me to a very good female lawyer down in Adelaide Terrace. I was ready to bring a defamation case against the main perpetrator.I flew to Perth with my files which had all the letters that had been written and the journal entries, minutes of meeting etc. I felt I was strong enough to do this and if this was the only way that I could ensure nursing staffs' safety, I would go ahead My dear husband was the only person who knew what I had intended doing.

Discussions in the meantime were held and this time, the General Manager finally organised a very experienced and highly regarded private consultant to come up to help the staff out there with dealing with difficult people and develop strategies for self-development and resilience. All the nursing staff where privately interviewed and the report that resulted was very disturbing. The nurses were very open as to how they were treated by a certain practitioner and his ongoing bullying and victimisation of certain nurses - in particular young graduates, nurse managers and nurses who would challenge or question, his rationale for treatment orders and how the District Director of Nursing had been 'crucified.' The nurses felt they had been finally listened to after this visit, as they were informed that The Commissioner of Health was coming up to deal with the perpetrator, which he did. At last, the visit from the commissioner paid dividends for the staff, which was amazing. The other outcome was that the nurse manager resigned to take up a post in my favourite place in WA, Rottnest Island and another restructure was decided. Roebourne and Wickham would transfer to the DON Health Service Manager model, I would then be totally safe and that my role would be changed to be solely responsible for Community Health and Nickol Bay Hospital. Whilst I was affected by this restructure professionally, I would be away from danger. They had got their way and I did not go ahead with going down the legal pathway for justice for nurses. I did not want the stress; I did not want ever to go back to where I had come from.

A very kind sincere and excellent experienced male nurse was appointed as the HSM/DON. He was married with a family; we had mutual respect for each other and I supported him when he needed help. We had a very good working relationship and today, we are still friends.

My role in the community was becoming busier with being asked to be on the Pilbara Domestic Violence Council, as well as the Roebourne Shire Domestic Violence Committee as well as The Drug and Alcohol Committee, and Safer WA Committee (Roebourne Shire) of which I was elected as President. I was also on the Local Emergency Management committee and on the Pilbara District Emergency Management Committee. These committees were where there had to be a very senior health service representative present. I was privileged to be on these committees which also lead to many professional development opportunities. I was also the Pilbara Nursing representative for the HDWA Performance Indicators development and sat on various HDWA and country health service projects. Life was busy; but I loved it. Another one of the roles delegated to me was to prepare and write the annual report for the West Pilbara Health Service which was a great learning experience. My favourite role was helping out clinically in midwifery, the emergency department and in theatre, when the need arose.

. . .

In 1998, JA was living in London for an extra year or two. Both Noddy and I decided to go to England to have Christmas with her. We were very lucky as Noddy's nephew and his family were coming home to Sydney for a month, so we were able to house mind his home in Highgate for him. JA had two weeks off over Christmas; she lived in a bedsit not far from where we were, so she came and lived with us for the month.

We three had a wonderful time and even though the days were short because it was winter and very cold, we did lots of exploring. It was Noddy's first visit there and he became engrossed in the history of London and exploring all that London had to offer. We would do day trips, when JA was at school to Bath and surrounds. We spent the week travelling to Stratford- upon- Avon, a medieval market town from the 16th century and enjoyed the journey of William Shakespeare's life. Noddy had never read Shakespeare, so he was not in seventh heaven there, as I was. We went to a Shakespearian play one evening, where he fell asleep and was snoring in the theatre serenading his neighbours sitting next to him as I tried to poke him awake. He did, however, enjoy downing a pint or two at Shakespeare's local pub.

From Stratford –upon -Avon, up we drove up to Beatrix Potter's country. The three of us also went over to Paris for a few days on the Eurostar. It was so amazing to be in London and a mere two and a half hours later in Paris. It was such a memorable holiday. From that time on we would go every second year, and JA would come home every second year for the 12 years she was there.

Once I had recovered, I started my social life again, connecting with all my friends and their families. They were non judgemental and life began to resemble normalcy again.

I had the biggest turning point in my journey of life in the middle of 1999. I heard about a Karratha woman who was doing healing sessions for the community in her little home, so I decided I would go to see her. She was a beautiful woman by the name of Francis Martin. I made an appointment to go and see her and I received a powerful wholeness healing and spiritual awakening experience that changed my life. Fran laid me on a massage table and started laying her hands on my head and I immediately closed my eyes and went into a very deep state of relaxation. I did not want to leave this state of internal ecstasy. I saw lots of colours circling through my body and felt sensations, I had never experienced before. It was so amazing that I had to know more about what Fran had done. She explained to me she was doing Reiki, and she would be guided as to where to lay her hands via an unseen guide. It all sounded very strange, I had never heard anything like this before in my life. I knew it was something I had to follow through. I felt amazingly light and clear when I left Fran's and returned for a few more sessions and started to learn everything I could about Reiki and Chakras; it fascinated me and gave me a new pathway into healing besides prayer and meditation.

I always felt like a different person after receiving one of Fran's treatments; I was very clear headed and had lots of energy. I was happier and very much at peace with myself and the world. I found a lady in Karratha who taught Reiki and I went and did the level Reiki 1 and Reiki 2 with her. In doing Reiki 1, further changes in my being were happening. During class, I was laying my hands on a woman's thigh and she said to me "oh my God your hands are so hot". I could feel heat radiating through her jeans and I was taken straight back to being a student nurse, because when I used to massage peoples backs, feet and limbs, the patients, young and old would say "Oh Nurse, your hands are so hot" I was awakened to the fact and realised I had had this gift of "Hands On Healing through the Power of Touch" all my nursing life. I was very excited about this and made a commitment I would start to learn more and practice this ancient healing art. I also had the opportunity of doing a certificate in reflexology by a trained reflexology teacher. This course I also did and loved that modality as well.

I went on to study the theory behind these ancient healing practices, and I read everything I could find. I stumbled across a book by an Intuitive Healer called, *The Anatomy of the Spirit* by Caroline Myss. It was another major awakening; her writings made so much sense to me. Caroline had written a number of books and created audio tapes on

Energy Healing. The more I read, the more I wanted to know. I started gathering a library of research based books on Energy Medicine by world leaders. I knew that this work was Sacred and a God given Gift.

I started practising on Noddy and others who were open minded enough and were my friends. Soon these friends started referring strangers. One was a beautiful old nun who worked out at Roebourne for years, (she was in her 80's). Every week, she would drive in from Roebourne for treatment. One day before she left Roebourne for good, she brought me a gift - a series of tapes by a Franciscan Priest whose name was Richard Rohr. What an awakening these tapes were and I still have them today. Many years later he became my spiritual mentor through the Centre of Contemplation in Albuquerque, US, through his meditation writings and books he has written over years.

Noddy had a special massage table made in Perth for me. He was very supportive as he could see the joy, I was experiencing. He could see the reconnection of Body Mind and Spirit happening within me at a very deep level.

Y2K

Y 2 K

Throughout 1999, fear overtook the world due to the Y2K bug which was expected to disrupt the computer age at the stroke of midnight. We had to prepare for the worst as doomsday experts predicted that all computer systems would fail as we transitioned into the new century. Many, many hours and millions and millions of taxpayers' dollars were spent preparing for the worst case scenario, that we would wake on New Year's Day with no computer networks, and all hard drives would have crashed in Australia and around the world. We spent hours developing up emergency management plans for every possible scenario. It was crazy. New Year's Eve came and I had to be at work by midnight for the clock to register 00:00hours. Guess what? No crash! No emergencies. Everything worked like it did one minute before midnight the same as it did one minute after midnight.I wonder if this was one of the biggest social engineering frauds the world has seen. I would suggest there would have been billions of dollars made out of the this event by both individuals and companies. Worldwide, everyone in Government, Federal, State and Local had to prepare for New Year's Eve's Y2K bug.

. . .

Noddy and I had been contacted by a Catholic Church agency, to see if we would be interested in going up to Papua New Guinea in the October of 1999. Our names had been mentioned to them through someone we knew in the Catholic Church community. This member had shown me an advert calling for interested people to volunteer in their areas of expertise. Noddy and I talked about it and said yes we would like to do it. In discussion with the organisation, I was asked to go up to an island off Alotau and mentor a young National nurse, who was being trained to take up all the management of the outlying islands Health Centres,(18 centres in all). The old nun, who had been there for fifty years, could not go out to the Islands any more, as the old darling was eighty years old and had had a hip replacement. We booked our holidays to go to PNG in April of 2000 and we committed to go for a month on this assignment. It was something we were very excited about and looked forward to.

During the years in Karratha, I would speak with my parents at least five times a week and the conversations invariably revolved around their health. Their depression and sadness just grew worse and worse. We begged them to come up and live in Karratha with us; however, they would not even entertain the idea. I knew they would have been so well cared for, as aged persons by the Home and Community Care in Karratha. The manager was a very kind and compassionate woman, for whom I had a great deal of respect. I would visit each time I went to Perth on business and we - Noddy and I - would take them out when we were holidaying in Perth.

It is probably one of the saddest scenarios that one experiences in life's journey; seeing one's parents suffer so badly. Poor old mum had severe osteoporosis, caused by a lack of calcium and other nutrients in the great depression of the 1930's and the subsequent rations of produce, like milk and cheese in the second world war from 1939-1945. Towards the end of her life, she lived on heavy opioid pain killers, up to 60-100 mg tablets of MS Contin BD ordered for her, together with oxycodone for breakthrough pain. This again caused so many other medical issues; she would have very bad falls, ending in hospitalisations and fractures. I tried to help her with meditation and breathing exercises and other techniques but to no avail; she had become too drug dependant. Dad would try his best to help her, and although many times social workers tried to put her into care, mum refused.

I know my Mum dreaded the thought of ever going into a nursing home. One day in November of 1999, Mum rang me and said "I am going to bed tomorrow and I am not going to get up, I will stop eating and drinking." She took control, so I flew down to Perth and when I arrived, my sister, Marion looked exhausted and was so relieved at my presence, she handed everything over to me.

I went to my mum's bedroom and sat on her bed, and as soon as I did, her facial expression suggested extreme pain. You could see it in her eyes, feel it in her presence, and hear it in her voice. When I gently asked her, her pain score she whispered 10/10. I asked her if I could ring her doctor, get a morphine pump for her and request for palliative care to come in. I assured her, she would not have to go into hospital, we would care for her at home. She just cried and said Peter thank you and yes, that is what I want. So I rang the GP and he agreed to her request. That afternoon she had a morphine pump insitu and was written up for breakthrough morphine hourly as required. She was a palliative care patient now.

Mum stopped eating and drinking, taking her destiny into her own hands, giving her power to no-one and died peacefully on the 24th November 1999. I so honour my mother for the last great lesson she taught me - how to die well. We went back to Karratha, sad but also with a great sense of relief and peace that she was no longer suffering. Noddy and I are great supporters of Assisted Dying for those who choose this pathway. His dear mother suffered with severe Alzheimer's and spent the last years of her life existing in a nursing home. I am a firm believer in that, persons know when it is their time for their spirit to leave and it is okay for the rest of us to say goodbye and allow them to go home.

. . .

We had a very heavy cyclone season through 1999/2000, with three Category 3 and 4 cyclones crossing the coast. As a consequence, I was very busy. Following the cyclones, the deluge in the Kimberley and Pilbara during this cyclone season was the worst I had seen in seven seasons. Just as I was about to finish work on the 30th of March before leaving for holidays on the 31st March, there was a car roll over with persons injured just outside our hospital. Staff had to be called in and I stayed until everything was under control. I was just about to go home at 2000 hrs when the phone rang. It was the head of the SES asking me, if a nurse would be available to go out with the SES helicopter up to the Shaw River in the morning at first light. They had a report from a Station Owner, on one side of the river that they had not seen their neighbour on the other side for four days. They wanted to ensure his safety, and just in case of an adverse advent they wanted to have a nurse with them. So, I said "yes, no trouble I can come." I was informed I had to be at the Heliport at 0600 hrs, so I picked up a disaster kit, rang the general manager and the nurse manager of Nickol Bay Hospital and informed them of the situation .

Next morning, I was at the heliport at 5.45am. The pilot was there and two state emergency personnel, the Manager plus his Deputy. We boarded and off we took very smoothly. This was my first experience in a helicopter. I had been in many Cessna's, but never a helicopter. I was a little nervous, so I said a prayer and sat back to enjoy the ride. What an experience!

The whole of the Harding River and dam were in flood and the dam was overflowing at the speed of a little Niagara Falls. It was magnificent to see the full force of nature, in all her glory. We flew over the ranges between Roebourne and Oske Roadhouse where we landed and refuelled. The waterfalls along the route were magnificent; the rivers, creeks and station land were flooded. The Shaw River was not far from the Oske Roadhouse, so fifteen minutes later, we circled the first station we came to, and dropped supplies.

We went over the river to the old man's place, circled the house and landed; we were greeted by an older man aged around sixty five years.

He was in his budgy smugglers and had a towel thrown over his shoulder; he told us, he had just been for his daily swim. He lived in a concrete type tank, an amazing construction and he had all the mod cons of living. He was a South African gentleman who was a hermit and a prospector. He had lived there for about thirty years and would only go into Port Hedland once every three or four months. He was a very interesting character who told us many stories over morning tea. After an hour, we left and he waved us goodbye, thanking us for coming out to check on him.

We were on our way up to Port Hedland, to drop off the SES people, as they were heading up to Broome. The pilot and I , were heading straight back to Karratha, when we got an emergency call to go out to the De Grey River Station, as there was a lady having a major anxiety attack . On arrival at the station, we landed by the back door. The whole area was inundated with thick brown reddish muddy water, and this included the homestead. The lady had barricaded herself in her caravan. It turned out that when she went into the house, she found black snakes were curled up everywhere. They too had come into the house, for refuge swept in by the flooded De Grey River. The poor old lady was terrified. I went to the caravan and she let me in, I gave her a big hug and calmed her down with some deep breathing techniques and a short meditation. She calmed down and we talked for an hour.

She had a son in Port Hedland and I suggested she come back with us to stay with him until the waters had subsided and then she could come home. She thought about it, however she would not leave her husband's side. So, she decided to stay and remain with her husband. She was safe in their big caravan, and her husband agreed, so all was well. I had to go to the outhouse before we flew off, as my bladder was tickling my chin. I was escorted through the water and mud to the latrine. I hated snakes and I would have been in a real state if I had seen one. The men looked out for snakes while I finished my business and ohh what a relief! I will never forget that adventure.

We were soon at the airport in Port Hedland and the SES gentlemen were dropped off to Broome. I had the privilege of sitting in the front seat of the helicopter with the pilot on the way home flying down the coast from Port Hedland back to Karratha, arriving back at the hospital at 1500 hrs, with lots of amazing photos. I had had a wonderful day and what a way to start my holidays - the next adventure.

    I handed over and said goodbye to all.

HOLIDAY BREAK

The 31st of March, 2000 came; Noddy and I left the Pilbara, flying to Perth then over to Brisbane where JD met us at the airport. We were leaving for Port Moresby the next day. We had a lovely evening catching up with him.

Next day, he took us to the airport and saw us off, promising to be there to pick us up on our return at the end of April. It was one of the best scenic flights I had been on, flying from Brisbane to New Guinea, into Port Moresby. We knew we were in for a very different holiday and we were excited, as we had never done anything like this before, visiting and living in a different country which was so far removed from the western mindset. We were going to live out on the remote Island of Kurrada off Milne Bay at the edge of the Solmon Sea. We arrived in Port Moresby around 1500hrs and had an hour to wait for our plane south. We were flying New Guinea Air, on an old DC3 that shook, rattled and rolled all the way down to Alotau.

The Bishop of the Region picked us up at the airport and took us to meet SR Ben, a small petite woman with a giant heart; she ran her organisation with love, compassion and care. At eighty, she was restricted to working on the mainland, running a health worker training school. Her protégé Ben was contracted for another four months on the

Island of Kurruda. We stayed in Alotau for a few days getting to know the organisation and doing a needs analysis on where I needed to focus on my management mentoring.

Once I had reviewed Sister Ben's management files, it appeared that I needed to focus on Quality Management, Submission writing for funding from Government, Develop a Disaster/Emergency Management plan, and concentrate on report writing skills.

Sister Ben had a few other management changes in mind which she wanted me to look at with Ben whilst I was working with him. We stayed in a humble little house in a compound inside the Church grounds. Sister Ben and Noddy hit it off like they had known each other all their lives and she even lent him her precious car, something she had never done before. We would have a meal with her every night.

The ferry to the surrounding islands including Kurrada only left once a week to do a supply run. The Bishop arranged our tickets and we were booked to leave at 2100 hrs four days after we arrived. We did a big shop, ensuring we had plenty of groceries and food to last us the month. Our only other option was a very small shop on the island with a sparse selection of food. We had only brought our old clothes with us, as we did not want to be over dressed in the community where the residents were so very poor materially.

The Bishop took us to the wharf at 2000hrs and our eyes popped out of our head. The ferry we were to travel on was an old wooden one with a motor in the middle of the deck. There were no cabins, one had to sit on the deck for the six-hour trip, and there were no benches or rows of seats.

Noddy looked at me and I at him; we had never seen anything quite like this before. The supplies and all the beds were loaded and there were lots and lots of nationals on board. We must have looked really different; chubby little white persons who had no idea where we were going. They waved us goodbye and off we motored out into the ocean. Everyone appeared very friendly smiling at us together as we sat holding hands and smiling back, the moon and stars lit up the gentle ocean and it was like we were gliding though the water.

We arrived at our destination around 3am, anchored off shore as there was nowhere to land - no jetties or wharfs. All the furniture like beds and chairs were thrown overboard to allow the tide to bring them to shore. Other supplies and our bags were handed to the persons on the out riggers who had come in to ferry us all to shore. Noddy was able to clamber down with a lot more agility than I. It would have been the funniest home video winner if anyone had seen this transfer. At least, I wasn't tipped into the ocean, thank goodness.

Ben and some of the village people were waiting for us on the shore on arrival. We were the first white people they had seen for well over a year and certainly the first for this century. There were no cars on the island, no bicycles - our transport was just our trusted physical bodies. Some kind men carried our bags to our humble little hut accommodation, a single bedroom with a double bed and a small kitchen, torches and candles lighting the way. We had to cross a deep large stream with no bridges, just logs at the crossing, to get to where our accommodation and the health centre was. It was a whole new different world.

Our welcome was so warm and gracious we knew we would just love the people and the environment. We snatched a couple of hours sleep, as the bed was already made up for us and the mosquito net was left hanging. We slept deeply and awoke about four hours later. Ben came round to orientate us to the community. There was no bathroom or toilet. He took us to the centre of the village and explained that this river which runs through the village is for all purposes. The river starts up in the mountain, the first pool closest to the top is where the drinking water and cooking water comes from, and the second is where the pots, pans dishes and eating utensils were washed. We would soon get used to the sounds and would wake to the sound of children's laughter as they washed the dishes in the river before they went to school early in the mornings. The river was a stone's throw from where we were staying. Then the next pool was where we washed our bodies, the next was where we washed our clothes and lay them on the rocks to dry, and then there was the "Long Drop" where we did our ablutions.

Living was different.

When I saw the pool, we had to wash in I said, "Oh no, I can't wash here in the middle of the village, I need to go somewhere a little more private." One old lady said I will come by and take you to another river for a bath. True to her word, she came at twelve o'clock; a very little old lady with hardly any teeth, and her mouth was red. The locals chewed beetle nut all the time, it left their mouth and lips a deep dark red. She was just wearing a grass skirt, no top, and on her head was a basket full of bananas she had brought over for us. We must have walked about two kilometres and ended up at this lovely wide river with a big crossing. The old lady took off her grass skirt and went into the river. I was very shy, got undressed and kept on my knickers. I washed my hair and body; we were just finishing when two women and a little girl approximately five years of age came around the corner. The little girl just started screaming and screaming. The old lady said to me, "don't worry she has never seen a white woman before" in her Pidgin English. I stayed submerged whilst they disappeared around the bend. After they crossed the river, I could still hear the poor little girl crying for some time.

We became settled and acclimatised very quickly. The weather was very humid, there was no electricity on the island so no air-conditioning or fans. The mornings were sunny with a clear blue sky, the surrounding ocean crystal clear, and a gentle breeze would blow to keep us comfortable. You could set your watch by 1200 for then the monsoon clouds would start to roll in, the heavens would open and the deluge would start for up to four hours of non-stop heavy rain.

Ben and I got along like we had always been friends. Ben, was a gorgeous human being. This young man had done his Nursing Degree by distance education through a University in Queensland and would spend hours and hours studying by candle light for his three year degree. We would spend four hours a day most days working together on management issues, writing submissions, looking and upgrading policies and human resource files. He really wanted to understand Emergency Management, especially if a major cyclone or tsunami came-as had happened in PNG some years before, where a whole island had been washed away. We studied evacuation of the community to the mountain regions, having meetings with key members in the community. Most nights Ben would have dinner with us and we developed a very strong bond.

The Health Workers were amazing. Both Ben and the other male Registered Nurse were brilliant clinically; they were far more skilled than I expected; They never had any medical practitioners come to the island. I witnessed them one day intubate a six-month-old baby who was in very severe respiratory distress and in an unconscious state. It was done perfectly and with precision. We had to transfer this baby to the mainland hospital in a small open motor boat. The trip took approximately three hours.

It was an evacuation the likes of which I had never seen before. We had to navigate the stream traversing over large logs with the intubated baby and a G sized oxygen cylinder to get to a little boat that was going to take us to the mainland. We had a small army of locals to help the operation. I went with the team in the open boat over to the mainland. We were met on the mainland by an ambulance, an open truck, and driven into Alotau General Hospital on a dusty dirt road. We had to wait several hours once we arrived at the hospital. The baby was so critical we knew she was dying; however, all the doctors and nurses were tied up looking after the chief of police and another police officer who had been very badly injured in a motor vehicle accident. They ordered us to wait in the waiting room despite the condition of the intubated baby. When we finally handed over the baby, we knew she would never come back to the island. The next day we received a radio message that the baby had passed away about an hour after we left. That was life in PNG, for all those who lived outside the capitols, like Port Moresby and Alotau. Naturally, we were all very sad, especially when a message came in from the Bishop's office that we should never have sent the baby over due to the costs involved.

I had the honour of helping the male midwife, manage and deliver a beautiful baby girl one day and the mother called the baby 'Peta'. I spent some time with her, in her post-natal period and I asked her if she was going to have any more babies. She told me no. I asked her what they did to ensure they had no more babies. She described a tree in the jungle up in the mountain. They would gather the leaves from the tree, boil them up and drink the juice - a natural sterility method.

I was fascinated and started wanting to know more about their traditional medicines and practices. One day, whilst at the village markets, there were all these older ladies sitting on the ground selling large prickly leaves. I sat with one older lady, as her command of the English language was good. She explained to me that if I rubbed this prickly leaf on my sore elbow and knee, it would take the pain away. It turned out that this was because the leaf had natural aspirin properties. I learnt so much whilst I was there. Just about every morning, I would be invited for a 'women's business only' meeting in the community, again a very powerful learning experience and which created wonderful memories. One of the things I was able to bring to these health meetings for women was pelvic floor strengthening exercises for incontinence, which was a major women's health issue.

A man came and sat down in the circle one morning while they were doing these exercises, and the women chased him away.

The family members of the people in hospital would do all the bathing of the patients, help with their meal preparations, feed their relatives if they could not feed themselves, and keep the wards clean. There was no other staff at all, just the two health workers and the two nurses. I saw tropical diseases I have never seen before and so much tuberculosis, not only of the lung but also of the spine and the brain. We had a few pass. I was honoured to sit with them and their loved ones by candle light until their last breath. The families did all the last rites and they would then take them home for their final farewell before burying them. It was all part of life.

Noddy was kept busy doing repairs around the hospital and also on the accommodation in which we were staying. Ben got a few of the young local men to help him. Noddy loved teaching them how to saw wood and do other little maintenance jobs. One job was to put back all the guttering along the long hospital building. The guttering needed to have all the screws replaced, but there was no drill or tools to fix the problem. So, after ten days, Noddy decided he would go back to the mainland with a list of items for the maintenance jobs. I was happy to stay by myself and I would spend the night in the little house where the female health workers were housed. It was very secure and there were security screens on their windows to keep the girls safe. There was a boat going one day, across to the mainland and had a spare spot for Noddy. They would return the next day. Noddy was happy to go to savour a couple of beers, and a good steak; he would come back with all the tools he needed to fix the problems that required maintenance. He did a great job. Often the men would invite him to someone's home for a game of darts. Noddy enjoyed this 'men only' time.

The headmaster even asked us to come down and talk to the school about Australia and where we lived. The kids were all friendly, disciplined and so very polite. They sang us a welcoming song in their language. The community was so clean you could eat off the ground. One of the jobs the kids had to do before school was to pick every leaf off the ground. Produce on the island was minimal as it was the growing season; our stable diet was rice, rice and more rice. Noddy would grind coconuts by hand and collect fern from the riverbanks with the nationals to give the rice more flavour. I think we lost about ten kgs during our stay. Also, it was very sad as the ocean had been fished out and there were no fish to be caught; their once staple diet was gone.

The weeks just disappeared and before long, it was time for us to leave. This was a very sad day for us, the people we met and with whom we shared a month of our lives, had given us so much love and respect, we really did not want to leave. The last night was filled with gratitude as the village had come together and put on a surprise farewell tea, sharing their meagre food supply with us, even catching and cooking one of their few chooks. A motor boat took us back to the mainland and then we waited and waited for a bus which never came; so we hitched a ride in a small covered wooden boat filled to the brim with food like coconuts and bananas which grew all year round for the markets up through Milne Bay to Alotau.

We ran out of fuel along the way and called into a little village to refuel, for which we paid. We finally arrived at our destination at 2200hrs, exhausted and fell into deep sleep as soon as our heads hit the pillow. We had two days in which I had to do a report and hand over to Sister Ben. I could not have spoken more highly of young Ben and assured Sister she had nothing to fear; that, in fact, this young man could end up one day as head of health in PNG. The Bishop and Sister Ben took us out to the best hotel in Alotau for a lovely dinner; they said we would be most welcome to come back anytime and expressed their gratitude for all we had done.. The kindness, acceptance, non-judgements and humility of these wonderful human beings had really touched us so deeply; we and they saw no colour - just brothers and sisters on the journey of life.

Next morning, we said our goodbyes to all and Sister Ben. She was genuinely sad to see us go. The Bishop took us to the airport and we flew back to Port Moresby, where we caught our plane that evening back to Brisbane. Our dear son picked us up and we headed back to the same hotel we were in on our way up to PNG, the three of us for the night.

We left for Sydney the next morning driving down the coast. We had a lovely road trip stopping over night at Byron Bay and Port Macquarie. We had a few days at Noddy's brother's home in Sydney waiting for them to return from Singapore. On the Friday night we arrived in Sydney, a major disaster struck.

We had a phone call from one very distressed daughter in London. She was at a supermarket checkout; she had her purse in her backpack which was on her back and someone had managed to open her bag and stolen her purse with our credit card (which we had given her a long time ago). We immediately cancelled Noddy, JD's and mine. We had left all other bankcards at home in Karratha. This meant of course we had just a few dollars between the three of us for the weekend. JD had about $30 dollars in cash, Noddy and I about $20.00 Young JD had his Commonwealth Bank card which he used, to take us to a Sydney Australian Rules Football game. On Monday morning, we went to the bank to order another credit card for the four of us, and we withdrew money to see us through to the next week.

Graham and Judy came home on the Monday. We had a couple of nights with them and then JD returned to Brisbane. From Sydney, we spent a few days driving down the coast road to Melbourne, a journey we did several times over the years, a most beautiful drive with lots of villages and towns along the coast to call into. We had a few days in Melbourne with Noddy's cousin, John Wundersitz and his wife Ada and then we returned to our home in Karratha. It was one very memorable holiday.

I returned to work in the middle of May, happy to be back. I had learnt so much and wanted to share what I had learnt from the wonderful program of training the health workers in PNG. It was so like the health worker program that we had in the 1970's in the Northern Territory. In WA, the training was very different. I met with the head of Public Health, a lovely older Indian doctor. Sister Ben had given me their training manual, which I shared with him. I had a vision of being able to take our Indigenous Health Workers on a tour to another country on an empowerment program. I documented how it could be done if we could get funding; but of course the whole idea was shut down from forces unknown.

Not long after, I was back at work, I had a visit from some senior managers from Woodside Petroleum. They were organising a major disaster exercise with an explosion and a major fire one of their platforms that was situated off the North West Shelf some 135kms northwest of Karratha. They asked whether we would be able to participate in the exercise? Woodside would pick up the full cost. The Burns Unit from Royal Perth Hospital, led by Dr Fiona Wood were to be involved too. I agreed. We would have three months in which to prepare. One does not know the work involved in planning for such an exercise. I contacted the Head of Emergency Management at the Health Department. He became involved and was a great support person. It was a positive learning experience for us all, and I was grateful for being fortunate to have done lots of courses in emergency management, which helped me to confidently coordinate NBH's participation in this exercise. The big day came and I got the call at seven in the morning. Everyone swung into action, the team from RPH arrived by plane that morning and we followed it through for the full eight hours that it had been planned for. The cost of this was in the vicinity of thousands of dollars.

It was worth it, because eighteen months later, we had a real live disaster at sea. I received a call at 1700hrs on a Sunday afternoon. An iron ore ship, anchored out at sea had had a massive explosion, and a fire broke out, with the report that men had been blown overboard and that there were several deaths and crew members badly burnt. We followed to the tee everything we had learned from the Woodside exercise. The staff were amazing. In the end, we only received one causality who had sustained 80% burns to his body. The doctors and nurses involved were highly skilled. They stabilised the patient and the RFDS flew the injured person to Royal Perth Hospital under the care of the RPH burns unit. Sadly, he did succumb to his injuries and passed away. I am so grateful to have had the experiences I have had and the honour to work with all these wonderful practitioners and support staff.

***

I had a friend in Karratha who was beginning her journey through breast cancer treatment. One of the biggest issues for her initially, was nausea post chemotherapy. We decided to do a small trial. I am not one of those academic nurses nor a researcher; however, we decided to trial giving her a Therapeutic Touch treatment the night before she was flying to Perth. I would see her after she returned to Karratha and then see her weekly. We did this for the whole of her chemo treatments. I am happy to report that she never had nausea again.

Jan owned her own company and she landed a contract with Woodside to evacuate their sick and injured staff from the rig to the mainland. So, she asked me if I would do some contract work for her, so I could be on call for evacuations. We had permission from the senior officials from the health service to do this. So, with two other lovely nurses, we provided a twenty-four on call service for evacuations. We were privileged to be flown out to the Goodwin A platform and to a tanker where other tankers could load gas from. We became familiar with the layout of the Gas Rig and the tanker. We had to fly out on Woodside helicopters. The callouts were very rare and I had only five call outs over the years I worked for Jan.

Even in my mid-fifties I, did the 'Huet Training Course', it was the scariest course I have ever done. I had to get dressed in boots, coveralls and a hard hat. You get strapped in a simulated cage and turned over in a helicopter look alike under water and you were supposed find your way out. It was so disorientating and the cabin was full of swirling water in the deep end of the Karratha swimming pool. I was having heart palpitations and I think this was probably related to fear. However, I was determined to push through and finally passed the practical and theory course.

Jan's company was growing and obtained a contract with some drilling companies out in the Western Desert. I received a phone call on a Saturday morning to go and pick up a man who was part of a drilling team out on the edge of the desert . This guy thought he had been bitten by a snake. The trip was four hours east of Karratha. When we arrived the man was absolutely fine, his bandage was loosely applied and slipped down around his ankle. This snake bite was said to have occurred around 5am.The man was up walking around and there was no evidence of any puncture sites. We had a discussion with the client and the manager. They wanted him to be transferred to Karratha Hospital. So, I re-bandaged his leg firmly from toes to the top of the whole limb and we flew back to Karratha with him. All his blood tests were fine and he was totally asymptomatic. He was kept in overnight and discharged fit and well the next day. Over the years that I was in the Pilbara we had a number of very bad snake bite victims who had to be transferred to a Tertiary Hospital in Perth.

In 1999- early 2000, I arranged to have a compulsory study day for all staff on Ethics to be delivered by a nurse ethicist. A very senior nursing ethics specialist came up from Perth and her visit was very well received by the nurses. She was a very gifted and wise nurse who was an academic and married the art of nursing with the science and art of ethics.

Again, during that time period, we had a visit from the Quality Management section of the HDWA. Their head was the doctor who had been the visiting doctor in Jigalong who had seen the old man with the traditional aboriginal doctor from the story told early from 1991.

The two men from Quality Management met with the Nursing staff and we received some very valuable insights into quality management from them. At question time, I raised with him the incident which had happened in the eighties. He asked to speak to me during lunch. I was informed that the HDWA was aware of the issues and problems that were occurring in relation to the continuation of the procedure that had been trialed at a previous hospital I had worked in. I knew absolutely nothing about the progress of what happened after he left that hospital. I told him what had happened. I remember he was so shocked to hear that this trial had been done in this period of time as there was absolutely no record of this ever occurring. After the conversation, the file was locked again in my mind. Not long after that I was having lunch with a visiting consultant, and the subject came up out of the blue regarding the visit from the HDWA, quality management team. During the conversation, the subject of the happenings of that time came up and what had happened before. He too was shocked as he had no knowledge of that specific incident ever happening in the 80s.

A year or so later, I was working at my desk and received a phone call from a lady chasing information of what had happened. Of course, I told her what had happened, and she asked me if I would be willing to testify in court. I agreed.

***

I had grown so much in the 'Healing Journey' I was on. This was even more reinforced deep within me, when in late December of 2000, I received an invitation to attend the National Community Nurses' Conference that was to be held in Bunbury in November 2000. I was hoping to go to the conference, however due to other commitments I could not attend. Two months after the conference, the presenting papers arrived on my desk. When I opened the conference book, the very first paper presented was a presentation on 'Healing Touch', by a nurse with whom I had worked with in the mid 80's.

I read and re read the paper as my heart was racing and I just knew I had to do the Healing Touch program. I rang Barbara and booked in to do the Level 1 course in early 2001. I took the papers home for Noddy to read; he read it and said to me "Darling, this is what you have being looking for all our married life. Go forth." It increased my joy in doing Reiki (I was up to Level2 Reiki by this stage).

I chose to follow this program because ever since 1995, The Western Australian Nurses' Board allowed nurses to use the following Complementary Therapies in practice. Healing Touch, Therapeutic Touch, Reflexology, Massage, Aromatherapy, Prayer and Meditation and Stress Management. So far, this knowledge had been kept out of mainstream nursing. It was the first I had ever heard of these therapies being used in nursing practice; so I started researching Healing Touch and Therapeutic Touch to find out that there were Post Graduate Masters and PHD – Doctoral Programs available in the USA for nurses to do after their graduate degree. Barbara had completed her Healing Touch Program and was a qualified teacher; she had done her program through Janet Mentgen's, 'Healing International' in Boulder, Colorado. She started (with another nurse) courses in Australia which were then accredited by Healing Touch in Boulder, Colorado. I started to study and read everything I could on Healing in Mainstream in the Medical Model. It was a Holistic model of Health Care - the only model of care I knew and believed in. I was so nourished by it, and that nourishment was to sustain me in some very difficult months ahead through 2001-2003.

***

In August of 2000, we had a very sad clinical outcome when a patient passed away. It became a Coroner's case. I met with the family and comforted them as best as I could. Next morning, I received a phone call from a heart centred nurse, Jane at 6am. The widow of the patient had rung her and wanted to talk to someone. The woman was so distressed, Jane said to her, "the best person for you to talk to is our Director of Nursing, I will ring her and see if she could see you."

Jane rang and asked me if she could give her my number. Arrangements were made and I met with her. I journeyed with her for her emotional, mental and spiritual needs; all out of hours and at her home, for many months during her grieving time. One day, she officially came to see me at work and asked me about the Freedom of Information Act, that I had mentioned to her, and she asked how she could obtain access to get her husband's notes. I directed her as to how she could obtain his notes.

Several weeks later, I received a request from the lady, for a meeting with the medical director and myself. Arrangements were made for a meeting to go ahead. I was called into the General Manager's office, and was asked if I had arranged a meeting with the widow and I said "yes".

He then, to my disbelief, said. "You have to cancel the meeting and you are not to have any dealing with the widow." It is a coroner's case and I forbid you to have dealings with her." I had to write her a letter cancelling the meeting and send a copy to the GM; my heart sank, and never before had I ever had interference in a clinical meeting/matter from an Administrator.

The meeting was cancelled and a letter was sent to the widow informing her of the cancellation. However, what I did do was keep copies of all the meetings we had had since her husband's passing and put them in a locked file in my office. Twelve months later, I received a phone call from a most delightful lawyer from the Health Department to tell me the State Coroner was coming to Karratha to conduct the inquest into the patient's death. She gave me the names of two nurses who would be called as witnesses. During our discussion, I informed her of the documentation, I had on file about the meetings, I had with the widow. She asked me to forward them on, so I immediately sent them as Registered Express Mail. As soon as she received and read them, she sent them straight over to the Coroner's office and called me a couple of days later to tell me that I too now was to be subpoenaed to appear in court. The hearing was set down for a fortnight later and she would be up to meet with us the evening before. This naturally caused the two nurses and myself a lot of stress. Not one of us had ever been to a coronial inquest and the stories we had heard about them since we started nursing were really frightening.

Court day came, and the Rescue Remedy spray got a very good work out. The coroner was a gentle looking man. I intuitively knew he was a fair man who wanted to find out what had happened to our patient and to make recommendations to prevent another person or family from losing a family member in similar circumstances. The clinical nursing staff were called first; they did very well answering questions clearly and distinctly when asked by counsel assisting the coroner. I was called to the stand after lunch. I took the oath and immediately felt strong, I was clear and articulate.

Counsel had finished asking questions, and then the coroner asked me the following question, "Mrs -----, I see you had a meeting booked with the widow. I have a letter here where you have written to Mrs -- and cancelled the planned meeting."

I replied" Yes sir".

He asked me why the meeting was cancelled.

I told him I was called into the General Manager's office and was told to cancel the meeting and write to Mrs ---stating the meeting was cancelled and I was to have no further contact with her due to the pending coronial inquest. He thanked me and I left the stand. I felt a weight lifted from my shoulders. The hearing went for a day and a half. I attended all sessions, and was present for the coroner's closing comments. The one thing he did say was, "If this meeting had been allowed to go ahead, we may not be here today."

Open disclosure was one of the recommendations from that inquest. Once the inquest was over, the widow continued to see me regularly for healing and today we are very close and great friends. I was glad I was able to help this dear woman through this very dark period in her life's journey. It didn't make me very popular with the bureaucracy; however, that was okay. As a patient advocate, I believe it was the ethical thing to do.

There was also another major crisis for the health service. The general practitioners in the town were contracted to provide a medical emergency service to Nickol Bay Hospital. They would also be on call to help the emergency nurses in case they needed any medical assistance. The GPs would have to leave their practice, which meant it would be expensive for them to provide this service to the hospital. (although they were to be paid by the hospital). There was an enterprise bargaining agreement being argued between the AMA and the HDWA. The GPs then demanded a flat rate of $1500 per day to provide this on-call service. The problem was solved by the HDWA, making a decision to have salaried medical officers run the medical services in Karratha Hospital. Port Hedland had salaried doctors, as did all of the other North West hospitals. The advertisements went out and the recruitment started, the selection criteria was extensive and thorough, this was to ensure it attracted a high quality team of medical officers.

I was the Director of Nursing on the panel of interviewers for the appointments. My faith in the recruitment processes was destroyed as I saw how things were mismanaged. I saw a mockery of the HDWA Human Resource Management policies and procedures. We had to read and review all the statements, addressing the selection criteria and write a report re the applicants meeting the criteria, to ensure all applicants were assessed impartially. I read every one and was happy to report that all, but one, met the criteria. One applicant met only one of the criteria; I could not in all honesty have approved this applicant. My report stated, "Not for interview - has not met or addressed the selection criteria"

The panel, made up of three very senior male managers and myself, met a few days later, and I was told that this applicant had never ever had to do an interview before nor address a selection criteria, and that the rest of the panel had agreed to give him a chance. I knew intuitively that I was fighting a losing battle, despite me pointing out that only one of the criteria had been met, that the candidate did not meet any other criteria other than the fact that the candidate was a registered medical practitioner and as a result could not be even considered for an interview. It went to a vote, I voted no, the other three voted yes; this candidate was appointed, so I will say no more. I was awakened as to how these people worked and I started to question management practices. I became very much on the outer. They were very nice to my face, however my intuition was telling me that they were discussing ways to get rid of me.

Noddy and I were very happy in Karratha, and spent our off time enjoying our lifestyle and the company of our dearest friends. Noddy had joined the committee for the North West Jockey Club. One year, the committee were fortunate enough to bring to Karratha the owner of a Melbourne Cup winner, Rogan Josh. The lady owner actually bought with her a replica of that Melbourne Cup for display at the Roebourne races. We had the very same replica of the Melbourne Cup on our dinner table one night as we had invited the owner for a barbecue with a few friends and neighbours. It was a great night and we all celebrated with a drink of champagne from the Melbourne Cup. We still have the photos.

We had some great camping weekends away with Sel, Charlie, Jane, James, Hudson and others down at the 40 Mile beach. Life was good. Our children were happy and on their journey. JA had met and moved in with her soul mate and we were very happy for her. John was to become a member of our family some years later.

Christmas 2001, was a very special one. Noddy turned sixty on the 21st December, and we planned a big Christmas reunion with his family in Adelaide. One of Noddy's sister and her husband flew in from the USA. JA flew back from London on the 19th December and JD arrived from the East Coast in his much loved Kombi van. We stayed in a beautiful apartment down at the beachfront in the heart of Glenelg. We had a great celebration for his birthday and a family dinner on Christmas day with his five siblings and their families. This was very special, as it was to be the last big family reunion we were ever to have. JA and Noddy shared a wonderful experience. She had given him two tickets for a hot air balloon ride over the Barossa Valley as his birthday present. JD actually went to the state library and searched through the microfiche for the day the newspaper was printed on the 21st /12/1941. He did it up as a special archive gift. Noddy was so amazed to receive such a beautiful document and treasures it so much. Our family unit had the best two weeks together. It was a sad day when JA, Noddy and I had to say goodbye to JD at Adelaide Airport. He was heading off back to university to finish his studies and had some work lined up, before university started while we were heading back to the West. Our holidays as a family unit were always the most precious times.

Throughout 2000/2001, I started writing healing papers and forwarded several off as submissions for the State Aged Care Plan and the State Domestic Violence planning committees. I never ever heard back from the organisations I forwarded them to; in fact, I think they were too left field for the powers that be at the time and would have ended up in file 13.(A common Aussie slang term for the rubbish bin.) I was also President of the West Pilbara Safer WA Committee and as such had to attend the annual state conference held in Perth one weekend per year. I was talking to the WA Chief Justice at our morning tea break about developing healing programs for juveniles' caught up in the justice system and prisoners in jail. He asked me to put my suggestions in writing.

It took me several months to write this paper as I didn't know where to start. For weeks, I would think about it before I went to sleep. Then one morning, I was woken out of a deep sleep at 4am with a few words, from a hymn we used to sing in church, the words were "Whom shall I send. Here I am Lord, It is I Lord, I heard you calling in the night." I had no idea what the significance of that was so, I rolled over and went back to sleep. The following night again at 4am, I woke up with words from another hymn, "and set the poor prisoners free".

This time I got out of bed and went straight to the computer and just sat down and wrote and wrote. Within thirty minutes, I had finished the paper that I was asked to write by the Chief Justice some months before. I was amazed with how the words just came together. This was the first time I had ever written anything like this and I have gone on to write many more over the years. The paper was forwarded on to the person who had asked me to put my thoughts and ideas in writing and several weeks later, I received a very lovely letter from the Chief Justice thanking me for forwarding the paper I had sent him. (*Today these three papers are more urgently needed in our society to be applied to the Aged Care, Domestic Violence in all its formats and for the Justice System Cohorts*).

I was also writing poetry again. Words were just coming, one after another, one poem was written while escorting a labouring lady by ambulance, who was being transferred to Port Hedland Regional Hospital, as she may have needed to have a caesarean section, and the doctor who did all the caesarean sections was out of town. The lady was sleeping on the way up and we were on the Port Hedland side of Whim Creek. The whole area was burning, fire leaping into the night sky as far as the eye could see. This was 2am and on the back of a hand towel, I wrote a poem about that fire. I love doing this when the inspiration comes.

The Fire
Her flames flicker tall and bright, an orange glow
Filling the night sky with a colour that's rare
Close to the road she creeps, looking so beautiful
Beneath that beauty, a deadly fear
A fear of all the destruction she will cause
Burning the spinifex and the life that lives there in
Oh! Mother Nature at times you can be harsh

Mother Nature, I am unsure whether I have misjudged you as the cause
Tonight, there is no lightning that you create
That lightening that at times set the bush in flames
So I have to ask are these your flames, or are they man made folly.
2002.

. . .

I attended an art exhibition in Karratha not long after this, and came across a landscape painting that was just fabulous. After I got home, I wrote the following:

"The Artist"
I look at her Artwork dressing the walls
I am taken to a place so pure and clean.
Caught on canvass all earthly colours gleam
Her hand so pure and clean.
She polishes the flowers, dirt hills, and roads
With colours abounding throughout the rainbow
To look at her Art alive fills me with feelings that set me free
to go to places of nature for total tranquillity.
Thank you Janine for sharing with us the gifts you have created
With your paintbrush.
November 2002

NEW GUINEA ADVENTURE 2000

Sister Ben

Noddy sharing a story
with 2 policemen in
Alotau, New Guinea (above)

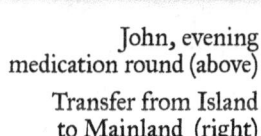

John, evening
medication round (above)

Transfer from Island
to Mainland (right)

Collecting Fern for dinner (left)

Washing Dishes the River
middle of the village (above)

HOLISTIC NURSING

In 2000/2001, the nursing shortages in Australia were really evident. Nurses were leaving the profession in droves and students coming out of high school were not enrolling into nursing. In 2001, the Federal Government called a Senate enquiry into Nursing Education in Australia and called for submissions to be sent to the Senate Community Affairs Reference Committee at Parliament House, Canberra. I forwarded to them a submission for that enquiry, never to hear back.

At the same time The HDWA launched a West Australian Nursing Study called, "New Vision New Direction" - this was a 12 month's study and I had forwarded the exact same submission I had sent to the federal government senate enquiry.

I only had a letter of acknowledgement to say the New Vision New Direction study had received my submission. However, I never heard another word, no report, nothing. My submission was based on what I believed could have been some solutions to the situation nursing found its self in, in 2001. The main points I wrote were: "Return to Caring, To Allow Nurses to Nurse Holistically, and Respect and Value Nursing." I need to add my opening paragraph that I wrote in 2001 and you will understand why.

A renowned information technology futurist and a British telecommunication analyst published his predictions for technology over the next two decades. Combining his predictions with what we know about nursing today and it is not hard to see what the nursing profession will look like in 2020.

What happens when computers are smarter than us? Pearson,(The information technology futurist) believes this will cause a shift to a "Care Economy." Computers cannot care. People will concentrate on the human interpersonal side of work.

Nurses will need to get back to their original and best strength – CARING. Although computers cannot care, they can help nurses define, quantify and administer the effects of caring on patient outcomes. Making sure that they do just that is crucial to nursing's survival.

Fast Forward to 2017 – 23rd of November 2017. The ABC News: The Jobs of 2027.There is a link pursuit.unimelb.edu .au (pursuit)

"In 10 years jobs we're familiar with now, will change as new technologies impact on how we work. Professionals like nursing will all need new skill sets to keep up with the technological revolution."

The nursing section of this article is reinforcing what I wrote in the submission in 2001, both to the Senate Committee and to the 'New Vision New Direction' study, that the HDWA were doing at the time. In 2001, mine was between business and heart centeredness. A lady studying for her masters of Nursing Science in 2017, writes, 'there's a balance to be struck between the march of technology and compassion.'[1]

After commencing the Healing Touch program, and finding out about the Nursing Boards all around Australia allowing nurses to use complementary therapies of which the modalities of touch, (Massage for example was one), I put out a memo to the Nursing Staff regarding the Introduction of a Complementary Therapy Policy for Nickol Bay Hospital - with the delegation for developing this policy to the Nickol Bay Hospital Best Practice Committee. At the same time, Sir Charles Gardiner Hospital was receiving accolades for setting up a Complementary Therapy Unit, fully funded by Browns Dairy for cancer patients and having a policy for nurses to use complementary therapies in their daily nursing practice. An Oncologist who specialises in Haematology was the founder of this unit. I was liaising with the manager of the unit as I had written an educational presentation for nursing staff on Holistic Care and Complementary Therapies. The manager of the Browns Unit asked me to send my presentation down and not long after, I received a phone call and an email back, requesting if they could use this as a patient handout for all the cancer patients and their families. I was so honoured to be asked for permission to use this information I said, "please do". Not long after, I received a phone call from the Albany Hospice asking if they could use it for their patients and families. The only other country health care unit that had a policy at that time was the Margaret River Hospital, who were very happy to share their policy with the NBH best practise committee. I was going to bring the Healing Touch program to Karratha at a later date as a number of nurses also expressed an interest in the program.

A memo was sent out on the 19th May to all the nursing staff about the plan for Complementary Therapies to be introduced later on in the year, once the policy had been developed by the Best Practise Committee. On the 24th of May, I received a very nasty letter from a senior official from the health service regarding this. The memo I had sent to the nursing division was at this stage only for the nursing division, so I wrote a background paper back to the person who sent me the letter. I pointed out in that paper that over the years and more recently, members of the Karratha community both European and Aboriginal supported the use of Complementary Therapies and had verbally approached myself and others to ask if this could be provided as part of their care in the hospital setting. I also included the fact that nurses have always used Complementary Therapies in practise, both as general nurses and midwives, and what we were in actual fact doing, was recognising and developing policies to ensure we were delivering the art of nursing and not just focusing on the science and task orientation side of the nurses' role. We were Holistic Nurses. Not another word was spoken apart from an order, given by this senior official, that

I was not to even discuss this any further with nursing staff. The policy would never be allowed through at Nickol Bay Hospital.

However, neither the nurses, nor I were fazed by this. We continued to do our research and the best practise committee developed a policy and signed off for presentation to the Medical Advisory Committee, to be put forward when the time was right. We went on also to liaise with the Frail Aged facility in Roebourne to include a policy for the Indigenous patients.

I was approached by a social worker to journey with a lady who was in the terminal stage with breast cancer. Her doctor approached me as he supported me in the healing work I was doing after hours. He told me, the dear lady had only about six weeks to live and she was in denial, so would I be able to help prepare her for her passing? I met with this beautiful soul and saw her every week for an hour; we had the most wonderful journey together over an eight-month period; she and her husband were just so happy.

I remember the day, a Saturday, I received a call, it was Denise and she said to me, "Peter I have reached my final destination, I am ready."

I went round to her home, rang her doctor and asked him to admit her into our new Palliative Care unit. A week later, she passed. I was so honoured, as the day before she passed, her husband came and asked me if I would do her memorial service.

I replied, "yes."

I then realised that I have never done anything like this before and thought crikey what have I said yes to? So, with sacred insight and help from her husband, friends and a nun friend of mine in Karratha, we put together this amazing program for her service. It was held at 1700 hrs in Cattrall Park, Karratha and concluded with the bagpipes playing just as the sun went down. I would have to say this was one of the best blessings I have had in my life, journeying with Denise and Michael and leading her final farewell.

***

. . .

In 2001, my father passed away on the 1st August. His passing too was a great blessing. He suffered so badly after losing my dear mother, the love and light of his life. After my mother died in November of 1999, he would say "I won't be here by Christmas," his heart had really broken. I could only pray for him. Although, we did ask him to come to Karratha and live with us, and he did think about coming for about two minutes after Mum died, then completely closed down. He took two years to pass. It was like, he was living in hell, and we felt so powerless to do anything for him, all he wanted to do was die.

He had a big argument with my sister who was living with him and who was also his carer. I was down in Perth at this time and my sister, Marie and I had to go out to mediate to enable peace to be restored. I had a long talk with my father and it broke my heart to find out that he had held a grudge against his mother and sister from something that occurred when he was nineteen years old. I never found out what that was; however, I realised it had affected him all his life for over sixty seven years. This insight made me commit even more to have healing in its true meaning, as part of the medical model. It was to become such a powerful passion for me. No one should have to live their lives buried in blockages that cause spiritual, mental and physical disharmony and disconnection. I felt nothing but compassion for him and prayed for a peaceful ending for him. It took another three months for my father to pass, after this argument with Marion, and he passed in an aged care facility, a broken old man. It was yet again a blessing and a relief and I actually saw someone called Father Des after my father passed, to deal with the emotional imbalance I was experiencing. I am so glad I did, as I was like a bird set free following my sessions with this wonderful healing Catholic priest who used to come to Karratha once every three months.

On the 5th June 2002, a consultation meeting was hosted in Karratha for a review of the Country Health Services. One very proactive member of the community was present, and presented questions. Her first question to the review panel was, "Is the Country Health Service review focused on genuinely seeking community input and then making an unbiased assessment of the suggestions received? Or is the focus about re-arranging the deck chairs on The Titanic? The supporting information I have from the West Pilbara Health Service, clearly states that the strategic plans have already been developed. Do the strategic plans include the provision of complementary therapies? That is, non-invasive therapies that complements the body's innate intelligence to heal itself."

I knew the presenter, but I did not know she would be present at the review, so I was surprised to see her there. In my heart, I was very happy though. I had never spoken a word about what the Nursing Division had tried to do and was still trying to do at Nickol Bay Hospital to anybody outside the nursing circles. Here was a community spokesperson stating exactly what I had put forward a year before to the nursing division, that had been shut down even before we had had a chance to develop a policy. In her presentation, this strong advocate had in the brief time she had to prepare, correlated examples of complementary therapies in the community and had secured five personal testimonials in support of Complementary Therapies from the Karratha community and also positioned the need to have access to treatments in the health service centres. There were no outcomes in the strategic plan and again the community was totally ignored, this was despite what was happening at SCGH and the evidence available through international research in Holistic Healing modalities being an essential part of health service delivery

I was also privileged to journey with a young couple who were on a journey through palliation, referred to me by another medical practitioner. This doctor would have to be one of the most caring heart centred doctors I have ever had the honour of working with.

I journeyed with the young couple for a couple of months and was with them the evening he passed. And I am still friends with Jeannie Kleynhans today, even though she lives in New South Wales and I in Perth.

I also had the most wonderful birthing experience with a couple having their first child using massage and Therapeutic Touch. I taught the father the techniques. It was like we used to do when we were student midwives. Not knowing back then we were using energy medicine, it was what we did in the 1960's and how I had always practised midwifery using The Power of Touch (the flow of love and light). As I write this paragraph, I can see them Mum, Dad and baby in the labour ward in my mind's eye and feel a warm glow in my heart. Thank you, Caroline Watkins.

On the 11th of September 2002, I took the Complementary Therapy Policy to the Medical Advisory Committee meeting. At the meeting, three issues were raised. One of the doctors expressed that potentially Aboriginal Healers would also be appropriate. This was music to my ears. One of the doctors had an issue with one of the points in the action plan of the policy. From this query, I was asked to contact the legal branch of the HDWA and it was tabled for review at the next meeting to be held on the 27th November 2002. I was happy inside as I thought, I may be starting to get somewhere. Next morning, I was at work early, formulated an email, and along with our policy, forwarded it to the HDWA legal branch. By 9am, I had a visit to my office from a senior official who told me not to send the policy to the HDWA legal branch. He had received a phone call from his boss and that there was no Complementary Therapy policy ever to be ratified at Nickol Bay Hospital. I informed him I had already forwarded it down to the legal branch of the HDWA. I still ask myself today why it ever had to go to the Medical Advisory Board?. This is what nurses and midwives had always done.The rationale given by the HDWA was that it was part of Complementary Medicine like Naturopathy and Homeopathy. They did not see it as Nursing Practice. Complementary Therapies are totally different to Complementary Medicine. Complementary Therapies have so much research based qualitative and quantitative data, that is available to all the Health Professionals and to the general public. If they look at the history of physiotherapy it also came from nursing practice. Many of the old nursing text books actually state this. [2]

I then received the following email.

"Hi Peter,

I have been considering the policy presented to the MAC, and after discussion with two of the most Senior Managers in the North West, (whose names I will not mention) would like to suggest the following course of action to progress it. I think we are all in agreement that we should not be sanctioning or promoting treatment modalities that are not evidence based and supported by scientifically proven research. I believe that we need to do a lot more work on this before it gets to a policy level. Until we have completed the following steps and have a policy in place NO Complementary Therapies should be practised within our Health Service.

Please gather the required evidence-based research, journal articles and documentation and collate it into a succinct format. This must be in place before we can even consider moving forward. I understand that some of the modalities are accredited by(?nurses board) as you mentioned in The MAC. I think you need to collect and present documentation outlining which modalities are accredited, who has accredited them and what basis they use to accredit the modalities themselves and the practitioners who deliver the treatment . This will form the basis of the Regional Director's approach to the Legal department (It should be done by him) to consider the proposal.

When this proposal is complete, we can present a policy to the MAC and take steps to implement.

Thanks Peter".

I really was starting to wonder what games were being played. I was happy to be going on leave as I needed some space to clear my head to get everything in perspective and be able to come up with what I was asked to do.

I received a phone call and an email one day from someone in Canberra - who I cannot remember - asking me to come to an Australian Nursing Conference in Canberra. The Conference was for the 13th and 14th of October 2002, I was very curious to find out why I had been invited and why I was was selected. I was told because I had submitted a submission to the enquiry into Nursing Education the year before. It was an Australian wide conference and had many leading professors of nursing from Australian universities presenting. I said I would love to come. It was fully funded and the venue was The Ridges Hotel in Canberra on Lake Burly Griffin.

I was so excited when I got home and told Noddy. He decided to take a few weeks off and after the conference, we would tour Tasmania. This fitted in perfectly with me as I had paid and booked for a four day Conference of the Holistic Nurses Association of Australia. Janet Mentgen (The Nurse Founder of Healing Touch) and Professor Dr Janet Quinn (RN –PhD Therapeutic Touch) were the International guest speakers. Janet Quinn, was doing a two-day Level 1 Therapeutic Touch workshop and Janet Mentgen was doing a one-day workshop on Healing Touch, so I had booked in to do both at the beginning of November, just three weeks after the Canberra Conference. The conference was to be held in Hahndorf in the Adelaide Hills. The next day I took my leave forms in to be signed by my boss only to be greeted with, "here comes Our Hippy DON." I was so happy in my heart when I heard him say this, as I knew where I stood, and knew that my days would be numbered.

The senior official resigned not long after that, and we got a replacement; a younger man in his thirties. But it was not long after that, another restructure was announced. This was the third since I had commenced in 1993. I was called to a meeting with the Senior Officials from the regional and local service and had the restructure explained. This time Onslow Health Service would be coming under the West Pilbara Health Service. They were appointing a DDON for the West Pilbara Health Service and the job description was to be redesigned for the DDON. All hospitals would have level 3 Nurse Managers running the individual units. I knew intuitively my days were definitely numbered because the questions I had asked in relation to the restructure made it very clear that I was not a suitable candidate by the answers given to me by the heirarchy. Work continued to run smoothly, with consultants being brought up to work with the DONs to develop the new model of Nursing Management which was to be implemented in 2003.

. . .

Noddy and I left for our holiday on the morning of the 12th October, flying Karratha-Perth-Canberra. JD picked us up at the airport. It was the day that Canberra was blasted with the biggest sand storm in its history. All the cars in the airport car park had the thickest layer of dust on them that I had ever seen, and every building, had their windows totally blocked out from the sand storm; even the top of the Rydges Hotel did not escape. We had never seen anything like this in our lives. We were quite shocked when we arrived to book in at the Rydges, to see my boss, an administrator sitting there. He too was sent to Canberra to the nursing conference. I will not document why here.

We settled in and spent the evening with our son. We all had a fairly early night but woke to the shocking news that eighty-eight Australians had been killed in a Bali bomb blast - three bombs detonated in the Sari Club and Paddy's bar. We were so shocked we could not believe what we were seeing on the morning news. Our country had been drawn into the world and age of terrorism. All we could do was pray for them, their families and the beautiful people of Bali.

I left the men at 9am to attend the conference. It was very enlightening and I was really heartened to see that in Karratha we were already running all the best practices and implementing programs that were being discussed here, like video conferencing for clinical problems in ED, the Labour ward and the operating theatres with specialists in Perth - we had this in situ.

In 2000/ 2001, I had put my hand up when they were calling for pilot sites, just as it was in its infancy. NBH already had the technology installed. Also, the HDWA was bringing in new computer programs in the operating theatres; we were also a pilot site for the introduction of a national program to monitor AIMS forms, where we would write up incidents if a patient had a hospital acquired problem due to an incident that caused harm to a patient by a staff member.

The conference was all very different to what we were used to in the past; it was very 'scientific' but not one presenter talked about caring or "Patient Centred Care" and the art of nursing. This disappointed me no end, and I questioned why not. I was saying to those present that we needed to marry the Art of Nursing with the Science of

Nursing, but no-one got it. (This is a discussion I would have with all new nursing staff both registered and students who would come to our health service worksites, ever since I became a DON in 1993).

Once the conference closed and we had all said our goodbyes, it was time to get into real holiday mode. We had the weekend in Canberra with JD and Noddy's brother, Graham and his wife, who drove down from Sydney for an overnight stay with us.

We left Canberra and drove down around the coast to Melbourne, where we caught up with family for a couple of days prior to flying to Launceston. We loved the rivers and valleys and the green sacred trees down around the Gordon and Franklin Rivers. All I can say is it is great that Australia had such wonderful advocates for conservation - "The Greenies who stopped the damming of the Franklin were saints." We had a wonderful ten days travelling all around down the West Coast. We were dismayed to see the permanent moon scapes scarring the mountains, just outside the copper mining town of Queenstown.

We loved Hobart and could quite easily have retired there. Whilst we were there, we went down to Port Arthur established in the 1800's for convicts. In 1996, a man massacred thirty-six people and injured countless others in a gun shooting spree in the Café. It was a very eerie feeling entering Port Arthur, the worst I have ever felt. The setting was absolutely perfect the old stone walls and heritage building so well preserved. We started to tour the old goal. Noddy felt sick at the knowledge of what happened back then and could not continue with the tour at the thought of man's inhumanity to man. We left not long after, quite shaken by the experience. Glad to say we have never been back. We travelled up the East Coast and on return to Launceston flew back to Melbourne and drove across to Adelaide through Horsham.

We arrived in Adelaide the day before the start of the Holistic Nurses Conference, and stayed with Noddy's older sister, Kay. He dropped me off at the Conference centre in Hahndorf, a magnificent little town in the Adelaide Hills, surrounded by beautiful gardens and enormous green valleys and hills. What a wonderful five days. I had never ever been to such a nursing conference in my career and never heard of all the research that had been done on Healing through the

Power of Touch and Energy Medicine. I met nurses who had either their PhD or Masters in both Healing Touch and Therapeutic Touch and I met amazing, knowledgeable, intelligent nurses. I realised how far Australia was behind the rest of the world in caring and healing in nursing practice.

I made two very special friends over those five days, Dr Janet Quinn and Bridget Kearne, both of whom had written their stories and had them for sale. I purchased them and also brought Janet's Quinn's teaching program, to be able to share with the nurses at Nickol Bay Hospital and my private clients. I still have those copies that I treasure. I did my level 1 Therapeutic Touch with Janet Quinn as my teacher, and fell in love with the modality. It is simple and it reminded me so much of what the traditional Aboriginal women healers had taught me in Yirrkala in Arnhem Land in 1972. I also did a day workshop with Janet Mentgen. Both Janet's were amazing, caring professionals and I could not believe, that I was sitting sharing several meals with them. I could not take my eyes off them when they were presenting and had my ears so tuned that I heard every single word they said and soaked up all the knowledge I could, absorbing all the science and research that they shared. It all made so much sense. It was so sacred. It was how I was trained in the 1960's without the science. I knew it was how nursing should be practised and from that time on I decided my career move would be, to be the best nurse healer I could be and that is what I was destined to become. I knew then in my heart that I was born for this.

I joined the Australian Holistic Nurses' Association and the International Nurse Healers' Association and accepted a position as the WA representative when the Annual General Meeting was held after the conference had finished. Sadly, the Australian Holistic Nurses' Association folded not long after because of low member numbers. I then joined the American Holistic Nurses' Association and till today receive all their journals and latest research and programs happening in the USA. There is a movement in Australia currently - the early beginnings of integrating healing; however, healers are not recognised by government or as part of the mainstream medical model.

Governments and Schools of Nursing at the Universities and Health Care Units, primary, secondary and tertiary have totally shut the door on allowing nurses to use complementary therapies in their daily practice and do not acknowledge what has been part of nursing practice for time and memorial. This is due to the lack of recognition of Holistic Nursing and Complementary Therapies as a speciality in its own right in Australia.

We returned to Karratha at the beginning of December to no news as to the restructure. Life was normal both at work and play but I did feel negative vibrations coming from the Executive. One of the nurses had been in to see me, as she was very upset about what was being said to her about me by a certain male member who held a position of power on the executive.

I started the long slow process doing what I was directed to do in relation to policy development to have our complementary therapy policy further developed. This work and research was done by Sir Charles Gairdner Hospital in Perth which is a Government Tertiary Institution. Having just come back from the Holistic Nurse Conference where the main theme was the Emergence of the Art and Wisdom with the Science of Nursing, I had all the latest research material available to me to begin what I had been asked to do in September 2002

Once well into the New Year, there were a couple of other incidents which brought me in conflict with the senior officials. I challenged an agreement when I was on a panel, arranging to bring a new allied health service person to the West Pilbara Health Service and allowing the provider of this new service to charge the West Pilbara provider for his airfare, accommodation, hire car etc. and this included his student practitioner. I argued that we did not do this for nursing students and other students like physios and medical students. I stated that the tax payers should not have to have to pick up this tab. The outcome from that discussion was that the provider was told to 'include it in your fee', and I was in trouble post teleconference for raising the issue.

I was also present at a big regional meeting in Port Hedland, where all heads of health in the Pilbara were present. Also present was a Senior Head from the Commonwealth Health Department. The head spokesperson for the Pilbara Health Service, after the formalities of the meeting were completed, stated that we provide a really holistic health care service - medical, nursing, allied health and community health services.

We provide all services. I reacted, put up my hand and said, "I am really tired of hearing the word holistic health care being used to describe what services we provide. I see that persons do not fully understand and recognise what Holism means and what true Holistic Health Care is about." I was shaking and bright red and sat down very quickly, once I finished speaking. The room was in a state of surprise to my standing up and saying what I said and I felt the daggers flying, metaphorically speaking. All of a sudden, some Aboriginal health professionals started to clap. The Head of the Port Hedland Aboriginal Service stood up and said, "At least one person in this room knows what she is talking about" and thanked me.

I had just put the last nail in my coffin.

I must write up a little story, about my own personal rebellion. The Health Minister at the time was a really honest and a sincere minister that you could talk to. He came up to Karratha in 2002 and it was funny because my office was different. I had a row of angels on the top of my big bookcase and in another a row of crystals. I had two very beautiful framed positive affirmations on a little table in front of glass panels that surrounded the office and many a community person would stop and read these beautiful messages.

The first message read:
What lies behind us
What lies before us
are tiny matter's
compared to
What lies within us.

Author : Ralph Emerson .

The second message read:
If there is
LIGHT
In the soul
There is
BEAUTY
in the person
If there is beauty in the person,
There will be
HARMONY
in the house
If there is harmony in the house,
There will be
ORDER
In the nation.
If there is order in the nation,
There will be
PEACE
In the world.

The day before the visit, I was told to put them all away before the minister's visit; I did not heed the order. The Minister came into see me the next day followed by the entourage of administrators. As soon as he walked in and shook my hand he looked around and said "What a beautiful happy feeling you have created here. This is the nicest office I have ever been in." I just gave him a big smile and said, "Thank you."

I had written to the Minister about an issue and on the 28th February I received a beautiful reply from him, which gave me faith, that there were open minded persons in positions of authority who supported my belief in improving the quality of health care. In my correspondence, I had raised the issue of holistic care. In his reply, which I still have, he stated. "With respect to the issue of holistic care, I'm in agreement with you. I know that holistic care is now taught in all undergraduate nursing education programs. I have also seen first-hand in our own public health system how a holistic approach is the way forward"

***

The Christmas and New Year period came and went very quickly; I had a ten day break which was very relaxing. JA did not come home this year as they were coming out for their long summer break for 6 weeks in the August of 2003. JD was going into his final year at Uni and doing extra units over the summer break. We had a wonderful Christmas out at Port Samson with Sel and Charlie, celebrating with Christmas dinner at the Red Rock Café in Wickham. Cyclone season was in full swing and one could actually see climate change happening and with each year passing, the Pilbara was becoming so humid and wet, so tropical.

On return to work in the New Year, it was business as usual. No further talk about the restructure; however, I was becoming more ostracised from management and executive decision making. Still holding my head high, I got on with the day to day routine of my position; I was beginning to not want to be there, however, this was only in the management area.

On the 21st February, a meeting was held regarding the New Model of Nursing Management in Karratha, Wickham, Roebourne and Onslow. The Senior Industrial Officer and another Project Manager –a nurse, came up from head office in Perth. The Directors of Nursing from the above health care units were there too. The JDF's were tabled and reviewed and assessment for the levels was presented. This stated that The District Director of Nursing and Community Health was to be a separate identity.

It became more evident that the role of the DDON was changing and with the changing role, the heart, spirit and wisdom had been removed from the role and it was now to become a business and systems model only. Therefore, I realised I needed to explore other options as to where I would fit into the organisation because I knew I could not work in this model of management.

I did have a discussion after the meeting with the Senior Industrial Relations Manager and from that discussion, I realised that he had been involved from the very beginning of this planned restructure. When one is awakened, they can absolutely read another person kinaesthetically; I was receiving very negative vibes from him. I knew I was being pushed out by a group of men that were the power brokers for the Health service and the HDWA. On March the 7th 2003, I had a meeting with the Senior Official yet again and at the meeting I spoke about the need for the DDON position to be integrated as a heart centred, business and systems management role. Lots and lots of emails started to go backwards and forwards between the Senior Officials from the region, from the head office in the HDWA and myself. However, I am sure many phone conferences were held not only with this trio, but I believe that there was also a hidden figure involved, who at the time was also involved in the formation of the restructure. My belief stems from the fact, that one day I saw him walking in with the Senior Official in 2002. I did not know that this hidden figure was coming to Karratha for a meeting. I was kept totally in the dark. I made the decision not to go near the Executive Suites that day; it was clear that I was not wanted nor was I supposed to know he was on the premises. I did not want a scene where I would be lied to or be embarrassed finding out about this visit.

I have to explain, my office had big windows on the side of the building opposite the executive office entrance to the hospital. I happened to be at my computer at the time and when looking up saw them both walking in, not long after the morning plane from Perth landed. One would think if this veiled figure from the HDWA was in town, he would certainly want to meet with The Director of Nursing Services and the nursing staff. In fact, I am sure that is why, he never answered my phone calls over the preceding months that I had made to him - leaving message after message and never receiving a phone call back. We only ever had one visit from him which was at the very beginning of his tenure. I had been trying for weeks, to speak with him for advice and assistance regarding the Complementary Policy saga; I ended up emailing him, to see if he would assist us with enabling support for the Nursing division on this matter of the introduction of the Complementary Therapy Policy into our health service. I never heard a word back. That email was sent on the 4th February, 2003.

I could not share what I had seen with anybody. So yet again, I went within and kept my own counsel, as I was unsure who I could trust. I know I could have shared it with Sel; however felt it would not be fair to her. So I buried it again deep within me at a cellular level. I had some very unpleasant, meetings and conversations with one particular senior member of the health service, and I left each time with increased stress levels. I had one meeting on the 7th March with him about the need to keep three components to the role which was the heart centred role integrated with the business and systems model role.

I spoke with the Senior Industrial Relations Manager at head office in Perth on the phone on the 10th March to find out that he was going to the Public Sector Management Office regarding negotiating a redundancy package for me on the Wednesday as discussed with the Senior Official.

Everything seemed to be already pre-determined without discussing it with me and I was stunned yet again. On the 19th March, I spoke with the most senior official in the Region, regarding options other than a redundancy or severance as I did not want to leave. There were no options.

By this time, I had decided I would just go. I could not work for an organisation such as the Health service or the HDWA who had absolutely no respect or valued staff in my opinion – especially staff who were different and thought outside the box; staff who would speak up and question decisions made, that one could see were not for the common good. I made some people uncomfortable with whom I disagreed or whom I was in conflict with. I was, not perfect I did live in the human condition which at times became a little imbalanced, which I learnt from and today I am still not perfect. However, I do remember the movie a "Few Good Men" and the words that were said in that movie. "When good men don't stand up and say anything, that is when evil prevails". I could not help challenging when (in my opinion) something was wrong. So I made many enemies over the years for being the person I am, and in the nursing positions I held in the Pilbara, first as DON of Roebourne and Wickham, then as the District DON for the Roebourne Shire for Nursing Services (Hospitals and Community Health) to the Director of Nursing Nickol Bay Hospital and Community Health.

So, on the 24th March I wrote this letter,

Dear Sir,

Re: Severance /Redundancy

"I am writing to confirm that following discussions with my husband, I would like to accept an offer of severance /redundancy from the health service at the abolition of the Director of Nursing Position at Nickol Bay Hospital and Community Health, Roebourne Shire".

The new position of District Director of Nursing Nickol Bay, Roebourne Wickham and Onslow Hospitals will take effect from July.

It would be appreciated if the above is kept confidential as I understand from our discussion last Friday you will be liaising with Bureaucrat X regarding the above and my subsequent decision."

Yours sincerely

Peter -Director of Nursing

Nickol Bay Hospital /Community Health.

I posted the letter and immediately felt this amazing peace just flow through me. I knew I had done the right thing even though I did not want to leave the Nursing Services. The Health Service to this date has not advertised the DDON position. I had made it very clear in my discussions and correspondence with the hierarchy that I would not leave until the new DDON was appointed. I had a phone conversation with the in-charge for the region and I said to him I would only accept a redundancy /severance if it was offered to me; I would do so only when the DDON was appointed so that it would enable a full handover to be done. I had further conversations with the Senior Industrial Relation Officials from the Head Office in Perth over the following weeks. This was ignored, as I was told to finish.

When I queried this with the Manager I had been dealing with, he became quite aggressive and told me that he has now brought forward my finish date. I reiterated that I had written and agreed I would accept the redundancy once the DDON model commenced; however, he ignored and refused to discuss this with me. I also expressed my deep concern about the speed with which all this was happening and the fact that the position had not yet been advertised. He reiterated that I was to be paid out before the end of the financial year and I asked why it could not be rolled over? This was a common practise in health services across WA. He stated that if I did not take it then, it may not be available to me. I took this as a threat, and it caused me some concern. I believed this had been an unfair process and they just wanted me gone. I do have to say I had been with the service for ten years and never once had I ever had a performance appraisal nor was I ever performance managed. I felt I had been completely shafted by the Health Department and the West Pilbara Health Service.

***

When I arrived home, I told Noddy and said I would see out the next two months with all the dignity I could muster. We had to arrange accommodation as we were not going to leave Karratha. Noddy loved his job and was not ready to retire and we did not want to leave our extended families – Sel and Charlie nor Melena, Dragon and the kids. Nor our friends and lifestyle. But we were looked after and we received some good news. The Catholic priest in Karratha offered the Catholic presbytery in Dampier which would become vacant at the beginning of June. We would also be the caretakers of the church and the grounds for a very fair and reasonable rate.

I also had to start the process of packing up all our personal effects that were being relocated to a storage company in Perth as part of my redundancy package. The weeks flew by and the closer the time came to my leaving, the happier I was becoming. We had decided that to keep me well and studying, I would go and do some contract work and in-between, continue with my private healing practice simultaneously, whilst I was doing my Healing Touch and Therapeutic Touch programs. We also realised that I needed my heart to heal to ensure there was no more disconnecting of Body, Mind and Spirit. So, I contacted a nursing agency in Darwin and put my name down to do a month's relief in a remote Aboriginal community commencing the 1st of July. We also realised that we needed to purchase another vehicle as the car I drove was a HDWA car that I could use privately. Again, we were very fortunate. We managed to find a little Daihatsu Terrios for sale. It was five years old and had only done 13,000 kms and never been off the bitumen.

JD's birthday was on the 11th April. We had arranged a huge surprise for him. We rang him on his birthday and asked him if he would like to fly over to Karratha and go swimming with the whale sharks down at Coral Bay with us. He was blown away. Over the long Easter weekend, I made arrangements with the DON of Exmouth to stay in the vacant DON's house for the weekend. We picked him up from the airport at 1700 and then drove 500kms to Coral Bay arriving safely at 9:30pm. All the beds were made up for us and there was a supply of coffee, tea and milk and cereal in the fridge. We were up early next morning and out to the dive venue.

We had the most amazing day and the experience was such a magical, spiritual experience. I had to be rescued a few times by the rubber ducky, which Noddy came out in. He doesn't like swimming under water, so he didn't do the dive. At one time, I had lost my bearings and swam straight into the whale shark's face staring it in the eyes. I got a real fright. He/she just kept on swimming; I took off to its right and swam as fast as I could. JD kept up with the shark, swimming with it, until his time was up. These animals are absolutely magnificent and thank God they are a protected species. found in one or two sites in the world, Coral Bay being one. We had a wonderful weekend, one that we will never forget. Swimming with this magnificent creature returned me to a consciousness that we are one with all. We returned to Karratha on the Monday and JD caught the early morning flight back to Canberra, we were so happy to have shared this experience with him.

In my last weeks at work I finished everything up and wrote a detailed report for the new DDON, sealed it and left it in the top drawer in the DON's Office.

The reality hit when I received an email sent out to our staff.

'It is with sadness that Nickol Bay Hospital and the Shire of Roebourne will be bidding farewell to Mrs Peter, the DON of Nickol Bay Hospital. Peter ---- will be leaving NBH. For those of you that have worked with Peter at any time over the last ten years (In her capacity as DON/ HSM Roebourne/ Wickham or as DON – Nickol Bay Hospital), you will know that Peter has been an excellent client and nursing advocate, who has always tried to steer us on the course of providing holistic care to our clients, patients and their carers. Peter will leave a vacuum both at Nickol Bay and The Roebourne Shire community which will be difficult to fill. I would like to invite all staff to an extra special morning tea on Friday at 10am to come and farewell Peter'.

Thanks

My dualistic mind could not help thinking this email, is so hypocritical of the author; he did not even know the positions I held in the Health Service, I was never the DON/HSM out at Roebourne Hospital. I was a District Director of Nursing for Roebourne, Wickham and Nickol Bay Hospital and for the Community Health Centre in the Roebourne Shire, and after a restructure in 1998, I was the Director of Nursing for Nickol Bay Hospital and Community Health Centres in the Roebourne Shire. I could not but feel sorry for this man.

I was sent a cc of the following reply that was sent back in response to the invitation:

"Thank you for the invitation, however I am at that time at the Ministry of Justice seeing clients, I would like to just let you know that I have had a lot of support from Peter over the last few years and I would also like to pass on thanks from my clients. My clients are often labelled as the trouble makers and the difficult to deal with clients with

other labels we will not mention. Those who have been admitted to hospital speak with affection and praise for Peter who often took the time out to talk to them or administer some other healing to them. Peter will know who I speak of. Pete as one of my clients calls her, has had a big impact on one young man who spent time in hospital. Peter may or may not be aware that this young man, currently doing addiction studies is over 12 months clean and sober, and has in the past said Peter had a part in his recovery. No doubt there are many more wonderful stories out there that will help Peter move on with pride knowing that she has made a great contribution to the Shire of Roebourne and had played a personal part in so many lives. I wish her wonderful times ahead and thank her for the support to me over the last five years".

For the first time, I just broke down and cried at the cruelty of what people who don't really care can do to heart centred persons. I know I had been targeted ever since I had my breakdown, recovery and returning to the workplace because my position was advertised in the West Australian newspaper as previously documented. It took five years to finally achieve their goal, to have me removed. It was good to have a good cry and I knew how strong a woman I had become and I realised I could now follow my true calling as a Nurse Healer.

Noddy and I were still building our nest egg for our retirement. I would still need to do some work besides running a not for profit healing centre.

Finally, the day arrived, and it was with great sadness that I said goodbye to all. My heart was hurting, my mind racing with both positive and negative thoughts, and my spirit ready to fly for the next journey /chapter of my life. Seleana was standing right beside me when I gave my final farewell speech to staff and visitors with her hand on my shoulder offering her support.

I returned to my office, pulled the blinds, picked up my bag and walked out the door to a beautiful clear blue sky, knowing that I had made a difference to the lives of many, I would not turn back and only move forward and live in the present.

TRANQUILLITAS HEALING

We had already packed up our personal effects, and on Saturday the 14th June we moved from our HDWA owned home and into the little cottage right next to the Catholic Church in Dampier. We settled into our new residency quite quickly and loved it. The beach was within walking distance at the end of the street and we were close to all amenities. Noddy became an active member of the bowling club and was surrounded by friends. Karratha was only twenty kilometres away, and we could travel out to Point Samson and Wickham. The little cottage had a meeting room and a sitting room attached and this we set up as a treatment room for 'Tranquillitas Healing' my private practice, and a new chapter began.

Two weeks after I had finished up, I received a phone call from the agency in the Northern Territory on the 27th June asking me if I would come for a month to a little community called Yarralin, in the West Katherine Health Service District 390 kilometres west of Katherine. The community was situated right on the Wickham River about 15 kilometres from the Victoria River Downs, a major cattle station in the Northern Territory. There was a two-nurse health clinic there; however, due to a shortage of nursing staff, there had been only one nurse there for a month and she was under severe stress and was having to be flown out as soon as a replacement nurse arrived. Could I start on the 1st July? The poor nurse. I felt so sorry for her when I heard this; it was her first post as a remote area nurse and she had never done anything like this before. In fact, she had very minimal emergency experience, if any at all.

Noddy gave me his blessing and in two days I left for my first fly-in- fly- out role. I was flown to Darwin on the 29th, had an overnight in a hotel and the next day, caught a streamlined passenger jet that took about thirty passengers down to Katherine. From there we boarded a two- seater tiny little plane and headed West. The pilot was very chatty, pointing out significant landmarks along the way and the three hour flight went very quickly. I felt free and excited about spending time out of mainstream western living. Our children were now grown up. I also knew that I would be so nourished by being in an indigenous healing environment and culture.

The poor nurse I was relieving was waiting for the plane to land. She looked very tired and stressed. Her eyes were red from crying and as soon as I put my hand on her shoulder, her tears started to roll. I just said get well again soon young one. She pointed to the troop carrier handing me the keys, and a mud map to get to the clinic and to the staff accommodation and with tears still in her eyes headed straight to the plane.

Such was my handover. I waited for them to leave and headed to the car and drove off down the road to the clinic. The community looked very pretty; lots and lots of green trees and bushes lined the small township with a population of about 240 people. The river was on the edge of town, and there were little kids swimming having a great time. I thought I would love to join them but had forgotten to bring my bathers.

I found the clinic without any problem. Then I drove to what was to be my accommodation for the next thirty days. The little house was fairly old and sparsely furnished. It needed a good clean and dust. I found some clean sheets, pillow cases and blankets folded in the linen cupboard. I got settled in, had a bite to eat and a cup of coffee and at 13.30 headed over to open the clinic. I had plenty of time to orientate myself, finding where ever thing was kept, and familiarise myself with the emergency room. The equipment was sparse with just a little automated external defibrillator. Nothing like what I had been taught to use. So I spent time ensuring I knew exactly how to use the defibrillator. Once I was happy, I went on to check out the pharmacy.

I heard the front door open towards the end of the day. An older aboriginal lady poked her head in to say she wanted some eye medicine, "dry eyes, sister, dry eyes." I found her notes in the filing cabinet and noted she had nothing documented regarding this dry eye problem but there was no mention of any eye drops being dispensed. The documentation was very different to what it is elsewhere. I saw her eyes were irritated where she had been rubbing them but there was no redness. So, I gave her a bottle of eye lubrication. She gave me a big smile and in her very broken English thanked me and left. She was my only patient for the afternoon. I finished mopping the floors of the clinic, as there was no cleaner and had the clinic looking fresh and in order as I liked, and then returned to my little home. I made some dinner, something I was not accustomed to do as my dear Noddy always did the cooking at home while it was my job to do the washing up.

I woke the next day, did my meditation and was up and prepared for my first day of work in a new world. I was excited to be back working in a remote community, a community where I could just be me. The community was very quiet; it was the school holidays, all the teachers had left town and a lot of families had gone to other remote settlements to stay with relatives. The population had dropped to around a hundred people. When the shop was open, I went over to introduce myself to the shopkeeper. It was the only provision store in the community.

On returning to the clinic, I reviewed the Policy and Procedure manuals, very well set out and clear so in situations where one was sent in to relieve, one could be up and running the next day. I found out that we would have a fortnightly doctor's visit from Timber Creek for two days; one was due that Thursday. He would stay overnight and do another clinic on the Friday morning. In emergencies, we had to ring the Aerial Medical Doctor. I rang the administration in Katherine to introduce myself and get instructions for what they needed from me on a daily basis. I was informed that they were trying to contract another nurse to come out as soon as possible to return to a full complement of staff, i.e. two nurses. There was no health worker, she was away.

At 10am a stream of patients started wandering in. They were really nice, warm and friendly. I addressed all their presenting complaints and felt very comfortable and relaxed. I loved the clinical work. It made me realise how fortunate I was to be able to maintain my clinical skills as a Director of Nursing both in a hospital environment and a community health setting. I was also blessed to have had previous experience working in remote communities. It felt good to be back in these earthy surroundings. I had time to talk and treat people holistically to be with them in a way that one cannot be in the western culture. I was using my senses of sight, touch, smell, hearing and intuition to guide me. We only had the most basic equipment.

I loved it when the old people would come in. I often would sit on the steps at the rear of the clinic and talk to the old drovers from the 50's and 60's listening to their stories. Stories so priceless, which may be lost forever. One old man used to keep me entertained with his stories of droving days, taking cattle down from Victoria River Downs to Wyndham. I developed a strong bond with these people, as we shared our journey in life together. I settled in very quickly and the people felt very comfortable coming into the clinic.

It was Thursday - doctor's clinic day and the community really liked this doctor. He was a man who had lived and worked in Africa for many years and worked with their traditional African healers. When he arrived, we sat and had morning tea and then lunch together. There was an instant connection as we shared our common interest in holistic healthcare and healing modalities. When he found out I was a Healing Touch, and Therapeutic Touch practitioner and believed in the traditional aboriginal healing model, he said he would send me some clients during his visit. One of his first patients, after lunch, was a very tall, well-built man who had injured himself in a rodeo on the previous weekend. He had come in from one of the surrounding stations to see the doctor, with a wry neck. The doctor came out of his consulting room, and asked me to come in and see if I could free the man's neck. I agreed and with the man's permission started to work with my energy medicine technique of Therapeutic Touch. Within fifteen minutes of doing what I practise, the man had full movement in his neck. The man couldn't believe it, as he had never seen a white person do this work. The doctor too was very happy. The man left with no pain, full movement of his neck and no drugs.

Needless to say, I was over the moon. I was a strong believer in the Power of Touch, through the modalities. During his visit, he referred a few more clients who came to me and the word spread in the community like wild fire, "new sister im do chucking medicine, like our medicine man and women." I was so honoured to be given permission to use the gift I had been given, being validated and acknowledged by these beautiful community members. I was accepted and trusted.

One Sunday, I was invited to have morning tea with the pastor in the community. When I arrived at his front gate, I was greeted by his two dogs - they were not happy puppies, barking and growling. He came out and shooed them away apologising for their behaviour. He made me laugh as he told me his dogs did not like white people. I made him laugh when I said our dog, a little miniature fox terrier, called Shamrock did not like dark people and would do exactly the same thing if he saw Aboriginal persons walking past our home. Honestly, living and working in communities like Yarrilin was just so rewarding.

Another day, an old Aboriginal lady came to the clinic and said to me in very broken English, "Sister you take us fishing on Sunday." I said yes, absolutely; I would love to do that. We made arrangements and Sunday came, I went around to where we had arranged to meet. I picked up five old ladies each with their walking sticks and headed to their fishing spot about twenty kms on a dirt corrugated road. As I had absolutely no idea where we were going and language was a communication barrier, I had to keep asking where to turn. I soon realised that directions were being given with a finger sign. If I came to a track going to the left, I would get a tap on the knee and a finger pointing to the left, if I was to go straight ahead it was a finger pointing straight ahead, and if to the right, a finger pointing to the right; very effective way of communicating directions.

The ladies were very happy to be going out especially when we eventually arrived at our destination, pulled up and disembarked, heading single file down the embankment onto the rocks where the water was flowing fairly slowly past us. It was such a peaceful place, warm rocks to sit on, and lots of green trees lining the surrounds and the bird life was in abundance. The women were chatting away in their dialect laughing and embracing life.

One old lady sitting next to me on the river bank said to me, picking up a strand of hair from my head, "Sister, do you colour your hair? I nodded - I used to have streaked hair at that time.

She said, "Sister you not colour your hair again, see this colour hair,(pointing to some white /and grey hair .) This colour hair means you wise old lady". I was all of fifty -five years old. I listened and from that time on never coloured my hair again. I smile when I reflect on the advice given by this very wise old Aboriginal Elder and her advice did save me a lot of money over the years. Well, we didn't catch one fish and no bites. They explained, "Water too cold sister." So, we headed back to the community, all very happy and I dropped them all home. I felt so blessed.

I had a call out one evening. A young mum had brought her baby in. "Baby getting cold sick, sister," she said. It was so good to see that the young mothers were on to identifying symptoms early and seeking assistance before the children developed bad colds leading to infections. They were very proactive in keeping themselves and their babies and children healthy. I asked her if I could do therapeutic touch on the baby and if she would like me to teach her how to do so. She said, "yes sister, I have heard about what you do, and please show me."

We had a very rich session with a very positive outcome for the baby with all the signs of a developing cold disappearing. The lass was very interested in where I had learnt this work. "Sister where did you learn this chucking medicine?" I explained all about the courses I was studying. It was such a free working environment, I could not help feeling so peaceful and I wanted to stay working here with these totally non-judgemental, non-materialistic people. But I knew it would be impossible as Noddy would never be settled or happy, living or working in such a remote area. He was an ocean person through and through.

It was in the last ten days of my assignment, I received a phone call to say that they were sending out another agency nurse to share the load. I was quite relieved as I was beginning to feel physically a little tired. Emotionally, mentally and spiritually I was feeling alive and connected. I was healed and just so happy to be able to nurse people integrating the medical model with the healing modalities through my hands. I picked up the new nurse two days after the phone call and we clicked instantly. She was a very nice lady approximately forty years of age from Queensland. I was having my first night off since I had been there and I was also getting excited. My beautiful daughter and her partner, John were arriving in Australia from London on the second of August, doing a trip down the East Coast and then to Uluru and then flying to Broome, where Noddy and I were going to meet them on the 8th August. I was missing Noddy too. We would talk on the phone every evening. He too was missing me and Shammy –the dog was fretting.

One day, we had a call to go to an outstation to the east of Yarrlin approximately 100kms inland to give vaccinations to two children living out there. There was no road, just a dirt track caused by the continual use of four wheel drives heading in the direction of the outstation. My colleague did not want to go as she had not been in an environment as remote as Yarrlin before. I of course, was only too happy to go. I was asking directions from a very old man, who had come into the clinic which way should I go. He told me, "Sister, I take you, you get lost". I could have kissed him, as he was so right, and we arranged to leave when the sun came up the next morning. Within ten minutes two other ladies came to the clinic and asked if they could come with us, as their sister lived at this community. Sure, I said. After we closed the clinic and went home, I packed a picnic lunch for all of us and ensured we had plenty of water, for the next day's journey

Next morning, we set off on our journey. The old man's English was very good. He sat in the front with myself and the ladies and a couple of children were in the back of the troop carrier. As soon as we left the community we had to take a dirt track that was quite overgrown. We had only gone about twenty kilometres when we had to pull up at a river crossing where there was another car also trying to cross. They too had pulled over and everyone got out for a chat. It was such a beautiful morning, clear blue sky, gentle breezes and the water just gently flowing down the spillway. I sat on the edge of the crossing and dipped my feet in the cool water - heaven.

All of a sudden one of the men told us all to be quiet, and as I stood up, he said stand still, and pointed to a big black snake curled up looking like a rock about twenty metres from where I was standing. I did as I was told, looked at the rock, then looked back at the man. He quietly whispered that it was a red bellied black snake. My heart started beating faster as snakes are my biggest fear. I started walking backwards as silently as I could and as soon as I got back to the car, jumped straight in. The others returned very quickly and quietly. We started the engines of both cars and headed off in different directions. I never wanted to see anything like that again. But I was blown away as always, about how nature protects her own, this snake was curled up just like a rock protecting itself from preying eagles and basking in the sun.

We arrived safely at the outstation after a fairly bumpy ride over rocks and boulders. It took us two hours. We were offered tea, boiled in a billy, as there was no electricity out there. I did the five year old's check-up and gave the little ones vaccinations. The kids were so good, no tears.

The women and children decided to stay out at the outstation, so the old man and I headed back to Yarrlin. He said to me as we were leaving, "Sister, I take you home different way." So, I followed his direction, this time no dirt track , just a road of boulders and the journey was harder to navigate than the one we came in on. It was much rougher. I prayed as he just kept talking; we rounded a corner and drove into this chasm; half way through this pathway, he said, "Sister, stop the car". I did and turned off the engine and we got out.

There was an eerie silence and quietly he said to me, "Sister this Sacred Site. In the 1880's this was a place which our men used for secret men's business. One day, they were here all sitting and then out of nowhere white men on horseback came with rifles and shot all the black men."

You could feel the ground vibrating. I was stunned and could not speak, tears started to flow and my heart was hurting. I had only heard stories of what the white people did to the Aboriginals in the Pilbara Region and there is a plethora of photos to prove the way the white man treated our first Australians there. I felt very heavy. I was so honoured to be taken to this place by this dear old man. I am so sure not many white people have had the privilege to be shown this sacred site. After spending five minutes in silence, we got back in the car and headed back to Yarrlin, arriving home safe and sound. The experience has stayed with me since that day.

A couple of days later, two old men came into see me; one had a very sore and painful foot. They were sitting on the bed and before I had even examined the foot, the patient said to me, "Sister you do like our medicine man work for my foot." I was blown away by this request. I spent twenty minutes giving him a therapeutic touch treatment and the outcome was very positive; he could walk with no pain. The two old men were just so interested in hearing about the studies I was doing and how a lot of the techniques in Healing Touch had been given to the RN, Janet Metagan and her team (the founder of Healing Touch), from the Hopi American Indians in the US. I also told them that I had been taught by an Aboriginal Medicine Woman in Yirrkala in Arnhem Land NT, when I was a young nurse.

The next day, I had an aboriginal elder come in to see the Doctor from Timber creek about his headaches. The Dr referred him to me and I did a Healing Touch technique called a Mind Clearance. Again, he had a very clear head and absolutely no pain, and on completion of the treatment, he was so happy, he gave me a big hug. The more I did the work I was doing with my hands, the stronger and stronger I became and my belief in the Ancient Healing Arts through the Power of Touch became totally cemented.

My last week came, and it was time for me to say goodbye to the lovely people there. I was asked to stay and be their permanent sister. It was hard to say, "no I am so sorry I am unable to do this as I have a family, but maybe one day. Please remember you will always be in my heart; you will always be with me."

When the day came for me to fly out, the RN from Victoria River Downs came by to pick me up and took me to the airstrip. The plane arrived, another light aircraft and this time the plane flew to Alice Springs and after several hours wait there, I took a flight back to Perth and then up to Karratha. It was so good to fall into Noddy's arms again, I had missed him and vice versa. It was great as I went right back to being balanced and very happy again and we had a few days to catch up with all our friends. Noddy had the mobile home –a twenty one foot Hino Bus all packed up, with the Terrios on the car trailer as we were going on a month's leave with JA and John.

ROUNDING UP

*H*olidays came and off to Broome we headed, stopping at the 80 Mile beach for a couple of nights. It was relaxing and it was great to be free from all the stress. We were excited to be sharing a month with our beautiful daughter and her partner. We arrived in Broome a day before JA and John flew in and had settled into a very nice caravan park. We had them booked into a cabin over the road from us. The big day came and we were out at the airport very early. The reunion was wonderful and we had a very memorable holiday with them. We spent a week showing them around this beautiful gem of the North of Western Australia.

Our next destination was Dampier for three days, to introduce John to the Pilbara Region and to our way of life up there. He found it very different to London and what he was used to. We headed then to Coral Bay for four days, before heading to Perth. It was so good to see JA so well and so happy but it was so hard when we had to take them to the airport and say goodbye. It is hard being a parent.

On our return to Dampier, I took a few more contracts for short periods of time. The first one was for the Sunrise Health Service in the Northern Territory to set up a Staff Development program for Remote Area Nurses and Aboriginal Health Workers. I found this quite challenging. It was not related to the kind of work I was used to, but I accepted that because many of the communities I visited were single nurse posts that had agency nurses working in them. Sadly, I perceived a lack of professionalism and knowledge. The staff quarters in these communities were not very conducive to maintaining permanent staff. A colleague and I were to stay over for a couple of days; however, we had to scrub the flat we were to stay in before we could even sit down for a cup of tea; and the clinic was not much better.

Talking with an agency nurse at this clinic, I certainly saw that he did not have the necessary experience to be working as a remote area nurse. It was a chance to make a lot of money, if you had a three month contract as an agency nurses; however, communities had changed too. For example, I was saddened when speaking to one young man who told me when I was talking to him, that he was addicted to *ganja*[1] and all his friends were smoking it. He described how there was just nothing to do in his community. He was bored and depressed. All I could do was pray for him and his community. I received quite a shock at how communities and health care delivery in remote areas had changed in the thirty one years since I first started as a public health nurse. I saw no evidence of any traditional medicine or traditional healers. Everything was the westernised medical model with the aboriginal health workers strictly following that model, as instructed by their RN.

I was very happy to leave this environment to go home to Katherine. I was witnessing the death of the great healing cultures that could really help and support our indigenous brothers and sisters. My colleague and I, on this trip, drove to visit all the clinics in the East Katherine district which included Roper River known as Numbulwar on the Gulf of Carpentaria. On the way back to Katherine we were on a dirt road and we got a flat tyre. My younger colleague, a fit and very capable woman was up on top of the Landcruiser in a trice. She did not have any trouble unscrewing the nuts on the new tyre; but when we tried to undo the nuts on the flat tyre, we could not move them. So, here we were stuck. It was hot and the sky was becoming very dark with rain clouds gathering. We ended up sitting under a big tree and waited for another car to come our way. About an hour and half later, with the heavens about to open, a bus full of Aboriginal men from Numbulwar pulled up, and several men got out and very kindly managed to undo the bolts and nuts. They changed the tyre and saw us safely on our way. Ten minutes down the road, the heavens put on a fabulous lightening show for us and the thunder crackled ominously; then torrential rain came down. We had not yet arrived at Mataranka and the rain was so heavy, we had a very slow long drive - 106 km- back to Katherine and by the time we arrived home, we were utterly exhausted.

The role I was employed to do, did not eventuate as the health service was in its very early infancy and the ground work for the service was months behind schedule. It was not related to the kind of work I was employed to do. I did manage to write up a staff development manual for the remote area nurses and the aboriginal health workers. I prepared and ran an orientation program for the first nurses they were employing.

I finished my contract and was very glad to leave. I knew I could not change anything; it was how it was.

My darling husband came up to Darwin for a ten day holiday over the Christmas period and I was able to get that time off. We did a lot of catching up with old friends and exploring a part of the territory we had never been to before. We did tours around Katherine and up the Katherine Gorge, a rather beautiful experience; it reminded me so much of the Kimberly. It was very hot and humid; we had New Year's Eve out in Kakadu National Park and took a magnificent flight out over the Kakadu Falls, first thing on New Year's Day.

We had the last two days in Darwin together and the night before Noddy left, I was awoken with a pain in my right upper right quadrant. The pain was excruciating. Noddy wanted to take me to the emergency department at the Royal Darwin Hospital. I refused to go and started to do self-energy work and laying on of my hands on my painful abdomen and within twenty minutes the pain had all but gone.

I told Noddy that while we were window shopping through Cullin Bay I had noticed a sign which indicated it was a healing clinic. The name on the window said it all, 'The Spirit Doctor.' I said to Noddy do not worry, I will go and see the Spirit Doctor after you fly home this morning. It was sad to see him go back to Karratha, but I had to complete what I was doing and knew I would be home in early February.

After his plane left, I drove to Cullen Bay and saw this Spirit Doctor. He was a lovely tall and big African American, who had worked in many places in the world learning traditional healing techniques. There was instant mutual respect for each other. After we talked for fifteen minutes, I lay on his couch and as soon as he started to work on me with his hands I could feel the energy flow, clearing around my right upper quadrant. I felt big changes within my physical, mental and spiritual body. I was so light when I left the clinic and very happy as I had no pain.

On my return to Katherine, I had committed myself to continue my healing studies in Healing Touch and Therapeutic Touch. However, I knew I needed to continue to work to pay for my studies. I also knew that I had to continue down this path as they were two energy healing modalities that nurses are allowed to use in practice, and to become a nurse healer, I needed to complete the programs.

After I had delivered my first two week orientation program in mid-January, I returned to Karratha. It was so good to be home with Noddy. While I was away, he and Shammy (our Tenterfield terrier) had a great time together walking every day and swimming after a day's work and kept the home fires burning. The kids were well. JA was very happy in London and young JD, who had just finished his second degree and was cementing his career, was doing well too. He had just returned from an adventure touring Peru and Bolivia.

Once back home, I was running my little private not for profit healing practice. I loved it so much and was being so rewarded spiritually. I met a beautiful young woman during this time, who had just finished a Swedish massage course. Noddy introduced her to me and we clicked straight away. We spent many happy Friday morning's swapping healings on each other. Jane Bartley was a gem and had great healing hands.

I had been liaising with a wonderful doctor at the Karratha Medical Centre. He could see the future in holistic healing and I was granted permission to have a room free of charge at the medical centre to run a clinic, two days a week. I was also contracted by the Division of General Practice to set up the Federal Government's care planning model for persons with chronic disease, two days per week for the GPs, and then train the practice nurses.

I had been working as a Complementary Therapist in the medical centre for two days and decided this was not the right place to be running a healing clinic. I found walls had ears, and I could hear exactly what the GP in the room next to me was saying to his patient. So, I went back and worked out of home, to ensure a sacred space of quietness and tranquillity.

I did enjoy setting up the chronic disease management program as I was meeting and talking with lots of older people. After the Care Planning Program was set up and the contract to do that was completed, I was then asked if I could set up a palliative care service for the remote towns and communities in the Pilbara.

Funding had been obtained from the Federal Government through the Division of General Practice to work with a project being run through a university in New South Wales. Again, I had to start the service from scratch. The first thing I had to do was write up a Palliative Care Manual with all the Policies and Procedures, order all the equipment and be office bound. The Pilbara Home care service ran the delivery service for Palliative Care in the Roebourne Shire.

Not long after the project had begun, I had a call to ask me, if I could provide a recliner rocker for a poor old man who was dying of lung cancer. At that stage, I did not have any equipment so I rang the nurse manager at Nickol Bay Hospital to ask for a loan recliner from the palliative care room at NBH as I knew they had two. The answer was no; the equipment belonged to Nickol Bay Hospital and was not to leave the premises.

I was also sent to Perth to do a week of up-skilling, visiting the Hospice in Shenton Park and speak with the Palliative Care Medical Staff. Again, I received such a shock to see how much had changed in Palliative Care management from the original model we had in the early 1980's. I found it overwhelming and I was disappointed about the medicalisation of dying. It was so alien for me. So, one night during that week, I rang Joy Brand the beautiful soul, who brought Palliative care to Perth in the early 80's. Joy too expressed the same thoughts and feelings. I felt so much better after talking to her, and realised that money was behind this change. The same thing had happened to palliative care that had happened to midwifery based nursing practice.

I managed to last three months in that role as there was no patient contact at all. I was in front of a computer and the changes that had taken place in palliative care did not sit well with me. So I decided after our 2004 trip to England, I would not be able to commit my heart and soul to this project. I decided to resign.

During this time, a friend who ran the Yulunya Nursing Home in Port Hedland rang me and asked if I could help her out for a few months. I said yes. Naturally.

We had a wonderful trip to the UK in June -July 2004 during which I was to experience several really interesting healing modalities.

As part of the Healing Touch program, we as student practitioners had to experience ten different healing modalities and write up a synopsis on each modality. I found a Chinese healer who had just opened a practice in Camden Town, London. My back pain at this time was crippling as the long flight from Karratha to London had played havoc with my spine. So I went and made an appointment at this clinic. The receptionist told me that the doctor did not speak any English and that I would have an interpreter with me. The doctor had not been in London very long; he had been working in Russia and Siberia for many years as a healer.

Noddy and I turned up for the appointment and I was ushered into his consulting room. The smile on this man's face said it all, and I felt totally at peace being there and intuitively knew he could help me. Working through the interpreter, I explained my presenting complaint; he took my blood pressure and found it to be sky high. He then beckoned me to lie on his couch. He started to work with his hands just off my physical body and after five minutes, I could feel the flow of the life force energy starting to pulsate through my body. He worked on me for thirty minutes, and when he finished I hopped off the table, bent over and could touch my toes. I had absolutely no pain at all. He also recommended I trial a herbal Chinese remedy to detox my body. I agreed to this. He asked if I wanted to make up the brew or take the tablets. I said oh no I will make a brew. What a mistake that was, I forgot we were having a ten day trip around the South of Ireland that next week and I purchased the herbs.

Well, we reached JA's and John's home, I cooked up the first brew of a week-long detox. Within five minutes, the smell coming from the stove was awful; but I continued cooking and left it to cool before drinking this vile tasting concoction. I had committed to the detoxing, so I had to finish the seven day course. It was okay for the first three days while we were still with JA and John; but then we had to discover a way to continue with the program in Ireland, as we were staying in Bed & Breakfast places.

I gamely asked our hosts if I could boil up my herbs. I told them it had a ghastly smell. Everyone was so obliging and I had no trouble continuing the detox for the next seven days. It was also a great learning experience for me as it opened up a Pandora's box of old Irish healing remedies that our hosts shared with us. I learnt a lot, and by the end of the week's treatment I was feeling well , full of energy, vitality and best of all, I had no back pain.

We flew over to Ireland taking a Ryan Air flight for 10 pounds and then we had a great week travelling around the south of Ireland. Once we landed in Dublin, we hired a car and headed for Galway Bay to see the sun go down over the Bay as the song was a favourite for both of us in the 1950's. I had been there on my 1971 visit and I just wanted

Noddy to see the spectacle; however it was not to be. It rained and rained all the way there.

Country Ireland is so beautiful; we loved the counties and the little villages we went through, the coloured houses and doors were just amazing. Going on to Cork, we decided to kiss the Blarney Stone so we climbed to the top lay on our backs and pretended to actually kiss the stone which was millimetres away from our lips; a guy would then clean it with a wipe - not very hygienic. Next to Blarney Castle was a woollen mill where my darling husband purchased for me a beautiful purple mohair cape and hat - that I never get to wear, because of our mild Perth winters; it has been lent to friends going overseas though.

Limerick was another stop we really enjoyed. We ended up in Waterford and spent a whole day visiting the Crystal Factory that I had heard about all my life.One trophy that was on display that really caught our eye was the The Wimbledon Tennis Championships Trophy. It was just too beautiful to describe. Of the little items I was able to afford to purchase there was set of rosary beads and a little Waterford crystal vase in the seconds' section of the shop. On returning to Dublin, we booked into a B&B for two days and had a wonderful visit to Trinity College. We spent hours visiting their library museum where the famous Book of Kells is displayed. This book has the most unbelievable history and is said to go back to the year 800AD. It would have to be the most famous book ever written, in my opinion. I would recommend that people Google "Library Trinity College - Book of Kells". It will be a wonderful read. I still have the photo I took of it and a copy of the book I brought there. I love flicking through it, every now and again.

JA had a week's vacation not long after we returned to London. We were also very lucky to have obtained tickets for day six of the Wimbledon Championships, a very special day for us, and we enjoyed our strawberries and cream there.

School finished and then JA, Noddy and I went for one very special holiday to Germany together - just the three of us .We loved travelling with JA, she was young and very pretty, so if we were lost anywhere, we would stay in the background, she would open her map looking for a famous tourist landmark and within minutes she would have about three guys helping her with directions; then we would join her, it worked every time.

We visited Berlin for three days, walking around this magnificent city, visiting and walking through the Brandenburg Gate and visiting Checkpoint Charlie. This was just such a moving experience for the three of us and going to the sites of where the Berlin wall stood, separating East and West Germany. It took our imaginations to that era and we prayed we never ever see a third world war. JA was so taken back reading the stories about the Berlin wall, and seeing the photos displayed brought her to tears and she could not believe this period in history of man's inhumanity to man had happened in her life time. From Berlin we caught a fast train down to Nuremberg.

Nuremberg was such an old and beautiful city. The Cathedral, and the castle were very old and spectacular. We visited the big arena were Adolf Hitler would give his famous speeches and visited the museum inside of the arena that depicted the history and stories, that were so horrendous from the atrocities of the time. It was a very sobering experience. We also visited the establishment were the military trials took place 66 years ago of 22 prominent leaders of Nazi Germany were brought to justice by the International Military Tribunal. An impressive building.

From Nuremberg we went to spend a few days in the historic and beautiful town of Heidelberg. This town won our hearts and we so enjoyed our short stay there. Heidelberg is on the Neckar River where we were fortunate to be able to go for a long walk and cross the old bridge that was built in 1786. This bridge was the ninth bridge built over this section of the Neckar River, in the Southwest of Germany; the history of this bridge is legendary and it is said that the Romans built the first bridge in the first century BC. Heidelberg is also famous because it is the home of one of the oldest Universities in Germany, known to all as Heidelberg University. It was founded in the 14th century. We took the train up to the famous Heidelberg castle, with magnificent views of the city and the old town with the famous bridge.

We were amazed to find the world's largest wine vat - a huge wine barrel which is said to hold over 100 kilo litres and is said to have been filled to the brim only once- worth seeing. From Heidelberg, we travelled on down to Frankfurt, Germany's fifth biggest city. JA only had one night with us here, before she had to catch the train back to Berlin in time for her flight back to London. What was so amazing for us, the day she left us, was that she was having breakfast with us in Frankfurt, lunch in Berlin and home for dinner in London that evening. We took her to the train station, which is really big, and saw her board the very fast train that travels up to 300 kms per hour back to Berlin. Parting from JA was not getting any easier I would have to say, however this time it was not too bad as she was coming home for Christmas and JD was coming over from the East Coast, so we would all be together again.

After she left, we booked a tour to go for a wine and boat trip on the Rhine. We had a great day out, enjoying all the great German hospitality and admiring the gifts of mother earth in all her glory. Looking back at all the movies we took and photos bring back to us beautiful memories. We left to fly home the next day, sad to leave, and knowing we would be back to this beautiful country one day. When we don't know.

Before I started at Yulunya, I flew over to Adelaide for a wonderful Therapeutic Touch workshop for 4 days. The visiting teacher flew in from Canada. She was a very learned and unbelievable aged healer, by the name of Crystal Hawke[2]. She was well into her 70s in 2004 and still flying and teaching around the world. It was here I was introduced to the Australasian Therapeutic Touch Association members; the beginning of my Australasian journey. Unfortunately, they were Victorian based and I being in the West and in a remote area, I was quite isolated; but we were connected in Spirit across the great divide.

In September, I had one of the happiest experiences that I had had in my nursing career for a long time, working in an Aboriginal Aged Care facility where the laughter was so infectious that I fell in love with it. The old people there were so cared for, healthy and happy.

Most were from outstations and remote communities. Anne Marie who ran the Nursing Home loved those old people, and she only employed persons who shared the love. This was their home and all sorts of activities and outings filled their day. All the staff put on a great Christmas party and we had to bring a present for a resident. I had one special one, a very old lady whose name was Nancy. I chose a new dress and a new broad brimmed hat for her. Nancy never stopped smiling; she could not talk except with her eyes, which were so pure and rich. It was so fabulous to see the smile on her face when she unwrapped the present and put her pink hat on.

They had a pet cat, which lived in the nursing home and whilst there, the cat gave birth to six little kittens. Great excitement was generated in the nursing home amongst all the oldies, when the kittens started exploring. One day a bobtail goanna, wandered in and the cat chased it quickly followed by yours truly. The old men sitting out on the veranda, nearly fell out of their chairs laughing at this chase. The bobtail eventually got away and the cat was put inside to prevent another game of chasey. I honestly loved the job and was so happy to be back in clinical nursing. Before long it was time for me to say goodbye.

What was one of the saddest parts of leaving was the fact that the Government was building a new multimillion dollar health campus at South Hedland and a brand new nursing home, so close to the shopping centre and where there would be no views ever like what Yulunya had. Yulunya was situated right on the sea frontage, overlooking the Port Hedland yacht club. The oldies would spend their day watching all the big iron ore vessels coming and going, there was always something going on and I loved sitting out there, on the big verandah overlooking the Indian Ocean, listening to the stories of their lives. People would be always walking by and stopping to say good day. BHP was buying the land, I was led to understand.

Whilst I was there, Judy the Director of Nursing at the Hospital asked me if I was interested in doing some relief work as the after-hours CNS /Nurse Manager for her. I said Judy "I would love to if this will not get you into any trouble with the regional manager", Judy assured me that she would be employing me, not the Regional Manager, so I agreed. However, I said Judy "I have a problem, I have been offered after our Christmas holiday with JA and JD a contract up in Balgo Hills in the Kimberley". The Balgo Manager for Mercy Care had offered me a contract to work as a remote area Emergency nurse and try to introduce and integrate traditional Aboriginal healing into the mainstream medical model in their clinic. Three weeks on and Three weeks off. Starting in January 2005. I had accepted that challenge and was very excited about the opportunity to try to make a difference. She informed, me that it would not be easy due to the 'Medical only' model clinic that the western nurses worked with. Judy was fantastic; she said 'we can work around this, how about we book you in for a few shifts on your three weeks off?' Judy's offer was immediately accepted.

We had an amazing family holiday the Christmas of 2005. JA had come home from London for two weeks and JD for a week from the East Coast. He could only stay for a week as he had planned a trip to climb Mt Kinabalu in Malaysia with a friend. It was a wonderful Christmas break with our two beautiful grown up children JA and JD, first in Dampier and then down at Coral Bay in our old mobile home. We had a campsite right at the front of the caravan park. Opposite our campsite, straight across the road there was the beach and the stunning clearest water you have ever swum in.

JD left on New Year's Eve by bus to Perth to catch his plane to Kuala Lumpur to meet his friend and do the climb; we were both happy and sad to see him leave. JA, Noddy and myself had another 48 hours there. On one of these days, JA and I went swimming out with the Manta Rays just outside of the reef beyond the Bay, and it was a wonderful day out. We left there on the 2ndst of January as JA was booked to fly back to London on the 3rd January and I to Balgo Hills on the 7th January.

I started in 2005, to do three week swings in Balgo Hills. On my three weeks off, I would do the middle week in Port Hedland Regional

Hospital, as the after-hours CNS /Nurse Manager. To get to Balgo, I had to travel from Karratha to Perth to Alice Springs and then take a light aircraft from Alice Springs up through the centre to Balgo Hills. I was walking out the door of the Alice Springs airport to catch the flight to Balgo Hills when my little old mobile phone rang. I answered it and it was the consultant with whom I had shared my eighties experience, asking if I would be prepared to go to court. I said yes, and said I would ring him back when I arrived in Balgo. With no pen on me, I could not ask for his phone number. I regret never ringing him back.

The approach to Balgo was so tropical with huge masses of green grass and trees spread over the landscape of very large hills, at the bottom of which lay a rather large community. We were picked up by the manager of the health clinic and taken to the nurses' units - small one bedroom units, adequate for one person with all the mod cons like television etc. There were two other nurses on this rotation. One, a nurse practitioner who was running a mens' health program and the other an emergency nurse. She was a 2nd year graduate nurse who had just completed her post graduate year in haematology. This was her first role and she had never been to a remote area nor worked in emergency. The only permanent nursing staff was the child health and a women's health nurse who was married to the manager of the health service. He was not a nurse and this was his first managerial role. All the after-hours call outs were to be done by the second emergency nurse and myself. We alternated every second night on call and also did alternate weekends. This I found very difficult as the young one would call me in for a second opinion when she was on call, and for any presentation that was a triage category 1-4. The manager and his wife would pack up at lunch time on a Friday afternoon and leave town most weekends.

After we were settled in to our respective units we were taken over to the clinic. We had our first meeting and I was designated to be the sexual health nurse for the community.

I said, "No, I have been employed to be an emergency nurse and to trial integrating Traditional Aboriginal Healing into the mainstream medical model here in Balgo."

They replied, "No, you are to be the sexual health nurse." So I suggested that the women's health program and the men's health program could encompass that role. I would be endeavouring to do what I was asked to do from the Mercy Care manager. That certainly did not go down very well at all, with the permanent staff. I rang the manager in Perth, who supported my stance and she rang the manager and directed him to do as I had suggested. I was not very popular at all.

I was even more unpopular when I did an orientation to the clinic that had recently opened. A brand new, very expensive modern clinic but I found it very unclean; so much so, I had to immediately go to work scrubbing down the beds in the emergency room with hot soap and water due to there being lots of dried blood stains on the trolleys, and dust everywhere. The floor looked like it had not been cleaned for a week. I called the manager in to inspect the place, before I started work on cleaning it up. He told me that they did not have a cleaner. I felt like calling the Mercy Care manager and saying, "please send up a relief; I cannot work in these conditions." I didn't, as I wanted to try and accomplish my goal of having the healers working side by side in the western model of care in this clinic. I thought it would go very well as they had started the production, (not through the health service)of making traditional bush medicine and giving the community the choice of Western medicine or Bush medicine, that was in its infancy, so I stayed and kept my opinion to myself. It took me four days to get the clinic to a state that I was happy to work in. My first week and weekend on call, was taken up seeing clients in-between cleaning and more cleaning.

During working hours, I would go out for an hour to meet up with two very old traditional healers called Helicopter and Barney. Helicopter was an artist and lawman. They were beautiful old Elders in the community. I knew that to be able to do what I wanted to do, I would have to have their trust first. They were very kind old men and I asked if I needed them in the clinic at any time, would one of them come? Helicopter smiled and said, yes. He had a big long white beard and piercing blue eyes. I knew I could trust him.

At first, I started very slowly with an old lady who had a nasty ulcer on her ankle for which she had been coming to the health clinic, for daily dressings for weeks. I asked Ms B----- if she would be happy for me to spend ten minutes per day giving her ankle a Therapeutic Touch treatment. When I showed her what I did with my hands, she immediately said "Sister you know our medicine." "Yes" I said.

I was then given permission to use Therapeutic Touch on the ulcer on her ankle. Within 48 hours she was as happy as could be, there had been a marked improvement in the ankle, and by the end of the fortnight she had one completely healed ulcer.

During the second week, one morning, Helicopter turned up in the clinic with a sore foot. The other nurse asked if she could help him, he said, "No, I want to see that sister", pointing to myself.

As soon as I was free, I saw Helicopter. He said "Sister, me got sore foot-you fix"?

I took Helicopter into a room and did a ten to fifteen minute Therapeutic Touch treatment. All of a sudden Helicopter said, "im better now, sister." The big thing I noticed during this treatment was that at the beginning of the treatment, Helicopter's foot was very hot to my touch. I noticed temperature changes in his foot and by the time Helicopter said, 'im better now', his foot was cold. He was very happy and left. He then taught me a number of healing practices, which were in fact very close to some of the techniques used by the energy-based nursing modalities of Therapeutic Touch and Healing Touch

I also had the opportunity of going out to the Mulin community to visit an African nurse on one of the weekends I was not on call. She had been employed in the community by Mercy Care as an emergency nurse. This was her first assignment in Australia. She was on the same contract- three weeks on, three weeks off. Poor dear, I felt she was very lonely and quite shell shocked, so I spent a weekend out there. Whilst I was there, I met a very old and beautiful Aboriginal lady; we talked and talked all afternoon and she invited us to go out to Lake Gregory for a swim on Sunday morning after mass. The Catholic Priest from Balgo would come over every Sunday for morning mass at 9am. There was no church there, so the service was held under trees and it was really quite lovely. The mass was in the local dialect. After mass, we packed a picnic lunch and headed off to the lake, some twenty kilometres from the community. The track out to Lake Gregory was through lots of long grass and pools of water from rain that had fallen over the preceding weeks, so I had to take care not to get bogged.

Once out at Lake Gregory, after we had a cup of tea and something to eat, Fatima offered me a healing session which I accepted. She started by laying her hands on my head for about ten minutes. I felt a quiet calm permeating through my body and felt a presence in my heart chakra. Then Fatima rubbed my body down very slowly front and back, settling her hands for some time where she felt heat and massaged areas like my lower back with the healing mud from the banks of the lake. This mud was soft and warm. Once she finished, I had to complete the treatment by having a swim in the lake. As I closed my eyes while swimming, I experienced green and pink colours swirling around me and this continued until I had finished my swim.

The water was very soft and felt like mineral water. The hands on treatment was very similar to the modalities of healing touch and therapeutic touch.

It was a wonderful afternoon. It was one healing modality that I will never forget. Later, I wrote this up for the synopsis of the program on experiencing different healing modalities on the 5th February 2005 as part of the Level 5 Healing Touch program.

The last week of the rotation went very quickly and it was not long before I was back home in Dampier with my beloved husband. I was rostered up at Port Hedland Hospital for seven night shifts during my second week back as the After Hours Nurse Manager and I just loved it. The night staff were some of the most caring nurses you could wish to work with and be nursed by. The ED doctors were respectful, kind and worked in unison with the nurses and the orderlies, especially a man called, Ian Robertson (RIP). It was such a pleasure to work there and being with them, I was very happy. The staff treated me with dignity and respect. Judy spoke to me when I went to say goodbye and they asked if I would be interested in the acting after-hours night CNS nurse manager's position that was being advertised in the next couple of weeks. I agreed to think about it.

I returned to Dampier and had a great week with Noddy, friends and clients, before heading off back to Balgo Hills, for my next rotation.

On my return nothing had changed. The clinic, was not like I left it and the staff were just so close minded; they only believed in the Medical Model. On arrival, I was called in by the women's health nurse who asked me why I had booked three young girls about 15 years old of age into see the doctor on his visit to the community, to have their Implanon implants removed. I replied because it was their choice and their right to have this device removed. They were finding the Implanon was making them eat too much and they said it was making them sad and unhappy. She gave me a lecture on preventing our aboriginal girls from becoming pregnant, so I just walked away, much to her displeasure. The girls had them removed. This contraceptive device was a practise that had started in early 2000 in Community Health in Roebourne, to prevent so called 'unwanted' pregnancies.

My first week back was pretty tough due to strained relationships; however, I enjoyed my next two weeks there, as the manager and his wife went on leave and the inexperienced nurse was held up coming back. She had some issues in Perth she had to deal with. The men's health nurse was also on a break. As a result, an older nurse came in to assist me. Her name was Glenys and she was originally from New Zealand. She was very experienced and knowledgeable. We connected very quickly and had a great fortnight working there together. We also had a lovely young locum doctor who came out for four days. I was very happy as Helicopter would come regularly to the clinic to assist me. He liked it while Glenys and I were there.

On my last weekend, I had another remarkable healing experience given to me by two old women from the community. The following is the synopsis of that Healing written up on the 5th March 2005 for my level 5 certification for HEALING TOUCH.

This healing took place at the Balgo Health Centre Kutjunga Region Kimberly, WA. The Healers were older women whose names were Patricia and Marie. Patricia did the first stages of the healing, by placing her hands on my crown chakra. She said she felt a lot of heat, so she cleared the energy field by using a similar technique I had learnt in Therapeutic and Healing Touch. Once Patricia had felt this region of my crown turning cold she moved down to my Solar Plexus- my third chakra region. Here she found lots of "Hot Spots" as she called them and commenced sweeping the energy fields of the Solar Plexus region which after a few minutes became quite cold and then very cold. Once this process had finished, Patricia rubbed Red Ochre with Mulan Tree Vicks and massaged that into my scalp, cupping her hand periodically and blowing into my scalp. This process was repeated several times and continued in the Solar Plexus region. At the same time, Maria was massaging my back using Red Ochre and Mulan Tree. Their techniques were by far the best I have experienced in massage therapy, their hands were very warm. The pressure they both used in massage was firm but very gentle at the same time. She worked her way up and down my spine and back muscles using a spiral technique. I felt a lot of energy movement, and once finished, they told me that I was not allowed to wash the red ochre off for twenty-four hrs. I felt very relaxed and had rushes of energy flow throughout my body that evening. I would really recommend these beautiful gifted healers to utilise their gifts within this community of Balgo. I am looking forward on my return to experience more hands on healing by these amazing healers.

I had several serious call outs during this rotation. One was an attempted suicide, a very serious one. I had to special a young patient for twenty-four hours before we could find her a bed in Derby or Perth. I also had a spur of the moment attempt at suicide by another young girl. It was a copycat attempt, after she had had a jealousy fight with her boyfriend. Her parents and I managed this and it resulted in her parents being able to take her into their care. There was no further problem with the boyfriend. He too went home with the parents.

This was on the last day before the manager left to go on holidays. I was in trouble again. Apparently, the mental health nurse was in town. I had not seen nor met him and did not know he was even in town. I was chastised for not calling him in at 01.30am. I was quite reactive to this aggressive chastisement by this person who was not a nurse and decided I was not going to be able to work in this environment. I resolved to apply for the position Judy told me about in Port Hedland when it came up.

One call out was at midnight, when a lady turned up at my unit with a piece of wood stuck in her head and a very painful jaw. I took her over to the clinic. She was pretty happy as she had been over to Halls Creek and had had a 'few sherbets'. Her group had another party at a creek crossing on the way home with some more amber fluid, and a fight broke out from which she came off second best. I cannot get over the stoicism of the indigenous people. She was so compliant and did not complain one single bit; there was no swearing, just the odd facial grimace.

I rang the doctor at RFDS in Derby. He was very supportive and whilst he was on the phone, I did an emergency assessment (under his direction) of the woman's mandible as I thought it could have been broken. It wasn't, thank goodness! I was able to insert local anaesthetic into the area around the head wound and gently removed the stick and a few small pieces of wood. Then I thoroughly washed it out three times with Betadine solution, packed it with gauze soaked in saline, and applied a head dressing. I then gave her a tetanus booster and said I would see her in the morning as she had no other head injury. She had not been knocked unconscious, so I took her home and went back to bed, tired but happy, but also sad that this was all I could do in my capacity. She came back the next morning very happy with no ill effects from the night before. She was reviewed every day for the next ten days, and the wound healed beautifully. The resilience of all the people in communities blows me away.

During the last week of the rotation, the A/CNS Night Manager position was advertised along with another Permanent CNS/Nurse Manager's position at Port Hedland Regional Hospital. I applied and was offered an interview for the A/CNM Night position.

I was notified and offered the position several days before my leave date. I discussed it with Noddy, Helicopter and the Mercy Care manager, who agreed we were ahead of our time and that one day when the time was right, we would all pursue our dreams. We came to the conclusion, that the time for us to pursue the dream was not now. There would come a time when mainstream medical people would accept the practice of the sacred healing arts in an integrated system with love, respect and non judgement. It would be best for me to resign and follow my dream.

Hence, I did resign, and left enriched by meeting and sharing with Fatima, Patricia, Marie, Barney, and Helicopter - who passed away in 2017 in his country. Sadly, he never got to see the integration. I am hoping I will live to see the day and he will be with me when that day comes, to celebrate. I had a sad but happy farewell to this community, rich in a culture both in daily living and in health and sickness. Their culture had been buried back then, but signs of revitalisation with the bush medicine were beginning to show signs of germination within the health system.

Glenys and I are still friends, and I value the time when we shared the Balgo chapter together.

***

On arrival back in Dampier, Noddy had the biggest surprise for my fifty-eighth birthday. Two tickets for a holiday in Bali before I started working in Port Hedland. He had arranged it all. What a fabulous week we had up there staying in a five star hotel on the beach, massages every day and regular reflexology sessions. I did hear about an amazing healer on the island, but sadly he was working over on the mainland of Indonesia, whilst we were in Bali; so, I could not experience his traditional healing. His reputation was second to none, I heard.

We had several adventures including a day out white-water rafting which was exhilarating; but oh! getting back up from the bottom of the river to the main road on the top of a mountain was a nightmare. There were so many steps and they were so high for us. We made it though, exhausted but triumphant. We had a great week, just relaxing around the pool which was just outside our room, eating some beautiful cuisine, sleeping a lot, having daily massages and just being with each other. It was over far too quickly and before we knew it, off back home we flew.

I started work in Port Hedland at the beginning of May 2005 on permanent night shift. I loved the role. It was mainly clinical and as a generalist nurse I could work anywhere - theatre, emergency, midwifery, medical/surgical, paediatrics and the like. I would be down at Yulunya to see the staff every night I was on. I loved all the staff who worked there in the health service and we had a very dynamic team that were just the most amazing truly holistic group of nurses young and old, I had ever worked with. Fortunately for me, Judy was happy to allow me to practice Healing Touch and Therapeutic touch in the clinical setting. I was extremely grateful to her for encouraging me to practise. There were some really great nurses who were so interested in therapeutic touch, natural therapies and holistic nursing who supported me. I fell in love with Port Hedland Regional Hospital-Staff and the patients.

I had some amazing experiences working with nurses like Lyn Sue, Jamie , Lindsay, Carol, Ann, Carol, Patsy, Jillian, Maggie and Julie and others I could not have been happier; the doctors too were great .The care given back then was exceptional, so much so that when in December of 2005, I had a surgical emergency and was being transferred to Perth via RFDS from Nickol Bay Hospital to a private hospital in Perth for surgery, I decided to say, "No, I will go to Port Hedland Hospital. I know the staff and I know I will get great care." I was right. I had the offending gall bladder and a gigantic stone removed, with no complications. I was home the next day and recovered during my week off.

In September of 2005, I had a voice say to me go, and have a Breast Screen as the pink mobile van was in Karratha. People may ask what is the Pink Van? The West Australian Government funds Breast Screen

WA, which runs a radiological van service to travel to the country and regional towns to do breast screening for breast cancer. Three times I went to the door of the van to make an appointment, I did not want to go in, I had not had a very pleasant experience on my first screening three years prior and after that I vowed I would not have another one. The voice kept saying you must have a screening. So on the fourth time I went in, made an appointment and had one. Sure enough, a week later I received a phone call to come to Perth for further testing as something had showed up on the mammogram. I thought about it and decided to wait awhile as I was sure it would go away.

I was in denial that there was anything wrong with me. Several weeks later, I received a letter from the Director of Breast Screen WA telling me I had to come to Perth, that I had breast cancer. I was very stubborn and contacted a dear doctor friend in Karratha. I wanted to be in control and manage this problem in my own way.

Dr. Peter arranged to meet Noddy and myself in his home for a discussion and to develop a plan. I had by then accepted the diagnosis and was ready to deal with it on my terms. Peter was great and supported me. We arranged to have another mammogram and needle aspirations, done in Karratha and once the results were through, he contacted the Director of Nursing at The Mount Hospital and asked her if she would recommend a top breast surgeon in Perth. Peter arranged it all, and I flew to Perth to meet her, seven days after I had had my gall bladder out. This doctor again repeated all the preliminary investigations, and said that it would have to be done urgently within the next few days. She would be doing a lumpectomy and I would have to undergo six weeks of radiotherapy.

I said to her, "No, I have just had surgery, my husband is not here. Until I am fully prepared physically, emotionally, mentally and spiritually, I would not put my body through another anaesthetic so close to the previous one."

So, we compromised and as she was going overseas in March, we decided that I would have the operation on the 10th February, 2006. This would give me six weeks to be back swimming my usual two kilometres per day and get my body ready. It would also give me time for researching what I could do as far as alternative and integrative management went. I had no fear and knew I was in no danger, I arrived home and Noddy was so supportive of my decision. We worked hard to prepare for the cancer journey, and I am so glad we did the research on radiotherapy. It identified for me the damage that radiotherapy can do to some people's ageing bones. I knew I was already leaking calcium from my vertebrae and did not want to take any risk of further weakening my spine. I ensured my diet was perfect for those weeks. I became a vegetarian and juiced twice daily, I meditated at least three times a day and did Therapeutic Touch twice a day.

I felt really well contented and happy. I was feeling very well and healthy. I didn't feel I had cancer. To be honest, I didn't know how I should be feeling. I had no fear, there was no history of breast cancer in my family, so I realised it was caused by the stress I had experienced over all those years working in some unhealthy and unfriendly environments. This stress was probably the reason for the cancer diagnosis.

I still believe that today. So after much discussion between Noddy and myself, I decided to refuse a lumpectomy (I had had a number of friends have lumpectomies and some had to return for further surgery due to the fact that they had not got all the tumour. One of my friends had to return three times, and have radiotherapy.

A week before surgery was booked, I rang and spoke to the surgeon and told her I had changed my mind and that I would request a full mastectomy of the affected breast. I have never forgotten her words. 'At least, you will be safe now,' she said. I took three weeks off work and the staff at Port Hedland Hospital were fantastic when I told them and Judy was so supportive.

Noddy flew to Perth with me and we stayed with our extended family, the beautiful Bultovics. We arrived at a private hospital in Perth at 6.30am for admission and I was booked in for surgery that afternoon, at 5pm. The surgeon came to see us just before her afternoon list at 12.30. We were very bored, so I said to her, "we would like to go for a walk down to the river which was just over the road from the hospital. "Oh no you can't do that" was the reply. About fifteen minutes later a nurse came in with a pre –med. Noddy rang one of my Healing

Touch Colleagues, a lovely woman by the name of Christine, who came in and gave me a beautiful treatment. Christine and I had done our Healing Touch course together. So next thing I remember was being wheeled into the OR.

I found it interesting how things had changed. There was no pre anaesthetic check done, and I met the anaesthetist, as I was laid on the OR table. I was a number, not a person. Everything went very well and I have to say the Surgeon was very good to Noddy, who went back to Milena and Dragon's home, a happy man.

I slept until 2200 and when I woke up, I was ravenous and dying for a cup of tea. I jumped out of bed only to find I could not go anywhere because of all these bottles attached to me - IV flask insitu and redivac bottles (A redivac is a bottle that is used to drain blood from the wound site.) I lost my balance and came crashing to the floor with the dangling bottles. I had no pain. I got back into bed; I had to ring the bell to get some help getting out of bed but as soon as the nurse left, I went to the patient's pantry and made myself a cup of tea and a plate of sandwiches, then went back to bed and slept until the morning. I was up and showered by myself and ready for the family to come in at ten. I felt great and wanted to go home, but was told I had to stay for another forty-eight hours. The physio came to see me and I asked her for a piece of tube grip just in case I could not get to the Lymphedoema Association to get a compression sleeve, before flying home. She gave me a small tube grip for my arm and I got charged $15 dollars for it - unbelievable. I was discharged exactly forty eight hours post-surgery and came home to the care of Milena, a wonderful nurse. I still had one redivac insitu and a very nice homecare nurse from the hospital would come every day to dress the wound and change the bottle. Fortunately, I had it out on day four and there were no problems.

Noddy had to fly back to work on the Monday after the operation. I had to go and see the surgeon a week after discharge. I wanted desperately to go home but she wanted me to see a radiology oncologist saying, "you may need to have some Tamoxifen as a preventative." I reminded her of her words to me a few weeks earlier when she had said, "At least now you will be safe." I got my clearance to fly home, day ten, post op.

I am forever grateful to the Bultovics, for their love and support for Noddy and I during that time. Once home, I felt a million dollars. The wound had healed, I was with my beloved husband, my dog and my friends, Seleana and Charlie. I was happy, back in the pool working hard, doing my exercises and within two weeks, back to swimming two kilometres per day. I returned to work exactly when I said I would; filled with gratitude for going through the experience as I learnt so much from it and now felt better able to support other cancer patients on their journey. Ensuring delivery of care with compassion and truth, doing as much research about treatments as I could and being fully informed, were the biggest lessons for me.

***

2006 was a great year work wise. I was really enjoying the role of the night manager and the Clinical nurse Specialist at Port Hedland Regional Hospital. I spent most of my time in Emergency as the activity there was very high, with major incidences. Mental illness, car accidents, domestic violence assaults severely ill people coming in from communities, snake bites surgical and medical emergencies, and industrial accidents to name just a few. There were only two staff members on with me for assistance and one doctor. Some nights were quieter than others. I was so happy, as I was often asked to give a patient a Therapeutic Touch Technique for pain management.

One night, as soon as I took over from the evening CNS/NM, I received a phone call from an RFDS doctor who had to go out to Jigalong to pick up a fourteen year old child with epiglottis. He asked if he could take the on-call anaesthetist with him. He explained that the boy had a short neck and he wanted the specialist to be there, to intubate him before he flew him out to Perth. I called the on-call anaesthetist and put the RFDS doctor through to him and he agreed to go.

Unbeknownst to me, the obstetrician had been called in to see a woman who was in trouble in the labour ward and needed an urgent caesarean section. Here was the anaesthetist on his way to the RFDS hanger. So, I rang the medical superintendent. (John and I had known each other for many years). I asked him to come in and be the anaesthetist for the caesarean. He came straight in. The obstetrician a big woman, who could at times be quite intimidating, came down to my office and said that as I had sent her anaesthetist off, and as I had called John to be the anaesthetist, she had no assistant, so I would have to be her assistant. "Sure", I replied. I handed the keys and my pager over to Lyn, the senior nurse on in ED, who let all the wards know that she would be covering for me. I went into the theatre scrubbed and took my place at the table.

I had not scrubbed for a caesarean since 1991, but scouted for many from 1994 to 2003. It was just like riding a bike. Not one person there knew I was an ex theatre nurse and the obstetrician who was talking me through it, said proudly, "you are picking this up very quickly." I thanked her with a smile.

At the very end of the operation, she said to me I could assist her at any time, and then I admitted I had started working in theatre in 1966, and had always kept up my theatre skills. She smiled and said, good on you and thank you so much. Once again, I realised how sad it was the young ones do not get the opportunity to become generalist nurses. It is such an important role in all facets of health care, primary, secondary and tertiary today, in my opinion.

***

Family life was wonderful. The week on, week off was a breeze and it meant I was only away from seeing Noddy six days per fortnight. I would drive to Port Hedland, leaving just after lunch on a Monday on the week on and leave Hedland at 07.30 for Karratha the following Monday, and be home by 11.30 am. I knew every bump on that road, and it was a very good time for a wind down from a busy working week.

JD had been posted to Cairns, and he invited us over to spend a couple of weeks over Easter with him. We had a wonderful holiday with JD and rediscovered Green Island which we had visited in 1975. I had plenty of leave and was granted time off. We caught the direct flight from Perth to Cairns. JD picked us up at the airport and settled us into his unit right in the heart of Cairns, whilst he took off to work. We crashed as we had been flying all night. Noddy woke well before I and went to have a haircut. To his astonishment he found all the shops shut and the barber shop had a big sign on the window, 'Shut due to a Tsunami.' But all was back to normal by lunch time. We went out to the volcanic lava tubes, this was something we had never experienced before, and we didn't even know they existed. From there we travelled up to Cooktown, the Daintree and back to Cairns. It was not long before it was time to pack up and say goodbye to our beautiful son.

Back to Karratha and back to work for both of us. We were very excited as we were counting down the weeks until we were leaving for Canada. Our daughter was getting married in Halifax to the love of her life, John Blaise Stewart in Nova Scotia on the 1st August. We had our leave booked and we planned a journey of six weeks.

Life in Dampier was busy with camping trips, dinner parties and barbecues; I was still running my healing practice and had finished my Level 5 for Healing Touch. I chose not to go on to become a teacher. I came to realise that I was not so much a teacher but more a coach and mentor. Therapeutic Touch was fast becoming my favourite modality and there were several techniques I could do in Healing Touch that would integrate very easily with Therapeutic Touch. Jane Bartley and I were still giving each other fortnightly treatments. We would see Chaz and Sel every fortnight and we also spent time with Dragon. Milena was in Perth with her beautiful daughter, Tanya who was studying at University.

We left for Canada mid-July and had three nights in Hong Kong with a very dear friend, Stephen Ha. Stephen and I worked together from 1987 to when I left Wanneroo Hospital at the end of 1990. He was the Staff Educator there. He ended up going back to Hong Kong to become the Director of Nursing of a 600 bed Acute Care Hospital. He had re married after his wife passed away and was very happy and settled. Stephen had made the accommodation booking for us in Hong

Kong. His wife was our guide for the three days we were there. We would spend long hours talking in the evenings over a nice meal with Stephen and his wife. Hong Kong was a great place to holiday; the city was so clean and the people so friendly.

From there we flew to Vancouver for three nights and loved touring during the day and crashing after dinner at night. From there we flew to Calgary where we were picked up by Pat and Moira McGuire and taken out to their property which overlooked the Rocky Mountains. It was heaven. Moira and Patrick were a couple whom we had billeted in 2001 in Karratha, when they were there doing some voluntary work for the Catholic Church. Sr Kath had told them we were coming, so of course, we were invited for a stopover. We had five glorious days traversing all over the Rockies to Lake Louise, Banff and everywhere in-between. Their back veranda looked out over to the Rocky Mountains and to sit having dinner watching the sun go down was a magical experience; we felt so blessed and privileged to be doing this, something we had never dreamed of. Too soon, time came to say goodbye to our lovely friends.

Off we flew to Halifax, and waiting for us at the airport were JA and John. There were tears of joy streaming down our faces, as we descended the elevator. This had been our longest ever separation, seventeen months. The joy at seeing her so happy and excited was overwhelming and we enjoyed a week of celebrations before the big day. JD had flown in and JA and JD had a couple of sacred days together before all JA and John's friends flew in from London. John's family were just the best. John's Aunt and Uncle Lester and Yvonne had done a fantastic job with JA - organising the whole week's celebration which included a massive Clan reunion. The wedding day came and oh what a day. First ride in a Limo for Noddy and I with the bride and her bridesmaids. The wedding ceremony was beautiful and a very happy celebration followed. We were blessed to gain a son-in-law.

After the wedding, we stayed an extra couple of days with JA and John. JD had to fly home to work. We visited Prince Edward Island and explored some wonderful sights around Halifax, including the Titanic Museum. We were also blessed to be staying with John's Aunt,

Shirley. A few days after the wedding JD and John went south to see his mother's family while Noddy and I headed up to Montreal for a few days. When we flew into Montreal, we realised we had not booked accommodation. Much to our surprise, they had a big board at the airport, where one just pressed a number and you were instantly connected to a B&B. The first one we tried was answered very promptly by a French speaking Canadian woman who offered us a room. We took a taxi to her address and was met at the front door by a plump short lady, with long grey hair done up in a big French roll and immaculately dressed. She beckoned us in and in her broken English, invited me into her formal lounge for a cuppa tea and said to Noddy, "You, Butler, take the luggage upstairs to room 3." This for the rest of the trip became a standard joke Noddy –The Butler.

It turned out the lady herself was one of Canada's leading Opera singers in her younger years. She took a shine to us and made us lots of great bookings for tours. We thoroughly enjoyed her company. One of the tours we went on was up to Quebec. What a magnificent city! It became one of my favourite cities in the world. From Montreal, we took a train ride down to Toronto were we spent four days, exploring that city. We had a great outing to Niagara Falls and a trip down memory lane on 'The Maid of The Mist'. Next, we visited the little village of Niagara and I could have bought a house there; it was just such a pretty warm village with lots of positive energy. We returned to Toronto the night before we were to fly to Thunder Bay where John's family lived.

Whilst in Toronto, we found a travel agent to book our tickets to Arizona where we were going to have a week with Noddy's sister, Pauline and her husband Wayne. We realised once again how small the world had become. We were served by a young Australian lad who was from Perth. He asked us were we lived, and when we told him we lived in Karratha, he was surprised. His uncle had lived there and he asked us if we knew Kevin. I smiled as Kevin was a dear friend of mine. He left us far too early from a sudden heart attack when he was campaigning to enter State politics in 2005. We had had dinner with his dear wife, Bev two weeks before we left on this trip. Kevin's nephew really looked after us, ensuring we got the right priced air tickets to Arizona.

After a week's holiday in Toronto, we left for Thunder Bay in Northern Ontario. We were booked on the same flight that JA, John and Anita were flying home to Thunder Bay on. All went according to plan and much to our delight when we boarded, we were in the two seats in the row in front of them on the plane.

John's family met us at the airport and that was the beginning of a superb week of relaxation, fun and new experiences which we will never forget. Cindy and Arnie and their two boys Jessie and Aj welcomed us into their family. We all went up to their holiday place up in the Lakes District and spent three nights relaxing, fishing and swimming. We also went out to his dear brother's property on the outskirts of Thunder Bay where Darryl lived in nature in a very humble little cottage with lots of acreage where wild bears roamed freely. He had two beautiful dogs and Darryl himself was a free spirit.

Soon we had to bid farewell to the family at Thunder Bay airport, promising JA and John we would be in London for Christmas 2007. Security was fairly tight at this airport; we even had to take off our shoes and socks and I had to hand over my little pot of tiger balm for my sore knees. I was not pleased. We had to go to Toronto to catch our connecting flight to Arizona, and the security here was even tougher. We had to go through the screening for the US, photos of our faces, fingerprinting and virtually a strip search. We were so glad we got through and boarded our flight down to Pauline's.

Wayne and Pauline were waiting for us when we arrived, and we had a very happy stay. It was the first time we had ever been in a gated aged residential community. It was so big, the houses very nice all on top of each other with no real gardens, but they had all the amenities.

The weather was truly hot; not one day under 112 degrees Fahrenheit. But that did not deter Wayne and Pauline taking us sightseeing. Sandy, Noddy's niece from Montana, came to visit us. It had been many years since Sandy and Warren Davis had been out to visit us in

Perth, so it was great to catch up. After a hectic week we had to pack our bags again and say final farewells and headed for LA. What a nightmare LA airport was! Security guards and police were everywhere, all carrying big machine guns. It was noisy beyond words. We stayed in the airport, as it was too hot to go into downtown LA. We were exhausted, and so we waited all day for our flight back to Australia, in the air-conditioning and watched the world go by.

We arrived back in Karratha three days later, and thank God, we had a couple of days to recuperate and enjoy real down time with our lovely little Tenterfield terrier before going back to work. Noddy returned to his job, and I to my beloved Port Hedland Hospital and my nursing sisters and brothers.

***

Whilst I was away, dark forces started to gather in Nursing Management Services, and this time Judy was in the firing line - for what, I do not know. Being on permanent nights, one is away from all the infighting and the politics. We would not get involved with the whispers and innuendos that were being bandied around. Our ship was tight and we stayed away from the gossip. I did speak to Judy and said I would be there for her if she needed to talk; she too was going through what I had been through in Karratha.

Work was such a joy for me; I was in a really good place. I spent a lot of time healing myself, juicing, eating lots of healthy nutritious food, studying energy medicine and reading healing books, as well as mystical books and running a little private practice in the lounge room of my unit for staff members as required. I would go to the pool after work and swim two kilometres every day at 8:00am. Meditation was part of a daily wellness practice. I would settle for sleep around 1:30pm and sleep until 9:30pm. I would wake up refreshed and be off to work by 10.00pm.

Judy never returned from holidays that year and another DON arrived. This DON was a nurse whom I had met and knew when she was a very junior nurse at a previous hospital where I had worked in

1991. Nursing services in Port Hedland Hospital, changed from a fully empowered nursing service to being shut down and micro managed. This change was supported by the region's senior official. What once was a very happy workplace turned into a very unsettled one over a short space of time.

Christmas came and went, and the cyclone season arrived; and what a cyclone time it was for Port Hedland Hospital that year. A big cyclone came and flattened one of the Fortescue Metals mining camps inland from Port Hedland. I received the call from the police around 3 o'clock in the morning of the event, two persons had been killed and they had a number of personnel injured. My emergency management training for disaster management, kicked straight into top gear. I rang the new DON and the operational manager and then went to plan for extra staff to come in, as evacuations from the site camp were being organised.

I was asked to come to an emergency hospital management meeting at 5am with the executive team and senior managers. I offered my advice focusing on the flow chart I had developed for the West Pilbara Disaster Management. The meeting went well, and we finished at about 6am. We had been notified that the first RFDS plane would be expected in around 8.30am; so I ensured all nursing staff who were off either on evening shift or on a day off were contacted and asked if they wouldn't mind coming in to assist in this disaster. I arranged staggered times for staff to come in to help in the clinical management and care of the patients. Not one nurse refused.

By this time it was 9am; everything was done and we were waiting for the first causalities to arrive. There was nothing left for me to do, so I went home to sleep, when I arrived at work at 9pm that night I was informed regarding the day's events. It was good to find that everything had gone very smoothly and that we were waiting for our last two patients to be evacuated to Perth.

Once again though, a couple of weeks later, I found myself in trouble. They advertised the acting Night Manager /CNS position for a permanent one. I applied and I was very happy with the panel. I turned up for my interview as per my letter to find out that the interviews had been cancelled and rescheduled, because the only other applicant had called in sick. I was not notified of the cancellation which threw me off balance.

The DON's attitude to me was neither friendly nor warm, her voice cold calculating and cutting. My intuition kicked in and my inner voice warned me that someone (a higher authority) had been talking to her and instructed her not to appoint me to the permanent position. About a month later, the interview took place and although I did very well, there was a new panel and I was not appointed. A new nurse manager/CNS came and within a month, it was mayhem.

Bullying started with full force and no one escaped her wrath. It was awful to witness what this woman was doing and she was fully supported by management. I was also on the receiving end until one night, I had enough and wrote out a formal complaint (drafted by a lawyer) and submitted it. We had had words and she told me that I was not allowed to practice Therapeutic Touch in my clinical work and that the DON had not given me permission to do so.

The next night, after I had had this discussion with her, we had a very bad night in which a patient I had been looking after, arrested and passed away. I knew immediately it would be a coroner's case as the death was unexpected. His care by all the nursing staff on the previous shift and our night shift had been first class; there were four of us by his side, when he arrested and despite our efforts we could not revive him. This had a devastating effect on all present.

Nursing Management were absolutely horrible to the nursing staff involved and made us feel we were responsible for this poor man's passing. I was not present at the debrief in the ED where the DON was speaking, about what happened; however, two of the ED nurses I had worked with there, they had been involved in caring for this man. They reported that the four of us had been singled out. It hit me very badly and I went into survival mode, and was told I could not work in ED ever again; this action by the DON crucified me yet again.

A month went by and I spent a lot of time working in the High

Dependency Unit. I had by then, swapped over to the opposite week of the bullying night manager's shifts, so I wouldn't have to work with her - other nurses also did this. If there were no patients in the high dependency ward, Susan would ask me to go down to help in ED.

A month to six weeks had passed from the time, I had put in the bullying compliant and I had heard nothing. Out of the blue, one day, the phone rang. It was the Director of Nursing, stating that in my letter of complaint, it was written that I would be happy to have a mediation session. I replied yes, I would be happy for this to go ahead, so the session was arranged for the following day.

On arrival at the meeting the next day, I was surprised, that the Director of Nursing was absent from the mediation session. Present in her place was the Assistant Director of Nursing and the Human Resource Manager, whom I had never met, together with the night nurse manager who was the perpetrator of the sustained bullying. I had a support person with me, a colleague by the name of Susan, who was a very good manager, nurse and colleague. When the meeting started, the perpetrator withdrew all of the statements she had made against me, that I had documented in the letter of complaint. She said I was one of the best nurses she had ever worked with and that she was so sorry for the way, she had treated and spoken to me and would I forgive her. I was very surprised at this turn of events and accepted her apology and the meeting was closed. The Human Resource Manager said he would send me an official letter regarding the apology -which incidentally is yet to happen, despite continuing to ask for it! I even asked through the Freedom of Information to have access to my personal file, but to no avail.

I went to work that night and was shocked and relieved to find out, that straight after the meeting this woman and her husband drove out of town never to be seen again. Now on reflection, writing these memoirs, this appears to me to have been a set up. There was no accountability for her bad behaviour, and I believe this continues today in management practices universally. I was also informed that I had not been the only one that had submitted formal complaints.

Worse was to come.

You can imagine my horror when next morning, I was summoned up to the DON's office and told that I had no contract at Port Hedland Regional Hospital. My services were no longer required. I was speechless, devastated and did not have a leg to stand on, as I had no contract. Yet, there were at least six very expensive agency nurses working there. I could see the week out but I was terminated as from my last shift on the Sunday. When I broke the news to my colleagues, no-one could believe it. I could feel myself starting to slip into a dark mind set again; however, I pulled myself back to the light and from that time on, decided I just could never work for Country Health Service again due to the lack of leadership, the lack of fairness and compassion, the lack of compliance to their Ethics and their Code of Conduct. At a senior level, nothing was worth anything - just like the paper it was written on. I was sad to leave my colleagues and I praise God these beautiful women are still in my life and I thank them for their unfailing love, light and support then, now, and always.

The toxicity of humanity settled inside me again; however, this time it didn't stay buried, as I had booked into a Therapeutic Touch Conference in Melbourne in early September to do my Level 2 and Intermediate certifications. Diane May, RN and Professor CheryAnn Hoffmeyer, both whom are world renowned Nurses, Therapeutic Touch teachers and leaders in Healing education, were coming from Canada to run the Level 2 and Intermediate workshops. It was just the right time. I went and had a very blessed time in workshops practising energy healing and meditation. The other practitioners all warm and sacred cleared all the blockages in my Body Mind and Spirit and after four days, I came home a very happy and blessed woman.

It was now time to rest and plan for the future. I continued with my healing clinic and journeyed with a dear colleague and friend, (who I had worked with during my time as a DON), who had terminal cancers and passed away several months later.

Noddy and I were in the middle of deciding whether to leave the North. The weather was becoming quite unbearable with the heat knocking us both around. Noddy was 66 and I was 61, so we made the decision to relocate back to our 'little golden pond' property in Perth. It was the opportune time to do this, as our tenants had been transferred so our little home was vacant. Noddy would come back to Karratha for three months after our trip as we had planned to go to Italy and then spend Christmas in London with JA and John.

I did not want to stop work, as I wanted to keep studying and I was not quite ready to retire yet. I saw a position advertised in the West Australian newspaper for Clinical Coaches for Graduate Nurses on a medical ward at a Tertiary Hospital that I had worked at, in 1992/93, before relocating to Roebourne and Wickham. It was a brand new position. So, I rang the Nurse Manager who was the contact person and she asked me to apply. My application was successful and my start date was booked for the 21st January 2008.

We finally packed up and left for Perth on the 19th November 2007, finishing an incredibly rich and rewarding experience as well as learning the lessons I had to learn through the experiences on my journey of life.

CHRISTMAS IN EUROPE

We settled into our little home and enjoyed a very quick visit from our dear son, who had come over for a couple of days, enroute to a major athletic competition in Singapore.

On the 8th Dec 2007, we boarded a plane and headed for a twelve day trip to Italy and to the East Coast of France where JA was meeting us after school had finished. We landed in Rome and found our way by public transport to the B&B we had booked, right in the centre of Rome; there we crashed and slept for twelve hours.

On awakening the next day, a new adventure started, exploring all Rome had to offer. We had five days in Rome and saw everything that we had talked about, read about and heard about from fellow travellers. Noddy was overwhelmed with the history and loved the visit to the Colosseum and Trivi Fountain. We were looking forward to visiting Vatican City and when we did, we were so disappointed; it was not for us and after a quick look around we could not wait to leave. The wealth, the pomp and ceremonies did not fit. There was the presence of security everywhere and the cost of everything within the Vatican City was outrageous. The Sistine Chapel though was really beautiful.

From Rome, we headed down to Naples for a couple of nights. That was an altogether different experience. All the Italian waste workers in Naples were on strike and no refuse had been collected for weeks. The air was offensive around the streets of Naples. I thought it quite a pretty town down by the water. The drivers were crazy and there were so many people. One of the highlights was a trip down to Pompeii and Sorrento. Italy, outside Naples, had it all: serenity beauty and very friendly locals.

From there we headed across to the East Coast to Bologna, where we had four wonderful days exploring the University of Bologna which was founded in 1088. It is the oldest university in continuous operation, as well as one of the leading academic institutions in Italy and Europe. The city was an archive of ancient Medieval times and Renaissance structures, that took us back to a time in history that we were unaware of in Australia. Noddy was in seventh heaven here, as Bologna is legendary for its traditional cuisine like spaghetti bolognese, lasagne and parmesan cheese, his favourite meals. From Bologna we headed cross country by train to Florence to see the famous works of Michelangelo and the statue of David. The views from where a statue replica of David was situated high on a hill overlooking the city. The view gave us the most panoramic sights of this magnificent city and beyond to the mountains. The marble statue of David at this magnificent site was sculptured in 1856 and taken to the site overlooking the city by nine pairs of oxen in 1873. It was a very educational few days as we learnt so much about the arts and history of Michelangelo and that period of Italian history. The original statue of David is housed in Galleria dell'Accademia museum.

After exploring this beautiful city, we headed for Pisa, one of the highlights of our Italy adventure. The City of Pisa goes back to 871 and we in 2007 were privileged to walk in and around this town, which has played such an important role in the history of Italy.

One of our highlights of the trip occurred here. As it was December there were hardly any tourists around. We climbed sixty metres to the top of the Leaning Tower. The view was out of this world. The history of the Leaning Tower of Pisa[1] is one of the most fascinating legends of the history of the world. In 1174, an Engineer, Bonnana Pisano laid a marble foundation and started the campanile of the cathedral and baptistery of Pisa. The Tower was actually the bell tower and was finally finished in the 4th century in 1399. The history of the Leaning Tower of Pisa was a very interesting experience for us. The lean commenced in 1178; the tower started to lean by the time the builders got to the third floor because of the soft ground on which the foundations were laid. At the time of writing this in 2018, it is 845 years old.

From Pizza, we caught a train up to Cinque Terra staying a night at various B&Bs in the five villages; Monterossi al mare, Vernazza, Corniglia ,Manarola and Riomaggiore. We fell in love with this section of Italy too. JD had been there on a Kontiki tour the year before and told us it was a must. We were so glad we listened to his advice as these five villages in this part of Italy had an energy and vibration that lingered with us long after we left the place.

From there we travelled by train up over the border to the East Coast of France to Nice, were our beautiful daughter joined us for a week's touring of Nice, Monaco and Cannes. It was amazing standing on the steps of where they hold the Cannes Film Festival; we loved the architecture, the French cuisine the people, the Christmas markets in the three towns we visited, the atmosphere of the whole region was electric and the weather extremely cold. Monaco was different altogether. When we walked up to the Monte Carlo Casino, we passed the Marina; the biggest we had ever seen. It was full of these unbelievable floating palaces and St Nicholas' Cathedral too was amazing.

The time to return to London came all too quickly and we arrived back on Noddy's birthday, December 21st. Christmas day was spent with JA and John in their new home and we spent lots of time visiting places in London which we had not seen on our previous visits. The highlights of this visit was doing a lovely day trip up to Cambridge, and an afternoon mystery tour of the wild side of London, and then the time came for us to return home. Again, the pain struck deep in my heart at having to say goodbye to our family of two now. Little did I know then, it would be our last trip to London.

***

. . .

Arriving back to the sun, surf and sand, I have to say it was such a relief, that instead of flying back to Karratha, we were able to go straight to our little home in Gwelup. Noddy flew back to Karratha to finish his three months which brought him to his long service leave. He was also able to pick up the mobile home to bring south, whilst I started the huge job of unpacking and setting up our new home. We had decided to live in it before doing any of the renovations and repairs. It was circa 1960's/70's and was looking tired and old.

21st January came around very quickly and before long I was back in a uniform and started work at a tertiary hospital as a clinical coach/mentor, which was an honour to undertake. The young women who were on their first rotation from University were a delight to be with. They were intelligent and born to nurse, and I was able to marry the science and the art of nursing with them from their very first day as a nurse clinician. Over a period of three years, I saw the growth and development of some of the finest young nurses one could meet - our future leaders. I also met there within the first weeks four soul sisters who are still close friends today - Abla Ruhal, Ailin Pinto, Theresa Morna and Mariyam Nisa.

Noddy retired in April 2008, and arrived safely home with the dog and the bus after a very harrowing experience on his way down from Karratha. He had blown a tyre, just outside of Northampton. His guardian Angel was with him that day. When the tyre blew, the bus pulling him to the near side of the Great Northern Highway to the other side of the road. Fortunately, there was no other transport vehicles on the road. This experience really shook him up.

It was so good to have him back home and he soon became the minister of interior and exterior affairs.

Noddy was blessed as he had been asked if he would like to come back every six months to be part of the Woodside Shut down maintenance programs post retirement. It meant him going back to Karratha for four to six weeks at a time working on shutdowns as a storeman. He loved it and it kept him young, going back and catching up with all his old workmates. I missed him like crazy while he was away.

I spent a lot of time with Milena and Dragon as they only lived ten minutes away. Abla and Ailin's husbands too worked away, so we three would have lots of lunches and coffees on our days off. I had found a new pool and continued my swimming regime and spending quite a lot of time down at my favourite little beach at Trigg. Life was good. I had a break from my Natural Therapies private practice as we did not have the space to set up a Sacred Room in our home, until we did some renovations. However, I kept reading as many books on my favourite subject - healing and meditation. I was able to give in-services at my work on Holistic Health Care and Complementary Therapies and run meditation sessions in Staff Development time .

In October, we finally worked out what we were going to do with our home and started an owner /builder program. We were ever so happy with the end result. At the end of 2007, JD had met the girl of his dreams, who became our dearly beloved daughter-in-law.

LIFE CONTINUES

In mid-2008, I received a visit from a police officer, asking me to write a witness statement for the death in ED in Port Hedland Regional Hospital a year before. I had written a statement at the time and kept it for when it was needed, I immediately contacted the ANF (Australian Nursing Federation) and received the best support and advice from a very nice legal officer, on how to write a witness statement. Once I had written it, I had it checked by the ANF and submitted it to the authorities.

In October of 2008, we had a phone call from JA and John; John had been a successful applicant for a headmaster's position at a private school in Perth that he had applied for. He would have to be in Perth for the beginning of the school year. Miracles do happen, I thought happily. JA and John were coming home. JA was coming home after twelve years in London so the excitement was out of this world. JA would be home three months later, as she had quite a lot of work to finish up and get their house ready for the market.

JD and his partner, Sarah were off to Burma before Christmas in 2008 and as always JD flew over to spend a couple of days with us. On their return we had a phone call to say, "are you sitting down?" We were knocked over with excitement and joy when they broke the news to us that we were to become Grandparents. We danced and sang all night; what a gift from heaven!

Oh! what a year 2009 was to be! Our life changed forever. John arrived in January and lived with us, JA arrived in the April so our little home was full and very happy. Even better news, we were to become grandparents again. So happy our family was home and even though JD and Sarah were over east they were only five hours by plane. We were all together in the same country. We were growing from six to eight.

JA and John were settled and happy to be in Perth, John settled into his new role and the Australian way of life. They found, a nice house on a big block in Duncraig eight kilometres from our front door, which they purchased and moved into. JA's first baby was due in early Jan, 2010. Work was great, and happily preparing for the arrival of the new babies. Noddy too was very happy as, the gardens were establishing and we were settling into city life again.

I arranged for holidays to go over to Canberra, for the birth of our first grandchild; we made it with an hour to spare. Sarah's mother and father, Anne and Nigel were there waiting too. We all met our first born grandchild, fifteen minutes after he was born on the 5th August 2009 at 18.20 hrs. What joy, what love.

We had a very blessed ten days with our extended family and cuddled one very special baby boy. We were overjoyed at becoming grandparents.

Our next grandchild was born on the 13th January 2010, at 14.10 hrs One beautiful angelic baby girl, so small with a mop of brownish hair. Poor little one had a pretty rough entry into the world which ended in an emergency caesarean section. Again, I took leave to help JA out for those first couple of weeks post-delivery and getting to know this very cute bundle of pure love and joy. JA was very fit and was soon back to normal before I returned to work. In November 2009, we received more heart-warming news our first born grandchild was to become a big brother.

2010 was a very blessed year work wise and our life pattern with our families and friends and our little granddaughter. We spent a lot of time doting over and babysitting as often as we could. The little grandson, growing very quickly, was just the most gorgeous little one too.

We flew to Canberra to be there for the birth of our third grandchild born 6th August 2010 so blessed when a little blonde bombshell with the two biggest dimples came into our lives. By this time JA was pregnant again and on the 25th February 2011 we were blessed with a delightful bundle of joy and a fourth grandchild an adorable little grandson, entered the world -this time a booked caesarean section. Our life was perfect.

It was in May of 2010, we received the worst news one could receive. Our beautiful friends, Sel and Charlie found out that dear Charlie (Chaz) had only six months to live with two very aggressive cancers growing within his body. Medically, nothing could be done. They stayed with us for a week before returning to Port Samson. They had to sell their home to come and stay in Perth.

Initially, they stayed with us when they came down until they bought a little place for Sel to call home. They found this home in Redcliffe not too far from us the week we were in Canberra celebrating our grandson's first birthday and awaiting the birth of our new grandchild. Charlie was the most amazing man, a realist, he ensured the love of his life was well taken care of and lived until he took his last breath. Seleana our dearest friend was heartbroken and she cared for her Chazie in all aspects of his life. Their best friends were there when he passed, Jane and James Best, Milena and Dragon and Noddy and myself. It was such an honour for all of us to be there with two of God's special people at this time. Life was even more precious after Charlie's passing in October 2010; the world lost a great soldier and humanitarian.

. . .

Work was progressing to some extent; I became one of the Peer Support Officers for nursing staff at this tertiary institution, I could feel the energy flow starting to slow and become blocked again in the workplace, as I was witnessing the management practices and the way some of the managers, clinical nurses, specialists clinical nurses and general nurses, treated their junior and seniors nurses.

In 2010 -2012, we had an excellent leader who was a beautiful heart centred nurse who had been acting in the role for two years. Sadly, she did not get the permanent position and things started to change when a new leader was appointed. The ward was not the happy place it used to be despite the efforts of the empathic senior nurses who kept supporting and watching out for those who were victims of the subtle workplace bullying and harassment that was occurring. There appeared to be an endemic of narcissism amongst a small cohort of nurses, at both senior and junior levels. I was also asked to go over to be a clinical coach and staff development nurse at the tertiary institution's rehabilitation centre. I did go to the rehab working there three days a week and on the medical ward two days per week. I really enjoyed the Rehab Centre period. The Manager was a very good woman who remembered me from the time when she was a graduate nurse on the short stay unit at this tertiary institution in 1992 where I worked. It is always such a joy to see the nurses who you mentored and helped as graduates, do so well. The staff were great and the patients delightful - all very keen to get back to their independence.

I had an amazing experience in this unit, which I will share here. I was with a beautiful old lady who was in her early nineties. She had lost her right leg in a bus accident. I used to do a round every day, and when I walked into her room, I observed that she was in severe pain related to phantom pains and she was very upset; secondary to the fact that the team had been in and had told her, she was too old to have a prosthesis. I asked her if I could help her phantom pain using Therapeutic Touch; she said yes so I pulled up a chair and started to work, with a very positive outcome. This gorgeous old lady told me a little of her life, her marriage to her best friend, her husband who had passed away some nine years prior to our meeting. I asked her "Do you talk to him" She informed me she did every night.I asked her 'if she had talked to him about her accident'. She said no, so I suggested that she do this. As I was leaving her, she told me she would tell him that night. I went on four days off, and on my return she called me in and was so excited. The team had been in to tell her that a decision had been made for her to have a prosthesis. She held my hand and said "Thank you". She informed me she had talked to her husband on the Wednesday night. We were both so happy and believed it was a direct gift from her husband.

***

2012 saw Noddy and I take our first cruising holiday - a 26 day voyage to Alaska around the Bearing Sea to a port in Northern Japan and across to Vladivostok in Eastern Russia down to Shanghai Tallin and finished with a three night stay in Beijing. What a trip we had. It did not start too well as we missed our 1am flight to Singapore. We had it in our heads that we were leaving at 1300 hours (1pm) instead of 0100(1am). Noddy woke me on the day we were supposed to be in Singapore and said," Honey we are supposed to be in Singapore on our way to Vancouver". All I could do was laugh, we were over organised and paying the price. We rang the travel agent at 9 am and by 10 am we were booked on the 0100 hours flight on the next morning. We were at the airport very early; our daughter saw to that. Yet again the realisation of how small the world is hit us, when we met a delightful couple from Sorrento in WA in Vancouver, who recognised me from the medical ward at the Tertiary Institution I was working in. We became good friends with Gary and Helen on our return to Australia.

We boarded the Diamond Princess and were so glad to have a beautiful cabin with a lovely balcony for this wonderful adventure, up the Inland passage of Alaska. It was the final voyage of the year as it was the beginning of the fall and the cruise liners were heading down south for the winter months. Our first Port of call was Ketchikan which is known as Alaska's first city. It is located on an island and began life as an Indian fishing camp. It is the first major community that travellers come to as they travel North. Here we did a tour around the village and went out to a famous waterfall near the town and a cruise around the fishing factories on the ocean. Fishing is their main industry.

Our next port was the very pretty town of Juneau. This town was where gold was first found in the 1880s, we saw many beautiful glaciers there and were very excited when told about the historic Red Dog saloon which boasts Wyatt Earp's Gun. I just had to go there for as a young child, I had heard so many stories and saw so many cowboy films about Wyatt Earp; he was a hero of my father's and of course one of my heroes' from that era. Juneau is the capitol of Alaska.

From Juneau we went to Skagway which was a lovingly restored frontier era village and we took a train ride aboard the vintage White Pass and Yukon Route Railroad to the Klondike Summit and Yukon. The display of International Flags up on the mountain is something that has remained with me today. I had brought a new walking stick in Skagway as the old back was playing up due to all the walking I had been doing. At one stage, I needed to get a bit of fresh air so I went out the door of the carriage to take in some big breaths of clear mountain air. The wind was very strong and cold and very quickly the wind blew the walking stick out of my hand and it disappeared down into the great canyon below us. I quickly retreated inside as I did not want to be blown away, like my new walking stick. The scenery along this six hour train trip was breathtaking, and truly a magnificent part of the world in which we travelled.

From Skagway we headed for a day of visiting the Glacier Bay National Park and College Fjords, seeing the spectacle of massive chunks of ice being calved into waters below the massive miles of huge icebergs all coming down from the mountains surrounding these wonderful National heritage parks. I am so glad to have had the opportunity to witness this magical event of Mother Earth which in years to come will not be here, because of environmental degradation due to global warming. We were also very lucky as we had perfect viewing because we had a balcony leading out from our cabin.

On board the ship, after a day of exploring, we would have wonderful experiences mixing and dining with such diverse people from around the world. Our next port was Anchorage; the history behind this city is very interesting. Captain Cook was one of the first Europeans to explore this region of Alaska; however, it was not until the Alaskan railroad was put in that it was finally accessible to the world. There is a wonderful Museum of History and the Arts and an Alaska Native Heritage centre where performers put on traditional story telling events and where the traditional artists would share their work. An amazing place to visit. Leaving Anchorage, the next stage of the voyage took us around the Bering Strait and around the Bering Sea, which is a marginal sea of the Pacific Ocean and it separates two continents. The Sea is boarded on the east by Alaska and on the west by Russia

During those six days the voyage took, navigating the Bering Sea, we had our 40th wedding anniversary, and as there was a Catholic Priest on board, we renewed our wedding vows. We were so blessed and so grateful to have made the 40-year journey through all the great times and through all the not so great times I had experienced. Noddy always by my side, a real Earth Guardian Angel. We have had so many great experiences that it would take another book to fill.

Before we entered the West, we berthed at the town of the most northerly port of Japan, a City called Kobe, and is one of Japan's ten largest cities. We only stayed in the Port area and did not go into the big city as it was a Sunday. I just loved this community, the Port town was small, and the town band was there to greet us. As soon as we were on land, we were invited into a community centre for a cultural learning experience, which was fantastic. The people were so warm and friendly, peace reigned around every step one had exploring what this section of Kobe had to offer. One of the videos I love to watch from this visit was seeing a Japanese man playing on a didgeridoo, outside his shop. After a wonderful day out and once we were ready for sailing, one of the schools' students in the town turned out for a display of band music and traditional dancing in the pouring rain, to bid us Bon Voyage.

Our next port of call was Vladivostok, a major Pacific city in Russia overlooking Golden Horn Bay, near the borders of China and North Korea. It is very well known for being the beginning or the terminus for one of the world's great train journeys The Trans-Siberian railway, a seven day journey that links Vladivostok to Moscow. It was fun, just to stand on this train station platform and visualise doing this journey one day. We took a tour here and were amazed at their military museums, including their submarine museum. We felt the city was quite a depressed city, people never smiled and always in a hurry. It did not feel relaxed like everywhere else we had been. We did receive one big surprise however, we were unaware the great actor, Yul Brynner was actually born and grew up in Vladivostok. We actually were taken to his home, where there is a lovely bronze statue of him, and I have a lovely photo of Noddy standing in front of that statue.

From here, we sailed around to Shanghi Dalin and Beijing. We took tours in these cities ,and I am so glad we did ,The amount of people the skyscrapers ,the cultural sights etc ,it was like being on another planet. The guides were excellent and their knowledge of the history and cultures were second to none. One of our stops was a top end of the market school for very bright and talented musicians and dancers as young as 6, they put on a show for us the likes of which we had never seen before.We visited the main tourist attractions and loved the experiences we had there.We had no idea how China had evolved to what it is today, over the years since the late 70's .Up until then for the period between 1949 -1974 the peoples Republic of China was closed to all but selected foreign visitors.In the late 70's when Deng Xiaoping decided to promote tourism vigorously as a means of earning foreign exchange .It was then China started to develop its tourist industry. We visited the venues for the Olympic games and were captivated by the most amazing sporting sculpture park I have ever seen.

I vividly remember walking into Tiananmen square and feeling quite distressed as it brought back all the memories of what was screened on our televisions in 1989, which became known as the Tiananmen Square Massacre[1] and I pictured the young man who stood in front of a big army tank in absolute defiance of the military assaults that killed over 1000 students. It is so important to know what happened to all these very brave brave young men and women who fought for their democracy. We visited other ancient buildings in the Forbidden City and other great sights. We were fortunate enough to go to a very ancient village situated 60 kilometres from Beijing. We were taken back centuries to what life would have been in 17th century China. We also had a wonderful evening out at a live production of the story of Kung Fu, the artistry and the athleticism of the dancers left us in awe.

The best experience we had on our three day visit was a day's trip out to the Great Wall of China. The construction of the first section of the Great Wall of China goes back to the Qin Dynasty (221 -226). It was finally completed in (1368-1644). We were not surprised to learn that The Great Wall is sometime called the longest cemetery on the planet because more than a million people died here while building it[2]. It was such an experience for us to actually walk a few kilometres on this sacred wall.

We left Beijing the following morning and flew back to Perth after an absolutely magnificent voyage and excited at the prospect of further cruises in our future lives after retirement.

***

Between 2009 and 2012, the State had some coronial inquests that involved nursing and medical staff. These were publicised through the media, and every time one was on the news and reports printed in the newspaper, I would become very stressed, knowing one day I would be called up to one. I would wake up with nightmares about the adverse incident that had occurred in 2007 while I was caring for a man who passed away in the ED I was working in. My mind really played games on me. I was seeing empty notes and observation sheets, fluid balance charts blank, and nightmares of TV cameras being pushed in my face when I left the court. It was awful. I didn't realise that this event had caused another post-traumatic stress disorder deeply buried at the time and I never sought any help, trying to deal with it myself.

I spoke to no one, not even Noddy. It was not until I received a phone call from the ANF Legal Officer, a wonderful young woman, who told me that the Coroner's office had set the date for the coronial inquest to commence in May 2012 - five years post the passing of our patient. I was to be the only nurse called, JD flew over from the East to be by my side, as Noddy was up North and JA wasn't in a position to help. The day came and I was really stressed. However, once I took the stand and the oath, all fear left me and I could feel a presence on my right shoulder, I am sure it was the spirit of the man who had passed away. My voice was strong and when I was asked to turn to a page in the file I had been given, I was asked if the hand writing was mine. I said, "Yes," noting that all documentation had been completely filled in - Observation Chart, Fluid Balance Chart and my notes completed.

The Lawyer for the ANF assured me at a meeting just before the inquest, I would be fine. Well, I was clear, confident and could answer all the questions asked of me by the coroner's assistant. I thanked the presence of the spirit on my shoulder for everything and his support; and I was so relieved to be able to return to be by my son's side after I was dismissed from the witness stand. Prior to the dismissal, the coroner thanked me for my documentation. I was so grateful as I had taken two weeks leave to deal with this; JD took me back to the East Coast with him where I could be with my family.

I never ever wanted to go through that again; neither did I want to ever see another nurse go through a coronial inquest. So, I started writing lectures and doing staff presentations for nurses to ensure that they learned from my experience. I started lecturing to third year student nurses, they were so grateful as they had done their law unit in their first semester, and did not fully understand the implications of what could be as they progressed into their nursing practice. My experiences working in a big institution made me realise that there was a real potential every day for an adverse incident.

I also started in 2012 to add to my qualifications besides the energy healing modalities. I had been studying and practicing since 1999; so, I decided to do an infant baby massage course, as well as life coaching studies through a Human Neuro Linguistics psychology course/program, run by a learned and practising Humanistic Neuro Linguistics, run by a very learned Master Practitioner, Gary de Rodriguez Both these courses were quite heavy going for me as no touch was allowed to be given to the babies or the clients in the HNLP program. However, I managed to get through the courses and pass the exams. I did these for the purpose of enriching my knowledge to be the very best healer I could be, so that, I would be ready to start my own healing practice in Perth.

I had leave over the Christmas period of 2012. We had a family Christmas for the very first time. All the family from the East Coast came over. We had a grand time despite the very hot weather. On return to work in early January, incivility in the workplace was increasing. Certain forces were making life very difficult at work for empathetic caring nurses.

In 2013, the lovely manager left the Rehab unit to take up another nursing position. Her replacement was very different and work became very stressful. I had had a back injury tearing my psoas muscle, at work in early January. I reported it and kept working, as I knew if I took time off that could be the end of my clinical nursing days, so I continued on, refusing to give in to the pain and took only very minimal medication. I was continuing to be an advocate for patients. Staff were coming to me as a peer support officer and I began to realise that I was becoming unwell again due to being on the receiving end of workplace bullying yet again and hearing what was happening to other colleagues.

As usual, I had everything documented and I took time off with the support of my trusted GP. Whilst on leave, I heard about the words "Laughing Yoga." I had no idea what laughing Yoga was all about. I contacted a gentleman by the name of Peter Schupp, who ran the programme and I met with him individually first to find out all about it. I realised this might help me on my next healing journey. I went for five months and began to be able to laugh again. Peter Schupp's program was just amazing, and I am sure had a wonderful effect on my wellbeing; I could feel a shift deep inside my being.

***

In October of 2013, Noddy took me on another adventure of the high seas. This time we travelled around the Baltic Countries. We boarded the ship in Copenhagen, Sweden; then we sailed on to Norway, Finland, Denmark and Saint Petersberg and Tallinn in Estonia. We sailed back to Estonia and from there, finished off the Baltic, and back in Copenhagen. We were enthralled by this amazing city. St Petersburg was once the Imperial Capital of Russia, before Moscow became the Capitol of Russia. St Petersburg is now known as The Venice of Russia. The city is built on a hundred islands linked by a series of beautiful bridges crossing a network of canals.

After touring all day, we had the choice of going to a Russian Ballet Production or a night of Russian folk dancing. We chose the Russian Folk Dance concert. The dance and music was explosive and highly energetic show. We visited the big museum there, the famous 'Hermitage' museum. It was big and its vast complex ranks as the second largest museum in the World. We were lucky to have two days here in St Petersberg. The difference between Vladivstock and St Petersburg is indescribable and the energy so very different. St Petersburg is very aristocratic and elegant and today is the cultural hub of Russia.

It was really an amazing experience, we never realised the history of these Baltic Countries; we did tours visiting many of the Viking Civilization medieval "Old Town" districts in Stockholm. Tallinn (my favourite) and we spent time in Copenhagen making a visit to "The Statue of The Little Mermaid."

From there, we sailed around to Warrnemunde, near Rostruck, on the North German Coast east of the Kiel Canal entrance and west of the Baltic Sea.

. . .

After leaving for Glasgow, Mother Nature intervened and brought a huge storm to the west coast of Scotland and the ship was redirected to Edinburgh. We chose to go on a tour cruising around Lock Loman where the famous mystical Lochness Monster was said to have lived. We had a wonderful day out in mother nature and attending a working sheep dog trial up in the mountains. Being out in the cool fresh air was just so beautiful, away from the hustle and bustle of a huge city busy city with all the pollution.

The ship from Edinburgh was redirected to the City of Cork's harbour for a couple of days. We had been to Cork on one of our previous trips abroad so we were happy to stay around Cove. It was an interesting place to visit. Cove, was the port that the Titanic sailed out of that fateful night on the 14th April 1912.

From Cove, we sailed across to Halifax in Nova Scotia, where John's uncle, Lester and aunty Yvonne met us. We had a great catchup with them. They had certainly aged since we last met them in 2006. I was really starting to come alive again and for the first time feeling balanced. I was much happier. I was healing, this I knew as I started writing creative stories for our grandchildren. This was a sure sign for me, I was returning to a state of total true wellness.

Our next port of call after Halifax was St John, where we took another tour that included the Horizontal Falls. We were given an overview of these horizontal falls to be told they were the only Horizontal Falls in the world. At one point during the walk, around the Falls, I could not help myself and I informed the guide that Western Australia had Horizontal Falls in the Dampier Archipelago in the Kimberley. I have to say after seeing both, Western Australian Falls are far bigger and superior. The guide was interested to hear this and thanked me very much for sharing this information with her.

I decided to resign from mainstream health as I realised my health was more important than working in a toxic environment. I awoke to the fact that I really needed to pursue my dream and commit myself 100% to my passion and open a little holistic not for profit healing clinic.

I had been off work since June of 2013 and resigned from the health service in April of 2014. It was for me a very sad day as I wanted to continue until 2017 to reach my fifty years of clinical nursing.

I was beginning to really feel like my old self again. I was receiving regular healing sessions and exploring deep meditative practices. I could feel the blockages had lifted and the gentle flow of the life force had returned.

In January of 2013, a Royal Commission into institutional responses to child sexual abuse was established in response to allegations of sexual abuse of children in institutional contexts that had been emerging in Australia for many years. I saw a need for healing programs for these victims when a man being interviewed came forward towards the end of the Perth hearings (April 28 - May 7, 2014). His comment, "I will go to my grave an angry man," disturbed me deeply.

I decided, after I heard this comment, I would go and have a talk to the Catholic Archbishop of Perth, to offer my healing support to victims at no cost, if they would be happy to see me. An appointment time was arranged and when I arrived, I was told, "The Archbishop was in the Eastern States and I would be seeing his secretary and the Vicar General." Talk about an inquisition. When the meeting was closed, I asked when I will be able to meet with the Archbishop. There was no reply. I asked again when I would be able to talk to the Archbishop.

This time I got an answer. "You won't. I will talk to the Archbishop."

Again, I reiterated that I would like to talk to the Archbishop.

"No, I will be speaking with the Archbishop" replied the Vicar General.

I could feel my blood pressure rising and left the building. Oh! what to do next? On the way home, after I had recovered from the ordeal through the practice of Laughing Yoga, I thought of Mary McKillop and decided to contact an old nun friend of mine and told her about my experience.

Her words are still ring in my ears as I write this, "You were being screened." she said.

I said to my friend, I feel like writing to the Pope. This very kind Nun said I will help you write the letter, so she wrote the draft for me. Once I had completed the formal letter, I sent it off by registered mail, and I have never heard a word back. I am sure it went into file 13 before it even got to him.

All I could do then was to pray for the victims. I often think of the poor man who started this fire in my heart; this was the door that opened my mind, to a new way of thinking in relation to religion, the dogma and the rituals of religious practices. I had to question and seek the real truth and de indoctrinate myself, from a religion I was born into and followed from a 12-year-old school girl. I really appreciated the ethos and values and the basis of Christianity from what I was taught at school; however, now I was on a new path of discovery of the purpose and meaning of life.

One morning, our dear neighbour, Peter Martin dropped by for a coffee. During our conversation, I was talking about writing our living wills. I was asked what a living will was. After explaining the purpose of a living will and showing him a copy of mine, Peter asked me if I would be interested in speaking at a meeting of an organisation in which he was an active member. The topics, we decided would be were the Living Will, Holistic Health Care and Complementary Therapies. I said yes, I would love to. So some months later I did the presentation. Post presentation I had a lovely older gentleman talk to me about his wife who was a healer. He had a very painful hip which was had stopped him from being able to play golf, his favourite pastime He asked if I could do some Therapeutic Touch on his painful hip. I agreed as his wife was away. He came back a month later and brought his lovely wife, she was in her early eighties. We had a lovely talk with them both. Before she left, we went into my little room and she looked around the room and she made a one comment, which so woke me up.

She said, "You are spiritually malnourished."

After they had left, I reflected on her words. Here I was practising and following a religion I thought I believed in. I had gone back to mass every Sunday. I would pray reverently and would do no harm to anybody. I believed in God the Father, Jesus the Son and Holy Spirit, and practised faith hope and charity.

I had moved in and out of the church over the years, however after this comment, I really had to find what was missing from my wholeness. At this time, there was a flyer on the church notice board. The flyer was advertising a Mission run by an Indian Priest, a Father Carlo Gilbert. I was curious and decided to go along. Well, I did and I was 'blown away' with his words on wholeness and healing and when he was preaching holistic prayer about body, mind and spirit and living in the whole, I had to just spend the next five days going to his mission every day. He spoke the same language I spoke and believed in. I had never seen written on an overhead, a priest give a recipe for natural pain management and I was so happy to talk to him after his presentations. I bought his book, *Meditation on Jesus for Healing and Joyful Living* and reading this book made me look at my faith differently. I started going to his weekly Yoga meditation sessions he was running. The foreword to the book really ignited me to start searching for what was missing in my life. The forward in the book was written by Leo Cornelio from a religious order called the 'Order of The Divine Word,'. He wrote, 'He is an Indian Priest from Bombay in India. He explained the use of Yoga in prayer and supported by inspiring quotes from the bible.

His book centres on using relaxation methods and scripture, to meditate in a Christian way. He brought from his native country rich spiritual and cultural heritage of his native India. Getting to know Father Gilbert through attending weekly yoga meditations was so wonderful for my own healing journey. His whole commitment was to share the importance of connecting body, mind and spirit. This time, the meaning of everything that I had practiced and learnt over my life, that sometimes closed the inside door to my soul many times over the years, suddenly came so alive and that my soul began to open and set me on a journey like no other I have had in the past. Father spends his time giving meditation through Yoga in India and around Australia and the World. It was such an honour to be able to repay him by giving him reflexology sessions. He loved the experiences.

Also, during this period of awakening in 2014, together with my sister, Marie and friends Dianne Silcock and Francesca Weston, we went on a day's womens' retreat run by The Fullness of Life Centre in Nedlands This was an amazing day and at the end of the day I spontaneously wrote a poem, after a meditation. God knows a fire had started burning in my Heart Centre. I was overjoyed and I immediately knew I had entered another awakening in my life's journey.

The Light.
Kindle my fire dear Lord of mine
Stoke it, stoke it with your Love
Watch the flame wavering now round and around, the Light a glow
Watch it glow dance and sing
Watch it circle throughout within
From head to toe
From heaven to earth
From toe to head
From earth to heaven
Watch it flow, feel it grow
See it spread through this room
From this room to the outdoors everywhere throughout the world
See the Light shining bright through the day and through the night
Through sunshine and rain, through summer and winter in every corner of Mother Earth
So the earth is alive with Grace Light Love Peace Joy Happiness and Laughter and Truth

A GIRL CALLED PETER

Thank you Spirit for bringing this great Light to shine through my Heart and Soul.
Peter Rebbechi

After this day, I had decided, I would upgrade my reflexology certification to a certificate of clinical reflexology at the Perth School of Reflexology, commencing Feb 2015. This was a nine month course.

I did a course in 2014, run by a woman by the name of Dawn Kelly who ran an Inner Compass Course. I learnt so much more about myself. I thank both Dawn and the women I journeyed with on that course.

In November of 2014, we decided to use up the credit owed to us from our last cruise. This time cruising the South China Sea, we had three days in Singapore prior to sailing. It was here that I had a remarkable experience on Sentosa Island.

We had just finished our meal, and walked outside the café when we noticed four people standing. Two men were supporting a distinguished looking older lady. Looking at her face, I realised she was in a bit of trouble, so I went up to her and asked her if she was okay. The lady had had a very bad fall landing on her right knee and could not weight bear on that leg. I asked the men to help her over to a nearby bench where we sat down. I informed her I was a nurse. Once there, I examined her knee and my initial intuitive thought was that she had torn her cartilage. I offered to help her manage the pain while they were waiting for a taxi to take them to the Singapore Hospital. I explained what I did and she agreed to try a Therapeutic Touch Treatment. Within fifteen minutes of the TT treatment, all pain had gone and she was able to fully bear weight on her injured leg. I advised them to still go to the hospital and have a medical examination and treatment as necessary. It turned out Bettye, and her lovely partner John with her two other companions were staying at the same hotel as we were, and were going on the same cruise we were going on, so I gave her my number in case she would like some further treatment during the night. Our phone rang in our room at 0800 the next morning; I didn't recognise the lady's voice. The lady was Bettye Anderson, the lady from Sentosa Island. They had gone to the hospital and after a medical assessment and an x-ray the medical staff could not find any damage and she had no pain. We met several times on the cruise for coffee, and I was able to give her a couple more healing sessions on her knee and to this day we remain friends.

I did not enjoy this cruise as much as I had the two previous ones. I was starting to change and see the world very differently as one does on awakening. Our first stop was Brunei. I had heard so much about this country but much to my surprise saw a great deal of poverty there which I did not expect. I had begun to experience compassion in a very different way. I felt for the people very deeply. I am glad we were only there for a day.

When we entered the South China Sea it was like a freeway of fishing boats out on the horizon. When one realises that the population of South Vietnam and Southern Thailand contains and sustains around 70 million people and their stable diet is fish, one wonders as to how do we keep our fishing sustainable? I was leaving a way of thinking, life, and western culture that I had been entrapped in for fifty-five years.

We were on one tour where we were taken to a coconut oil farm. I saw people, westerners, just trudging through the middle of these people's homes without permission. I felt so embarrassed and vowed I would never do another booked tour again; we would do our own thing. We had two stops in Vietnam and two in Thailand. Bangkok was so busy with people everywhere. We went for a Thai massage which was really painful. Poor Noddy could not walk properly for a few days. Mine was not so bad, thank goodness; this cruise was only for fifteen days, so it went very quickly.

On arrival back in Perth, my energy was flowing from within and I could feel the reconnection with my physical, emotional, mental and spiritual body was continuing. I was feeling very well and happy. I was ready to commence the next journey of my life, starting my little not for profit healing clinic.

In March of 2015, I realised my dream and opened my healing clinic.

Slowly, I started to build a clientele. I loved what I was doing and I was able to nurture people to reconnect with their true self again.

I had also at this time commenced the clinical reflexology certification course. During this course, I was asked by a very beautiful Mercy nun to participate in a five day retreat for country women giving hands on healing modalities to the women taking part in the spiritual retreat. The nun who normally did the healing therapies was sick and unable to do them. My name was given to her and so she rang me and invited me to take the sick nun's place. I was so honoured and privileged to do my work and partake in a week's retreat. It was a real spiritual growth time for me, as it was the first five day retreat I had been on since my high school days. I came away feeling very nourished with an increased awakening of consciousness. I was very grateful for the opportunity to administer Therapeutic Touch and Reflexology to these beautiful country women.

In the clinical reflexology course, there were twelve of us in the class. We journeyed together over the nine month period and I was asked on the last day by a very special lady, Nandita d'Cruz, if I would mentor her in healing. I immediately said to Nandita, "yes, I would love to." That was to be the beginning of a dream that I had had in the year 2000. At the end of the course, we were offered to upgrade our clinical reflexology certificate to a diploma of reflexology. I accepted the offer and finally completed the diploma in 2016.

***

To Hell and Back

To open up this section I have to say, that my darling husband wanted it all deleted, saying this book is about Peter, and not him. I, on the other hand, replied that me being his medical advocate, nurse, carer 24/7 and his wife had experienced nearly as much as he had and that the story should be told.

The year 2015 turned out to be a very challenging one for Noddy and myself. During the two week break in April of 2015 from the School of Reflexology, we packed up the caravan and headed down the South Coast of WA from Perth to Esperance for a holiday. It was while we were in Esperance, that Noddy was not himself; I had never seen him so tired and fatigued, despite a very restful trip down the coast, stopping in Denmark, Albany and Hopetown. He never complained about anything, his appetite was good; however, I just knew something was not right; he didn't look well and I rang our GP, Dr Craig Berg and booked an appointment for a review as soon as we returned home

A CT scan was arranged and we received the news that my dearest friend and soulmate had prostate cancer with lymphadenoma (metastases through his abdominal lymph nodes). Noddy took the news unbelievably well. As soon as Craig told us, he went straight down the beach on his own and walked, meditating on the news for about an hour. I too was very calm and started praying so hard for peace and healing for us. When Noddy came home we had gathered our thoughts. He decided to follow the Medical Model, together with the Integrated Healing model I practiced and do whatever we had to do to fight this insidious disease. He totally accepted that his lifestyle in the first thirty years of his life, had finally caught up with him at seventy-four years of age. I promised I would support and look after him all the way, no matter whatever it took. We decided also that we would continue our life patterns, and it was to be business as usual.

In June, we had to see a specialist urologist. A very interesting experience and what an insight into how the business side of medicine works in the private system. Our meeting occurred the day before we were flying to Canberra for two weeks of looking after our beautiful grandchildren for the school holidays, and have some Canberra family time.

The specialist told Noddy he had to have an urgent biopsy and a bone scan. We informed him that we were going to Canberra the next day.

He replied, "no, you can't go."

Noddy said to him, "We are going, please write us a referral to a

Urologist in Canberra and I will have both the biopsy and bone scan done in Canberra."

Immediately, then it was not so urgent; and we were told it could wait until we came back to Perth. When we got back to Perth, he had to go through all the tests that one does when one is faced with a cancer diagnosis. Noddy was diagnosed with a grade 4 prostate cancer and secondaries in his lymph nodes giving him a Gleason's score of 10^3.

We had been advised by several of our friends to ask for a referral to a Radiation Oncologist at a teaching hospital in Perth, as he had the best reputation, but did not have a private practice. This we did and our request was granted. The Oncologist immediately referred us over to a Medical Oncologist at a private hospital for the lymphadenoma cancer management.

What a journey it turned out to be! The Chemotherapy started mid-September and on week two of the first dose Noddy ended up in hospital with severe neutropenia. I saw things from a totally different perspective in the medical and nursing model being practised in 2015. I realised the absolute importance of having an advocate at the bedside when one has a loved one in hospital at all times.

I saw very little empathy on our first day with the exception of the ward clerk and the booking clerk who met us as we came in. As soon as I left Noddy, in his allocated room, I had to go down to another floor to book him in. It was then I started showing some emotion, with tears starting to flow as I realised how sick Noddy really was. The ladies booking Noddy in were very understanding and without asking questions completed the paper work and I went back upstairs via the lift. And in the lift going up was our beautiful daughter; that was it for me. The flood of tears came unchecked, as did hers.

I knew it was okay to have a cry. I had written a poem "Tears" back in 1991. When the specialist came into the room, he spoke to Noddy in a jovial manner and slapping me on my shoulder, he said, "What are you crying about he'll be right in twenty-four hours after the antibiotics".

I did not react. I was not worried or stressed; the tears were tears of pain for seeing my beloved lying in this bed so sick, I have never ever seen Noddy sick before. In forty-three years of marriage, he had never had a sick day off work, so when the specialist came back to insert the cannula, I said to him, "these are not tears of worry nor stress these are tears from seeing my husband in this bed in this condition. He has never been sick in his life."

He then apologised much to his credit. The nursing staff tried their best, I am sure; however nursing practice had changed and I certainly met and saw a couple of good nurses; however, due to the golden dollar there weren't enough to go around, especially on the weekend with skeleton staff on. '

However, I did note the standard of care as I knew it, was not evident. Fortunately, he never succumbed to this neutropenia again, due to the fact that we could afford to purchase a medication that was not on the PBS, an injection that I gave for five days after each treatment cycle .The cost was $600 for five injections. He had three more cycles before the chemotherapy had to be stopped. The cost of these injections ended up being $2400.

I decided to go after the admission and meet with the Quality Manager of the hospital to tell my story of my time spent with Noddy during his hospitalisation and am glad I did, as I was most unhappy with the lack of standards of care he received which included a adverse event caused by a problem with the administration of medication.

I was asked to come in and tell my story to the staff. Several weeks later, I prepared a paper and did the presentation as requested. One of the nursing staff said at question time after I had finished my presentation, to the manager of the unit. "It is not only us that needs to hear this, the Executive and Management need to hear this too."

I thanked the staff for attending and I was presented with flowers and chocolates and left, never to be asked back to speak and share the paper I had presented to the ward staff to the Executive and the Management team. Fortunately, he never had to go back to that hospital.

During Noddy's entire journey through the chemotherapy regimens, I was giving him reflexology every few days and I wrote him up as a case study. I spoke to the oncologist just before his fourth round as

I was very concerned regarding his cardiovascular system. On both feet, I noted during the treatment his chest reflexes were severely crunchy and his heart reflex felt very spongy. During my query about the cardiovascular system, the specialist closed me right down and completely ignored me. I knew he didn't believe in reflexology or complementary therapies as he had told us as much on our second visit, after I had said to him we have added that to Noddy's treatment plan.

What I found interesting during the whole journey was that not one specialist ever spoke about the value of complementary therapies, either in the public or private system, and yet Solaris Care was based in SCGH a government hospital and as mentioned earlier has been operational since 2002. It is also on site in one of Perth's biggest private hospital where they also have a big cancer centre. The volunteers from different healing modalities keep these centres running and have been doing so since 2002 when the Browns Centre was opened.

The practitioner spends the most time of all the paid workers with the patient. I did a shift at one of the centres and found it not a sacred place. I was placed to work in the kitchen area doing reflexology, where there was a lot of noise. All practitioners involved in the clinical management of cancer patients including the manager of the volunteers' therapies are all paid. All the volunteers are amazing people and are professional health practitioners; many of them have nursing backgrounds. It made me even more determined for the integration of healing modalities within the mainstream medical model.

The next major emergency happened on his fourth round of chemo. He had a massive internal bleed one night, three nights after we had seen the medical oncologist. This again was the worst possible experience we had ever gone through. JD flew in from the East Coast to be with Noddy, JA and myself. Prayer groups all over the world were praying for him. It was during this experience that I understood what other people could see what happens in the health system and why there was so much dissatisfaction with the mainstream medical model. No-one had time to be kind or show compassion. Your loved one was just a number, and in some instances, to a few nurses, a nuisance.

Noddy came home with a hospital acquired infection that the RN did not even notice when she took out his IV. However, I did and managed to get a Medical Officer to see it before he was discharged. He was put on antibiotics and slowly after three weeks the cellulitis around his IV site had cleared.

Noddy had been home three days when we received a letter from this hospital asking us for donations to fund their research centre. I do not understand the people who make these decisions to target vulnerable patients and families during such an adverse time of their lives. I as a nurse, who had worked in the system for forty-seven years, had no idea that requesting money in this way was ever occurring; apparently that was standard practice that happens in our tertiary institutions. I was becoming even more disillusioned with the system. We saw the medical oncologist and all chemotherapy treatment from that time on had to be stopped, much to our relief, a week after this experience.

During Noddy's journey, a Medicare review was announced by the Federal Government. I found this out by accident, so I called the enquiry line and asked to be involved in the review. My goal was to try to ensure that Medicare would consider funding for Holistic and Complementary Therapies namely Clinical Reflexology, Therapeutic Touch, Healing Touch, Massage, Aromatherapy, Meditation, and Stress Management for the patient and their loved ones. No one from the review team ever contacted me, however being very persistent in my phone calls to the review organisers, I was finally interviewed via phone as to my queries, and was invited to be a recipient of all the minutes of meetings, regarding the review which would take several years, and I could then make comments back.

Noddy and I decided we would go down and have a meeting with our Federal Member, who was a Minister in the Liberal Government. This meeting did take place. It was here that we were surprised by the lack of respect that we felt was shown to us, by this politician. We were directed into a room to sit down by a young woman who did not introduce herself to us. We took our seats and we were asked to wait for five minutes. Exactly five minutes later, this man walked in with this young lady, and both sat down, he immediately asked us what we were here to see him about.

I answered with the question, "You are Mr X, aren't you?" This is my husband Brian and I am Peter. I am pleased to meet you."

He got up and shook our hands and introduced himself and his assistant. Then we had a discussion with him regarding the inclusion of Holistic Complementary Therapies in Medicare payments, to enable all persons - not just those suffering from cancer or those who could afford to see a Holistic Complementary Therapy Practitioner in the community to benefit from these therapies. e.g. chronic pain, chronic diseases etc.

I received a letter from him on the 21st December 2015, with a copy of a response on behalf of the Health Minister written on the 15th December. The letter was very informative, however at this stage of our journey we were exhausted, and I put the letters away to deal with the advice when the time was right.

We also had a discussion with him on Seniors and the aged with no or very minimal Technology Skills only being able to have access to services like Medicare and other Government services through 'My Gov'. This is a major issue today in Australia for all non-technological persons of all ages ,and races. It has become a sleeping monster eating away at humanity, at a very fast pace and we are very much losing the art of communication. One sees jobs disappearing and small banks closing their branches in country towns. One wonders where it is all going to end. We were told by the Minister, that anyone over 60 did not have to use the computer system; this did please us, so we were able to reassure a lot of our friends and strangers who we met on the journey, whenever the conversation came up.

We had an appointment with the Radiation Oncologist in mid-December and when we walked into his consulting room, he looked at Noddy, and said "You look like you have been to hell and back."

Noddy informed him, "yes, he had and was still in hell with what the chemo had done to him".

The Oncologist looked quite concerned and made the comment, "They did not follow the Harvard treatment."

He asked us to document Noddy's journey. This I did and I handed it to him at our next visit, we never heard another word about this and we never followed it through. Like everything else, the report I wrote was filed in the back of his notes. What was done, was done. He was alive and we had put it behind us. 2015 came to an end and Christmas was a quiet one this year, spent with family and also our friends Seleana, Milena and Dragon.

Now it was time to look at starting the Radiotherapy Treatment Program. Several weeks after the chemo stopped, we had a phone call from a medical secretary of a gastroenterologist, stating Noddy had to come to his clinic for a gastroscopy and a colonoscopy due to the massive internal bleed he had had. He had been referred by the medical oncologist unbeknown to us. Noddy had not heard of this man and he said no I will not have this done. "If I need it done, I will not have it done by any other person other than the specialist", who he had seen in the work up to his diagnosis. (We had chosen him as I knew him from Karratha Hospital).

A week later he had a phone call from the Urologist's medical secretary to come in for gold seeds that had to be inserted prior to radiotherapy commencing. They had booked him in as a day surgical patient at a private hospital. Again, Noddy said "no I will not have any invasive procedure done until I have this chemotherapy cleared from my body."

In the meantime, we found out radiotherapy was due to commence late February. We had done a lot of research on the side effects of radiotherapy so we could look for preventative measures together with the natural therapies I would administer to him. We were blessed to read an article in the Western Australian newspaper on a scientific study done in London on the use of colostrum in medicine. It really caught my attention and I started my own research. My conclusion was it was worth trying to access some.

As synchronicity would have it, I met a wonderful man Paul Dent who was the state importer of a medical grade Alph Lipid Colostrum.

We had a long discussion and we were prepared to trial colostrum for the 38 days of the radiotherapy treatment. Paul was so kind and gave us two weeks supply so we could start before our order arrived. This gave a lead in time of two weeks before the treatment commenced. By this time Noddy was feeling much better, and getting stronger every day. He was back in the pool, although we were dealing with very severe side effects of the chemotherapy and the hormone treatment he had to have. We also tried Chinese Medicine Acupuncture.

The worst of the three severe side effects was the killing of all the nerves from his feet all the way up to the tops of his legs. Also, the continuum of the hot sweats as a result of the hormone treatment, and the lymphedema. None of these life long side effects were mentioned in the treatment plan by the Oncologists. Fortunately, we found a gifted Physiotherapist who specialised in lympheodema massage. In the two visits we had with her, she taught me to do the full lymphedoema massage, so I was able to treat him at home.

Right after that, Noddy had his gold seeds inserted after his chemotherapy.

Noddy sailed through his radiotherapy with no side effects whatsoever; in fact, he was so well one would not have known that there was anything wrong with him. His hair had grown back and still not a grey hair. Noddy decided to continue with taking the Colostrum on completion of all treatment and till today takes a daily dose. I did write a Synopsis up of this and gave it to his Radiation Oncologist with the hope he would share it with other men. All he could do was laugh, at the thought of Noddy on mother's milk. The synopsis was filed in his notes. From this time on Noddy and I would always keep our own power when it came to matters related to our health and never stop asking questions, so we would always be fully informed. We even re wrote our living wills ensuring our children knew our wishes regarding our health care.

***

. . .

I promised Noddy we would do a road trip in our caravan in 2016 when he was fully recovered. We had arranged to go to Darwin to spend time with Dave and Lyn Barclay, and two other mutual friends, Dave and Robbie McNeal would also be joining us. This fitted in very well with the Reflexology and Energy Medicine workshop that I had booked into in July in Melbourne, as part of my ongoing Professional Development. So we planned a trip across the Nullarbor, down around the Eyre Peninsular to Adelaide for a few days catching up with family and friends. Then, up to Darwin and home via the West Coast. We booked to leave Perth on the 5th June. After this caravan trip, we were also doing a major sea voyage in October from London to Fremantle as a celebration of Noddy's life and recovery.

Our life continued as before all the events of 2015. Noddy was just amazing; he was keeping the Minister of Interior and the Minister of Exterior roles, picking up grandchildren from school three times per week and running them wherever they needed to be taken for their extra-curricular activities. My little healing practice was moving forward very well, I would only see one or two clients a day. Another Reflexology student who was completing her Clinical Reflexology Certificate contacted me, and asked if I would mentor her in healing. Her name was Devi Laloo, a beautiful young holistic nurse. I was only too happy to say yes and it was not long after that I was able to introduce Devi to Nandita.

I also was very happy to become involved with Anne Carey's "Courage to be Kind" campaign. I had met Anne not long after her interview in the Sunday Times early in 2016. Synchronicity at work again. Anne had been honoured with the Western Australian of the Year award for 2016 and her theme for the year was to bring to focus the epidemic of Bullying and Harassment in the Health Industry and in particular the Nursing Profession. I rang the Sunday Times after I read the article and asked the journalist to please ring Anne and to ask her to call me. This she did and that afternoon Anne contacted me. I became part of her support team and we offered our home for Ann to bring together Health Professionals who had been bullied to have a safe place to meet.

I found journeying with Anne over this time very healing for me due to the fact that the Victorian Government in 2016 called a Senate Enquiry into bullying in the Health Industry. Anne asked if I would write up a submission for the Inquiry, based on my experiences. I was only too happy to do this. Anne informed me the submission had to be de-indentifed. I prayed about it before I started it, so happy I did' as I found if I handed it over to my higher inner power, words just flow. So, I sat down and wrote a full presentation of the physical, emotional, mental and spiritual effects on a person being bullied and harassed in the workplace, and sent it off to her. Anne then submitted that with other people's submissions to the enquiry.

I went to a lovely nurse healer for a healing several days later, as I was feeling rather unwell. After that healing, I had an energy healing crisis which culminated four days later when on the Saturday night I started to become very nauseated and my abdomen was so swollen and painful. On awaking at 1am, I vomited up two buckets of black bile. You may well ask what is black bile? I knew nothing about black bile until I did my research into the History of the Ancient Healing Arts and learnt about Hippocrates 4 humors- blood, sputum, yellow bile and black bile. From then on, I felt like a new person; renewed with a zest for living life to the fullest. It was like, all that had been buried down at deep cellular level since I was a young girl, had been cleansed from my body. I had absolute clarity of thought and was so light and happy. [Please do your own research on medieval physiology].

Another dear friend, Challis Wilson, asked whether I would be happy to present a lecture on Complementary Therapies and Pain Management for an organisation's she worked for. It was a study day on Dementia and Alzheimer's disease. I was so honoured to be asked and was very happy as the organisation went on to offer us, Nandita, Divi and myself, short term contracts to provide Reflexology to their client base in Nursing Homes.

I was asked by the Western Australian Reflexology Association in May, to present at their September study day. It was an hour's presentation on The History of Reflexology. I was also asked by an organisation to come and assist in working through a workplace issue of bullying in a small department within the organisation. I was unsure where to start this project, until one day I received a very intuitive message at the end of a healing session I was doing. I just felt my neck turn towards 'The Virtues Board' I have hanging on the wall in my healing room and the first word I saw was 'Assertiveness'. Later on that evening, I was contemplating the word that was presented to me so clearly in the morning and realised the opposite to assertiveness was aggression; so I went to bed thinking that I would base my talk around the difference between assertiveness and aggression. I was woken by an inner voice around 3.30am and got out of bed and wrote my first paper on addressing bullying in the workplace. I was ever so happy with the outcome. It was well received.

I was seeing very special and amazing women and men come in treatments and I was more than ever convinced that healing had to be integrated into main stream medicine, and post graduate programs developed here in the Schools of Nursing just like they have in the United States for heart centred nurses, doctors and other health professionals to be able to study Holistic Health Care and Healing. I spoke to many people and tried to get appointments to speak to Deans of Nursing schools at the four Universities in Perth. No one would ever ring back. One could get disillusioned; however, I know one day (and maybe not in my life time) this will come to fruition.

I also had a dear lady who is another nurse, discuss with me the Clinical Reflexology Course. I was so happy when she told me she was booked in to do the course, I asked her if she would like to join our healing group. I was very happy for this lady as she was just such a beautiful person to be with. She had done her level 2 Healing Touch Program many years before and was in a leadership role in her nursing speciality. Now we were four.

It was not long after this I was approached by another lady, Shona Robinson who loved the idea of the concept of the dream I had seventeen years ago to develop a program to bring healing through the complementary therapies that nurses were allowed to use in their practice. Shona offered to become involved in being the admin assistant for our little organization, I was planning to launch and shared the dream with Nandita d'Cruz, Devi Laloo, Jan Ryan and Shona Robinson.

At the beginning of May 2016, 'The Healing Insights' Organization was formed. We had a month to set up as Noddy and I had a caravanning trip planned leaving Perth on the 9th of June. So lots of discussions and meetings occurred. We developed our ethics, mission statement etc. We started to promote ourselves and were requested to participate in an open day with an aged care organisation and participate in a Nursing Speciality Study day promoting and doing Reflexology for persons who requested one - in July and October respectively.

***

Noddy and I left on the 9th of June and travelled across the Nullarbor Plains. Our last trip across had been in 1985. I had totally forgotten what the drive was like and was looking forward to experiencing the drive in the winter. Our first night was spent in Norseman, the gateway to the Nullarbor, and this brought back many memories for me from 1991. It was very cold; fortunately our little heater in the caravan kept us very warm.

Our first stop for fuel was Balladonia. Oh my God! what a surprise I was in for. When we entered the little museum there, I came across all the newspaper clippings and a car that had participated in the 1954 Redex Car Trial. I couldn't believe it and to think I was actually at Marble Bar as a little girl, handing out sandwiches to the drivers and the support teams as they passed through on their way around Australia. There was also the NASA Skylab Station debris that crashed in Balladonia in 1979. I had completely forgotten this part of Australian history. I enjoyed this little museum so much.

Our second night's stay, was at Caiguna Roadhouse. I woke up in the morning unable to open my right eye. Once I bathed the eye with salty water, I was able to open it. It was very red and painful. So, we headed for Eucla as there was a Silver Chain nursing post there. On arrival, we found we were too late to see the nurse as she had flown out on leave that morning. I had to go to the hotel to receive the help I needed. I thought I needed some chloromycetin eye drops. I was advised by the barmaid to ring the RFDS service in Kalgoorlie. This very polite young woman took me to the RFDS phone they had in the hotel, and I rang the number, leaving me to speak to a lovely young doctor who answered the phone. After explaining my symptoms I was told to go to the staff and ask for the key to the emergency box; the chloromycetin eye drops would be there.

"Just take the number down of where you got it from and ring me back with the number so it can be reordered", the doctor requested.

Sure enough I found it, rang the doctor back with the number and we were on our way again. I had to say it was the easiest consultation I have ever had and after three days of treatment, my eye infection was cured. From there, we had a night at the Nullarbor Roadhouse. On leaving the roadhouse next morning, we detoured into the Head of The Great Australian Bight. We were so amazed to see what had been done here. A big tourist centre had been built with a large boardwalk down to the viewing platforms for whale watching, that was also disability friendly.

We stayed there for a couple of hours just watching mother whales and their calves playing. It was a glorious day just being with mother nature, the ocean the huge white cliffs of the Bight; the birds and the whales made it a perfect place to meditate and be one with the Universe. One does not mind paying taxes when you see such fantastic government projects as this. Once we left the Bight, we drove to Ceduna in South Australia. I have to say the trip across the Nullarbor Plains was the best. It was cold and we drove through lots of rain and the environment was very green, the ranges were just amazing. Ceduna is very well known for its fishing and oyster industry; a very pretty small country town.

As planned, we headed down to Streaky bay at the bottom of the Eyre Penninsular. We fell in love with this town, lots of history and old buildings. It is a very large pastoral region. From there, we headed up to Port Lincoln where we were booked in for four days. It is here that you can swim with the great white sharks. You are lowered down in a cage and can have an eye-to-eye experience with these masters of the ocean. This was something I was really looking forward to doing, much to Noddy's horror. He was very relieved when we went to buy the ticket for me to have this adventure, to find out that all the charter boats had been fully booked for the whole week, by the American soldiers who were participating in a big exercise with the Australian Army out in the back blocks of Coober Pedy. Never mind, I said to myself, a great excuse to come back.

We meandered through to Adelaide, where we had a wonderful week catching up with Noddy's family and friends. After a couple of days there, I flew to Melbourne to attend a one day workshop on Energy Medicine and a two day Reflexology workshop, which I really enjoyed. I was gladdened to see that energy medicine was now being talked about in the modality of reflexology; something which I had always believed in since 2000.

I stayed in a B&B not far from the venue where the workshop was held and the owner of the B&B was an astrologer. She was lovely, we connected straight away and she treated me like a family member and not a paying house guest. She took me to the venue each day and picked me up at the end of each day, even taking me out to the airport for my return flight to Adelaide, after the workshop had finished. Honestly, loving kindness was so alive and well in all I was meeting on my journey.

On return to Adelaide we headed up the centre through to Darwin, visiting all towns along the highway. For the first time we explored Coober Pedy. Coober Pedy is the Opal mining capitol of Australia and it was amazing. Most of the houses are built underground and we could not believe what we discovered, a total new way of living, no heating or air-conditioning required - a mean temperature of 25 degrees 365 days a year. We were really taken in by the underground Churches; they were out of this world. The Serbian Church was our favourite, built into the rock and underground, it was spectacular. The really upsetting part of the drive up to Darwin, was the lack of rehabilitation of the environment. As one drives out of Coober Pedy on the Stuart Highway, there are kilometres of slag piles everywhere. What a way to spoil the pristine, arid, flat desert. We could not understand how the miners were allowed to leave the dirt without rehabilitating Mother Earth, and it went on for kilometres and kilometres. Even in the 1970's, Nabalco had to return the bauxite mine site in Gove, back to its original status; so why not here in the desert?

We did a day trip out to Ayers Rock from Alice Springs; I had heard about the Rock so many times and we had flown over it many times too but never actually visited it. We had a wonderful day and were overjoyed at the spiritual energy that we experienced there .We went for long walks all the while being cognisant of the sacredness of the site and the rock including the differentiation of women's business and men's business meeting places .It was worth all the years of waiting to walk within the sacredness of the environment. Alice Springs was very quiet and it had a different vibe to it than when I was there last in 2005. It seemed sadder and many shops had for lease signs on, I was glad to leave as I did feel a negative energy around the malls.

From Alice Springs we headed up to Tenant Creek. Noddy had a mate, Peter Pointon Wales up there, who he heard lived up there. He was Noddy's best friend from the age of four, through their teenage and early 20's. They lost contact and Noddy had been trying to contact him for as long as I can remember. He seemed just to have disappeared off the face of the earth. We asked everyone who had been in Tennant Creek for a very long time if they knew of his whereabouts. Only one lady spoke to us and said that Peter had left years ago and no-one knew of his whereabouts. Another dead end.

On our way up the highway, we spent a night in Mataranka. We were up early and drove into Katherine the next day. We could not believe how Katherine had changed. It had grown, new buildings and the town was very clean. It looked very busy and a hub of activity as it was still the middle of the tourist season. We did not stay this time and slowly drove up to Livingstone via Daily Waters. I just love this part of the Territory. Whilst we were passing through their territory we experienced the first rains for months. Everyone, it appeared, were very excited about the rains.

Dave and Lyn were waiting for us when we arrived at their property several hours later. Our other friends, Dave McNeil and his partner Robyn had beaten us by a day. We had a great catch-up with telephone calls to many old acquaintances and friends from the Gove days. Dave and Lyn Barclay have done a wonderful job of keeping in touch with many Govites from the early 70's. We on the other hand dropped out, but still holding special people in our hearts and minds, over the thirty-seven years since we left Gove.

We had a full day out exploring in Darwin. It had just exploded into one new suburb after another and high rise buildings were everywhere since we were last there in 2003. The Oil and Gas industry had changed Darwin; it was no longer the Darwin we knew and loved. One thing we wanted to do, was to fly over to Gove for a weekend. But when we rang to find out the price of the ticket we could have been knocked over with a feather; The cost of the flight 1hour and 40 minutes =$900 return per person! So, we had to forgo this little dream; but the memories that are so precious from our time there will be with us forever. We had a wonderful rich laughter filled week with our friends. We left them on the 22nd July 2016. They made promise they would be in Perth in April 2017.

The drive along the Victoria Highway between Katherine and the WA border would have to be one on the most scenic rugged drives in Australia. The beauty is indescribable, the rugged mountain ranges, took me straight back to Dorothea McKellar's poem, *A Sunburnt Country*. No human could have created the environment through which we drove. We were drawn into the whole consciousness of creation.

We spent a night at Timber Creek, a very pretty little town where the caravan park was run by an Aboriginal Corporation; it was so good to see, it was very clean and well managed. Our next-door caravanning neighbours were a lovely couple from Victoria travelling with their seventeen-year-old son, who had some disabilities. He was just a lovely gentle young man crazy about football, and as Noddy was a football fan they really bonded; We were so happy in their company, and we bade them farewell early next morning as we were heading up to spend two nights up at Lake Argyle. We needed a rest after ten days on the go, non-stop.

I was amazed what they had done to Lake Argyle. The last time I was there was in 1969 when they were constructing the first stage of damming of the Ord River. When I looked over the wall of the infinity pool there, I recalled walking on the rocks and soil, where the Ord River had been drained forty-eight years ago. We were overjoyed when our neighbours from Timber Creek turned up and when they were placed right opposite us, friendships were cemented.

We loved our stay there and we would have stayed; but we still had 2,300 kilometres to go home and after being on the road for six weeks, I was starting to want to just head home. Noddy had not ever been to Wyndham before, so we went from Lake Argyle to the Wyndham Caravan Park. We had two nights there and I took Noddy on a trip down memory lane.

We went into the old court house which now housed the Wyndham museum and sitting on the table in the back room were two photos of my dear mother. The tears started to roll down my cheeks. Dad was also listed on the headmasters' honour board. The new court house was on the old school site and the police station was where the old goal was. I took Noddy through the old hospital; a private buyer had brought it and was renovating it to turn it into tourist accommodation. They gave us permission to go over the whole building. I really loved taking Noddy on this trip, down memory lane and I am sure he enjoyed it too.

It was so hot - 36 degrees at the end of July; so we spent a few hours in the caravan park pool in the afternoons. After we cooled off, we went exploring again, I showed Noddy the old school I went to and recognised our home from 1958, were we lived out at the Three Mile. Now the Three Mile is the town of Wyndham and the old Wyndham I knew as a child in the fifties is now known as the Port of Wyndham. It was really good to go back .It still had a very good down to earth energy about it and the people we spoke to all very friendly and proud of their town.

From Wyndham we headed south to Halls Creek, a very sad town, lots of buildings boarded up and streets desolate, however the surrounding bushland was very beautiful. We had an overnight stay in the caravan park there. From Halls Creek we drove South to Warnum, were we were going to take a helicopter flight over the Bungle Bungles, but sadly the office was closed that day so it was a no go. But never mind, it was still a great excuse to go back one day.

The next town on the highway south was Fitzroy Crossing, one of my favourite places. A community where I spent some healing time in 1991; it was lovely. I did try to find a traditional healer there; however, the only one recommended to me by the locals was an old man who was out at bush meetings. We had two nights camping at the Fitzroy River Lodge and we took an afternoon cruise up Geikie Gorge, which was an amazing experience. We saw lots of fresh water crocodiles along the banks of the river and birds you do not see anywhere else. Mother Earth and Nature at her best.

The next day we went into Derby as Noddy had never been there either. One very rarely hears of Derby anymore, Broome has become the mecca of the Kimberly whereas up until the 1990's Derby was the hub of the Kimberley. I felt a sense of nostalgia, as Derby just like Wyndham and Roebourne in the Pilbara were little towns that were swallowed up as Government Departments made Kununurra, Broome and Karratha the centres of the Universe. We thought Derby was great and although a poor cousin to Broome, these days, it had a Spirit about it that Broome once had before it became a Tourist Mecca. Derby was a small vibrant community and the people were so happy and very friendly. Nothing exorbitantly priced like the Broome of today. If I had a choice, I would prefer to live in Derby.

Once we had explored all Derby had to offer, we decided not to go into Broome and headed straight for home calling into Karratha for lunch with friends. Oh! what a shock we received on arrival in Karratha. High rise buildings, traffic lights and I could not believe where they were building the new health campus. It was being built right on the marsh. In 1995/96, a big study (that would have cost hundreds and thousands of dollars) was done in relation to flood zones in the town of Karratha. One modelling of the flood zone, extended up nearly to the Dampier road out to the Burrup and Dampier. I shook my head that here, was this campus being built right in the major flood zone. We haven't been back to Karratha since the new hospital was opened. I was reassured that the new hospital has been built to be flood proof.

It was lovely to see our friends. However, I was very glad to leave and head straight for home. We arrived in Perth two days later on the 5th August 2016. We were so happy to be home again, with JA, John and the grandees. I had a number of clients waiting for me when I got home, and meetings for 'Healing Insights .'I knew I was going to be busy as we were leaving Perth for London on the 16th October for a fifty-four day voyage on the MV Astor from London to Fremantle - a trip we booked back in December of 2015 to celebrate Noddy's recovery from cancer.

I was honoured to present a paper on the History of the Ancient Healing Arts whilst focusing on the History of Reflexology at a workshop for the West Australian Reflexology Association. It took me four months to research this presentation that took me on a journey from 60,000 years ago through to 2016. What a spiritual journey that turned out to be for me. I knocked very loudly on the door of my soul, and the door was opened and has remained open ever since, and it awakened the Spirit in me, that had been buried for so long. I could feel the full reconnection of my whole being starting to happen .

One of the awakenings I had which was the common denominator of all ancient civilisations was the constant flow of the Life Force-Energy. After that, awakening and writings started to come very easily for me and it was the continuation I realised of my own healing journey, taking me to a new level of consciousness. Healing Insights was slowly progressing forward and planning was starting for 2017.

Sadness and happiness was also in our lives at that time. Our dear friend, Seleana Powell was preparing to return to live on the East Coast at Fingal Bay. We could not imagine what life would be like with Sel living on the other side of the country, and not sharing our lives together as we had done for the last 23 years. However, we were very happy for her, as she had a seven-year plan after dear Chaz passed of returning home to the Newcastle to be close to her very close family. Her house was put on the market and sold very quickly. It was arranged for Sal to move into our home whilst we were away and she would leave on our return home on the 8th of December, 2016.

I finished my client bookings on the 10th of October, as we had so many social engagements to catch up with friends and family before flying to London on the 14th October. The 14th October arrived and off to London we flew. Modern day flying is so easy, however very stressful, with all the security checks and balances here in Perth Airport. Within 24 hrs, we were in London's Heathrow airport, where there were no security checks. We just collected our luggage and walked out the front door to a waiting taxi, to take us to our Hyde Park Hotel. We were so exhausted, we went straight to bed. We had to be at Victoria Station by 0900 on the 16th to catch the bus to the Tilbury Docks where our ship was leaving from at 1300 hrs that afternoon. Once on board and having done the passenger drill we slowly made our way down the Thames out to the open sea. We had a very nice cabin, no balcony this trip, however we had a nice big porthole. The Ship was so much smaller that the big cruise liners we had been on before. There were only 500 passengers and crew and we settled in very quickly and everyone, passengers and staff ever so friendly. It took about a week to find our sea legs and join in the activities on board, it was not nearly as formal or commercial as the big, floating cities that we had been on before this voyage.

Our first port of call was the Port of Funchal on the Island of Madeira - a three-day sea journey from London. We had a great day out and travelled by sky train up to the top of the mountain directly where a big fire earlier in the summer had gone through, destroying everything in its path. It was lovely walking through the historical gardens and buildings listening to the history of this very old Spanish Island. We came down from the top of Island in a very unconventional way, via a road toboggan. It was great fun turning through narrow windy cobblestone streets, arriving at the bottom of the mountain at a very fast rate.

We then had a very long seven day voyage across the Atlantic Ocean prior to arriving in Antigua on Friday the 28th October. The seven days went very quickly, lots of activities were offered on board, if you wanted to become involved. I joined the choir which was on at 08.30 every morning. This was followed by a quiz, morning tea followed, and if one wanted to, one could attend the talks that were held in the big lounge on board. The guest speakers were all very good and knowledgeable on their subject that they were experts in; they even had a lovely guest artist on board, whose work was just amazing, and whom you could have art lessons with. Often, I would disappear and go for quiet time meditations. I had a book called, *God Alone Suffices*, an autobiography of a 15th century nun who started the Carmelite order- St Theresa of Avila. I had this book in my library for years; however never bothered to read it. I had not long before this, read Caroline Myss's, *Entering the Castle*. Caroline Myss was an avid supporter of St Theresa of Avala. Once I started reading it, I could not put it down. I also took the opportunity to start to write up lectures and holistic healing papers after listening to my inner voice that was becoming stronger and stronger very night.

We arrived on the island of Antigua on the scheduled date. Noddy and I as usual fell in love with the place, the culture and the people. Stopping to talk to as many locals as we could. Antigua is one of two major Islands in the Caribbean. We berthed in St John; here we took an organised tour and explored the Cathedral that housed many geological and historical artefacts. The history was really interesting. After the four hour tour we walked and talked to all we met around the little city and returned to the ship an hour before departure and we so grateful for a wonderful joy filled day out. Our next port of call was St Lucia at the Castries Harbour; here we did a tour up to the Pitons, two lush volcanic spires that rise up above the coastline, that are listed as a UNESCO World Heritage Site. Once back at the ship we had three days at sea and then entered Barbados, here we did our own tour. We were talking to some locals, who told us of a huge celebration happening at the Sir

Viv Richards cricket grounds .We were directed to where to catch a bus, and headed out to see all the schools in Barbados doing a big marching competition at the Viv Richards stadium. What a great few hours we had there. Following this we caught the bus back to the port, and explored the surrounding community for the next few hours, until we were ready to set sail again.

Once we left the West Indies, I could feel myself coming down with the beginnings of a cold/flu. Initially, it was not too bad; it had started to go around the passengers and crew on board, and so many people were affected. Noddy was one of the few, who did not get it and we put that down to the daily colostrum intake; one thing he did as a preventative measure was to double his dose. His immune system was so strong. During this time we sailed through the old Panama Canal, a highlight for Noddy as the engineering feat is too unbelievable to describe. We passed the New Panama running alongside built to cater for the huge ocean liners, tankers and cargo ships that pass from the Atlantic Ocean to the Pacific Ocean today.

From there we sailed up to Acapulco in Mexico. Once our feet were on *terra firma* we were shocked to see soldiers and police every 500 metres patrolling the streets. We hired a taxi driver, an honest man, who took us to so many tourist sites for a very reasonable price for six hours. He explained that the police and soldiers were there to protect the people from the drug cartels and the drug wars that could occur at any time of day or night. We did not expect this and to be honest it shocked us. Well we felt very safe. Noddy had one of the many highlights of the voyage here. We had a meal at the hotel that Johnny Weissmuller (Tarzan -1932 - 1942 film era) owned, and where John Wayne would spend a lot of time with what was known as "The Rat Pack" of that era. John Wayne lived in a very nice house overlooking the Caribbean there, as he was married to a lady from Acapulco; the house was pointed out to us where he lived. We were also taken to the Cliffs and saw the most amazing Cliff Divers ever, it was quite a hair rising feat, their diving skill was just so precise, not missing a beat. They must have had nerves of steel. I had my photo taken with these very brave and fit young men at the end of the evening.

The day after we left Acapulco, I started to feel very unwell with a sore throat and a severe ear ache, and developed a cough. I decided to hibernate in the cabin until I recovered from what had developed into a severe upper respiratory tract infection. I was feeling so unwell, all I could do was sleep and read for a while and spend a lot of my waking time meditating and praying. My dear husband kept me nourished. I was determined not to go to see the ship's doctor; but I had to succumb, when I started experiencing severe chest pain, when I lost the hearing in my left ear and the sinuses became very painful. So I went to see the ship's doctor, a Ukrainian man, whose command of the English language was negligible. He wanted me to have blood tests etc. I refused and said no, I just would like a course of antibiotics. I was given the antibiotics and told to come back in 2 days' however I didn't go back and started to recover within 4 days.

Our next port of call was the French Polynesian Island of Nika Hava. There I knew I could have a swim and let the salt water work to clear my sinuses in the ocean and I would maybe find a traditional healer.

We arrived in Nika Hava on schedule where Noddy and I had a most remarkable experience. We had to be tendered in as the island was very small and had only a very small jetty. Once we arrived on the Island we went for a swim where I was able to clear my head, following this we had a bite to eat in the local village and found a lady who knew a natural healer on the Island. She kindly rang him and 10 minutes later a car pulled up and out came this rather big gentleman, he beckoned to us to get in his car and he took us up to his home in the Mountain. A humble home overlooking the South Pacific Archipelago.

When we arrived at his home, he indicated to me to get up on his massage table set up on his back verandah, from where we could see the MV Astor. He started to work while Noddy filmed his treatment. The treatment was amazing, just like the Traditional Healers in Balgo gave me. The "Chucking Medicine" - it was just what I did in my Energy Healing Practice, when doing Therapeutic Touch or Healing Touch. He worked on my face, and oh my goodness, I could feel him breaking up all the swelling in my sinuses and when he went around to my left ear I had my hearing back, and no pain. After I turned over, he beckoned to Noddy to come over and he showed Noddy how my left leg was shorter by 1-2 cms from the right leg. He went to work on my back and by the time he finished my feet were absolutely equal and all pain from my chest wall and my back had vanished. I was so happy; I could breathe, my sinuses were clear, I could hear, and I had no pain in my body. Noddy was blown away by watching this gifted man work.

He reminded him of an Islander he visited in Adelaide back in the early sixties. He had had an extremely bad knee and it was just when he was training with the South Australian Lacrosse Team. He had been told about this man through word of mouth; so he went to see him. He could hardly walk, going in. This man went to work on him and Noddy walked out an hour later and never ever had any problems with that knee again. He played in the international game, a week later. Thinking about this, I believe it is why Noddy has been so supportive of me in my chosen pathway as a nurse healer practising natural therapies. The man took us back to the wharf and we went back to the ship via the tender boat. I was a new woman.

From Nika Hava we sailed to Moree and we had a great day exploring the island on our own, catching local buses and heading out to see the real communities; we had the full day and chatted with lots of locals, returning in plenty of time not to miss the sailing time. We had a day at sea prior to arriving in Papeete a very different place to when I visited in 1971, it had become so westernised. We decided to go and catch a bus and head out of the capital. We travelled out to a little village to chat and meet with the locals. We had coffee with them and returned to the capital for lunch and a wander through the markets.

Back on board, we had another six day stint at sea. I was at last feeling my old self again and had finished a couple of books including St Theresa of Alva's autobiography. One night, I woke at 0300 with a voice talking to me. It was a beautiful message and I had to get up and go to the desk and write up what I was told. This was to totally change me spiritually, and I continued throughout the rest of the voyage writing and growing in total reconnection of Body Mind and Spirit. I would be woken most morning around 0300hrs and would get up and go out on deck to have a deep meditation, being absorbed into the full consciousness of the universe with no one else around. The ocean, the night sky, moon and stars and I became one. Then go back to bed and sleep very deeply until Noddy brought me a cup of coffee around 7am.

We arrived in New Zealand in Auckland on the 27th November where we had to say goodbye to a number of people leaving the ship with whom we had become travelling companions on the journey. We did the Hop-on-Hop-off bus for the day and had a great day out. One of the best stops was the Auckland Maori Museum where I learnt more about the history of New Zealand before the white settlers than I have ever recalled seeing in Australian Museums about the Indigenous Australian Aborigines. That museum was a wonderful historical treasure trove.

It took three days to cross the Tasman Sea to Sydney. We were very excited on arrival as JD, Max and Harper had come up from Canberra to have the day with us. Again a joy filled day we had. Prior to us arriving in Sydney we had arranged for them to come on board to have a look over the ship that had been Grandpa and Grandma's home for the last 47 days. They loved it and wanted to come back to Perth with us. They were made so welcome by all the staff they met on board. Sydney was so busy so we took the ferry over to Manly and spent a very happy few hours there. Then 1600 hours came too quickly and we had to say goodbye to them as they had a 3 ½ hour drive back to Canberra. Sailing out of Sydney down the harbour and out through the heads was a very special experience.

After two days at sea we arrived in Adelaide were Kay, one of Noddy's sisters, came out to pick us up, and had a very relaxing day with her. Sadly, we didn't catch up with his other family members as they were all unwell. From Adelaide we went to Kangaroo Island, an Island we had been meaning to visit on our many holidays to Adelaide. JA had booked us a Hyundai i load van, which we picked up and with two other couples, we drove around the island. I loved Kangaroo Island; it was quiet and unpopulated and I could have quite easily moved there; we travelled over 400 kilometres throughout the day, visiting all the tourist attractions that made Kangaroo Island so special.

By now, I was becoming very excited, three days left on board and knowing that JA, Inaya and Blaise would be waiting for us at Fremantle's passenger terminal on the 9th December, this had been the longest time we had spent away from home and grandparent duties. The last few days were spent sharing time with friends, we had made on the voyage and saying goodbye to all. We arrived into Fremantle Port at 10am on the 9th December, however due to a sudden death earlier in the morning in a cabin not far from ours , we could not disembark until 1400hrs. JA, Inaya, Blaise and Billy were patiently waiting for us as we ran to gather them all in our arms. It was so strange being back on land, with the traffic and volumes and volumes of people.

We were so happy to pull into our drive way and walk into our little home where dear Seleana was waiting. Home sweet Home.

***

Seleana was leaving on the 11th December with her dog, Honey to cross the Nullarbor on her journey to her new life and home in Fingal Bay, New South Wales. That evening we went to dinner, the three of us to the Bulatovich's for our final meal together. We had a lunch party on the Saturday over at Kevin and Kim's, our friend Jane's parents' home with Jane, James, Hudson, sadly young Elly could not join us and Len and Rita. It was really sad as this could well be the very last meal we would all share together. Sunday, the 11th came very quickly and at 07.30 we waved Seleana goodbye, as she drove out of our drive way to her new life. Both Noddy and I had two sides of the coin, crying with sadness, as our bestie drove off into the sunrise and happy she was going home to her family and her new life. We would be seeing her at the end of January 2017 as we were booked for school holiday grand parenting in Canberra for a couple of week's mid-January.

Work for me started on the 12th December and it was not long before we were back in to the swing of life again; although it took us a week to get our land legs again and settle to sleep without feeling the gentle rocking of the ocean. Christmas came and went and before we knew where we were, we entered into 2017. We had our street

Christmas party in that first week in January and how grateful we were to live in a small rich community of this section of Gwelup; all the neighbours came and a great night had by all.

Tranquillitas was open; however, as we had to go away to Canberra on the 11th January, I could only see a limited clientele. We had a great 'Healing Insights' meeting and decided to have our first Parent –Child Introduction to Reflexology Relaxation workshop (age group 5-7) on the 26th February 2017. I would write the presentation for the parents, and each member accepted responsibilities for planning and running the two hour workshop I was also asked by the International Therapeutic Touch Association to write and submit for their International Newsletter. An article as to what we were doing in Western Australia, this was due by end of April for their Bi-Annual International newsletter.

We left for Canberra on the 11th January, flying Tiger Air. They had a really good special on between Perth and Sydney and home again. Once we arrived in Sydney, we travelled by bus down to Canberra, a three hour journey JD was there to meet us at the bus station, and we were straight back into grand parenting duties .Max and Harper were growing very quickly and very mature for 6 and 7 year olds, it was easy to keep them entertained. We always have so much pleasure spending time with the family.JD unfortunately was away a lot of this trip so we didn't see too much of him .We caught up with a cousin of mine in Canberra whom we met for the first time in 2015, a member of the extended Rebbechi family, a lovely lady- Nina Craven, who we met through a cousin who contacted me via phone when he was arranging a Australian Rebbechi reunion in Daylesford in Victoria.

Here was a family I had not heard of and cousins I did not know existed. Nina, her husband, Noddy and I clicked straight away and would sit for hours telling stories over coffee. I was still having 'Peter' time, writing papers and enjoying writing so very much. Where the family live in Canberra, lends itself to creativity, looking out to their backyard into the wondrous nature park of Mt Ainslie, with beautiful bird life and lots of gullies and trees, that all have stories to tell.

Whilst I was in Canberra, on this visit, I had a phone call from a very nice lady from the Western Australian Symphony Orchestra asking me if I would be interested in being their preferred provider for Reflexology in their Staff Health and Wellness program. I was overwhelmed with this request and said I would be honoured to. I arranged to be in contact when we returned to Perth.

One day for a change of scenery, we decided to drive down to Batemans Bay with the kids for a day at the beach and have a meal at our most favourite fish and chip café in Australia, before returning to Canberra. The time flew and before we knew it, school was back again and we left to go up and spend four days with Seleana in Fingle Bay. It was so good to see her so happy and settling into her new home. Members of her family came up from Newcastle to visit us as did an old mate of Sel and Charlie from Newcastle. Noddy's brother and his wife also came down for a quick visit from Port Macquarie to spend a night with us.

We left Fingle Bay to return to Perth on the 2nd February. This time straight back into work. Catching up with clients and planning for our very first 'Healing Insights' education workshop. I was invited to the Nursing and Midwifery board meeting to hear the outcome of the Nurses, and Midwifery Board focus group meeting for the new Code of Conduct and Ethics for nurses, that was held in Perth on the 7th of February 2017. As I had been involved in the original focus group meeting in Perth for the review, on the 14th of April 2016, I was selected to attend this focus group as well. I felt so strongly about where nursing had gone professionally, I flew back from Canberra just for the meeting that day. My friend, Abla picked me up and I stayed with her overnight. She so kindly took me to the meeting and on completion of that, took me to the airport for my flight back to Canberra.

I was so glad I attended this meeting as it gave those of us present, a voice. It was no surprise that bullying and harassment was the number one issue at that initial meeting.

February was a fairly busy month; socially and work wise 'Healing Insights' meetings were being held in preparation for our first ever workshop.

I was seeing my regular clients. I had an amazing experience at the end of a session when a client a most beautiful young woman said to me "I am finding it so hard to surrender when I say the words, Let Go, Let God,"

I listened to her and agreed, "yes, it is a very long journey and I too find it difficult to surrender to living in the present."

That night I went to bed thinking about surrender. At 2am hours I was awoken from the deepest sleep with sacred words coming to me and a couple of days later sat down at the computer and just wrote a paper on the word, 'Surrender'. The words were like music to my ears, a real awakening to actually what on a spiritual level, it meant. Such joy filled my being when I finished the paper, because for me it was an answer I had been searching for since leaving my internal world as a young girl. This was to open up a whole new world for me in terms of more writings. I am so grateful to my young traveller on the journey for sharing the difficulty she was having with surrendering I sent her the paper when I had finished it.

I met with the West Australian Symphony Orchestra (WASO) human resource management team towards the end of February - what a wonderful organisation. Their health and wellbeing program was something that I was so impressed with and I acknowledge them as great role models for other organisations in health and well-being. We held our first trial workshop for mums and children on the 27th February and we were very happy with how the afternoon went, and the very positive feedback given. Nandita and I had a meeting with Juniper Health Care at the beginning of March and arranged to have a Senior's workshop in their village at Bentley on the 11th April 2017

I spent many hours trying to contact persons, to try and arrange meetings, to introduce 'Healing Insights' to Health Professionals and Schools of Nursing at several of the Universities. Again in Perth, organisations, such as Health Services Providers and University Schools of Nursing trying to arrange a meeting was impossible .There was such a need to start a conversation on integrating Holistic Health care and Healing into mainstream medicine, but to no avail. It is quite disheartening when no-one answers your emails or rings you back after a phone call.

In 2017, a Senate enquiry had been commenced into Aged Care, and the head of the enquiry was a Senator from WA. I rang her office to see if I could get an appointment to see her as the submission I had written to the State Aged Care Plan in 2001 was so relevant for aged care today as it was back then. However, I was told no I could not see her, but I could come and meet with the person to whom I was speaking to on the phone. So, I made an appointment and was just so taken aback and disappointed by this young lady's attitude. I was asking for help as I wanted my voice to be heard and I was not politically savvy at that time. She did not have the courtesy to read my submission, and told me to go away and modernise it. This was after I had spent half an hour with her discussing the issues I was seeing in the aged care industry. I would have to say it was a complete waste of time. I still requested a meeting with the Senator, for when she would be in Perth next. I never heard back again from this young lady, so I tried again several weeks later and still no joy, in getting an appointment with this Senator.

The young lady asked if I would like to come and see her again. I agreed and this time I gave the aged care submission written in 2001, with no changes to it. She accepted it and said she would give it to the Senator. Again, I sat talking to her for some time. It was still the same behaviour and I felt totally ignored and there was absolutely no respect, just platitudes, to keep me quiet again. The whole time I was there, she was just looking at her mobile phone, I never heard back. On leaving the office I noticed a poster on the board with a picture of a woman the caption was, "Tell your Story."A month later I rang the Senator's office to see when I could get to see the Senator yet again, this time I got a very short shift from a young man. I have to question why, and ask what does it take to have a voice and have someone listen to what you are trying to do for the betterment of humanity.

At the announcement of the Aged Care Senate enquiry I had

contacted the Federal Minister of Aged Care who was also the Federal Minister for Aboriginal Health to see if I could have an appointment with the Minister on one of his visits to his electorate in Perth. I received the same response from a young man, an advisor to whom I spoke with. He was also disrespectful, and not interested. I never got an appointment.

One wonders, why the politicians do not have senior older advisors who have experienced life and not just young ones who have gone to school-university and into an advisory role. The three I have spoken to were all in their mid to late 20's and very unhelpful.

Despite coming up against brick wall after brick wall I was very happy. My reconnection of Body Mind and Spirit was at a level I had never felt before and I was really understanding surrendering and as synchronicity would have it I had the most unbelievable transformation after I received a meditation out of the blue from the Centre of Action and Contemplation in Albuquerque in New Mexico. The Centre is run by a Franciscan Priest, Father Richard Rohr, a very special mystic, who works in unison with a group of mystics from all religions around the world - Hindus, Muslims, Buddhists, Jews. His writings were just amazing . This totally freed me and I knew I was actually so close to being finally healed and I started writing again paper after paper and sharing with a few very special people.

Noddy was so happy and so supportive. I now knew what St Theresa went through in the 15th Century and what Caroline Myss's book, "Entering the Castle" was actually all about. One thing that hit me when I was on this journey, people walked away, many I whom I had known for a long time. I am sure they did not understand what was happening to me and I could not explain it myself in language that persons would understand. I had changed and had found the place of tranquillity within, a place so different to the external world. It was okay, I was so fortunate that my special friends stood by me.

I had a phone call on the 22nd March from a mother who had heard about the work I was doing in healing and came to interview me to see if I could help her son. The next day I had a phone call from a very distressed young man .I saw him the next day and journeyed with him over the next four months and what a journey we had together and today we have a very special bond.

April came, and JA, John, Inaya and Blaise flew out for the school holidays to Italy and London. We took the opportunity to move into their home, so we could have our home painted and the jarrah floors stripped and polished. My clients were very good and continued to come for their treatments. I kept on writing as new messages were coming through. I was really listening and loving and caring for myself Body Mind and Spirit. Something I had done during periods in my life before being drawn back into the outer world. Now I was living in my inner world and being so nourished from the well that was overflowing with Unconditional Divine Grace Love Light Peace and Harmony, Compassion and Healing, deep within the Soul.

The 'Healing Insights' Aged Care workshop at Juniper was presented on the 11th of April, 2017 and it was very successful. We were very happy and committed to progressing slowly, with the education side of our organisation, knowing how hard it is to be change agents. We knew that it would be a very slow progression. We had to just keep the faith in our vision and ourselves.

I turned 70 in the May 2017. My family wanted me to have a big party, however I did not want one. I was beginning to want to spend more and more time getting to know my inner self and rediscover the real depth of my soul. So a celebration with a very quiet family dinner with Noddy, JA, John, Inaya and Blaise was held with our Canberra family being with us in Spirit. Noddy and I disappeared up to Kalbarri for 4 days, it was so peaceful and I had on my birthday a lovely quiet day visiting Kalbarri Gorge and in the oneness of the universe with my dearest friend and soul mate, Noddy. The team from Healing Insights had a little celebration at our May meeting. I gave a talk to a retirees meeting, organised by a friend I had met on the Astor trip in 2016 which went really well .The interest by the aged present, was amazing with lots of stories of what treatments their mothers and grandmothers used on them with touch when they were young. One lady, in her 80's, was telling me how she recovered from polio as a young girl by her grandmother giving her massages three times a day when the doctors, back then said she would never walk again. May came and went so quickly, life was gentle and I was enjoying just being.

Simon Molan, the young man I was journeying with was improving slowly with his weekly reflexology therapy. He was such a beautiful Soul and I was talking to my inner voice one morning and asked for a little advice regarding his treatment. I had an answer back "Start from the Soul /Spirit on the inside and work out". When he arrived that afternoon, I told him about the message I had received in the early morning, and I asked him if that would be okay with him. He immediately said" yes."

I opened the submission I had written for the Senate Enquiry into Bullying in the Health Industry that had been sent to Anne Carey for the enquiry and read to him, "The Physical Emotional Mental and Spiritual effects that Workplace Bullying and Harassment has on a Person. His reaction was, "Peter the whole world needs to hear this."

A month later, he rang me to say, "You have to write a book, I am paying for it to be published".

I procrastinated and said, "no, you can't do this, and no you cannot pay for it to be published" However, he persisted and four weeks later, he rang and said I have paid for your book to be published.

After much discussion, I finally accepted I would write my memoir as the main purpose in my life had really developed into a deep passion to see safe workplaces for our four beautiful grandchildren, their peers and all the beautiful heart centred children that were transitioning into the world in which we live and to have healing integrated into mainstream health. I was being offered an opportunity to do this by writing and sharing the story of my journey from 1950 to 2017. I then embraced the challenge, knowing we would be away on a four-month road trip over in the Eastern States. I also realised I needed to go away to enable me to write freely.

***

In 2017, the Federal Government announced a national inquiry into events that had happened in the 1980s. A client sent me a copy of a newspaper report regarding this Senate Inquiry. This unfortunately brought a flood of emotional and mental imbalances in me that I had buried right down at a deep cellular level. The file, so deeply buried, came back into my human consciousness again. I had no idea what progress had been made in relation to those events in the eighties until I read this newspaper article. In addition to the article that night, the ABC 7:30 report gave a background into the history of the upcoming senate enquiry.

I decided, this time, I would finally once and for all heal from the events that had so affected me. I decided I would send a submission to the Senate Enquiry, as I still had kept my diary and offered my support to persons so tragically affected over the preceding years that followed. Fortunately at this time , I was surrounded by energy medicine practitioners from the Healing Insights Team, present to walk with me through this valley of darkness .

I sat and wrote my submission in relation to this event, again feeling a great release doing so -I documented my diary entries and once completed forwarded it to Canberra.

Again a great weight was lifted .

Three weeks post the announcement of Senate Enquiry, I received a phone call from a journalist from the East Coast -(she is a journalist I admire so much for her work), and after several conversations I trusted her enough to forward to her copies from my diary entries from that time . It took me a few weeks of healing time and to have received the Power of Touch through Reflexology was such a blessing.

I certainly became a firm believer in writing as a healing art.

I was completely shocked on reading the information that was now open for all to read. I really felt for the women and wondered why a medical professional was allowed to proceed with this procedure when the Australian Therapeutic Goods Administration (TGA) flagged the harmful effects that had developed in relation to this procedure? [4]

Why was it not stopped and how was it allowed to happen? Where was the accountability? Surely what I uncovered over a few months was not picked up in the early stages. How did this end up all over the world destroying the lives of so many women and their families?

I was so fortunate to have my 'Healing Insights' members there to help me through this period.

It took me some weeks to come to terms with what had happened and it played on my mind for some time. I followed the reporting of the enquiry right the way through and was so shocked when I read of the newspaper article of the Australian Medical Association president confirming AMA WA's role in the scandal during the senate hearings in Perth, WA.

I was fortunate enough to do a two-day course for Mental Health First Aid I had read about it in a professional Reflexology Magazine and could obtain CPD points required for my annual registration with The Reflexology Association of Australia. It has been a recognised course in Australia since 2000 and I had never ever heard of its existence. I would have to say it was one of the best presented courses I had ever done and in my opinion an essential course for all; just like The Physical First Aid Course which is run for all. The lady who presented was just fantastic. She had had a very similar experience to mine through workplace bullying and it really hit me how powerful a course is when the teacher has actually walked the walk and then goes on to talk the talk.I came away on such a high and was awoken at 0300 with my inner voice talking to me. Out of bed I hopped, and wrote another paper I also got an inspiration to develop another project and write a book on Spiritual Health.

Bullying in the health workplace was in the Western Australian News yet again - this time at Princess Margaret Hospital (now Perth Children's Hospital) and Armadale Hospital. I decided I would try to arrange a meeting with the newly elected Health Minister as I had seen him at Parliament House when he was in Opposition. I shared with him at that time, parts of my journey that involved workplace bullying. He said, there was nothing he could do in Opposition and if elected, there would be changes in healthcare culture. On finishing the meeting, he invited me to come back to see him anytime. He took a copy of my paper on the History of the Ancient Healing Arts.

I could not have a meeting with the Minister, once he was appointed to the position of Minister of Health in 2017. He was no longer available; so I decided I would go to see the Minister of Health's advisors - the Senior Advisor and the Mental Health Advisor to offer some of my ideas for the prevention of bullying in the work place.

This was just a couple of weeks after the Mental Health First Aid course I had attended, and I was granted a meeting. This meeting was so different from the previous meetings I had with other advisors. The advisors were mature gentlemen who had the ability to listen and show respect. During this meeting I mentioned to them about the Mental Health First Aid Course and informed them of my thoughts about it and said in my opinion that it needed to be compulsory for all who work in the Health Industry. They too had not heard of it and they asked why it was so good. My reply, "It was the presenter; she had walked the walk so she could talk the talk." I spoke at length with these two very pleasant gentlemen and was assured the Minister was committed to making a difference to the working lives for Health Professionals.I was also informed of a Health Department of Western Australian Community Consultation for a Sustainable Health Care plan that was being developed .

I also rang the AMA to ask if I could have a conversation in relation to Holisitc Healing Complimentary Therapies with a leader of the AMA. When I rang, a young receptionist answered the phone. I explained to her the reason for my call. I was asked if I was an expert in my field,I replied, "yes I am". I was then asked what was my PhD on. I said, "I do not have a PhD; however, I have a PhD in the university of life". Much to my disappointment, she just hung up on me.This was an awakening for me as to how some think and totally ignore people who do have not a tertiary education. I wondered too if this was ageism at it's best.

It was not long after the meeting I had had with the Health Minister's advisors that the Minister announced the HDWA Sustainable

Health Care Review and was calling for community and individual submissions. I then spent weeks preparing a 4000 word submission focusing on the integration of holistic health care practices and the introduction of healing practitioners in the medical model - be they western healers, traditional aboriginal healers or other cultural healers. I was interested in applying for a community representative role on the committee, however knew I could not, due to our absence from the State from October to the end of January 2018.

I was also very fortunate to be invited to the Australasian Therapeutic Touch Association for their annual retreat and conference/workshops to be held over a week, down at Portsea on the Mornington Peninsular in August. It was here that Diana May, a world leading teacher of Therapeutic Touch, was coming to Australia to run the Advanced Practice unit for Therapeutic Touch Practitioners. It was her first visit back here since 2007 when I did my Level 2 and Intermediate certificate with Diana and Cheri Ann Hoffmeyer. This course was the Level 3 Advanced Practice Therapeutic Touch Spiritual Healing Course.

I had said to Noddy, "why don't you come with me and you go up to Queensland to see your two really good mates, one who lived in Biggenden and the other at Dingo Beach on the Whitsunday's, while I go to the conference and do the Advanced Therapeutic Touch Course?" We discussed it and he said, "Why don't I go now and then you can help out with the school pickups/child-minding and when you go to the Conference and retreat I will do the Grand parenting duties." I said sure, knowing he really does not like the winter months. So Noddy went off to Queensland on the 13th June for 2 weeks. What a wonderful time he had with these two amazing friends he had known since the late 60's. Life was full on for me whilst he was away.

In July of 2017, Healing Insights were privileged to be invited to attend a presentation by a visiting Professor of Nursing from St Christopher's Hospice in London that was held at Bethesda Hospital. The presentation was on the Power of Touch - "The Namaste Approach." It was a brilliant presentation and we were very happy as this Professor of Nursing validated all the practices philosophies and ethics Healing Insights was about.

The weekend of the 29th and 30th July was a big one for 'Healing Insights.Org.' The very first Seniors Expo in Australia was held in the Perth Convention Centre and Healing Insights was there. We had a great weekend doing short reflexology sessions for persons who wanted to trial it.I did lots and lots of talking and networking. All the team members participated and we thoroughly enjoyed the experience. We were asked back for the 2018 Expo
***

Before I knew it, I was winging my way to the Mornington Peninsular. The first workshop was held in Seaford at one of the Therapeutic Touch Practitioner's Home. It was just wonderful to catch up with a couple of colleagues I had done previous workshops with but had not seen for 10 years and to meet other practitioners I had never met before. Being in their presence one could not help feeling so much love and peace. Diane's workshop was brilliant and so validating yet again for the work and pathway I had committed to do and will follow for the rest of my life. The next day we headed down to Portsea and had five glorious days being nourished in education healing and affirmations of where I was in my journey in life that had moved from a journey to a voyage of everlasting life.

This was a real healing time for me and I realised that I could now completely let go of my workplace injury that I suffered in the late eighties. I was now free and with the mystical experiences that I had experienced intermittently since that night on the Astor in November 2016, I was finally transformed into a total free spirit and was fully reconnected in Body, Emotion, Mind and Soul/ Spirit I was finally fully healed.

During this time away, there was a series of very sad and negative stories in the media from the most beautiful community of Roebourne both in print and on television. I really felt for the community that I knew so well and loved from 1993-to 2003. I thought of all the positive outcomes we had back then and again wondered what went so wrong I decided to contact the Minister of Child Protection, Women's Interest, Prevention of Family and Domestic Violence; and Community Services, to share with her with the paper I had prepared for the State Domestic Violence Council in 2001 and start a conversation regarding healing for broken people and communities. I received a very positive email back stating a senior member of her department would be in contact with me.

I never ever heard another word no phone call, no email, no letter.

Noddy and I had another health encounter, towards the end of September that was a real eye opener to the way our health industry works that had shocked us and made us wonder why we are paying exorbitant fees for private health insurance. One Saturday evening we were at home and he told me he felt a "flutter" around his heart. He said my mum used to get these all the time for years and years. His mother lived until she was 99 years. I assured him he was not having a heart attack and we would go and see Craig, our GP next week and follow it up, if he would like to do that. Sunday, he had further flutters and said he thought it would be best if he would go and have it checked.

"I said no worries," and we went to a medical practice and he ended up being referred for review at a private hospital by a cardiologist as we had private health insurance. Noddy was admitted for monitoring and was told that he would not see the cardiologist until the next, day as it was Sunday. The whole experience was a disaster from admission to discharge thirty-six hours later and we were so shocked to receive the financial details from our private insurance company. The whole 36 hours cost $7000. For nothing except an echo cardiogram and a sleepover in a hospital bed, and a 5 minute visit from a cardiologist who booked him in to come and see him in his rooms in January.

After we found out the cost of this sleep over, I rang to speak to the hospital's Quality Manager and told the full story. I was asked to write to the Director of Nursing. Something I did not follow through due to knowing that platitudes would only be given "it is as it is." It is a big big business - the health system. This would have to be one of the greatest over servicing of any medical provider I have witnessed in my fifty-three years in the health industry. Funny thing is Noddy never has had another flutter. We decided we would not see this cardiologist and go on our return in 2018 to see his cardiovascular surgeon, who has been looking after Noddy's cardiovascular system for five years. He trusted him.

I saw an advertisement for free acting classes in Perth for an afternoon on the 16th September. I had not done anything like this before and decided it might be a fun thing to do as a hobby and enrolled to go along to see what it was all about. Well I had a ball and really got into the action very quickly no inhibitions and loved it I came home bubbling with excitement about it and received a follow-up email and decided to do a weekend course early next year after our trip .So I booked and paid for a level 1 weekend in February 2018. I think my family are shaking their heads at Grandmas freedom. Inaya, my Perth granddaughter loved the idea.

Noddy had finally by this time organised and planned the first month of our trip leaving on the 5th October to travel across the Nullarbor and follow the Murray River from Morgan to Corrong, on our way to Canberra . We had to be there by the 1st November, so he was very busy ensuring the Car and Caravan were serviced and packed ready for our adventure.

Meanwhile. I was finishing up all my work for Tranquillitas Health and our healing organisation. The International Reflexology Week was celebrated from the 18th to the 22nd of September. Healing Insights" had three activities organised and we did our first in- service on holistic health and healing modalities to a speciality unit in a Perth Hospital. I was so happy.

The young nurses were so interested in a pathway for nurses that they had never ever heard of. The next activity was to provide reflexology for an aged care organisation at their Seniors Open Expo. This expo was a just so wonderful for our healing org. From participating in this day, we were asked if we would consider being the organisations' preferred provider of reflexology to their home care clients. A dream coming true. We of course, said we would love to provide this service to their clients.

We immediately realised we could no longer continue as an organisation and that we would need to start a company. Something that was so foreign to all of us. We were blessed as Noddy and I knew a very professional business accountant. We contacted him and he immediately offered to come and meet with us and help us set up the business for our healing organisation to be a certified company. We also had a friend who was an insurance broker and he set up all our insurance policies. Things moved very quickly. I had to give my apologies for leaving all the business set up planning and all that goes with setting up a company, with the team; however, I knew I had to go and be without any other distractions to write up my memoirs.

The third activity was presenting and giving reflexology experiences to a sporting club. We were moving forward slowly and were very happy at the end of the reflexology week. We knew it would not be easy too, as clinicians we were not very business orientated; it was all so new for us. For me at seventy and being completely computer illiterate except for typing and sending emails and receiving emails and having left the budget and business side of health in 2003, I was completely at sea with it all. However, the team really took up the challenge and had it all under control and by mid-November, we were a registered company.

On the 5th October, we left on another road trip to traverse across the Nullarbor to travel the whole of the Murray River system and followed the Murray to the top, then on to Canberra for a month of child minding and then continuing our trip on to Queensland. This trip across the Nullarbor was the best we had done. The weather was perfect and we met some lovely personalities on the way. We arrived in Ceduna forty-eight hours after we had left Perth. We had a three night stay and explored Ceduna - something we had not done on our last visit. Again we absorbed the history of the town and its surrounds; we could understand why the town was so popular with Australians. From Ceduna, we headed for Burra, a town I had never heard of. Oh my goodness what a beautiful old town and the Heritage buildings just so well preserved.

Noddy was so happy as he had memories of his time here as a young man and was able to recognise roads and buildings and told stories of his wild days and his experiences there fifty-five years ago. I had never heard these stories before. We had some lovely chats with the locals in the couple of hours we spent there. From there we headed to Morgan a very historical town. We set up camp and booked in for a couple of days. The History of Morgan was just so amazing ,it was the heart of the transportation hub in the mid 1800's, and oh the museum there was just "mind blowing." I remember sitting on the veranda talking to an 90 year old man who had lived there all his life I was in 7th heaven, just listening to his stories and allowing the imagination to take me back to that time, although I did history at school in the 1960s, it was all British and European History .I never knew or heard of the towns and the history of Australia. In fact all the towns on the Murray were like this. There was not one we didn't fall in love with, spending hours meandering through old buildings and museums. We talked to the old timers and the intergenerational community member's .We just loved how the old towns were re-inventing themselves.

One of our favourite experiences was visiting Swan Hill were there was a night light and sound show. Very impressive - giving the history of the creation of the world, starting with the Murray cod and the rainbow serpent, through to the dinosaurs era and then through to today. The cleverness of persons who develop theses light and sound shows filled us with admiration for the imagination and creativity of the artists and the production teams who put them together. Noddy had spent some wild weekends up on the Murray as it was so close to Adelaide. He was totally amazed at this journey as he had spent too much of his time in the Local Pubs having ales, he had not realised the magnitude of the beauty and history the Murray River had to offer.

I really enjoyed visiting Glenrowan, here the spirit of Ned Kelly lives. There is the most brilliant museum and light and sound show of Ned Kelly's life. We even went through the house he lived in.We met this old man in his 80's that had a dream of developing a living memorial to Ned Kelly. Sure enough he followed his dream and has this very large Ned Kelly story house all computerised. His 19 year old grandson helps him manage the business and with the running of the show. The other highlight for me was visiting the town of Corryong where the story of the Man from Snowy River was filmed .The museum was so full of memorabilia and so so interesting. I have always had the greatest admiration for our Indigenous People .I was really only aware of the history of Northern Australia of our Indigenous brothers and Sisters however I was unaware of the history of the Aboriginal People in the Southern States of Australia. My admiration moved to another level.Visiting the museum in Corryong[5] opened up another chapter for me of Australian History and deepened my admiration for our pioneers of this beautiful country we call Australia. The ingenuity and the feats to build Australia in the 1800's that our forefathers and mothers are beyond comprehension. The strength, physically, emotionally, mentally and spirituality of the women, their children and the men displayed, I wonder if we could ever replicate their resilience in today's world. I was fortunate to have visited communities in remote areas in the North West of WA and the Northern Territory. Living in these communities, opens a world of Australia History that 90% of Australia's population would have not heard of. Noddy and I both felt so privileged for our life's journey and where it has taken us.

Arriving in Canberra, from where we had just been immersed into early Australia was a shock to the system. The rush, the cars, and busyness of the city was too much. We settled quickly into our grand parenting role and to see Max and Harper now 7 and 8 who had grown so much since we saw them at the end of January, was just so wonderful. Our son was in good form. Our dear daughter was away for work; however, her Spirit was very strong in their home. We had a very happy month being there with and for them and I loved going for long walks up in the National Park spending a lot of time just being. I also managed to type and type and type the manuscript of " A Girl Called Peter" while the kids were in school. The month had no sooner started and it finished. Anne and Nigel returned for the last three weeks of term and Noddy and I headed up to continue our journey up to Queensland.

Our first stop was to visit our dearest friend, Seleana Powell in Fingle Bay. We had a very restful fun filled relaxing time with Sel. Sel had settled in very well and became a great tourist guide. Showing us all these beautiful communities and beaches she had discovered this year. We were also honoured that Seleana's family – Her sister Jeanette and her daughter Taylor came up to spend a night and day with us and her sister Shirley and her husband came up to visit one day. An old friend of Chaz and Sel's we met at Chaz's farewell came up to have lunch. God we miss her in the West; however, to see Sel so happy and settled into her new home and community with her family so close, was just so fantastic.

After a week with Sel, we headed to our next stop which would have to be one of my most favourite places in Australia, Byron Bay. We stayed in the caravan park where we had spent a week celebrating Noddy's 70th birthday with our son and his family. Byron Bay is a mecca for the world, the people just so friendly, and polite .

Our next destination was Kawana Waters were we were having two nights with a very dear couple Bettye Anderson and her partner John. Bettye was the lady who had the fall at Santosa Island and injured her left knee, and whom I had been able to help with Therapeutic Touch, as I have previously written about. On our way to Kawana waters, we had arranged to have lunch and a Reflexology session with a beautiful soul and healer, Sonia Bailey.I was first introduced to Sonia in 2015 when I communicated with her on the phone in relation to Reflexology. At that time Sonia was the President of The Reflexology Association of Australia. We have become friends over the last couple of years. Sonia lives North of Brisbane and boy didn't we get lost. We missed the turnoff Sonia had given us per text, as we approached the city from the

South .We kept going round and round in circles of the airport. It was like one big maze. However we called into one of the industrial sites and this lovely man gave us very clear directions and once we followed his instructions we went straight to Sonia's home. We had a lovely visit and I a very relaxed Reflexology treatment, and I reciprocated with a Zone reflexology treatment I had been developing through 2017. I felt so grateful to having Sonia as my friend.

We found Bettye and John's place very easily. It was good to be there and blessed to have a friendship that developed so quickly following the mis-adventure that Bettye had. They are in their late 70s and beautiful people. We also managed to have lunch with a very beautiful young woman by the name of Lindsey Cox.(We had worked together at Port Hedland Hospital from 2005-to when I left in 2007) in Caloundra. Sadly, she has left nursing and is a partner now in a very successful innovative business with her fiancée. It was lovely to catch up with her and see her so happy.

From Bettye and John's we drove up to Gympie were we were staying with a friend of Noddy's from Adelaide from the 1950/60s. Noddy caught up with Leon whilst at another old friend's 70th birthday party in Victor Harbor in 2016 on the phone, as he could not be there in person. I had never met Leon, nor his wife but after meeting them, it felt like I had known them for years. Noddy had been reminiscing of him with much affection. When we arrived, we were met by this absolutely gorgeous lady, who introduced herself as Jenny Pethick.

Leon was busy on his motorised lawn mower mowing his glorious five acre property. He had seen us pull up and immediately got off to walk back to the house, which was a very lovely renovated Queenslander overlooking valleys and hills. Jenny and I were inside making a cuppa when Leon arrived and the greeting these two seventy six year old men gave each other brought me to tears. It was so heart felt. They had not seen each other since 1967 when Noddy went to Darwin and Leon to Tenant Creek. What a visit it turned out to be and we could have stayed for a week. Leon, like Noddy, had met and married a nurse in Tenant Creek while he was working in the construction industry. Jenny and I had very similar career pathways and had worked in many remote areas .We talked and talked and talked all day and late into the night. Their life's journey was very similar to ours and we were so honoured to be made so welcome into their lives. While we were there Noddy asked Leon what happened to their very old mutual friend ,who was Noddy's best friend from the age of four, up until Peter went to Tennant Creek in the mid 60's to work for Peko Mines. Noddy had been looking for Peter ever since I can remember. It seemed he had simply disappeared off the face of the earth. God is so amazing. Jenny and Leon told us that Peter was still alive and a very happy man, living the simplest life of anybody they knew. Leon rang Peter and Noddy spoke to him on the phone. It was such an emotional and joyful reaction.

We were heading to Nimbin after we left our next destination, Biggenden; and as Peter lived very humbly on a small acreage in Lismore, only a 30 minute drive from Nimbin they arranged for a meet up. Noddy was thrilled and so excited at being able to make a reconnection with his best friend from 1945.

We had a wonderful three day visit with the Leon and Jenny and so reconnected. Jenny and I have become friends and email or message regularly. A beautiful Soul Sister. We left early in the fourth morning as we were heading for Biggenden in South East Queensland inland from Maryborough. The farewell was very moving and to see the joy on the faces of Noddy and Leon also bought so much joy to Jenny and I.

We had a great drive through, to Biggenden, arriving at our friend Pauline Dakin's home just after 1300. What a wonderful woman who breathes love patience and kindness to her disabled Uncle, a beautiful 71 year old man. Pauline's hobby is collecting antiques and memorabilia and she showed us her museum in the huge shed out in her yard. The old memorabilia she has collected over many many years was equal to any of the wonderful historical museums we had visited along the Murray. After lunch the four of us headed out to Tony Farrell's (Bumper) property, approximately a 30 minute drive from Biggenden. What an honour it was to spend three days/nights out at Bumper's cattle property with Pauline and Len. Bumper is an amazing man and to see this man deal with his cattle and work, brought me back to the four days I had out at the Gibb River Station in 1970. This was Noddy's second visit to Bumper's Property this year. We stayed in the 100 year old home that Bumper's grandfather had built. Bumper had a land line, however mobile phones could only be accessed intermittently from a particular corner on the back veranda. We were lucky as we were able to speak and say goodbye to our beautiful Perth family, who were leaving to celebrate Christmas and holiday over in Canada with John's family in Thunder Bay on the 18th December, 2018.

It was so peaceful. Lots of bird sounds and the landscape and air were so pure. We were blessed to hear all the wonderful stories Bumper had to tell, of his life's journey growing up and having a ten year break from the property (It was in this time Noddy met Bumper in the late 60's and I in 1972) Of course Pauline and I had so much in common as we were both Nurses. Pauline chose to do her training as a mature aged graduate and trained through the university model. She was such a heart centred caring nurse, however she too had to leave the profession due to the lack of caring she had witnessed through out her career. She totally understood all the issues relating to bullying and harassment in the health industry. Her passion was aged care. After a very full and fun filled weekend having to say goodbye to these most down to earth amazing human beings was sad. We hope to see them back in Perth again this year. I really understand now the plight of farmers, station owners of cattle and sheep properties, when the droughts come. Thank God this year the district received big rains in October and November following a large low pressure system off the east coast in Southern Queensland. The country was so green and rich pastures were so evident. It was good to see the surrounding dams full around the properties in the district.

Bumper and Pauline directed us down the inland road, to Brisbane to the M4 and then onto Lismore. No traffic and we went through some very old towns on route, many we had heard of before like Kingaroy made famous by Joh and Flo Bjelke-Petersen -Premier of Queensland from 1968-1987 and Flow's pumpkin scone recipe. The greenery and beauty of the inland from the Sunshine Coast and Gold Coast was very captivating. We called into Lismore and how it had grown from when we were last there in the 1990's! It is a big inland city now; the energy was very vibrant and the city had a really good feel about it. From there we drove through inland country that was so beautiful one was left in awe of God's creation of the earth.

Driving into Nimbin, I felt my heart beating joyful vibrations, taking in the landscape and the Nimbin's main street. The first little cottage I saw was painted in rainbow colours as was the wooden fence at the entrance to the cottage. We drove past the hospital – (the same one that I wanted to apply for as the Director of Nursing position during my recovery in 1997-1998, as previously described). We arrived at the caravan park and booked into a cabin for two nights. Once booked in we called Peter Pointin Wales, to say we had arrived.

Peter arrived around 1500 and oh my God what an experience it was to see these 2 fit and well 76 year olds greet each other, the connection love and energy was absolutely an experience I will never forget. The evening was so rich and vibrant with the journeys of their lives, these two beautiful souls shared. He even brought us a gift and this gift is one of God's gifts, given to all of us to share for our health and wellbeing, Peter had to leave around 2100 hrs as he had business to attend to in Lismore in the morning. He promised to return at the completion of his business. To see the happiness in their eyes and visibly showing on their faces will be with me forever.

I had never met Peter before, and the man I saw was a man who had the freest spirit of any person I have had the honour to meet. His wholeness, living simplicity, his physical, mental emotional and spirituality just emitted light and love. He really lived from the inside out and not from the outside in. This statement living from the inside out instead of the outside in was given to me by Spirit, when I was writing a paper I was presenting at the Aboriginal women's meeting in Roebourne in 1993. The next time I wrote these words was the submissions in 2001 as I have written about in a former chapter.

We were so happy that he could come back the next day and spend the day and night with us; he said he would be back around 11.00 am.

The next day we went down to one of the lovely cafes in town and had a very healthy and filling breakfast. We wandered down the street chatting with the locals and retailers. The energy was fantastic and I even booked in to have a Reiki from the Reiki practitioner in town at 1800 hours that evening. I went into every little shop in the main street, everyone was so lovely, helpful, kind and the people had wonderful auras around them.

Noddy after 20 minutes of strolling, returned to the cabin as Peter was expected around 1100. He said, "you come back when you have finished honey." The community members I talked to certainly affected me and I could foresee what a role model the Nimbin community, other remote Indigenous communities, and little towns scattered around the world have to offer our society. Peace, Joy and Love shone through all I met.

I also visited the hemp shop where I had a wonderful conversation regarding hemp seeds for health and well-being. Earlier, in 2017, the Australian Federal Government passed the law that retailers could sell hemp seeds from their retail outlet. It made me realise yet again how far behind the rest of the world we are. The control and banning of natural healing medicines and therapies, by government leaders, the pharmaceutical companies and the medical fraternity that have had the sacred plants buried and burnt until now.

Peter was waiting for us at our cabin, when we arrived home. We had a great afternoon discussing cultures and philosophies and marrying them up with our journeys through life. Noddy had a poppa nap, whilst I gave Peter a Sacred Reflexology. I have only felt feet as healthy as Peter's once before. The flow of the life force was just so strong though this beautiful soul man and Peter's feet that I have ever felt. I connected it straight away to the wholeness of this man - Body Mind and Spirit. He looked after his physical, mental and spiritual bodies through exercise diet/nutrition, mindfulness and living in the "presence".

I was seeing the connectedness to the oneness and consciousness to all beings. I am so blessed to be witnessing this awakening in many many little ones especially the little ones who are different to the accepted normal outside world and systems of education and society; the children who have the wonderful gift of imagination. It reminded me of the most beautiful quote written by Albert Einstein, "Intelligence is not knowledge, intelligence is imagination". The young people of today with whom I meet, and talk, hear and see who have no blockages in the flow of their life force (Energy).The men and women who are awakening to follow a pathway of healing, is just amazing. When I reflected on my time in my 40's 50's and 60's when I had awakenings, the door to my soul opened. I was searching for God and the meaning of life, and due to the human condition, I kept shutting the door each time and became entrapped back into the outer world. I realised this was my journey, and I had to learn the lessons for my own transformation and reconnection to wholeness and truth.

I had a very blessed healing from the reiki practitioner. We had a wonderful evening with Peter and we all went to bed very happy. After an early breakfast we had to pack up and say our goodbyes as we had to be down in Dunbogan that afternoon. Peter hopefully will be over to visit us this year and all being well we will be seeing him in 2018.We said our goodbyes Noddy Peter and myself to the owner of the caravan park, and she was delighted to hear the story of Noddy's and Peter's reunion and did not charge us for the spare bed Peter had slept in.

Peter gave us directions for a straight drive down to connect with the M4 .This was so easy and before we knew where we were, we were driving into Ann and Nigel's, our son's in laws' parent's drive way. We had detoured on the way through to Port Macquarie to say a quick hello to Noddy's brother, Graham and his wife, Judy. We were blessed there too to catch up with their beautiful daughter, Shelley Davidson, whom we had not seen for many years. Arrangements were made for the change of venue for the celebration of Noddy's 76th birthday, the next day. We were so happy again to be in the presence of Anne and Nigel and our grandchildren, Max and Harper. We had a long chat and a cuppa tea, to be joined by JD and their four legged love machine, a kelpie -staffy cross at 1800 hrs. He had been driving all day from Canberra to be there for Noddy's birthday and Christmas celebration and have a holiday with Max and Harper, Anne and Nigel in Dunbogan. Sarah was also there not physically, however her presence was very much there.

We had a special birthday lunch celebration, down at the Laurieton Hotel with our dear son and his beautiful children and Anne and Nigel, Graham and his family. We were blessed to have Shelley and Tony, Noddy's niece and nephew and their children present.

Christmas too was special, starting our day at a church service. On arrival back at home, it was present opening time and the kids very very happy and excited. Ann is a very gifted cook and we so enjoyed the cuisine she nourished us with It was so great to be able to Skype with our beautiful daughter –in-law and our family in Canada We spent six nights with our family there and I have to say it was the most beautiful time really being in wholeness. Anne and I had very deep life conversations, so enriching to have these very deep honest conversations sharing our individual journeys. Both Anne and Nigel are very special people. We had to stay goodbye on the morning of the 26th to go to Fingal Bay to spend two nights with Sel, before we returned to Canberra to cat-sit the family cat until JD and the kids arrive home. I was full of joy and love saying goodbye to our family, and full of gratitude for the gift of family.

The trip down to Fingal Bay was very easy, the traffic negligible going south and, we experienced, a huge thunderstorm that brought a deluge of rain to the earth along the M4 to Coffs Harbour. We arrived at Seleana's late in the afternoon exhausted but very happy. We had a very relaxed evening and celebrated Christmas again. The next evening, Sel had invited a lovely little family up from Newcastle to meet us; something she had wanted to do for a few years for me to meet one of her friend's she has known since her younger years, prior to her leaving to travel with Charlie. She often spoke of this lady as she too was a healer. What a beautiful joy filled night we had.

Another late night. We were up early and on the road again heading for Canberra. We had a very smooth journey down the highway, arriving in Canberra in the afternoon. Oh what a greeting we received from the family's three legged cat; her reaction was something I had not seen since top- cat came home to us.

JD, Max and Harper arrived home on the 2nd of January. We were very tired and exhausted so we had a few days rest before we started the next section of our travels homeward bound.

I had a goal to have the memoirs finished by the 31st of January so I continued writing and writing, as I knew I had so much more to write and I would not be able to achieve the previous goal I had set for the 31st December 2017. I was just loving the flow of memories and words that were coming through for me.

We spent the first few days of 2018 repacking and preparing the caravan for the journey home. The days just slipped away so quickly and before we knew it, the 8th of January was upon us. Again, the pain of separation from family was there, however the pain was not severe and it was balanced with the joy of knowing that we were all one in being and we are always connected in the oneness of the Universe, no matter where we are.

We said our goodbyes and headed down to Gundagai, and to visit "The Dog on the Tucker Box". Like all the stops we had along the Murray River, we fell in love with Gundagai. I had heard and been singing, "The Road to Gundagai[6]" since I was 4-5 years old. Dad used to sing the song to us all the time for years when I was a little girl and I was pinching myself I was actually there, standing in front of the famous statue of the dog. We did to not spend to long here as we had a long drive ahead to get to our overnight destination. We promised ourselves that on our next visit to Canberra, we would come down and stay a couple of nights with Max and Harper, the history[7] there just pulsates one's being. By 1500hrs, we decided to pull up for the day, we were both very tired, so we drove into a very nice clean caravan park at Seymour. We had not heard of this town before and went on a discovery tour once we were set up. Seymour is right on the Goulbourn river and a very pretty old town which formally was the service town for the Puckapunyal Army Base. Again we learnt a lot by chatting to the locals. Everyone was so friendly and after a meal you could not 'jump over' at the local historical hotel we retired for a good night's sleep. Our destination the next day was Robe on the Limestone coast of South Australia .

We were up nice and early following the Hume Highway to the ring road around Melbourne. One of the locals had drawn us a map so we did not get lost and his words to us were 'stay in the middle lane.' We listened and sure enough we followed his directions and after spending an hour driving through the traffic and all the closed roads due to major transport infrastructure works, we safely arrived back on track to the Ballarat freeway on our way to Horsham through into South Australia The freeway was brilliant and we so enjoyed driving through the picturesque landscapes Western Victoria is renowned for. Once we passed over the border, we drove down through all the wine growing regions, through Penola and down into Robe.

Our last visit was in 2012 and we had fallen in love with it back then. When we first went there it was a very quiet historical old town situated right on the shores of Guichen Bay. Not anymore, it is now a very busy seaside holiday town. The town was packed, and just so busy. New businesses had opened and the main street looked a picture. The community had expanded with lots and lots of new estates and it had the feel of a retiree's paradise. The caravan park was situated a short drive from town and oh my goodness it was so full. Caravans were being packed in like cans of sardines; however, we decided to stay for the two nights we had booked in for to try and rest.

Never again would we go to a caravan park during school holidays, due to the noise, little kids on bikes with no parental supervision racing round as kids do; it was quite dangerous as the little ones are so fast and do not watch were they are riding darting from this side of the road to the other.

We were packed up and gone by 06.30 am as meandered up the Coorong to Middleton. We have travelled the Coorong several times before but this time we saw it through new eyes as a part of the consciousness's of the universe, taking notice of the ecology and the environment .The Coorong is a long shallow saline lagoon that stretches more than 100 kilometres and is separated from the Southern Ocean by a narrow sand dune Peninsular. This time we saw the beauty of the birds and the bushes along the side of the road. We also found lots of maroon bush. This is one of the most powerful bush medicinal plants, used by our Indigenous brothers and sisters for thousands of years and is well known for the curing of cancer and other diseases.

Scientific research was done on this plant by both Griffith's University and the HDWA in the late 50's and 60's. The research has since been buried and burnt for decades. Noddy had been on Maroon Bush for over two years during his cancer journey in 2015-2016. It grows in semi-arid regions all over Australia. I have to ask why do Australians, not know about the benefits of traditional bush medicine and why we cannot have access to it through the mainstream medical model? We have free will, and we should have an informed choice of whether we get treated with drugs such as chemotherapy as laid out by the scientific pharmaceutical and medical industry.

Leaving the Coorong, we came to our last river crossing on the Murray River and headed for Middleton on the Fleur Peninsular. Noddy had another retired eighty year old mate, John Pilcher, who he had to catch up with. John was another man whom I had never met. The caravan park there was lovely, quiet, clean and privately owned and run by a young couple who caters for older families and retirees. I would certainly go back to that one in the school holidays.

We went to dinner at John Pilcher's home and met his beautiful wife and little boy. The men had a wonderful night reminiscing, and the ladies thoroughly enjoyed discussing women's business. Honestly, it has been such a pleasure to meet Noddy's mates from the 40's, 50's and 60's and hearing all the stories these young Adelaide men and Chiton Rocks Surf Lifesavers from that era had to tell. It was a window opened into the life of my dear darling husband prior to our meeting in 1972. They may have got up to a lot of mischief when they were not on patrol, however all were true gentleman and had aged with dignity and grace.

Up early and on the road again, this time heading to Victor Harbour to stay with Harry and Rosemary for two days. Noddy had kept in touch with them on some of our trips to Adelaide in the past. We had stayed with Harry and Rosemary last back in 2016. This time, we could really see why Victor Harbour had the honour of being called God's waiting room. The amount of ageing and aged people in the community really hit us. One can see how this cohort of the population is growing that quickly that the infrastructure to cater for their needs cannot keep up. What a reality check. We had forgotten that we are already in that cohort.

Again we did something we had not done before; we caught the Cockle Steam train that runs down the coast from Victor Harbour to Goolwa to see the final section where the Murray River meets the ocean. The old train was a magic ride, bringing back memories of the times I have ridden on trains before the electric ones. We sat in the royal carriage that the Princess of Wales, Lady Diana was in when she did this train trip on her visit to Victor Harbour in 1988. I sat on a seat on the ocean side and was shocked to see the effect of climate change on the sea front here.

The beaches and bays are disappearing with the rise in the ocean. Noddy, Harry and I were very surprised to see this. The beach they used to patrol back in the early 60's was so different to the beach now. Nowhere else was the effects of change in climate more evident than Port Elliot near the cliffs, with beautiful homes that sit on top of them. I could see in my mind's eye the picture of what happened in Los Angeles when houses slipped into the ocean in 2016/17. I prayed it never happens here. We arrived in Goolwa, and I was excited to be greeted by the beautiful waters of the Murray River and the Ocean dancing in unison as one. We had a cup of coffee and meandered back for the return trip to Victor Harbour. We had our final meal with Rosemary and Harry and retired fairly early as we were all a little tired. Next morning we said our goodbyes until our next trip to Adelaide or their visit to Perth.

By 11.00 hrs and a short drive, we were at our next destination in McLaren Vale, to spend the night with one of Noddy's nephews and his wife, Peter and Lorraine Field. Their home and property was situated very high on a hill overlooking a sea of green green vineyards, extending down virtually to the crystal blue Southern Ocean on the Fleuri Peninsular. There was clear blue skies and a breeze that was just right. There were no words to describe the beauty of the scenery below. We had a great visit there talking and talking as we so enjoy doing intergenerational visits with extended family. There was lots of laughter and storytelling with them reminiscing over their journey in life. The night flew by and before we knew it, it was nearly midnight. We had a great night's sleep and woke early in the morning breathing in the fresh fresh air, the birds too here were chirping to their hearts content.

After a nourishing breakfast, with eggs straight from the chook pen, it was time to make the last leg into Adelaide. We were surprised as to how easy it was compared to our last visit here as at that time there were road works everywhere; but now the freeway takes you straight into Adelaide. We had arranged to leave the van at another one of Noddy's nephews Michael's in his workshop grounds. Once parked, we had a quick chat and arranged to have a meal with him and his lovely partner that evening. The afternoon was spent with his sister, Kay with whom we were staying as we had always done on our visits to Adelaide.

We also spent a few hours with June and Harry, Noddy's oldest sister and brother in law. It was great to see them all. Both looked well and happy much to our delight as both had been very unwell for such a long time over the last couple of years. June is a great role model for me to age gracefully. She is very humble with a very sharp mind and witty at 85 years young.

That night we had a lovely meal with Michael and and his partner at one of their favourite local's. On Tuesday we had to go into the city to the Apple store to try and find out what was wrong with my iPad. There were no bookings available until later that afternoon, and as we had a luncheon to go to, we were told to come back in for a 0900hrs opening the next day to be able to see a technician. On the way out we looked at a new Pro iPad. A young man came to speak to us, we had a chat and he said , 'I will have a look at this now for you'. Well, I have never before come across such a kind, caring, helpful, patient young sales person as this young man.

He told us the iPad was not dead and although it was 8 years old and very slow, that it had about 15 months life left in it, the initial problem he had not dealt with before, however he went out of his way to have the problem sorted, and within 30 minutes the Ipad was working again much to my joy. We expressed our gratitude and appreciation for his assistance.I was relieved that it would give me hopefully time to save for a new one before 'the old girl dies'. The afternoon was spent sharing a lovely lunch with Noddy's sister Shirley and her husband Don. Every time we had been to Adelaide we had always spent time with the family as a whole, all talking with different conversations happening, this trip was different. We had one on one time with each couple and it was so good to have meaningful and deep discussions that we had never had before. We were so blessed to be able to share this time with them. Shirley never ages, however Don was not so strong.

The weather was really warming up and the temperature was up around 38 degrees. It was hot and expected to stay very hot for a few days. Noddy was getting worried about driving in the heat and booked the car in for a service, ensuring the tyres were in good condition to handle the hot bitumen and the long drive home. Noddy had made a travel plan to fit in with the temperatures expected Thursday and Friday 44 and 45 degrees respectively. I had a luncheon booked on Thursday with another nurse friend .

Noddy then decided to leave Adelaide Thursday afternoon around 1500 hours to go to Gepps Cross on the outskirts of North Adelaide and book into the hotel for the night. Rising around 01.30hrs and driving through the wee small hours of the morning, and instead of taking the inland road from Port Augusta to Ceduna we would hug the east coast of the Peninsular and spend the day and night in the coastal community of Cowell, leaving for Ceduna in the early hours of the morning. Wednesday was a day of rest for us; however we had one more nephew we were hoping to catch up with whom we had not seen for years. We were fortunate he had just finished a shutdown at an industrial plant and was able to join Noddy, Kay and myself for a very nice lunch down at Glenelg, one of our favourite places in Adelaide.

Thursday came around too quickly and following a sad farewell to Kay. Noddy dropped me at Shirley Jackson's, a friend's home. Well put two old nurses together, both who had walked similar paths and had similar experiences in our careers - one can just imagine the joy of sharing such rich fulfilling and rewarding lives and come through all the heartaches and tears we had both experienced in the workplace. In her last years she had been working at Flinders University and she had become a life coach. Noddy came, lunch was completed and we said goodbye yet again to another very rich and beautiful lady.

On arrival at 1500 hrs back at Michael's, we hooked up the van, waved goodbye and headed out to Gepps Cross. Oh my goodness it was so hot. The temperature was up to 45 degrees and they even had to shorten the leg of the Tour Down Under International Cycling Event. Noddy's plan came together perfectly. We had an early dinner and into bed and asleep by 2000 hrs. Sure enough we were up and hit the road by 01.30 am. We had a very smooth hassle free run down to Cowell. Arriving just before 0900hrs. By this time the temperature was already 40 degrees, not a breath of air anywhere. We booked into a little cabin and hibernated, only coming out to walk to the pub for a meal at 1800hrs. The hardest thing we were having difficulty with was daylight saving. Forty degrees at 1800hrs was just too much for us; we thanked God for not having it in the West. The West has had 3 referendums over the years and after 2 trials it was still voted out. I would consider day light saving for the winter months, but definitely not for The West's long hot summers. Climate change is definitely affecting the planet and as temperatures continue to climb each year so too will it affect us all even more. We had a very restful night and left Cowell at 0500hrs.

The drive from Cowell to Ceduna was very very pretty. The landscape of green rich pastures with lots of very happy and contented livestock, and more rich vineyards for the thriving wine industry was again too beautiful to describe. We passed through some very old towns and before we knew it we were pulling into the caravan park in Ceduna.

The temperature had dropped by 15 degrees from the day before, the sea breeze was in and it was just so pleasant. We had a drive through site so we did not have to unhook making it so easy to set up. We spent the afternoon washing and emptying the fridge etc we gave our spare fruit and vegetables to our neighbours, as we would have to surrender all at the border in Eucla. We had dinner at the pub and an early night as we had planned an early exit at 06.00 hrs. Right on schedule we were on the road by 0600 and took the leisurely drive across to the border where we had to have the car and caravan checked for fruit and vegetables. We got the all clear from the Inspectors at the border and headed West. Oh what a feeling heading home as we had only driven home once before from Adelaide across the Nullarbor, in 1985. Back then we were young and on a very strict time frame and we drove from the Border straight through to Perth, not realising what we were missing out on. The road ran parallel to the cliffs and the ocean of the Great Australian Bight. A magnificent journey when one has the time and takes the time to notice the beauty that surrounds them. We had a problem however as we gained 2 and ½ hours. We arrived in Eucla at 13.30 pm, in the afternoon; however it was only 11am in Western Australia. We decided to continue through and pulled into Caiguna road house that night. Whilst we understand the cost of running a roadhouse on the Nullarbor is very expensive, we found paying for '1500mls of water' very exorbitant so we had to say no thank you. Fortunately we had enough to see us through to our next overnight stay which was Southern Cross. We had had 2 big days so we were very glad to say goodnight to the world. The sun was down by 19.30hrs, thank God' ensuring a good night's sleep before the last 380 kilometres drive home.

We were out on the road by 0600 hrs, the sky was very black and by the time we reached Kellerberrin the thunder and lightning started. We experienced a wonderful sky works show, the rain was giving us a miss however, falling quite heavily about 5 kilometres to the West. The traffic started to build just outside Mundaring and already we knew we were back into a far less leisurely life. Cars, trucks, people all around us. The road systems in Perth are just fantastic and we were soon on the Reid Highway. The road works around the suburbs there were in full swing and we got such a shock as to how quickly things had changed just near Ellenbrook and Whiteman's Park. Twenty five minutes later we turned into our driveway.

Home at last to a great welcome into the arms of our beautiful family. It had been so long since we had seen them. Inaya and Blaise had grown so much. I felt so wonderful, I arrived home, totally healed and free, "Fully Human Fully Alive". I was so balanced, with a constant flow of the Life Force pulsating through my being. I had found God and the true Meaning of Life. That I had been searching for this since that day in year 12, in 1964, when I was told God is everywhere, 53 years ago.

I am finishing *A Girl Called Peter* here, and I will continue writing a sequel from January 2018 until the Transition to Everlasting Life when I take my last breath. God willing. I would like to say thank you to every single person whom I have met and walked with on this very long life. For my dearest husband, Noddy and those who have remained with me during the journey Thank-you for all your loving support and kindness during my life, and I would also like to thank all who taught me great lessons by sharing the human condition during the periods of being surrounded in the darkness that had consumed my Soul during the dark times.

I will finish here with the poem, *The Weaver* by B M Franklin.
The Weaver.

My Life is but a weaving
Between my Lord and me
I cannot choose the colours he weaves so steadily
Oft times he weaveth sorrow
And I in foolish pride
Forgets he seethe upper
And I the underside

Not until the loom is silent
And the shuttle ceases to fly
Will God roll back the canvas?
And explain the reason why
The dark threads are as needful
In the Weavers skilful hand
As the threads of gold and silver
In the pattern He has planned
Author-B M Franklin

THE BEGINNING OF THE DREAM

ALBANY COMMUNITY HOSPICE

COMPLEMENTARY CARE UNIT

OVERVIEW OF COMPLEMENTARY THERAPIES AND HO___ CARE

PRESENTED BY:

PETA NOTTLE, DIRECTOR OF NURSING
WEST PILBARA HEALTH SERVICE
4TH SEPTEMBER 2001

Australasian Therapeutic Touch Members with Crystal Hawke Adelaide

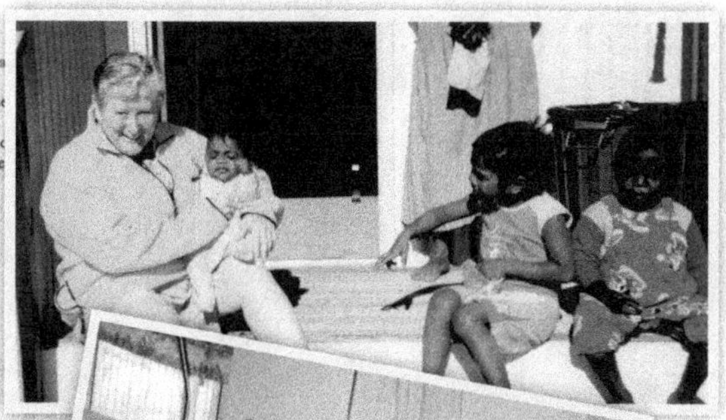

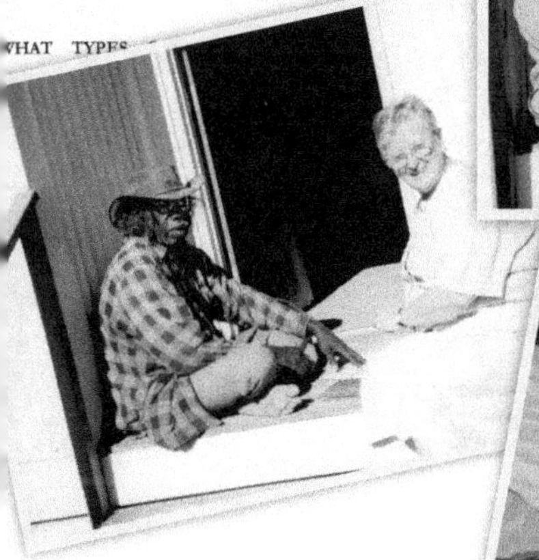

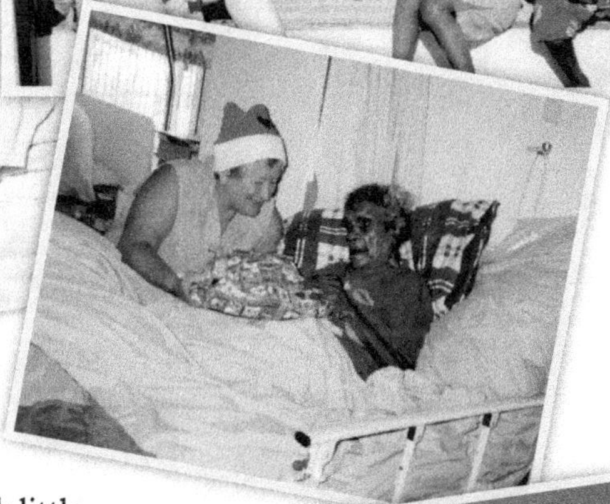

COMPLEMENTARY THERAPIES:

- Are used as an adjunct to or in conjunction with traditions interventions to enhance client outcomes.
- Do not interfere or replace traditional therapies, and, in this se___ health practices.
- Are based on an approach to health that blends body an___ traditional and cross-cultural avenues of diagnosis and treatme___
- Unlike Western Medicine, complementary therapies ___

WHAT TYPES

NT -Yarralin Health Clinic with little ones - 2003 (above right)

NT -Yarralin Health Clinic - Old drover sharing stories - 2003 (above)

My favourite elder in Port Hedland Nursing Home- 2004 (right)

Camel riding at Cable Beach Broome - 2003 (above)

Myself on Spill way on the Roper River at Nujkkara Community - 2003 (left)

ADVENTURES CONTINUE

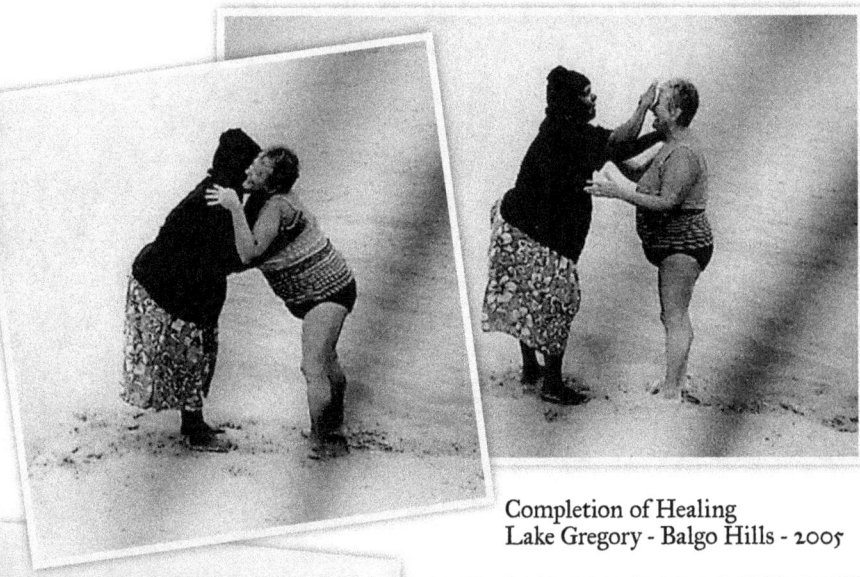

Completion of Healing
Lake Gregory - Balgo Hills - 2005

Seleana Powell, Chas Bulmer,
Jane and James Best,
Noddy and I (from left to right)

Presenting before computers -
1994 (below)

Traditional Healer, Helicopter (Long Beard) &
Friends, Balgo - 2005 (above)

Arriving in Oslo Norway (below)

EPILOGUE

I started to write, " A Girl Called Peter " in 2017. It has been a journey like I have never undertaken in my life before. Several drafts later, I had it ready, to finally hand it over to a West Australian Editor I had met at a meetup in Perth City in March of 2019. As soon as I heard Shoma speak, I knew she was the Editor for me, as I had my inner voice say to me "Shoma is to be your editor. I listened and several days later I called her and asked her if she would be interested in being the editor of my memoirs. The rest is history, and I am honoured and grateful to have journeyed with the book "Midwives " Shoma , the editor and Andy the graphic designer to bring 70 years of memories, wonderful, good and bad to birth .

I have so much to share since I completed this manuscript; the next manuscript of the Voyage to Everlasting Life will be written over the coming years , until my Soul separates from my human body to return home .

In writing the above paragraph, I have to add a synopsis of several wonderful pathways, that have opened and brought me so much joy both personally and professionally in 2018 and 2019.

. . .

2018

On returning home in January of 2018, life took on a new meaning for me, I walked many different pathways and read many different deep and life changing books. One day in early February 2018, I had doubled booked myself for two events. My intuition and my heart were telling me to go to an event at the University of Western Australia (UWA)which had appeared mysteriously on my iPad. It looked interesting but my mind told me to go to the Toast Masters Meeting that was being held that evening.

I decided to listen to my heart and my inner voice and found myself sitting in a lecture theatre at the UWA School of Business.This lecture was an awakening for me in more ways than one. It opened a whole new world I had never known of nor had I ever heard of before.

After that night, I attended many different breakfast meetings at the UWA, University Club. I learnt so much of the wonderful happenings in Perth, in relation to Homelessness, the future of Palliative Care , Aboriginal Health and many other programmes to improve the quality of life for people in need of assistance in their daily lives. I spoke with many good people who were making a difference in the lives of people not as privileged or fortunate as we are. The people with whom I shared a breakfast table and talked to, were very sincere and heart centred people, and I saw kindness in all, everywhere. It seemed to me that our future is in very good hands with the graduates involved in the Social Impact Studies and Humanities at UWA.

Healing Insights was invited to participate in the Good Market, an annual event held at The University of WA. We were kept very busy all day, administering Reflexology to those who wished to have or experience Reflexology for the first time. And it was here I met a beautiful lady, Rashmi Patel with whom I have become very good friends. Now we spend many hours philosophising and discussing the need to integrate Holistic Health Care and Healing into Humanity and planet Earth, into both the Mainstream Business Bio Scientific Medical Model and our Environment. We attended many lectures together from a Health and Well Being perspective.

I am happy to report, that there is now an incredible movement towards this model both here in Australia and overseas.

I do believe that one day (may be not in the time I have left on mother earth) that the Art and Wisdom of Nursing, Medicine and Allied Health Practitioners, will be integrated into the Medical System we have in this country. Spirituality and the Complementary Therapies of Touch (therapeutic touch, healing touch, reflexology and massage), Prayer and Meditation, Aromatherapy and Stress Management will include therapies of Music, Art, Dance, Yoga, Laughing Yoga and Storytelling and Writing to Heal will become part of patient care, in Primary Secondary and Tertiary Care. Care and Compassion will be at the forefront of Health Service Delivery including in all health and well being programs as well chronic disease management be it physical, emotional, mental or spiritual health.

Whilst writing the above paragraph, I received the March 2020 Special Edition of the American Journal of Holistic Nursing : Special Issue - Spirituality . The Editorial – SPIRITUALITY, THE MISSING LINK FOR HOLISTIC HEALTH CARE

During August of 2018, Noddy and I headed up to Darwin for eight weeks to visit the family. The first month was great; we were out and about catching up with family and old friends, including visiting Joe's grave site which was a very emotional experience for me. Having special time with our Darwin grandies[1] whom we adored. Darwin in the Dry Season is a great place to visit with lots and lots of festivals happening. The best one for me was the Australian Aboriginal Arts Festival, where Indigenous Artists from all over the Northern Territory and from the North of Western Australia presented their artwork. I met a couple of very old ladies who remembered me from Balgo Hills. It was great to introduce my grandchildren to them. We met an old couple from Jigalong and we spoke to the representatives from Yirrkala, all young happy , intelligent women .

During time this time, I read an article on the Traditional Aboriginal Healers from the YPA worksite by the Doctors at the Royal Adelaide Hospital. This stoked the Fire in my heart. I forward a revised edition of the submission I had forwarded to the HDWA Health review in 2017 which was a submission titled, 'The WA State Sustainable Health Care Plan'. (See Appendices)

Whilst in Darwin, I did a silly thing and worked out too hard in the swimming pool. I woke up one morning unable to put any weight on my left leg; the pain was excruciating. I ended up in the New Darwin Hospital with trapped nerves at the level of lumbar 4,5 and Sacral 1, 2 and 3 nerves (caused by me exerting myself doing breast stroke, thinking I was 18 years old and it reminded me of the old saying, 'the mind is willing but the flesh is weak'). I just could not walk. I was admitted for two days to get the pain under control. The experience was not a good one from a holistic health point of view. One lovely young nurse in the emergency department who showed deep empathy and compassion as she had just returned from leave after injuring her back in the line of duty. She said to me, "I know what you are going through".

The next day I was visited by two pharmacists who wanted my Pharmacist and GP's names and telephone numbers in Perth, to get my history from them. Why, I did not know. I kept my own power and did not disclose my service provider's details. A physiotherapist came to see me. She did not do an assessment nor lay a hand on me, told me to get up and just start marching as I was living in a two storey house and to go up and down the stairs. The physiotherapist did not suggest any ultrasound or physiotherapy as I have had in the past, when I had nerve entrapments. The nursing staff would not spend any time with me, like giving me a back rub or offering hot packs for pain relief. They just came in to give the opioids and left. I was discharged the next morning and we went to stay with our dear friends, Dave and Lyn Barclay who looked after me very well. It was a really bad experience for me being an elderly patient in need of care. It took months for the nerves to be free again.

I had a meeting with a senior person in governance here in WA on my return from Darwin that had been arranged prior to us going North. I met him after a breakfast meeting on mental health at UWA. I happened to stand up and ask a question at question time. The question was about why I had not heard the word 'healing' mentioned from anyone during the entire presentation and why did we not have a Holistic Healing Model of Health Care which would include balancing the Art and Wisdom of Healing and Wholeness integrated into the Scientific Business Model of Health Care practised in Australia. I finished with saying this needs to be part of the Medicare system, so it is available for everybody, not just for those who can afford it.

On the way out, the senior person in governance, stopped and asked to see me and to call his scheduler for an appointment. This I did. I arrived at his residence to see him and was taken to a big parlour. I handed him a copy of The Sustainable Health Care Plan, plus a copy of a paper I had written in 2016 titled, 'Something Old is Now New - The History of The Ancient Healing Arts', and a paper on Therapeutic Touch.

Once I explained my submission to him, his words to me were, "When I heard you speak at the University I thought you wanted to bring something new into the health system, now I clearly see you want to bring something back".

"Yes, Care and Compassion," was my reply. I was told that he would read them thoroughly and then call in the Senior Health People. I never heard back.

I contacted CEO's from organisations -government funded, government departments and Universities that teach nursing throughout this time. Between 2018 -2019, I hibernated for a while and waited in silence.

2019

The Organisation I founded in 2016, that became a Company Pty Ltd in 2017 has flourished with developing programs for providing complementary therapies for clients of three large service providers in aged care.

I have met and enjoyed networking with absolutely amazing people who have walked with me throughout this period, with a special mention to my healing partners, lifelong friends and new friends.

I decided to try acting classes as a relaxation project, something I had not done since high school. An advertisement for The Perth Acting School caught my eye and I went along to a free three hour workshop. The workshop was being run by the owner, a really talented acting coach. I just loved it and went on to learn more. During the level 2 weekend, Loren was doing his critique on my acting skills in a scene I was in. Loren said, "Peta, you are a storyteller".

I replied, " I am. I was brought up with story telling and I have never stopped telling stories.

After a Level 3 class, I Googled local story tellers in Perth, and the first name on the page that came up was Lisa Evans—Speaking Savvy Public Speaking and Story Telling. I called Lisa and after a discussion, enrolled into her next Story Telling Workshop, and went on a fantastic ride with Lisa and fellow travellers on the Journey of Life. I have been so privileged to be a storyteller at two of Lisa's events, the last one being at the Perth Fringe Festival 2020

2019 brought me an honour I will never ever forget. I was selected to be a presenter at the 5th International Congress of Therapeutic Touch in Toronto, Canada. The theme of the Congress was, 'Deepening our Practise as Compassionate Healers.'

The first presentation was, " An International Sustainable Health Care Plan " (adapted from the plan I had submitted to the HDWA Health Care Review in 2018). During the International Panel Presentations from around the globe, I reflected on the day I met Professor Janet Quinn. I reconnected with Crystal Hawke, Diane May and Professor Cheryl Hoffmeyer. The second presentation was in the plenary sessions, the topic was, 'My Healing Journey. This was a story telling presentation.

Looking back, when I first started studying Healing Touch in Perth in 2001, I would never have envisaged or believed that I would ever end up on stage at the 5th International Congress of Therapeutic Touch in Toronto.

To see energy medicine now becoming part of the main stream medical model through integrated holistic care throughout the world is amazing. This was evident by the weekend TT practitioners had their Congress in Toronto. There was an International Energy Medicine Conference for pyschologists happening in Vancouver. And yet, our Australian Government does not recognise healing modalities and holistic health care practitioners in our health care system nor in nursing schools or medical schools either at Universities or Nursing Schools at Technical and Further Education(TAFE's).

I was honoured to have brought the first Therapeutic Touch Course to Perth in May of 2019. Jane Hall from Healing Dimensions in

Melbourne came to Perth to deliver the Level 1 Therapeutic Touch course for our Healing Insights Company Directors. Jane is a learned academic in Energy Medicine and Healing, and has been studying and working with Therapeutic Touch since 1983. Jane has been at the forefront of the Australasian Therapeutic Touch Association in Australia for many years, and I am honoured to be assisting Jane in mentoring others.

In November of 2019, Jane and another qualified Therapeutic Touch Teacher, Virginia Kingsford came and ran a second level one class workshop where we had the honour of three new beautiful souls completing their level one workshop and they will be working towards becoming practitioners. Jane also ran the level 2 - Intermediate workshop for the two of our Company Directors. So we will have two Therapeutic Touch Teachers in Perth in the future. Currently, a trainee mentorship program is also underway .

Before concluding this update of happenings I have to write about the whole world which has been turned upside down and is in turmoil, with the evolution of a very new contagious virus connected to the Corona Virus family. This virus was named COVID -19. It first appeared in the city of Wuhan in China in December 2019 and very quickly spread to many countries throughout the world. Initially, the World Health Organisation declared this virus an epidemic but in March of 2020 a major international pandemic was declared. January 19th 2020 onwards, the Australian Government and State Government started to warn the Australian Population regarding the seriousness of this pandemic and started to prepare for the worst case scenarios to prevent the transfer of infections and deaths from Covid that were occurring in Wuhan and in Italy, The United Kingdom and the USA .

Strict Hand Hygiene, Social Distancing, Staying At Home, Self-Isolating and Quarantine are now the norm, here in Australia. Interstate and Overseas travel is now forbidden. Many businesses have been closed and many hundreds of thousands of Australians have lost their jobs throughout this pandemic. Schools have been closed, although some are open for essential workers' children. Education is being delivered through on -line learning. Many of our students are suffering. Teachers are under great strain as are our police force and our health professionals . They are also advertising for retired doctors and nurses some of whom have not been registered for a long time to come back into the workforce. I would love to be able to offer my speciality and clinical skills to all who are in so much distress in the clinical setting for their well being; however, as I am in the over 70 cohort, we have been confined to our homes. Our house in Perth has a front verandah, and I have to say so we are blessed and happy to be able to spend as much time in nature day and night as we wish, either working from our front verandah or walking over the road to our Lake and Reserve .

In Western Australia, The State Government has made WA an island within an island and has closed off WA from the rest of Australia -except for very few essential services. Within WA, Regional Boarders have been closed. Gone are our travel plans for this year because the Government is trying to balance the Health Crisis and Business Crisis to help Australia and Australians get back to normal as soon as they can.

Noddy and I are at home , spending our time, decluttering our home and our big shed. It is a huge job and I am finding it really difficult, as we have Australian history stored from many of our collection of treasures. Noddy's mother was a keeper, and we have found his school reports from 1947 through to 1954. I have a lot of my Grandmother's and Mother's China. So we are really having to sort through our accumulation of treasures.

We go to the beach most days and keep to the strict rules of isolation. I am reading a lot more, and working on my computer.

. . .

I have been so fortunate and blessed as by accident I found out that I can, through technology, administer The Power of Touch using the Modality of Therapeutic Touch Healing Touch Hand Reflexology and Meditation. I am happy for we are able to stay connected to our family (now living in Sydney and Adelaide) and friends via the phone, Zoom or Skype. Australia is almost in total lockdown and hundreds are losing their jobs daily. All elective surgery has been cancelled and tele-health has become the norm. All sport events, including the Tokyo Olympic Games, Wimbledon , all International and National Football codes have been deferred or rescheduled. My ten year old granddaughter, Inaya had a virtual sports day last week run by her school in Adelaide.

Kindness and goodness is emerging from so many individuals, community groups, organisations and businesses. I thank all who have participated in sharing their Care and Compassion with Love .

One of the saddest things that have emerged during this pandemic is the fear and the isolation of many people of all ages and especially those in their later years. Stories are being shared of people dying alone without a family member being present. My heart goes out to all, as fear has consumed our world and it has the potential tipping point for a New World Order .

Today, as I write this on the 18th of May 2021, the COVID-19 pandemic continues to cause havoc throughout the world with very few countries not affected. The COVID-19 virus has changed with many variants coming through in a second and third wave. Thousands upon thousands have lost their lives and so many more affected. The poor countries have been the hardest hit and have run out of essential supplies of oxygen, medication and beds. The first world countries, have lost many of their citizens; however they are not so deeply affected as countries like Brazil and India. Vaccinations are now available - mainly to the western countries. Please God, these countries will share with the poor countries of the world to alleviate this scourge of the corona virus pandemic.

I will finish this epilogue now and say my thoughts and prayers are with all humanity .

It is with deep gratitude that I finish by saying thank you to my wonderful husband and to both our daughter and son and their partners, our four precious grandchildren and finally our family of friends and colleagues who have joined with us on the Journey of Life and will be with us as long as we are on Mother Earth.

Peter (Peta)

APPENDIX 1

A Better Future for Our Children.

I was asked in 1993 to present a paper to an Aboriginal Women's workshop in Roebourne for the Aboriginal Medical Service .The title for the workshop was "A Better Future for Our Children."

The Presentation:

I have done a lot of reflection on what to say on this topic over the last couple of weeks and I have based my talk not on health issues, e.g. housing, education, alcohol and drugs sexually transmitted disease etc. I have written this from the heart.Knowing what I now know at my age (45) and what life has taught me I have come to believe that if we are to have a better future for our children the number one most important thing for us to do is to believe we can achieve this. Before I continue I would like to share with you a few of my golden rules.

1. You can't love anybody unless you love yourself.
2. You can't care for anybody, unless you care for yourself.
3. You can't believe in anyone unless you believe in yourself.

No person is born great; just ordinary people achieving greatness because of their great determination. If we are to join together in wanting a better future for our children with determination that goal

APPENDIX 1

can be achieved. We must first know what we want for our children and start working towards that.

So many people die with their dreams within them. Think big and believe in yourself.

It is what you do with what you have that counts.

Know what you do **not** want for the future and aim for what you do want for the future of your children.

In continued reflection I would like to share my personal thoughts for change.

I believe change must come from within us.

We live in a world full of constant negativity. Negativity daily intrudes into our lives through many different ways - television, newspapers and radio are often full of negativity intruding into our lives with news of wars, shootings and killings etc. The commercial TV stations are continually bombarding us with TV shows of an unreal world. That TV program Beverly Hills 92101 is a classic example. Advertising is constantly telling us we must have this, have that. We can't live without this or that. 'Your mother needs a microwave for Mother's Day.'

Money and material things have taken over the way we value people and their lives.

We have become conditioned to live from the outside world in; therefore, we are so caught up in the material world we forget we have an inner self.

I will stop here for a minute to mention that in our Western culture we are not conditioned to get to know our inner selves and I believe if we are to change for the better, we could start by getting to know the real 'Me'.

I personally believe I am made up of three parts:

1 A physical part-my body

2. A mental body –my conscious mind

3. A spiritual part – my subconscious part –my soul/spirit.

An equal triangle - to make one holistic unique human being and to be a better person, I need to have my triangle equal. I need to get in

APPENDIX 1

touch with my inner self daily because I found by having that time out I can create a better place.

I have certainly changed over the years and this change process has been achieved since I was introduced to Raj Yoga and Meditation – (sacred gift of dream time) 10 years ago. That changed me to live from the inside out. However, I must admit being human. I at times (and for long or short periods of time) go back to living from the outside in. I wonder if we are to develop a better life for the children whether we need to take a step back from societal norms and introduce dream time and meditation again for our children.

In helping to create a better life for our children, perhaps the focus lies in focusing one's energies into positive outcomes to break from the cycle of negativity and to concentrate on what we are good at. People do not really want to know your problems. People want to see your talent. We need to take a close look at ourselves - inside and out. Take stock of all the good points. Know your best qualities and the things you are most proficient at - anything about you that makes you a little bit different, that makes you unique.

It is by knowing this, you can draw up a plan as an individual to improve your weaknesses and capitalise on your strengths and then I believe if the community united with the same principals, we could make a better world for our children.

Where do we start?

A few suggestions.

1 Dream Time and Meditation workshops .

2. Traditional aboriginal cultures in dance and music into schools curriculums.

3. Motivational education

4. Systematic Training for effective parenting from the cradle to the early adult years.

Thank you .

APPENDIX 2

Vision Towards Developing a Holistic Approach in the Rehabilitation of Prisoners

In wondering where to begin toward a new vision to make a change in the lives of prisoners and their families both in prison and on release into the community, I believe that a solution can be found in the introduction of Holistic Healing approach as part of rehabilitation whilst prisoners are incarcerated.

Setting the Stage – Definitions

Rehabilitation – According to the Oxford Dictionary rehabilitation is defined as:
 'To restore to normal life by training, especially after imprisonment or illness, and to restore to former privileges or reputations or to proper condition.'

Heal – According to the Oxford Dictionary, to heal is to become healthy again, to cure or put right.

APPENDIX 2

Holism – According to the Oxford Dictionary, holism is the theory that certain wholes are greater than the sum of their parts.

Philosophy

As we know, we as people are not just made up of the physical body. We are unique being made up of a physical body, a mental body, an emotional body and a spiritual body. If parts of this whole is broken then we have a breakdown of our wholeness.

Life is a development

As infants, we are born whole and it appears (to me) that as infants and little children that wholeness remains intact. It is only as we grow that outside influences start to impact on our wholeness.

When does this start? I think it starts when we reason and make choices. And as we now a percentage of young people will and do make the wrong choices. As a consequence little chips appear and cracks in the various sides of their 'square'. If this continues as a person grows eventually parts of the square break and the consequence of that are seen in our society today.

I would like to suggest the theory that it may be that a breakdown in a prisoner's 'wholeness' is the reason he is in custody in the first place. For example, a breakdown in the emotional body that had caused the person to lash out in anger resulting in injury to another, a charge of grievous bodily harm and a period of imprisonment commences, if found guilty.

Rationale

In today's society, more than ever the need for Government and Institutions to take a different approach to the way we look at things. By taking a heart centred and holistic approach to rehabilitation and healing we can make a difference to not only the lives of prisoners but their families and the community as well.

Possibilities of such an approach
How can this be introduced to the prison system?

APPENDIX 2

In the first instance, there needs to be a major commitment for change by the persons responsible for administering the prison system and there needs to be an education process in place to enable growth and development of all staff within the system.

No formal education is required to become a holistic person. The holistic approach requires that the individual learns to accept people as they are, without judgement, with unconditional love and with compassion.

This approach starts with self acceptance, which can be achieved by focusing inwards. There are various methods available that can help a person develop this focus, such as meditation, visualisation, contemplation and spiritual practice.

Self responsibility also leads the person to recognise the interconnectedness to all individuals and their relationship to the human and global community. This recognition and awareness further develops healing.

Complementary therapies can be learned to enhance self development and healing.

Once this philosophical shift takes place in a system then it will flow out into the persons in our care. Then holistic rehabilitation process can become a reality.

The goal of holistic rehabilitation is to restore and promote health, facilitate healing and alleviate suffering. To do so the custodian focuses on rehabilitating the whole person – the body, mind and spirit during the period of confinement.

According to holistic philosophy, wisdom and healing comes from the prisoner, not the custodian. The custodian facilitates the process of healing by creating a heart centred environment in which healing can occur.

Whilst we are focused on treating all parts of a person separately and not interconnecting the parts as a whole, then nothing will change. It is imperative that a new approach is adopted via developing a heart centred healing community.

APPENDIX 2

This paper was inspired by Mary Mackillop, a prominent Australian woman and the first Saint whose operational philosophy was, "Never see a need without trying to do something about it."

Peta Nottle

18 November 2001

APPENDIX 3

37 Lady Douglas Way
   Karratha WA 6714

Ph: (08) 9185 3236

27 June 2001

Mr Elton Humphrey
   Secretary
   Senate Community Affairs Reference Committee
   Suite S1 59
   Parliament House
   Canberra ACT 2600.

Dear Mr Humphrey,

Thank you for this opportunity to submit a submission into The Senate inquiry into the Nursing Profession.

I am aware that the inquiry is focusing mainly on Nursing Education, Nursing Retention and Recruitment issues; however, I believe that

APPENDIX 3

before these issues can be addressed successfully there are 3 essential elements that any Nursing study needs to take into consideration if there is to be a successful outcome .

These elements, if incorporated, will bring Nurses back into the profession and certainly, will retain a highly skilled professional empowered nursing workforce.

These elements are as follows:
Caring Profession
Holistic Nursing
Valuing and Respecting Nurses and the Nursing Profession

Unless the above are considered and integrated into a plan, Nurses will continue to leave the Profession as they are doing now and will not be incited back into a workforce which does not respect or value them. Nurses need to be able to deliver holistic care in a caring and nurturing environment.

I am of the belief that if the above can be integrated into a total holistic approach to the Health Industry then there may be a chance for the future to be improved.

Please consider the attached submission as part of a solution to the issues confronting the Government and the Health Industry in relation to the Nursing Profession.

I would like to have the opportunity to appear before the Senate Select Committee if the Senate Committee travels to remote Western Australia for public hearings .

Yours sincerely
Peta Nottle (Mrs)

New Vision – New Direction

I have been thinking about the Nursing profession for many years now and wondering about solutions. I would like to take this opportunity to outline what I believe could be solutions to the current situation that nursing finds its profession in today.

Return to caring, Nursing is a heart centred profession.

To allow nurses to nurse holistically.

Respect and value nurses.

1. Return to Caring

To nurse means to care for or to nurture with compassion.

"Mr Ian Pearson, a renowned information technology futurist and a British telecommunications analyst published his predictions for technology over the next 2 decades, combines his predictions with what we know about nursing today, and it is not hard to see what the nursing profession might look like in 2020.

What happens when computers are smarter than us? Pearson believes that this will cause a shift to a "care economy" computers can never learn to care. People will concentrate on the human interpersonal side of work.

Nurses will need to get back to their original and best strength – caring. Although computers cannot care, they can help nurses define, quantify and measure the effects of caring of patients outcomes. Making sure that they do just that, is crucial to nursing's survival.

Caring defined

"Step 1 – Nurses must refine and adopt a standard language for nursing specific practise. The language of physicians and ancillaries will not work. If you can't define caring, you can't measure caring. In today's accountable health industry you can't measure caring and therefore caring does not count. Since caring should be nursing's primary purpose 20 years from now, it makes a lot of sense to define it now."

(Reference and quotation taken from an article on information technology in the Nursing Management Journal – Springhouse Corporation April 2000).

2. Holistic Approach to Nursing

Florence Nightingale expressed a holistic view of nursing when she said that nursing should "put us in the best possible conditions of nature to restore or preserve health, to prevent or cure disease or injury".

APPENDIX 3

The goal of holistic nursing is to promote health, facilitate healing and alleviate suffering. To do so the nurse focuses on the whole person – body, mind and spirit when delivering care.

Many many nurses today are expressing a feeling of frustration and failure. Nurses see themselves spread as pawns across a health care system too large to control or understand. Today's health system is a business and is run as such. This has had a major impact on encouraging young men and women entering the profession. There are so many other professions and trades that young people are choosing to enter, rather than the nursing profession.

Traditionally, nurses have found it hard to provide holistic care in institutions that are focused on purely the medical model. In this environment, care is typically symptom and disease oriented, focused more on the diseased part rather than the person with the disease.

I am of the firm belief that we in Western Australia need to focus on a model such as the innovative program called the 'Healing Web'. This model of Holistic Nursing was developed by a group of Nurse Educators from South Dakota in the US.

(Reference – "Nurse's Handbook of Alternatives and Complementary Therapies", Publisher Springhouse).

In conclusion to the above, I cannot emphasise enough for the Committee to recommend that Nursing remains a heart centered profession and that is I believe crucial to the healing of the profession, once this philosophy is grounded then we can really assist in healing the people entrusted to our care, whether it be at home, in the community or in our institutions – hospitals.

3. Respect and Valuing Nurses

I think a fundamental component for addressing the issues related to the Nursing profession is the valuing and respect of nurses. In 1991, I wrote the following:-

The Clinical Nurse
   Nurses by the bedside are very special, are they not?
   Appreciated by their clients, by management they are not

APPENDIX 3

Treated with a lack of respect and dignity
I wonder if this will ever change for you and me
Our focus is on patient care not on numbers like the top
You work here, you work there. It does not matter if you are in a specialty, or not
Happiness in the workplace should a priority be
For then, and only then, will the best come deep from within me
Respect your colleagues, a cry to management be
For then and only then will we be a true fraternity

In 2001, I ask myself, "What has changed?" My career path has taken me to the level of Director of Nursing; therefore my reflections come out of my experience. I find that today Senior Nurses are not always respected by the corporate sector. In my position, I see what is happening to our nurses, and I constantly ask myself, why is it that senior nurses are not consulted, listened to or involved in decision making at a corporate level, even thought they are part of the Health Service Executive? Nurses are heart-centred people and there is a need I believe, for heart-centredness and business centredness to be integrated so that our profession as nurses can bring a holistic approach to the health industry. This will have major benefits for the health industry with a resultant flow-on effect to our communities and institutions. It is interesting to note one of Western Australia's most successful companies, practise this model of Holistic Management at the highest level.

A good place to start is that we truly listen to each other. Nurses are the backbone of the Health Industry – they are intelligent, responsible, accountable and according to the Bulletin's magazine ranking, among the ten top professions, nurses are "the most ethical of professionals".

It is imperative that Nurses are supported, valued and respected by the whole of the Health Industry.

Peta Nottle
    Director of Nursing
    Nickol Bay Hospital

APPENDIX 4

The History of Bullying of a Nurse during her extended and extensive nursing career, and how the continuation of the bullying and harassment had a profound effect on her mental, emotional physical and spiritual self, causing a total breakdown in her "wholeness".

The Nurse is now a 69 year old woman, who describes retirement to be the happiest, most contented peaceful place to be in. For the sake of the confidentiality of this woman and other stake holders in her story she has called herself "Dina Souris".

Dina Souris was brought up in remote Australia, a very free spirit, who loved nothing better than running free. She was trusting and loved people and life. She was sent to boarding school at 12 and realised that not all persons were like her. She had a very difficult time settling into an up-market all girls' school environment. Things were very strict and her free spirit realised that this was too hard for her; so she ran away, only to have to ring the front bell of the convent at 1100 pm after several hours on the outside she escaped over a very big brick wall on the night as she had nowhere to go and she had no money in this big city. The trouble Dina Souris got into for this misdemeanour was very harsh. Her parents kept her there; despite her pleading to go back to her

APPENDIX 4

country. They were adamant because they wanted her to get a 'good' education.

Dina Souris realised that she had to conform to rules and regulations. She started to learn and practise tennis and became a very good tennis player. It strengthened her body and mind as she could take out her emotional pain on the tennis ball.

Having survived five years at boarding school, Dina Souris decided to go into nursing school; something she had dreamed of since a young girl. She was offered a place in a very famous hospital and even though it was a tough life, she loved it, with her passion of caring through nursing. She had great tutors, mentors and most of all colleagues - all young mostly straight from school, living together in nurses' quarters - always having someone to talk to if needed about a bad day. Dina Souris states that her training days were some of the happiest days of her life.

Dina Souris on completion of training went straight back to the bush and spent many many years working in rural and remote areas. When Dina Souris's children were of an age to have the opportunities of a good education, Dina Souris and her husband decided to leave and return to mainstream living in a city, which was an alien place for them; however, their children came first. For the first time, Dina Souris had to go to work in a city secondary hospital and as a senior clinical nurse, blew the whistle on an experiment that was being trialled in theatre at that time. The ramifications of her doing this, started an avalanche of harassment bullying and victimisation by parties involved with the practitioner involved.

This came as a shock to Dina Souris and unfortunately management were supportive to some extent initially when they realised the predicament they could have been in. However, nobody was ever held accountable.

Dina Souris suffered very badly from this and left the workplace to follow her dream of becoming a country matron.

Once the children were at University, Dina Souris who was very much an "old school" nurse and who had practised the art of caring, did become a Country Matron –a DON; however, her main goal was to

APPENDIX 4

ensure that the patients were administered the highest standard of care by all involved. She also cared very deeply for her nurses; she led from the front being there on call 24 hours a day, 7 days a week.

During her time as a DON, she had to address major issues with a very very small cohort of practitioners whose practices at times were questionable and changes were made in policies and procedures to bring Health Care Units into the 1990's, in units that were being run on the 1970's model of care. This cohort of clinicians set about destroying her career. There were many incidents of malicious untrue statements being spoken and written about her and leaked out to the communities in which she worked over a period of four years. These ended up in the Council Minutes, Medical Advisory Meeting Minutes and when a local politician brought these in to the political arena, discussing her in parliament, this was the final straw that broke her back.

The health department knew all about what was going on, however, covered it all up and ignored the issues despite calls and cries for help from Dina Souris and others for a proper investigation into the bullying harassment and victimisation issues that would not stop.

Dina Souris finally broke into a physical, mental, emotional and spiritual wreck. Dina Souris was heavily sedated and on very strong antidepressants. She would not go outside the front door of her home for six months and would have severe nightmares of a perpetrator knocking on the door and throwing acid into her face. Her light nearly went out. And if it was not for the love of her devoted husband, family and friends, of the care of a caring GP and a very caring visiting psychiatrist, she may not be here today. Dina Souris was sent to a private hospital in a major city and referred to a very highly respected psychiatrist. It was this psychiatrist, who helped her start on her healing journey. After the psychiatrist, listened to her story, the psychiatrist said to her ,"It is not you. I know this person ("one of the main perpetrators of the abuse."). It was then the light in her heart started to become a little stronger, and the healing process began.

It took nine months for Dina Souris to recover and heal from this break-down. It was not helped by her position being advertised by the

APPENDIX 4

General Manager of the Health Service during her rehabilitation period. This was done two months before the planned RTW day. By this time, Dina Souris was so much stronger mentally emotionally and spiritually, she immediately contacted the Health Service and sought clarification of the advertisement and that she was not resigning and would be returning to her gazetted position. Dina Souris was told it was a misunderstanding and a mistake. To this day, Dina Souris does not believe that.

This was fully accepted as a WC Claim.

Restructures followed on Dina Souris's return to work and although things had settled for her in some ways, other good senior nursing staffs were receiving the same abuse, she had been subjected to. Again, the Health Department did not support the staff until it was too late. Eventually six years after the abuse first manifested, the Health Department sent up a consultant to help the staff deal with the continuum of this perpetrator's behaviour and the head of the Health Department came up to deal with the main perpetrator personally.

Dina Souris knew her days were numbered when she became a target for senior bureaucrats. She always stuck to her ethical and holistic management practices and would not bend to suit the wants of administration services. A redundancy was arranged and Dina Souris left her community, and the role she was so devoted to.

Dina Souris finished her last years still being bullied and harassed by administration in other roles she had undertaken, in a tertiary institution where she worked. Her role as a peer support officer, brought back bad memories for her and the lies and malicious gossip that were spread about her in this setting amongst persons whom she challenged for poor clinical governance, where reminiscent of the 1990's. This period lasted for three years. Dina Souris began to feel the way she did in 1997.

Fortunately, for Dina Souris, she had a very supportive kind and compassionate GP who knew how she was suffering. Finally, at the age of 67 she left the profession which she had devoted her life's work to.

Whilst she had very hard times, she also has wonderful memories of her journey in nursing and has had amazing experiences and blessed with wonderful friendships. She freely admits her husband and life partner of forty-five years, has been her rock and brought her where she is today.

Dina Souris is proud to write up this synopsis and hopes it will help others to see light at the end of the tunnel. Her biggest message today is to care for and love yourself; and that it is okay to put your hand up and say I am broken, as it is then that the healing begins and you begin the journey in returning to wholeness. It takes time. Journey through a passion-music, art or whatever makes you happy. Work on all parts of your spiritual, mental, emotional and physical body.

You can do it.

Before I complete this I will share a little poem with you.
To God
Please untie my knots that are in my heart and my life
Remove the can nots, have nots and do nots that I have in my mind
Erase the will nots, may nots, might nots, that might find home in my heart
Release me from the could nots and would nots and should nots, that obstruct my life
And most of all Dear God that you remove from my mind, my heart and my life all of the am nots, that I have allowed to hold me back
*Especially the thought **I am not good enough.***
Amen
(Author known to God)
In the stage of my life , I now believe at 70 years old I have changed from the life being a journey to now **Life is a Sacred Journey to Everlasting Life**

May God bless you all and please remember, we are all on the journey and we are all here to support each other on the journey.

Thank you.

Peta

APPENDIX 5

Submission –Health Department Sustainable Health Review 2018.

This submission, is an update to Submission 2, submitted in 2017. There have been changes that need to be documented in this edition for 2018. - See Aboriginal Health and recommendations for change.

Having read the information sent in reference to the HDWA for the community to have an input into the formation of a Sustainable Health Care Plan for The State of WA, the author is writing this submission in two parts.

The first part is in relation to the current medical model of health service delivery as presented on the YouTube presentation of the Australian Health Care Medical System.

The second part is in relation to the Traditional Aboriginal Holistic Healing Model of health service delivery.

The author of this submission has been thinking about the challenges the Health System faces for many years now and has been developing and implementing solutions to some of the emotional, mental and spiritual challenges providers and consumers face. The author would like to take this opportunity to outline what could be solutions to both patient challenges and the current situation the health industry finds itself. The author has worked in remote aboriginal communities, in primary, secondary and tertiary hospitals and now finds great joy in providing Holistic Integrative Healing Support Services as a Nurse Healer to clients who choose to be reconnected in Body, Mind, Emotion and Spirit.

The Vision.

A fair and balanced reading of the literature will give the foregone conclusion that holistic integrative therapies are financially and ethically worthwhile using a patient - centred care approach. There is much evidence to support holistic nurse healers /practitioners delivering integrative therapies and their positive outcomes. The goal of holistic care started with the nursing profession when Florence Nightingale stated the purpose of nursing is to promote health, facilitate healing and alleviate suffering. To do so, the nurse focuses on the whole person - body, mind and spirit with compassion when delivering care. Most holistic healing integrative therapies use hands on approach and there has been evidence in the past and now more evidence of the power of touch to an individual's health and well-being. For example, the research that looked at the effect of human touch on premature and newborn babies, led to decreased length of hospital stays and decreased number of hospital readmission rates within the current Diagnostic Related Group (DRG) funding model. The same is true for small children, teenagers, adults and the elderly. For those in the last days of their lives, touch is an ethical obligation that should not be ignored.

By introducing a holistic integrative healing therapeutic approach to mainstream health service delivery I believe many of the problems today summarised in the Sustainable Health Review information package could be addressed. This could result in Western Australia becoming a leader in the creation of the best practice model of health service delivery not just nationally, but internationally.

I will now put forward a vision I have for the delivery of patient – centred integrated, high quality and financially sustainable healthcare across the State of Western Australia, that fits into The Western

APPENDIX 5

Australian Government model of healthcare within the range of key areas as listed on the first page of the Sustainable Health Review Document.

The author recognises that this submission may be very different; however, I will not be writing in the style of academia. I will be writing from a heart- centred and healing perspective.

As we know, people are not just made up of a physical body. We are unique persons made up of a physical body, a mental body, an emotional body and a spiritual body. If parts of this whole are broken or missing then we have a break down in our wholeness.

On a broader scale, our communities are the same, made up of unique persons and when sections of our communities are broken, e.g. respecting, valuing and listening to the wisdom of our children, our elders and not knowing our true self, then communities have a breakdown in their wholeness.

As infants we are born whole, including babies who are born with physical disabilities (such as Down syndrome and cerebral palsy). It is only as we grow that outside influences start to impact on our wholeness. In 2017, the influence begins as young as 3 years of age, I believe, and sadly younger, in some cases.

From the beginning of life, children, adolescents, young adults and adults are being conditioned by outer world influences to live totally in the outside world and not from the inside world (the heart centre) out; the true self that they were when they were born.

The consequences of this are seen constantly in our societies, clearly evident through the Senate Enquiries and Royal Commissions that are being held today. Examples include the Royal Commission to The Aboriginal Deaths in Custody, The Royal Commission into Child Sexual Abuse, and the Royal Commission into the WA Inc. years, here in Western Australia in the late 1980's; the latter leading from restructure to restructure depending on who was in Government and whether the Government supported regionalisation or centralisation for The HDWA. The current Royal Commission in Victorian Senate Enquiry into Bullying in the Health Industry in 2016, the Senate Enquiry into

APPENDIX 5

Aged Care, 2017, followed by the Royal Commission into Aged Care Service Delivery; and then the Senate Inquiry into the Vaginal Sling and Pelvic Mesh operations in 2017, which had its origins in a Government Hospital in WA.

In 2018, there have been a number of Federal Senate enquires into PTSD in the defence force, the ambulance services and the first responders to name just a few, costing so many millions of dollars. Despite these enquiries, problems continue to be reported and appear to be increasing.

The pandemic suicide rates, homelessness, violence including domestic violence (which includes not only physical - it also includes emotional, mental, financial, sexual, and spiritual abuse), alcohol and drug addiction, bullying/abuse are in all facets of living from the very young to the aged, infirm and dying members of our society. Now we are witnessing it in Parliament, both at State and Federal Level.

This also includes nurses and doctors as regularly reported in newspapers and on a recent Insights Program on SBS, 2017. I have been a victim of this insidious horizontal and vertical violence and have suffered very badly on two occasions. Many, many nurses are still currently being bullied in the health industry throughout Australia in 2018.

Sir Charles Gairdner Hospital in 2012-2013, invested many thousands of dollars on a research program to build resilience in nurses through Curtain University. I was involved in the study and put forward a proposition for a solution to develop a healing centre offering complementary therapies to nurses. I, however, succumbed to the stressors of workplace bullying and seeing other nurses being broken, in particular heart-centred nurses, before the outcome of the project was completed. The cost of bullying on the hospital budgets are enormous and to the Government, as seen recently in a nurse being awarded over $1,000,000 in compensation in Queensland. Please make the workplace safe for our gifted caregivers and the future generations of gifted caregivers. In 2018, a few organisations in Australia are trying to bring about changes; however, it appears very little has changed.

APPENDIX 5

The physical, mental, emotional and spiritual brokenness of the individual and societies manifesting in physical disease, mental illness and broken spirits will continue if change does not happen.

The cost of health care delivery today could be absolutely reduced by introducing a truly holistic health care model. This could be achieved by taking an approach whereby individuals and communities are empowered to learn the true meaning of holism, healing and embrace holism in its deepest and purest form from cradle to grave.

The possibilities of such an approach.

In the first instance, there needs to be a major commitment for changes by government institutions, bureaucrats and persons responsible for administering health care services. will take this opportunity to congratulate and thank The Western Australian Premier The Honourable Mark McGowan, The Health Minister The Honourable Roger Cook and Policy Advisors for their commitment to implement a truly sustainable model of health care.

The journey towards this vision could begin with an education program in place for all staff within health for the growth and development in holistic health care in the integration of the healing arts with the science of medicine and nursing. The current medical model is not meeting the needs of multicultural Australia.

To begin with, it must be noted that no formal education is required to become a holistic or empowered person. The holistic approach requires the individual to learn to accept people as they are, without judgement, with unconditional love, compassion and harmony.

This approach starts with self-acceptance, which can be achieved by focusing inwards. There are various methods available that can help a person develop this focus such as meditation, visualisation, contemplation, prayer and spiritual practice. Self-awareness also leads the person to recognise the interconnectedness to all individuals and their relationship to the human and global communities. This recognition and awareness further creates a fertile ground for personal and professional development.

Once this philosophical shift has occurred in the system, then it

APPENDIX 5

will flow automatically into our service delivery and communities and then the holistic rehabilitation of health care can become a reality.

The goal of rehabilitation for a Sustainable Health Review is to prioritise the delivery of patient and community centred integrated high quality and financially sustainable healthcare across the State .This will take many, many years.

The goal of this submission to this review is to restore and promote health, wellbeing, facilitate healing and alleviate suffering. In doing this, strategists, financiers, planners, administrators and service deliverers focus on rehabilitating the WHOLE Person, the WHOLE Community in Body, Mind, Emotion, and Spirit.

According to holistic philosophy, wisdom and healing come from the individual, not the service providers. The service providers help the process of healing by creating a heart - centred environment in which healing can happen both in the individual and the community.

NB: The integrative (formally complementary) therapies such as Therapeutic Touch, Healing Touch, Clinical Reflexology, Stress Management, Massage, Aromatherapy Yoga, Kinesiology Meditation Art and Dance can be learned to enhance self-development and healing. (See Nurses and Midwives Board New South Wales: Complementary therapies in Nursing and Midwifery Practice-. http://www.nmb.nsw.gov.au/Complementary- Therapies/default.aspx)

The Nurses and Midwifery Boards of Australia regulated by AHPRA have accredited and endorsed the above Integrative (complementary) Therapies in nursing practise. (This has been endorsed since 1996 in Western Australia) The Alzheimer's and Dementia Association and Bethanie Aged Care Service Providers in Perth are leaders in developing a patient-centred model of service delivery. The Healing Insights team was honoured to attend a lecture at Bethesda Hospital recently, presented by a visiting dementia nursing consultant and senior lecturer at St Christopher's Hospice in London and the primary author of, T*he Namaste Approach The Power of Touch.*

She gave insight into caring for people with advanced dementia to improve the quality of life for those who can no longer move, or have the capacity to communicate or who have totally ability to communicate. The insight into what is happening in St Christopher's in London was so validating for the WA Healing Insights Organisation, as this is exactly the model of health care delivery members of the team practise in their individual private practises.

All people are inherently good and that goodness exists in every single human being as a permanent and inseparable element, quality or attribute. I believe that by taking a holistic approach to living from cradle to grave we can create a better future for our health industry providers and service deliverers and to all we serve.

There are a so many incredible organisations and corporations within our state, doing wonderful work and I am of the belief that the Department of Family and Children Services, The University of WA School of Business Social Impact and others are doing a fantastic healing work in the State of WA, that could be integrated into community Health and primary care programs as well as in local, regional and tertiary hospitals. Attending many breakfasts at the University Club of UWA, has given great insight into the work that would be of great value to the State Sustainable Health Care Plan.

Aboriginal Health

Traditional Aboriginal Healing. There is an absolute urgency to integrate traditional Aboriginal healing practises, with mainstream health practises, to turn the issues relating to aboriginal morbidity and mortality around from a system that is failing in the delivery of healthcare that is not compatible with Aboriginal Culture and Healing.

I was privileged to spend part of my childhood in both the Pilbara and the Kimberley in the 1950's. My friends were mostly made up of Aboriginal children.

I have worked very closely with traditional Aboriginal Healers in my extensive career as a nurse both in the Northern Territory - Yirrkala/ Nhulunbuy- Arnhem Land: Yarrilin West Katherine Aboriginal Health Service. Western Australia in the Kimberley, Wyndham, Fitzroy Crossing hospitals and the remote community of BalgoHills. In the Pilbara Region, in the remote centre of Jigalong. Roebourne, Wickham, Karratha and Port Hedland Hospitals and community health centres in the Roebourne shire.

During my first appointment as a public health nurse based in Yirrkala on the Gove Peninsular in 1972, as a naïve 23 year old registered nurse and midwife, I was introduced to men and women of high degree. A old Aboriginal health worker/healer taught me many lessons in relation to culture and healing, and on many occasions I would liaise with this beautiful wise woman, and another male traditional healer.

I have been very blessed by being embraced and taught by Traditional Aboriginal healers throughout my career when working in remote communities, towns and regional centres. Today I am a practising nurse - healer who has studied and practised the Ancient Healing Arts in the Laying on of Hands with the modalities of complementary therapies/modalities that nurses are allowed to use in practise. The modality that encompasses in my opinion the closest to traditional aboriginal healing is the energy based healing practise of Therapeutic Touch.(Australia is very fortunate to have very learned and experienced teachers in this modality.) I am not a teacher; however I am a mentor and coach in the integrative modalities that nurses are allowed to use in practice. I chose to pursue studies in the healing arts, rather than upgrade my diploma in nursing and midwifery to a Bachelor of Nursing which I obtained in 1968 and 1969 respectively. I was privileged to be able to study healing from 1998, recognising I needed to be healed after suffering from a breakdown directly related to workplace bullying and harassment, sustained over a 4 year period

I find it very sad and am deeply embarrassed when oversees researchers from European countries come to study and work with the traditional Aboriginal healing cultures and practises. Two such researchers come to mind:

Helmut Petri

The research for the history of traditional Aboriginal healing, lead me to a book called, *The Australian Medicine Man* written by a German anthropologist, Helmut Petri. *The Australian Medicine Man* is an extensive survey of literature to the Aboriginal Medicine men or as Elkin was to term them "Men of High Degree"

APPENDIX 5

Dr Francesca.

Dr Francescesca, an Italian researcher came to Australia in 2014, to study how international legal standards related to Aboriginal traditional medicine. She was amazed at the lack of research or recognition of this 60,000 year old body of knowledge. "I had been aware that globally Australia is recognised as having advanced policy development and support for traditional medicine 'she says "but it turned out this was because of the official embrace of Chinese medicine I could not believe that there was a complete dismissal at an official level of Indigenous health practise."

Reference – Aboriginal Healers are working to keep traditional medicine alive –AWAYE –ABC Radio National http://www.abc.net.au/ radio national /program /awaye/aboriginal –healers-working –to keep – traditional medicine alive.

For Further reference see www.Creative Spirit website. Korff J.,11th March 2016, Traditional Aboriginal Health Care www.creativespirits.info.

In 2018, The Royal Adelaide Hospital in Adelaide, South Australia, have now employed Traditional Aboriginal Healers to work alongside doctors. See - "Ngangkari healers" 60,000 years of traditional Aboriginal methods made headway in medical clinics-ABC News (Australian..... www.abc.-Aboriginal Healers. Posted 28th March 2018

Welcome to Country March 1st 2018."Meet the Traditional Aboriginal Healers working Inside Australia's Hospitals-Impressive results of Traditional Aboriginal Healers are starting to gain attention and respect of western health professions "

ANTACA Anangu Ngangkari TJutaka Aboriginal Corporation.

I must document here that the best practise committee for nursing practice at Nickol Bay Hospital in Karratha had formulated a Complementary Therapies and a Traditional Aboriginal Healing Policy in 2003 and it was passed by the medical advisory committee and subjected to a review by the legal branch of the HDWA.The outcome was a very negative one. This is despite SCGH having just opened the Brown's centre - Complementary Therapy Unit for oncology patients; now

APPENDIX 5

Solaris Care at Sir Charles Gardiner Hospital situated in Nedlands, Perth WA. Currently, there are Solaris Care Units at SCGH and St John of God's Hospital, Subiaco.

I wrote the first patient hand out on Holistic Health care and Complementary Therapies for the Brown's centre in 2001. This handout was also sent to the Hospice in Albany at their request. Margaret River Hospital was the only other hospital who had a complementary therapies policy at that time.

On reflection, while writing this submission I contemplate what could have been the outcome if this policy had been implemented back in 2003-14 years on. One looks at the situation from Wyndham to Esperance and (in particular, now in Roebourne). In remote areas, townships and regional centres, together with our urban brothers and sisters, one does get a deep sense of sadness and shame for the burning and burying of The Great Indigenous Healing Arts.

There are white clouds appearing in the rainbow of Life's Journey. I would ask persons who are responsible for planning, developing and implementing the sustainable health plan that they will have an open mind to exploring the possibilities of opening the door to an integrated holistic healing model with the mainstream medical healing model.

I conclude this section of the submission with a poem by Kevin Gilbert, called:

"Losing Bush Medicine"

Oh what if all the doctors died Elena thought then cried and cried and what if modern medicine fails

to keep the virus from this vale of what if secret wisdom stays a secret all our many ways

our bush food and our medicine will be forgotten and lost to men I truly

cannot understand

how can we keep? Elena wept and wept

and wept and wept.

- Kevin John Gilbert (1933–1993), First Nations human rights defender, poet, playwright, and artist, was born on 10 July 1933 to the

APPENDIX 5

Wiradjuri Nation on the banks of the Kalara (Lachlan) river near Condobolin, New South Wales.

Recommendations.

1. Request assistance from credible positive healers.

Aboriginal Healers, Other Cultural Healers-Indian, African, Indonesian, European Healers and Therapeutic Touch Healers in developing accredited healing programs to be incorporated and introduced in the Sustainable Health Care review/ Plan.

2. To develop educational awareness of holistic self-care and empowerment

3. To liaise with:

a. The Australasian Therapeutic Touch Association

b. The International Therapeutic Touch Association based in New York

c. The American Holistic Nurses Association

d. Peta Nottle –Tranquillitas Health Clinic-

To develop integrative therapies programmes approved by The Australian Nursing and Midwifery Boards to be included in the Sustainable Health Care Review

Submitted by Peta Nottle: Holistic RN/ Nurse Healer, through the integrative therapies of Therapeutic Touch Clinical Reflexology, Healing Touch , Massage ,Prayer Meditation and Contemplation Coach: Humanistic Neuro Linguistic Psychology Master Practitioner Life Coach-Stress Management Coach. Healing Mentor.

Associations: Registered with The Nursing Board of Australia.

Professional Member of the Reflexology Association of Australia. Member of the International Therapeutic Touch Association Member of the Australasian Therapeutic Touch Association.

Member of American Holistic Nurses Association

Peta Nottle. Tranquillitas Health Clinic.(Founder of Healing Insights -Healing Insights Company Pty Ltd.

I was recognised by the International Nurses' Association in 2015 and was featured in the February edition 2016 of World Health Leaders in Health Care.

APPENDIX 5

I have included two stories to demonstrate The Power of Touch through the Healing Modality of Therapeutic Touch."

1 An Old Aboriginal Healer's Story:

There was an old traditional Aboriginal healer originating from deep in the western Desert of the Kimberly region .He spent many years in Balgo Hills. In 2005, I was privileged to be contracted to Balgo Hills as a clinic nurse, and I was contracted as part of my role to introduce Traditional Aboriginal Healing into the mainstream medical model at the Balgo Clinic. I was introduced to this man who had never seen a white person do the kind of work he did in his healing practice. One day, he came into the clinic and asked to see this sister, (pointing to me). He said "Sister me got sore foot, you fix.

I took him to the consulting room, and did a 15 minute therapeutic touch treatment. All of a sudden, he said, "I'm better now Sister. I took my hands off and he went away very happy, never to have the pain again. The old Aboriginal healer then taught me many of their traditional practises.

The Singapore Holiday:

I was holidaying in Singapore in 2015. I was over at Santosa Island, when a 70 year old lady had a heavy fall, injuring her left knee. The lady was in severe pain. Her pain score was. A 10/10 and she could not weight bear. I offered to help her, until arrangements could be made to transfer her to Singapore Hospital. The lady agreed, and I did a fifteen minute therapeutic touch treatment on her knee. After fifteen minutes, the pain had completely gone and she was able to walk normally.

The lady and her friends were just amazed. It turned out, the party was staying at the same hotel and were going on the same cruise that my husband and I were going on. I recommended that they go to Singapore hospital and have a review to ensure the knee had no diagnosed injury. This they did.The all clear was given after x-rays and a medical review. Confirmation of this story can be validated by contacting the lady herself, who lives in Queensland and would be only too happy to validate her experience with Therapeutic Touch.

Thank you for the opportunity of submitting this update to submission one.

Peta Nottle

"In every culture and in every medical tradition before ours, healing was accomplished by moving energy."

Albert Szent-Györgyi - won the Nobel Prize for Medicine and Physiology in 1937

APPENDIX 6

18 June 2019
    Secretariat
    Educating the Nurse of the Future
    To whom it may concern,

Thank you for this opportunity to submit a submission into Independent Review of Nursing Education: Educating the Nurse of the Future into the Nursing Profession.

I am aware that the inquiry is focusing mainly on Nursing Education however I believe that before these issues can be addressed successfully there are 3 essential elements that any Nursing study needs to take into consideration if there is to be a successful outcome.

These elements if incorporated will retain Nurses in the profession and result in the development of highly skilled professional Nursing workforce with subsequent improvements in the health and well-being of Australians in primary, secondary and tertiary care.

These elements are as follows:
1. Caring Profession
2. Holistic Nursing
3. Valuing and Respecting Nurses and the Nursing Profession

APPENDIX 6

Unless the above are considered and integrated into the review, Nursing will not progress causing nurses to experience burnout and lose their ability to care with compassion that they once had. Nurses need to be able to deliver holistic care in a caring and nurturing environment.

I am of the belief that if the above can be integrated into a total holistic approach to health service delivery then there may be a chance for the future of nursing to be assured.

Please consider the attached submission as part of a solution to the issues confronting the Government and health service delivery in relation to Educating the Nurse of the Future.

I give permission for you to include this submission on the Independent Review website. Yours sincerely

Peta Nottle (Mrs)

Holistic Nurse Healer, Complementary Therapist, Owner Director Tranquillitas Healing Clinic & Director Healing Insights WA Pty Ltd

Independent Review of Nursing Education: Educating the Nurse of the Future

Australian Government Department of Health

This submission addresses a number of factors that fall into the various categories set out in the Terms of Reference for this enquiry. These comments are made under headings relating to the Terms of Reference.

Effectiveness of current educational preparation of and articulation between enrolled and registered nurses and nurse practitioners in meeting the needs of health service delivery

Current educational preparation and articulation between enrolled and registered nurses and nurse practitioners (hereafter called EN, RN and NP)

Although there are still experienced RNs, it is the practice of primary, secondary and tertiary health care for the future of not employing ENs. All nurses are expected to have a Bachelor of Nursing Science degree. This is evident in the model of practice for education in WA by educating ENs at TAFE and transitioning to university study

APPENDIX 6

once they enter the workforce. Graduate programs for ENs are very limited in terms of availability and scope.

Many ENs end up, on completion of their TAFE studies, as care givers in Aged Care and Community Care with very limited experience in this area.

Due to the diversity of students there is often a lack of understanding of the needs of the elderly physically, mentally, emotionally and spiritually, in addition to the cultural and environmental contexts.

There is no screening of suitability of these students as to their personality type, the result being often a lack of empathy and compassion.

There is no differentiation between the care given in hospitals between ENs and RNs apart from the fact that ENs cannot give intravenous medications, nor access scheduled drugs without the presence of a RN.

There is often a lack of communication and respect between ENs and RNs due to not valuing each other –and this leads to a breakdown in communication and compromises care.

The present model deems a nurse with three years' full time advanced practice with an additional year specialised practice, along with completion of a Master's degree in Nursing, an expert as they then qualify to become a Nurse Practitioner (NP).

Some become experts in name only. There is a deep lack of holistic patient centred care in the current model. There are many anecdotal instances where this is evident. It appears the role of NP lies between a RN and a doctor however in many instances is purely focused on the business model.

Health service delivery is currently ineffective, secondary to the lack of holistic and patience centred care.

Factors effecting the choice of nursing as an occupation, including for men.

Most nurses begin their formal education with this ideal of becoming a holistic nurse. Many nurses retain this orientation after graduation, and some manage this guiding principle of caring throughout their professional life. However, many nurses through the hectic pace of their professional lives, may forget this ideal, become discouraged and feel a sense of burnout. It appears that this is what is and has been happening in the Western Australian nursing profession over the last 30 years. Unfortunately, the nursing profession is in need of a total holistic approach to Nursing if it is to survive.

Many nurses express a feeling of frustration and failure. Nurses feel themselves spread as pawns across a health care system too large to control or understand. This in part could be directly related to having forgotten their true role as holistic nurses. Today people choose nursing as a career and this includes both men and women. Attractive factors include job flexibility, security, remuneration, transferability of skills with travel, and career progression. In the past, nursing was seen as a vocation.

The role and appropriateness of transition to practice programs however named.

There is a lack of clinical expertise on graduation for nursing graduates as they enter graduate programs, if they are available. 380 students graduated from universities in WA in 2018, with only 80 positions available. As an outcome, RNs are only able to obtain work as carers for Aged Care and Home care providers. Many RNs end up leaving the profession and open small businesses in cleaning or choose to gain certification in complementary therapies such as Reiki, reflexology and massage and open their own practice with no experience in their profession of choice.

This is an infective use of resources.

The competitiveness and attractiveness of Australian nursing qualifications across international contexts.

Nursing needs to be empowered in Western Australia. This movement – empowering of Nurses has been happening in the US for years. The evolution in the US has seen the emergence of a new model of nursing and that is the holistic nurse. Universities in the US now offer undergraduate training programs for holistic nursing. The definition of nursing equals care with compassion and sadly this has slowly been eroded as focus has changed to the science and technology of nursing.

In practical terms, this shift has removed the art and wisdom of

APPENDIX 6

nursing from nursing education at all levels – EN, RN and NP. The result is a total lack of person centred care.

Regional needs and circumstances

Nursing staff who work in rural and remote areas must have a broad range of experience and skills to meet the full gamut of health care delivery. The absolute need to bring back education in the form of a generalist nurse able to work in emergency care, paediatric care, palliative care, aged care, surgical care, medical care and midwifery care, is clear. One solution is rotational programs to encourage nursing staff to obtain skills in all facets of nursing care in the specialities described above. This ought to include primary health care nursing staff. Nursing staff today do not access this experience in the tertiary system as it stands.

National and international trends

The international trend in nursing is the transition from a science based model only to an integration of the art and wisdom of nursing with the science of nursing. In the US, the American Holistic Nurses Association (AHNA) vision is 'every nurse is a holistic nurse'. The mission statement of the AHNA is to 'illuminate holism in nursing practice, community, advocacy, research and education.'

This includes:

Engagement Opportunities
Committees Networking

- Practice

- Research

- Health (advocacy)

- Education

APPENDIX 6

- Awards

- Nurse networking calls (quarterly)

- Conferences

- Local chapters

- Social media

Leadership
- Serve as a Board member

- Serve as a local chapter leader

- Serve as a Committee Chair

- Become a Conference Presenter
The strategic goals of the AHNA for 2018-2022 are as follows:

- Increase AHNA membership and expand influence on holism in healthcare

- Increase and unify holistic and integrative research, practice and education
  opportunities

- Strengthen and empower the voice of holistic nursing

- Expand and increase communication and awareness about holistic nursing

- Optimise and leverage resources to strengthen AHNA infrastructure.
The AHNA has a detailed reference book: Holistic Nursing: Scope and Standards of Practice. 2018. (2 edition) nursesbooks.org, Silver

Spring Maryland. This would be a useful resource to guide the implementation of the above mentioned principles for education of the nurse for the future.

In October 2019 in Tokyo, Japan a Conference on Traditional, Holistic Medicine and Holistic Nursing will be convened. The conference theme is enhancing the excellence in traditional and alternative medicine. This might provide great insight into international developments.

The need to consider and adopt a similar approach to that of the US is absolutely fundamental to the future of nursing in Australia. From the nursing staff perspective this approach provides a greater range of opportunities resulting in a broader richer career path with various pathways for staff to pursue. This approach would lead to greater retention of trained staff as they can see opportunities for advancement and further development.

In addition, this would benefit the community as staff would have the flexibility to meet the needs of people in their care, particularly required in the regional and remote WA.

Research policies and enquiries and previous reviews relating to nursing education

I made a submission to a previous Senate inquiry into the Nursing Profession in June 2001. The main themes and changes I saw and commented on related to three areas:

1. Return to caring - Nursing is a heart centred profession.

2. To allow nurses to nurse holistically.

3. Greater respect and value of nurses, especially by the Medical Profession.

Sadly, since 2001 the change in nursing education to a science only based program has had a significant effect in the removal of care and compassion in health service delivery. An example of this is the introduction of care in the form of checklists. The disappearance of the nursing process and the NANDA diagnosis language has ruled out nursing language that is compatible with the medical and allied health professionals approaches.

Nurses must refine and adopt a standard language for nursing specific practices. The language of physicians and ancillaries does not work. By nurses returning to their original and best strength – 'caring' – true patient centred care will be the outcome.

In conclusion, I cannot emphasise enough for the Committee to recommend that Nursing remains a Heart Centred Profession and that is, I believe, crucial to the healing of the profession; Once this philosophy is grounded, then we can really assist in healing the people entrusted to our care, whether it be at home, in the community or in our institutions – hospitals.

APPENDIX 7

INTERNATIONAL SUSTAINABLE HEALTH CARE PLAN.

Thank you. It is an honour to be here today, to present to you a vision I had for an International Sustainable Health Care Plan, which resulted from a submission I had forwarded to the Health Department of Western Australia for their Sustainable Health Care Plan.

I am led to understand that health systems around the globe are under insurmountable pressure, especially in Western countries, where health is based on a business/sickness model and not a preventative one.

In Australia, I see the need for holistic health care and the true meaning of 'holism' together with healing practices to be integrated with the scientific evidence based, business bio medical model that is practised in Australia. This integration is paramount to the health and well being of all Australians

For a population of 25 million, the cost of the Australian health care system for 2018 /2019 is over $180 billion dollars - 10 % of GDP. If the current system does not change , the system is, in my opinion, unsustainable.

The vision I am presenting today is based on a wholeness model,

APPENDIX 7

commencing with a picture of our wholeness at birth. As we know, we are made of up of the physical, emotional, mental and spiritual body. This is our true self, totally connected in being. The environment in which we live is also part of our being .

When a baby is born, all people see is the physical body, we do not see who the baby really is . The door to the baby's soul is open, the spirit is free, the baby's emotional and mental bodies are at the very beginning of development and as science now tells us, the development to full maturity is not complete until the age of 28 - in some persons earlier, and in others, later .

The connectedness to who our developing little one truly is affected by outer world influences and the majority of the littles one start to lose their individualities and become conditioned to conform to societal expectations .

I have been so privileged to be blessed with four beautiful grandchildren and they have taught me to see and live as a little child, in my inner world.

What I have observed is what external worldly influences can have on their wholeness .

I have observed that changes start to appear in kindergarten. This has the potential in many, to develop into a lack of heart centredness. Some children learn to develop a total separation from their inside world. I have also observed in my experiences, some children have changes well before kindergarten .

Life's journey will take them on various different pathways and if there is a breakdown in their young lives, and the child is NOT nurtured in non conditional values and virtues, then this could have major ramifications in their lives .

As they grow, continuing on in their life's journey without a positive framework for living this has the potential to lock his or her life into a very negative framework of living .

Many traumas that young ones are exposed to, also have major influences on their predispositions to emotional mental and spiritual brokenness which, as we know, can manifest in this continuum of a negative framework of living.

This brokenness leads to a loss of the true self and the closing of the door to the soul. This could leave a person with a severe addiction or addictions - drugs , alcohol leading to domestic violence, either as a receiver of violent actions, physical , emotional , mental , sexual financial etc from the very young to the aged, or a perpetrator .

This leads to stress, anxieties PTSD, depression both reactive (exogenous) and endogenous, broken homes and families, societies, homelessness and ultimately suicides, to name just a few.

In Australia, the responses by Federal, State, Local and Governmental Bodies has been to have Senate Enquires and Royal Commissions month after month, at the cost of millions of dollars to the Australian taxpayer with ultimately no real sustainable outcomes .

Therapeutic Touch, in my opinion would, if implemented into a global model of health care, enable education of Holistic Healing Programs to be developed from the cradle to the end of life. Holistic therapeutic touch practitioners as we all know do embrace this model of care and have a deep understanding and practise with deep care and compassion.

This model of Care does have major cost benefits for consumers who receive holistic care and healing through the power of touch; as it does for health care providers who allow practitioners to practise holistic care and use therapeutic touch in their daily work schedules, be it in the public or private sectors, in primary health care, hospitals, aged care institutions and hospice care.

There is a real need to collaborate with funders , and universities that teach nursing, medicine and allied health professionals, together with other health and well-being institutions to enable education on holistic health care and healing to be at the centre of their chosen field of study and practice .

APPENDIX 7

The International Therapeutic Touch Association and the Australasian Therapeutic Touch Association, are in my opinion the world leaders in the education of holistic health care and healing practitioners .

There is a need to build a National Health Code of Practice to ensure that countries who are signatories to the World Health Organisation's policy on CAMS and the Environment comply with their policies. Australia is a signatory to their policy; however, does not comply in any way to include the policies in the business bio - medical model.

The Australian medical model of health service delivery does not meet the needs of Indigenous or CALD persons or cultures as per the WHO policies .

In Australia, (as in other Indigenous Cultures and Practices) there is much to be learnt from our indigenous traditional healers and their practices. This is now at the very early stages of development .

IN CONCLUSION

We need a paradigm shift in the way we manage health and well being from the beginning of life - the continuum of life which includes all persons with disabilities and chronic disease to end of life care. This paradigm shift needs to be considered by not only government departments responsible for health service delivery, but a whole approach with all service deliverers for all persons and cultures - this includes the current education and justice systems plus others .

Health Specific

A. Development of a International Sustainable Health Care Plan

B. Plan and Implementation the shift from a purely scientific model of Care to a Model of Curing and Healing with a real, focus on the prevention of illness and disease.

APPENDIX 7

C. The development of an education system , teaching the true meaning of holistic healthcare and healing .

I do believe that the vision I had of a International Sustainable Health Care Plan for all nations would be achievable for all persons and for the environment if implemented and enable the total reconnection to wholeness and finding the 'immortal diamond' within them . The immortal diamond -the Divine Self - Divine Love Light Energy Peace Truth and Happiness .

Thank you.
    Peta Nottle

GLOSSARY

References [to do]

Wanjuk - (Look up on Safari/Google See National Museum Australia " Yalangara "art of the Djang 'kawu". The Marika Family look for Wunjuk

(Google Galaru Yunipingu).

Billy (pg 67)

Pg 68 (.A google .search on Groote Island today has a site called the Anindilyakwa Land Council. This site is well worth reading .The history of Groote is so old dating back to the 15th Century)

Pg 87 There is a very good article one can search on the internet that was presented to the Government then on the 18th of August 2005, called Shenton Park Cottage Hospice –Grievance, regarding the closure of this essential service at that time.

Pg 92 - –see Nursing Text books from 1914 to Toohey 1965.'Medical Nursing'.

Pg 96 - Pelvic Mesh disaster

Pg 105 – Rabbit proof fence

NOTES

2. TREESVILLE

1. Andrew Barton "Banjo" Paterson, CBE was an Australian bush poet, journalist and author. He wrote many ballads and poems about Australian life, focusing particularly on the rural and outback areas. Source: Wikipedia

3. HERITAGE

1. https://en.wikipedia.org/wiki/Operation_Chastise

4. MARBLE BAR

1. https://en.wikipedia.org/wiki/Spinifex_(plant)
2. The **Round Australia Trial** was a motorsport rally which was run on multiple occasions between 1953 and 1998. The theme of the event was to stage a rally which circumnavigated Australia. Its early years were tremendously popular as the roads linking large portions of the country, particularly west of Adelaide, were not in good condition. Automobile manufacturers enthused over the event as it provided a particularly severe test event for their products, proving their cars were able to stand up to whatever conditions remote Australia could provide. Source: Wikipedia
3. https://www.australiasnorthwest.com/business/eat-drink/ironclad-hotel
4. Shrubby Australian acacia trees

6. WYNDHAM

1. **Grog** is any of a variety of alcoholic beverages. The word originally referred to a drink made with water and rum, which British Vice admiral Edward Vernon introduced into the naval squadron he commanded in the West Indies on 21 August 1740. Source: Wikipedia
2. https://en.wikipedia.org/wiki/Drover_(Australian)
3. https://simpleflying.com/milk-run-flight/
4. The Brolga is a large grey crane, with a featherless red head and grey crown. The legs are grey and there is a black dewlap under the chin. Females are shorter than males. The energetic dance performed by the Brolga is a spectacular sight. Displays may be given at any time of the year and by birds of any age. The Sarus

NOTES

Crane, *G. antigone*, another species of crane found in Australia, can be identified by its dull pink legs and the red of its head extending down the neck. Source: https://www.birdsinbackyards.net/species/Grus-rubicunda

8. TRIP TO LONDON

1. The **line-crossing ceremony** is an initiation rite that commemorates a person's first crossing of the Equator.[1] The tradition may have originated with ceremonies when passing headlands, and become a "folly" sanctioned as a boost to morale,[2] or have been created as a test for seasoned sailors to ensure their new shipmates were capable of handling long rough times at sea. Equator-crossing ceremonies, typically featuring King Neptune, are common in the navy and are also sometimes carried out for passengers' entertainment on civilian ocean liners and cruise ships. They are also performed in the merchant navy and aboard sail training ships. Source: Wikipedia

10. THE EUROPEAN EXPERIENCE

1. https://en.wikipedia.org/wiki/Hurley_(stick)

11. YIRRKALA

1. Wandjuk Djuakan Marika was born in 1927 on Bremer Island (Dhambaliya) in the Northern Territory.[4] He was the eldest son of Mawalan Marika and his wife Bamatja.[1][4] Marika was a member of the Rirratjingu group of the Yolngu people.[4] Marika was educated at the Methodist Overseas Mission at Yirrkala. His paintings expressed his people's traditional religious beliefs, and included *Djang'kawu Story* (1960) and *Birth of the Djang'kawu Children of Yelangbara* (1982).[2][5] Djang'kawu is the founding ancestor of the Riratjingu in traditional stories.[1]

    He co-founded the Aboriginal Arts Board in 1973, and became Chairman in 1976.[6] He was appointed an Officer of the Order of the British Empire that same year.[7]

    His name was given to the Wandjuk Marika 3D Memorial Award, a category of the prestigious National Aboriginal & Torres Strait Islander Art Award, awarded annually by the Museum and Art Gallery of the Northern Territory.[8] His portrait hangs in the National Portrait Gallery in Canberra,[9] and several of his paintings feature in the Art Gallery of New South Wales.[2] Source: Wikipedia

2. The **billy** is an **Australian** term for a metal container used for boiling water, making tea or cooking over a fire. By the end of the 19th century the **billy** had become as natural, widespread and symbolic of bush life as the gum tree, the

NOTES

kangaroo and the wattle. 'A Halt. Source: https://www.nma.gov.au/exhibitions/symbols-australia/billy

3. **Groote Eylandt** is the largest island in the Gulf of Carpentaria and the fourth largest island in Australia. It is the homeland of, and is owned by, the Warnindhilyagwa who speak the Anindilyakwa language.

Groote Eylandt lies about 50 km (31 mi) from the Northern Territory mainland and eastern coast of Arnhem Land, about 630 kilometres (390 mi) from Darwin, opposite Blue Mud Bay. The island measures about 50 kilometres (31 mi) from east to west and 60 kilometres (37 mi) from north to south; its area is 2,326.1 km2 (898.1 sq mi). It is generally quite low-lying, with an average height above sea level of 15 metres (49 ft), although Central Hill reaches an elevation of 219 metres (719 ft). It was named by the explorer Abel Tasman in 1644 and is Dutch for "Large Island" in an archaic spelling. The modern Dutch spelling is *Groot Eiland*.

12. ONE BECOMES TWO AND THEN SIX

1. https://www.surgeons.org/en/about-racs/about-the-college-of-surgeons/in-memoriam/obituaries/alan-bromwich

17. WHEATBELT ADVENTURES

1. https://en.wikipedia.org/wiki/Rabbit-Proof_Fence

18. NORSEMAN

1. The **Aussie salute**, also known as the **Barcoo salute** (after the Barcoo River) [1] or **Bush salute**, is the waving of one's hand in front of the face at regular intervals in order to prevent bush flies from landing on it, or entering one's nose or mouth. Source: Wikipedia

21. ROEBOURNE AND WICKHAM

1. (see press –files.anu.edu.au "A Good Life: Human rights and encounters with modernity" 6.Ordinary people enduring extraordinary things.)

26. HOLISTIC NURSING

1. See appendices for the 2001 submissions.
2. See "A Complete System of Nursing "by A Millicent Ashdown,1939 .

NOTES

28. ROUNDING UP

1. **Ganja** is another name for marijuana. The word is ofter times associated with the west indies, but the truth is that it originated in India.
2. https://tlhealingpathways.com/about/

29. CHRISTMAS IN EUROPE

1. https://en.wikipedia.org/wiki/Leaning_Tower_of_Pisa

30. LIFE CONTINUES

1. https://en.wikipedia.org/wiki/1989_Tiananmen_Square_protests
2. https://sublimechina.com
3. https://prostatecancerfree.org/
4. https://www.lawyersalliance.com.au/opinion/the-urogynaecological-mesh-scandal
5. https://www.visituppermurray.com.au/places/corryong/
6. https://indigenousx.com.au/the-heroes-of-gundagai/
7. https://www.thedogonthetuckerbox.com/poemsfolk_songs

EPILOGUE

1. Grandies is often the affectionate term used for grandchildren in Australia

www.ingramcontent.com/pod-product-compliance
Lightning Source LLC
Chambersburg PA
CBHW071552080526
44588CB00010B/877